KU-575-298

COLLINS FIELD GUIDE TO
ARCHAEOLOGY

COLLINS POCKET GUIDES

COLLINS POCKET GUIDE TO BRITISH BIRDS
by R. S. R. Fitter   *Illustrated by R. A. Richardson*

COLLINS POCKET GUIDE TO NESTS AND EGGS
by R. S. R. Fitter   *Illustrated by R. A. Richardson*

COLLINS GUIDE TO BIRD-WATCHING
by R. S. R. Fitter

COLLINS POCKET GUIDE TO WILD FLOWERS
by David McClintock and R. S. R. Fitter

COLLINS POCKET GUIDE TO THE SEA SHORE
by John Barrett and C. M. Yonge

COLLINS GUIDE TO MUSHROOMS AND TOADSTOOLS
by Morten Lange and F. B. Hora

COLLINS FIELD GUIDE TO ARCHAEOLOGY
by Eric S. Wood

A FIELD GUIDE TO THE BIRDS OF BRITAIN AND EUROPE
by Roger-Tory Peterson, Guy Mountford and P. A. D. Hollom

A FIELD GUIDE TO THE MAMMALS OF BRITAIN AND EUROPE
by F. H. van den Brink

A FIELD GUIDE TO THE STARS AND THE PLANETS
by Donald Menzel

A FIELD GUIDE TO THE BIRDS OF EAST AND CENTRAL AFRICA
by J. G. Williams

A FIELD GUIDE TO THE BIRDS OF NEW ZEALAND
by R. A. Falla, R. B. Sibson and E. G. Turbott

THE BIRDS OF THE WEST INDIES
by James Bond

THE BIRDS OF TRINIDAD AND TOBAGO
by G. A. K. Herklots

A FIELD GUIDE TO THE BUTTERFLIES OF BRITAIN AND EUROPE
L. G. Higgins and N. D. Riley

A FIELD GUIDE TO THE LARGER MAMMALS OF AFRICA
by J. Dorst and P. Dandelot

A FIELD GUIDE TO THE BIRDS OF SOUTHERN AFRICA
by O. P. M. Prozesky

A FIELD GUIDE TO THE SNAKES OF SOUTHERN AFRICA
by V. F. M. FitzSimons

A FIELD GUIDE TO THE BUTTERFLIES OF AFRICA
by J. G. Williams

COLLINS
FIELD GUIDE TO
ARCHAEOLOGY

ERIC S. WOOD
F.S.A.

WITH AN INTRODUCTION BY
SIR MORTIMER WHEELER

*Illustrated with 59 photographs
and 189 maps and line drawings*

BOOK CLUB ASSOCIATES
LONDON

TO H.J.S.
WHO HELPED ME TO LOOK,
AND SEE

This edition published 1973 by
Book Club Associates
By arrangement with Wm. Collins Sons & Co. Ltd.

© *in revised edition Eric S. Wood and R. S. R. Fitter,* 1967
Printed in Great Britain
Collins Clear-Type Press
London and Glasgow

Introduction

Like tribal lays, books about archaeology may be constructed in nine and sixty ways, and quite a number of them are right. Amongst these I am happy to introduce the present book, though—or because—it is of a somewhat unusual sort. It adheres to the British landscape, but within that scene its range is remarkable, extending as it does from barrows and bronzes to boiling-mounds and bowling-greens and bee-keeping. It even has a section on the hideously neglected subject of ancient milestones, which have been so sadly reduced by war, authoritarian wickedness and neglect since, many years ago, the late Sir John Myres campaigned for them. What a wealth of interest and humble craftsmanship they represent!—with their optimistic 'customary miles', their antique phonetic spelling and their delectable lettering.

I mention these things at random to stress the wise catholicity of Mr Wood's outlook. But he is no mere purveyor of trifles, however entertaining. He has set out to produce a solid, useful and readable book for the beginner or so-called amateur; a book in which anyone with a lively interest in his homely environment may at some point find information and stimulus, and a hint of new methods of understanding. Nowadays only a daring and devoted student would venture upon so ambitious an enterprise. At no previous time have so many critical specialists been at work in so many and various fields of enquiry; at no previous time, with advancing techniques, have chronology and inference been so prone to new fixation; and yet again, at no time have chronology and inference been more mobile and precarious. Mr Wood faces these risks with unostentatious courage, fortified by wide reading, unimpeded by footnotes but with a considerable bibliography. His summary survey deserves wide circulation at a time of properly increasing curiosity and concern in the human make-up of a countryside which is, at an unprecedented rate, being gouged out of existence.

Mortimer Wheeler

Contents

Water Supply

Canals and Marshes

Sites re-used

Odds and Ends

Deceptive Natural Features

Plates

The photographs for plates 16 to 19 were specially taken by Mr M. B. Cookson, using subjects of which some were kindly lent for the purpose by the University of London Institute of Archaeology

Text Figures

Tables

Regional Maps

Preface

This book is about the visible remains of man's occupation of Britain from the earliest times to almost the present day. It seeks to show how man has affected the landscape and what he has left behind in the course of his long story.

The area covered is England, Wales and Scotland, with Ireland and other places mentioned only where this is likely to be helpful. Houses, castles, churches, abbeys and their contents are excluded, but it has not always been easy to avoid treading very close to this necessary but somewhat arbitrary frontier.

The book begins with a short summary (pages 21-2) which makes clearer what it covers and how it is arranged, and may help the reader to find his way about it.

A book of this kind can be no more than a brief introduction, and is in no way a substitute for further reading, local enquiry and observation. The selection of examples is not meant to be exhaustive, but only illustrative. The reader should visit as many sites as he can, build up his own knowledge, and note his own comparisons, at first hand.

The facts are of course almost all to be found in more detail in other people's works. The list of books to read (pages 335-47) refers to some of these, which I gladly acknowledge having read and used. I hope the authors of articles etc. not mentioned in this list will accept a general acknowledgment here.

I can only trust that the need for compression over such a wide front has not distorted the facts nor squeezed out the very real interest of the subject.

I am very greatly indebted to those who have had the kindness and the patience to read large parts of the manuscript: Mr H. J. Stickland, F.S.A., Dr J. X. W. P. Corcoran, F.S.A., who read it from their respective amateur and professional standpoints; and Mr R. S. R. Fitter, to whom is due the genesis and much of the inspiration of the book. They not only removed error and inconsistency, but suggested innumerable improvements. The section on the Law was read by Mr James Cunningham, Barrister-at-law, and that on canals by an expert who wishes to stay anonymous. A large number of people, experts in many fields, have gone out of their way to answer questions and fill gaps; they are very numerous, and I hope will not mind not being named.

The staffs of the libraries of the British Museum, the University of London, the Institute of Archaeology and the Society of Antiquaries have also been most helpful. The book owes most of its value, but not any errors which may remain, to these friends, and I should like to say how much I appreciate their ready help.

I am not only honoured, but greatly encouraged, by Sir Mortimer Wheeler's generous introduction, and cannot adequately thank him for writing it. Several improvements in the text are due to his suggestion.

December 1962   *E.S.W.*

Foreword to Second Edition

The first edition of this book, and its reprint, seem to have filled a gap in the general literature of British archaeology, and to have proved useful to the enquirer into the subject. But during the past few years great progress has been made in the understanding of almost every period of the past, and in the application of new scientific techniques to the solution of its problems. Archaeology, in fact, is as lively as ever.

Some passages of the book have therefore needed amendment or even re-writing, and a few new topics have been included. The Sites to Visit section has been recast for some counties, and the Books to Read have been brought more up to date.

I am most grateful to all those who, in reviews, in letters, or orally, have suggested corrections and improvements, and to those who gave advice and answered questions; and to the publishers for allowing so many alterations to be made. The result can only be a more useful book.

October 1967   *E.S.W.*

Foreword to Third Edition

Since 1967 a great deal has happened in British archaeology. The application of advanced technologies still gathers momentum, and our understanding of the sequence, relations, nature and dating of events in prehistory is being revolutionised thereby. The spate of books runs on unchecked.

Amid all this I have tried to mention some of the more significant developments, but this book can never be complete or final, and in any case its main object is to draw attention to the (fast disappearing) field monuments of Britain, which in themselves do not change, even though their interpretation does.

October 1971   E.S.W.

Glossary

It is impossible to avoid all technical terms in a survey of this kind. Most of them have been defined where they first occur, or in the Background sections, but a list of a few perhaps unfamiliar words may save referring to these places.

Barrow (tumulus): a mound of earth, chalk, earth and stones, etc., covering a burial.

Beaker people: the first Bronze Age immigrants, about 1800 BC, called after their characteristic pot, of beaker form, which held a drink of the beer type.

Bell pit: a pit, narrower at the mouth than the bottom, for the extraction of clay for iron-making, etc.

Berm: a platform round a mound or along a bank or wall.

Bivallate, multivallate, univallate: having two, many (two or more) and one rampart respectively; said of hillforts.

Burin: a flint tool in which a sliver is taken off from one corner to make a tiny transverse edge.

Cairn: a mound of stones.

Clunch: a hard chalk used as a building stone.

Culture: the totality of the material equipment of a given people at a given time, and as much of its social structure, religion, customs and way of life as can be deduced from the material evidence surviving, or from any other reliable source.

Ecology: the relations between living organisms and their environment—soil, vegetation, fauna, climate; e.g. man in his physical setting.

Food Vessel: an Early Bronze Age culture called after its characteristic pottery (*c.* 1700–1500 BC).

Henge: a monument consisting of a circular bank and ditch (or more than one), with one or more entrances and sometimes with a stone circle inside; used for religious etc. functions in the Secondary Neolithic, and in the Early Bronze Age (*c.* 1800–1400 BC).

Jurassic Ridge: the limestone ridge which crosses England from Dorset to Yorkshire, providing a highway for early man.

Lynchet: a bank accumulated on a slope, owing to creep of soil loosened by ploughing.

Marl: an earthy chalk, used for liming the fields.

Megalithic: made of very large stones; applied mainly to the

19

tombs of certain Neolithic cultures, mostly in the West of Britain.

Mesolithic: of the Middle Stone Age—the last phase of the hunting and food-gathering cultures, from the end of the last glaciation to the coming of the first farmers (*c.* 12,000–3000 BC).

Microlith: flint tools of very small size and often geometric shape, used mainly by the mesolithic peoples.

Moraine: a bank or layer of gravel, stones and mud deposited by a glacier.

Motte: a conical mound with a flat top, on which stood a Norman fort.

Neolithic: of the New Stone Age, the period and culture of the first farmers, before metal was used (*c.* 3000–1800 BC in Britain).

Palaeolithic: of the Old Stone Age, the first million years or so of man's life on Earth (until *c.* 12,000 BC in Britain).

Pax Romana: the state of peace and civilisation imposed by the Romans on the peoples they conquered and absorbed into the Roman Empire.

Secondary culture (Neolithic, etc): one where a native people adopts features from the superior culture of an immigrant people, and adapts them to its own way of life, producing a new culture of mixed character.

Spelt: a grain of the wheat type, grown as a staple crop in the Bronze and Iron Ages.

Tree ring: (a) the annual growth-ring in a tree-trunk, which varies in thickness and denseness with the weather of the year in which it grew; (b) a bank and ditch surrounding an ornamental clump of trees, on which was put a fence to prevent damage by animals when the trees were young.

Windmill Hill: the first neolithic culture of Britain, that of the first farmers, called after the site, near Avebury, where its features were first recognised.

Zones, highland and lowland: the broad geographical division of Britain into two (see p. 28 for their significance for human settlement).

How to Use this Book

In case the mass of information in this book should appear confusing and unwieldy, the following guide will assist the reader in finding what he wants.

First comes a very brief *glossary* (p. 19), although most if not all the terms used (and technical terms cannot be avoided altogether) are explained in the background sections or where they first occur.

Then follows a *general background* (p. 23), which provides a theoretical framework within which the field antiquities described in the central part of the book can be fitted. This background begins with *Man's Influence on the Landscape* (p. 23), what man has made of the countryside in successive ages—followed by the converse, *The Two Zones* (p. 28), and its pendant *The Patterns of Settlement* (p. 32), the geography as it affects the various occupations of the land. *Climate* (p. 34) describes its effects also, such as the remains of the glaciers of the Ice Age. *Cultures of Britain* (p. 41) outlines the life and influence of the various peoples who have lived in this country from the beginning until after the Norman Conquest.

The next section, *Identifying Earthworks* (p. 85) brings in the actual types of earthwork—banks, ditches, etc.—which can be seen in the field, and this is in many ways the most important part of the book. It should be referred to first when seeing an earthwork of any kind, and its reference followed up. Familiarity with it will greatly increase the excitement of the chase, and underline the interest of a country walk.

The various earthworks and other objects are then described in the succeeding sections, *Types of Field Antiquities* (p. 97) which also sets them briefly in their background. Each group of major objects is treated historically, so as to make clearer any development there may have been. *Odds and Ends* (pp. 203–52) speak for themselves—these are the other objects, of all kinds, mostly not earthworks, which can be seen. *Surface Finds* (p. 254) are the flints and small portable objects which can be picked up in the fields.

Deceptive Natural Features (p. 253) explains itself.

Technical and Legal (p. 281) comprises a few aspects, mostly of practical importance in field archaeology, but some included by way of supplementary interest only. *Techniques of Archaeology* (p. 281) mentions the principles of excavation and some of the modern scientific aids to archaeology; this is followed by *How Sites get Buried* (p. 294). *The Law* (p. 296) and *Scheduled Monuments* (p. 299) although not possibly very popular subjects, are yet important to know the essential points of, and it may be helpful to have them.

Following Up (p. 302) contains under this heading hints on libraries, museums, archaeological societies, periodicals and other sources of information. *Sites to Visit* (p. 308) is a very abridged list of major sites or typical examples of their class, in every county of England, Wales and Scotland. *Books to Read* (p. 335) gives those likely to be of most help, and which are reasonably easy to read and to get hold of (many of them are quite cheap and a library will have or be able to get the others).

Finally, full use should be made of the *Indexes* of both *places* (p. 368) and *subjects* (p. 376), as the reference to a particular object in the book cannot always be deduced from the title of the section which contains it.

Part I: General Background

CHAPTER I

Man's Influence on the Landscape

It is far from easy to visualise what a countryside looked like at any given period, or what changes there have been in it, but it is important to try to do so if we are to see the men of past ages in their true setting. This is particularly difficult today, when the great majority of us do not have to wage a continual battle against our natural environment in order to live a civilised life at all; but until the last century or so that was the normal condition of most Britons. Occasionally one comes across a stretch of country, or a view, which appears to be primeval, never to have changed for hundreds of years; but this is rarely actually the case. In more ways than we usually realise man has affected the landscape, and what we see now is the product, in all but a few places, of a long series of man-made changes.

Broadly, these changes have been made in the interests of farming and industry.

Man's effect on the countryside is itself influenced by the slow changes of climate which are always going on, and which determine the amount of water available, and the temperature, which in turn affect the sort of vegetation and other wild life able to colonise those places where man also wants to live. Indeed, man's story has been essentially one of progressive control of this natural environment, which, in the long *palaeolithic* and *mesolithic* periods, had it all its own way. Man was then a hunter and food-gatherer, living in small groups where he could in the vast, trackless, undrained wilderness from which he had to get his uncertain living. The few hundred humans (only about 3,000 even by the *Mesolithic*) who wandered about this country during these long years could make no impression on its appearance at all; their huts or shelters of branches and skins, their game-traps and fish-weirs, were all engulfed by the forests when they passed on to fresh or seasonal hunting-grounds.

The coming of the *neolithic* farmers early in the third millennium made a clean break with this primitive helplessness; farming needs space, which was gained by the 'slash and burn' method, by which the bushes and smaller trees were cut down with the polished stone or flint axes of the newcomers and burnt on the spot, their ashes enriching the soil. In addition, man's animals, cattle and sheep, roamed widely and helped to clear the land of woods by eating the young shoots of trees and bushes. But even so, the neolithic population of Britain has been estimated as not exceeding 20,000 at any one time; they had to occupy the lighter soils, and could not tackle the forests and marshes. So, although they made a beginning, their influence on the landscape was slight. The small corn-plots of this period were cultivated by a simple digging-stick, and have left few traces.

The uneven distribution of early remains is sometimes due to early man himself. For instance, Neolithic and Bronze Age farming in northern England destroyed the birch cover and started soil erosion; this poor farming went on to Scandinavian times. The scarcity of traces of early man in the Lake District is due, not to the absence of settlement, but to the remains being covered with peat, hill-wash, etc., owing to the removal of the tree-cover.

In the succeeding *Bronze Age* there was at first a tendency towards more cattle-keeping in a nomadic or semi-nomadic way of life, but although the population was increasing, their corn-plots and stock-runs still took up only an insignificant amount of the available land. The next impetus was given in the Late Bronze Age, by the development of the digging-stick into the ard-plough, a light plough which still only made shallow furrows in the soil, but was drawn by oxen along and across a squarish field. Man was now a settled farmer, and groups of these 'Celtic' fields can still be seen on the hills of southern England, and in some places further north also. But the total population of Britain was still less than 100,000; this continued to grow during the *Early Iron Age*, and farming became more varied, and in some regions very prosperous, but on the same techniques. The *Belgae*, in the first century BC, brought with them the heavy (possibly wheeled) plough with a share to turn the sod, which enabled them at last to tackle some of the heavier lands in the valleys and plains. In 100 BC, the population was possibly about ¼ million, but by AD 43 had nearly doubled; the potentialities of Britain were becoming recognised, but it was left to the *Romans* to transform the country, and lay the foundations of its later development.

This they did by laying down a network of roads which could be used in all weathers, building towns of all sizes, which needed greatly intensified farming to feed them, and developing trade. In order to expand farming land they drained the marshes in many parts, and cleared much more of the valleys and heavy soils than the Belgae had been able to do. The Celtic nobility, and some foreigners, established huge farms, for corn and sheep, which were the basis of the villa system. Meanwhile, the natives continued to farm in the old way, and many of the Celtic field systems date from the Roman period; similarly, the old trackways remained in use to serve these native villages. Later, the Saxons used both in founding their new pattern of settlement. The villas created large clearances; in all about 100 towns needed feeding, and contained about 200,000 people out of about a million or $1\frac{1}{2}$ million in the province. The rest of these people lived in 1,000 or more native villages or homesteads or on as many villas; but even with this great increase over earlier times, still only about 2 to 3 per cent of the possible land was used, and most of that in the southern half of the country. The highland zone was still in the Iron Age or even earlier type of economy. The almost modern appearance of the map of the province, with its network of roads, makes figures of this order hard to grasp; but undoubtedly much of the country through which the roads passed must have been still wild and uncultivated.

In the late 4th century and during the 5th some even of this land went out of use, and the incoming *Anglo-Saxons* had, except in certain areas, a practically free choice of land to colonise. Some of the deserted British lands were reoccupied in the first three Saxon centuries, some not till the 12th and 13th centuries. The Saxons lived mostly in villages; this became the normal pattern in the Midlands, but in areas with considerable native populations the pattern was more mixed, with hamlets and isolated farms dotted about in the Celtic manner. Some Saxon villages also were on the sites of earlier settlements, particularly those on hilltops; but most of them were on new sites, along the valleys.

The new villages normally had open fields (two, sometimes three), surrounded by waste, which was gradually encroached on as the population of the village expanded. The forest, which still covered most of the country, was cleared, as in the Neolithic, by fire, axe and grazing. The large fields were divided into sections (furlongs), each containing strips for cultivation; a man's strips were distributed over the village land to equalise the advantages. There were also a few large estates and deer-parks.

The *Scandinavians* who colonised parts of northern England in the 9th century followed much the same pattern, and cleared and drained some new land. In Lincolnshire and Norfolk the pattern is one of scattered settlements, with small compact farms.

By the time the Domesday Book was compiled in 1086 there were about $1\frac{1}{4}$ million people in England; East Anglia was the most thickly populated area. But vast areas were still underpopulated, and much was still primeval. But the population was steadily growing, and moor, forest, marsh and fen were being tackled and gradually pushed back. This had the effect of lowering the water-table, but throughout the Middle Ages the rivers and streams were larger than they are today, and could be used for a variety of purposes. Nearly every modern village was already in being by 1086, except a few made during the forest-clearances of the 12th and 13th centuries, and those created by the Industrial Revolution. Towns also were established, some on Roman sites, many new and most of them very small. There were now about 25 people to the square mile.

From the 12th to the 14th centuries the clearances went on. The wastes were colonised, including open spaces within city walls, even in London itself; pigs were kept in the forests, open fields extended, new farms built.

There were also new features. The Royal Forests—these were tracts of country, not necessarily, or even mainly, wooded (the New Forest was wooded, but Knaresborough Forest was open country), reserved as hunting grounds for the King and his licensees and nobody else; by Henry II's time (second half of 12th century) these had spread over a third of England, hindering farming by their restrictive laws, and in some places actually destroying villages and farms. The great monasteries particularly in the north and west (and especially the Cistercian houses such as Fountains and Byland) cleared and drained widely, and set up vast sheep-farms and tracts of arable, with granges to manage them.

By 1349 (the Black Death), there were 4 million people. About 1½ million died from the plagues of this time, and the number of monks was halved; this had profound and lasting effects on the life of England. Already some 300 villages had been deserted as a result of clearance for the royal forests and the monastic farms, but now another 1,000 disappeared. The scarcity of labour led to a great increase of sheep-farming, for which open fields were enclosed. By 1500 there were 3 sheep to every human being (8 million to under 3 million), and there were too few people to exploit the land or its minerals properly.

The peak of the wool industry in the late 15th and 16th centuries led again to widespread enclosure of open fields in areas as yet unaffected, such as the Midlands; about a sixth of the villages were deserted as a result of this. But the remaining ones thrived, and much building and rebuilding was done, particularly from 1570 to 1640. During this time also great parks were created, which had their effect on the local villages, and caused diversions of roads. Forests were attacked now in earnest, not only for normal clearance, but for the needs of the growing industries, such as iron, glass and pottery.

By the late 17th century, when the country had settled down after the Civil War, there was at last enough population for a stable and prosperous rural life. Another wave of building occurred from 1660 to 1770, the rest of the open fields were enclosed, this time not by local agreements, but by private Acts of Parliament, and the country began to take on its modern appearance. In 1700 half the arable was enclosed, but the Acts dealt with another 4½ million acres; at this time also there were still about 5 million acres of waste.

The parliamentary enclosures, which went on until about 1850, a high proportion between 1760 and 1800, mainly affected the central belt from Dorset to Yorkshire; in the highland zone there had been a different land history, where small farms and irregular fields were the norm. But in the areas affected they transformed the appearance of the country, laying down the present pattern of straight ash or hawthorn hedges, new roads and farmhouses, and squarish fields of 5 to 10 acres.

Industrial development, until the 18th century, was on a very small scale, and had little effect on the landscape. Few quarries or factories were large, and the wildness of the country was such that they were absorbed in it. Only with the great industrial organizations of the Industrial Revolution, coupled with the growing bareness of the countryside, did industry and its communications become an inescapable feature of the landscape. The enormous growth of towns too completes the picture, but not the problems, of our present times.

CHAPTER 2

The Two Zones

Frequent mention is made in this book of the Highland and the Lowland Zones. In *The Personality of Britain*, a pioneer work in which the relation between the geography and the human settlement of Britain is investigated, Sir Cyril Fox elaborated the significance of the division of Britain into two geographical zones (fig. 1, p. 29). The lowland zone includes all the south and centre of England, Lancashire, and Yorkshire east of the Pennines; it consists of the more recent rocks and deposits, and has no great heights. It contains land easy to settle and cultivate (chalk, gravels, sandstones, soft limestones). The highland zone is the rest: the south-west of England (with the Mendips and Malverns as 'islands'), Wales except the Vale of Glamorgan, the Pennines, Lake District and north-east of England (the North York Moors are a borderland with features of both zones), and all Scotland (although the east coast has some of the characteristics of the lowland zone). The rocks are old and hard, the climate is wetter and windier than in the lowland zone, and much of the area is bleak moor and mountain difficult to settle.

Most of the invasions of Britain have entered the lowland zone and rapidly occupied it, spreading slowly into the north and west. Fox deduced from this that in the lowland zone new cultures tended to be *imposed* on the earlier ones and to *replace* them; in the highland zone they tended to be *absorbed* by the older culture and to create new patterns of *fusion*. Although Professor Piggott has urged caution in applying this principle rigidly—the full facts are not so clear-cut—it is undoubtedly helpful and illuminating. In any case the geographical concept of the zones is valid and useful. Whatever its strictly archaeological merits, it is too neat and too familiar to discard.

THE STRUCTURE OF BRITAIN

It has become a commonplace, thanks to work like that of Professors Trueman and Dudley Stamp, that Britain's scenery is determined by her geology. And with the scenery goes the vegetation which itself governs the areas where early man could settle, and from where he could extend his living-area when his resources so allowed. It is therefore

FIG. 1. The highland zone of Britain (shaded) and the lowland zone
with its hill-features

important to have a broad idea of the main geological features of the country, although what follows is so simplified that it should be supplemented by detailed works on particular regions or localities. Moreover, any general account ignores the many small patches of alluvium or boulder clay (the 'drift'), which could often make human development possible, irrespective of the underlying rock. To a surprising extent the main concentrations of population are still in the lowland areas, and away from the regions of the older rocks, these being mountainous and still difficult of access and communication.

Broadly, the older and harder rocks of Britain are in the north and west, the newer and softer in the east and south. We are not here concerned with the geological history, the processes of deposition, volcanic action and land movement which have given rise to what we now see, but merely with the resultant conditions in their relation to man and his cultures.

Taking Scotland first, the most conspicuous mass is that of the Highlands, from Wester Ross to the Forth-Clyde line, including most of the counties of Perth, Argyll, Inverness and Ross and Cromarty. The central part of this large area was hardly settled at all, except for a few favoured and accessible valleys, but along the west coast are a maze of sea-lochs, submerged valleys with easy land at their heads. These have long been settled, with intercommunication by sea, and there are a few broader valleys, such as Crinan in Argyll, where settlement has been intensive since the Neolithic. The Hebrides, both Inner and Outer, and other large islands such as Kintyre, Bute and Arran, are in general easier.

In the north of Scotland are the bare limestone uplands and sea-plains of Sutherland and Caithness, which are thickly dotted with remains of early occupation sites—it may be said that such concentrations are partly accounted for by the accident of survival, but none the less the essential pattern is there. Orkney, and to a lesser extent Shetland, also have a continuous human history since the Neolithic. Another great concentration is at the head of the Moray Firth, from the Beauly district of Cromarty to Inverness and Nairn. Settlement is scattered along the Moray coast. The East of Scotland is easy of access, and has some of the characteristics of the lowland zone; human settlement is intensive in Aberdeenshire, Angus and Strathmore, and in Fife.

Central Scotland, the Forth and Clyde valleys, are a great highway and belt of settlement. The Southern Uplands, although broken by rich valleys, have considerable blocks of bleak mountain, and in the southwest at least most of the early occupation was near the coast, and is very intensive in Galloway. In the south-east the Lothians and Berwickshire are low and open; settlement is also intensive in much of Roxburghshire, in the shelter of the Cheviots. Selkirkshire, Peeblesshire and much of Dumfriesshire are difficult country, even today, and are thinly populated.

The North of England is largely taken up by the mountain masses of the Lake District and the Pennines, with exposed and rather sour land extending from them into Northumberland and Co. Durham. Nonetheless the better parts of these areas were settled early, as were the great Pennine dales and through routes (the Stainmore and Aire gaps). On the west the sea-plains were of easy access. This highland zone country occupies all the western side of Yorkshire, and includes Derbyshire and north-east Staffs. In the Pennines the tracts of limestone are more hospitable than the grits, but the latter, with their bleak moorlands, were occupied by mesolithic man.

Cheshire makes a break between two highland blocks, and forms the outlet of the Midland plain to the sea. Wales is an area of highland character, a complex jumble of mountain blocks and more or less fertile valleys. Human penetration was for the most part by way of the coasts, and then up the valleys, larger areas of easier land being reached in Anglesey, Lleyn, Pembrokeshire, Carmarthenshire and Glamorgan. Monmouthshire is part of the Severn settlement area, and Brecon is in some ways an extension of this. Central Wales centres mostly round the Newtown-Machynlleth valley, and inland north Wales along the Dee-Mawddach line.

The highland zone is completed with the south-western peninsula of England, from the Quantocks and Exmoor through Devon to Cornwall. Early settlement was thick in Cornwall, partly for its mineral wealth, partly in the landfall area of Penwith.

East of all this is the lowland zone, which falls into two parts, that north-west and that south-east of the Jurassic ridge, the belt of limestones which run from the Tees to the Devon-Dorset border. North-west of this is the Vale of York and the Midland Plain, for much of their history difficult country, covered with damp forests and cut up by marshy valleys. This could not be fully occupied till post-Roman times. South-east of this are the younger rocks, limestones, sandstones, chalk and later deposits which make up the whole of south-east England. Its frontier, partly followed by the Fosse Way, was the North York Moors, the Howardian Hills, the Lincoln Edge, the Northamptonshire heights, the Cotswolds, the Mendips, of which the first and the last have a somewhat highland zone flavour. Inside this is the great line of chalk, from the Wolds in Yorkshire and Lincolnshire, and then—after the break caused by the Wash and the Fens—along the Chilterns (the line of the Icknield Way) into Wessex, and reaching the sea in west Dorset and east Devon. From this belt the East Anglian chalk stretches out, and the two long fingers of the North and South Downs into Kent and Sussex. The North Downs have a capping of clay-with-flints etc. which carry heavy forest, but south of them (see map 3, p. 352) runs a belt of greensand which formed a highway for early man. Of all this considerable area only the Fens, parts of Essex and the Weald (these

last two being heavily-forested claylands), are difficult lands for settlement; the rest has been continuously occupied from earliest human
times. Wessex forms a solid block, central to many early cultures, and
the long ridges running from it carried men and ideas in all directions.
The Thames valley was a major thoroughfare also. The east and south-
east coast of course saw repeated influxes of settlers from the Continent.

THE PATTERNS OF SETTLEMENT

This rapid sketch of the country enables us to look for the main areas
of settlement in each successive culture-period. These periods and
peoples are described in the section *The Cultures of Britain* (pp. 41–84).

Palaeolithic. The conditions determined by the glaciations kept most
of these people in the Thames valley and south of it, particularly in the
early phases. In the later phases they moved further north to NE
Wales, Derbyshire, Yorkshire as far as Nidderdale and the East Coast.
The terraces of the Thames and its tributaries are particularly rich.

Mesolithic. The peoples of Sauveterrian tradition (see p. 48) lived on
the open heaths and moorlands of southern England (e.g. the Surrey
and Hampshire greensands), East Anglia, the southern Pennines, the
North York Moors. There are coastal settlements in SW Scotland and
Argyllshire. The Forest peoples (see p. 49) occupied mostly the eastern
side of England, particularly the river valleys.

Neolithic. The Windmill Hill farmers (see p. 54) entered Britain along
the south coast, and spread on to the chalk lands of Sussex and Wessex,
and similar cultures occur on the lighter soils of East Anglia, Lincolnshire and Yorkshire, and the south-west. The megalithic tomb builders
(see p. 55) approached from the south-west, and settled the drier lands
in Cornwall, round the Bristol Channel, both sides of the Irish Sea,
SW Scotland, and round the Scottish coasts to Orkney, the Moray
Firth and Aberdeenshire. The Secondary Neolithic peoples (see p. 57)
appear in much the same areas as all these.

Bronze Age. Sir Cyril Fox's famous distribution map, in *The Personality
of Britain,* although composite and covering over 1,000 years, shows the
possible settlement in an early stage of agriculture, using most of the
lighter soils. The main concentrations are in Wessex, Dartmoor, Cornwall, Sussex, the Thames Valley, much of East Anglia, the southern
Pennines, east Yorkshire, Northumberland, much of SE Scotland,
Galloway, east Cumberland, much of N Wales, Pembrokeshire and

1. EFFECTS OF GLACIATIONS. *Above*. With changes in sea-level, rivers alternately build up gravel terraces and cut down through them. *Below*, the successive shore lines of a lake, still visible across later erosion gullies (The "Parallel Roads" of Glenroy)

2. *Above*, rock grooved (striated) by the movement of a glacier. *Below*, the exposed remains of a megalithic chamber tomb, one of the earliest types of stone structure

Glamorgan. Within this composite picture, the Beaker peoples (see p. 59) spread from the east and south-east coasts of England and Scotland, and are strong in Wessex. Food Vessels (see p. 60) are found in three main areas, East Yorkshire and the coastal regions from there into Scotland, Wessex and N Ireland. By the Late Bronze Age most of the lighter soils had been occupied.

Early Iron Age. This pattern is intensified, and some slightly heavier soils are tackled.

Roman. Direct Roman influence was essentially in the lowland zone.

Saxon. The Anglo-Saxons were lowland farmers, and their area is again mostly the lowland zone; for the first time the heavy lands of the English Midlands were effectively colonised. The Danes settled eastern England from Tees to Thames; the Norse entered north-west England up to the Pennines, and also occupied Man and Orkney (with Shetland and N Scotland).

Middle Ages. As the population grew, colonisation was pushed on to the poorer lands, marshes were drained and forests cleared. But to this day the higher moorland and mountain areas of the south-west, the North of England, Wales and Scotland are still largely uninhabited. About one-fifth of the total area of England and Wales is in this category, and a further considerable acreage is very sparsely occupied—the two together exceed a quarter of the total area. In Scotland the proportion is even higher.

CHAPTER 3

Climate

Not only is Man's way of life affected by the type of country he lives in, and the kind of food it can produce, but these two factors are also partly governed by the climate. The interaction of all these factors forms the ecological background against which all living things, and not least man (until a very short time ago), have had to develop. Throughout the time that man or sub-man has lived on earth, nearly two million years, the climate of north-west Europe has undergone many violent fluctuations. The whole of this time is also the bulk of the Pleistocene period, when alternate phases of heat and cold provide a chronological framework within which can be set the development of man and his cultures. This framework can be seen in the terraces along our rivers, and the raised beaches of the coast, and has been set in a reasonably reliable time-scale by reference to the solar radiation received at the earth's atmosphere, the fluctuations of which have been plotted by Milankovitch and dates assigned to them. In spite of criticisms this scale accords with other evidence, and can be accepted for practical purposes, except for the Last Glaciation, which is now fixed by reference to radiocarbon dates.

ICE AGES

When, for complicated reasons, solar radiation in summer is lower than usual for long periods, and winter radiation higher, the increased winter precipitation falls as snow, and on the high ground does not melt so rapidly in the summer. If this continues, ice-sheets are built up in the mountains, which themselves set up weather-cycles perpetuating the glacial conditions, which spread and maintain themselves until the radiation itself changes. A mild 'interglacial' period then follows, often very long, and the cycle is repeated. This has happened four times in the last half-million years, and indeed has been the background of the whole of man's life on earth. We are not concerned with earlier ice-ages at all; indeed, only the last glaciation has left effects which are still fresh in the landscape. The four ice-ages have each been split into two phases, and the last into three—each phase separated by short mild periods ('interstadials'). The gap between the second and third of the four glaciations was very long. The chronology of all this may be shown as follows, the figures being approximate, and liable to adjustment in the light of other methods of dating (e.g. by radioactivity):

Table 1

GLACIATION AND HUMAN CULTURE-PERIODS

Peak of Glaciations (Milankovitch dates) (*no. of years ago*)	*Glacial phases*	*Human Cultures* (*for details see p. 42*)
590,000	**Early Glaciation (Günz) phase I**	Lower Palaeolithic
550,000	**phase II**	
	Antepenultimate Interglacial (60,000 years long)	
476,000	**Antepenultimate Glaciation (Mindel)**	
	phase I	
	phase II	
435,000	Penultimate (Great) Interglacial (190,000 years long)	Middle Palaeolithic
230,000	**Penultimate Glaciation (Riss) phase I**	
187,000	**phase II**	
	Last Interglacial (60,000 years long)	
115,000	**Last Glaciation (Würm) phase I**	Upper Palaeolithic
72,000	**phase II**	
25,000	**phase III**	
12,000	Final recession of ice	
	Postglacial	Mesolithic onwards

See also Table 3, p. 51

Although it is not strictly accurate to do so, British archaeologists still use the same names as those of the glaciations in the Alps: Günz, Mindel, Riss and Würm. Attempts have been made to use local British names—such as North Sea Drift (Mindel II), Great Chalky Boulder Clay (Riss II), Little Eastern, Newer Drift, Scottish Re-advance (Würm I, II and III)—but such names are not universally agreed upon. The general descriptive names, Early Glaciation, etc., were given by Zeuner, whose book *Dating the Past* (4th edition, 1958) should be referred to.

THE EFFECT OF GLACIERS

During the antepenultimate glaciation the ice-sheet covered the whole of Britain and Ireland north of a line roughly from Cardiff through Gloucester, Stratford-on-Avon, just north of London, and out into the then dry North Sea near Ipswich. The greatest extent of the last glaciation (phase II) was north of this, excluding southern Ireland, south-west Wales, the Welsh borders to about Shrewsbury, down to Birmingham, then north to the Pennines, where the major dales had their own local glaciers, to the sea at Scarborough, and touching also the coast of east Yorkshire, Lincolnshire and Norfolk. In the less severe glaciations, such as phase III of the last glaciation, the ice was confined to the mountain masses, but its influence in the shape of tundra, frozen subsoil, etc., extended over most of the country. A vast quantity of ice was involved in these glaciations, running into thousands of feet thick in places. (The thickness of the present-day ice-cap of Greenland is of the order of 10,000 ft.) This had two important effects. Its enormous weight depressed the earth's crust, and the huge quantity of water locked up in it depleted the sea. So during the cold phases the sea-level was low, and it rose again when the ice melted and released its water back into the sea; at the same time the crust of the earth gradually expanded when the weight was lifted, rising to its normal level, but slower than the sea. The changes in sea-level are known as 'eustatic', those of the land as 'isostatic'.

The sea-levels in the three interglacials have stood at about 200, 100, 60 and 25 ft. respectively above the present level (the last two figures represent two different levels in the last interglacial). These levels have produced the raised beaches of (e.g.) the south coast of England, between Brighton and Portsmouth. The rivers, such as the Thames, have reacted to these complex changes of level by the building up of terraces along their lower courses (Fig. 2, p. 37). This is because during the warm phases the sea rises and the river flows slower, depositing sheets of gravel up to the new sea-level; then, in the cold phases, the sea falls and the river cuts down into this gravel, leaving a terrace on either side. When the sea-level was lower than it is today (as in the cold phases of the last glaciation), the river cut a channel which was later buried by the next deposit of gravel. (pl. 1, p. 32).

As the sea-levels are lower in each successive warm phase (for uncertain reasons), the terraces form a series of which the highest is the earliest. For the lower Thames, the series of terraces is complete, and can be studied in the gravel-pits of north Kent, near Dartford and Northfleet. The Ambersham terrace (200 ft.) represents the antepenultimate interglacial, the High or Boyn Hill terrace (100 ft.) the great interglacial—the Swanscombe human remains were found in this—the Taplow terrace (60 ft.) and the Upper Floodplain terrace (25 ft.) the last interglacial, and two low terraces the interstadials of the last glaciation. These terraces are of course obscured in some places by downward soil-movements. Early man settled on the gravels, and the terraces are therefore good hunting-grounds for his tools, which can be dated by the age of the terraces themselves.

In its upper reaches a river reacts quite differently to glaciation. Here, it was in the warm phases that the river had enough water to cut down into its bed. In the cold phases it ran slower, and vast quantities of material were put into it by hill-wash and solifluction (soil-movement due to the upper layers of earth creeping down a slope over a frozen subsoil); these were deposited as sheets of gravel, called aggradation-terraces.

All these processes are seen clearest in the periglacial areas (the areas not actually covered with ice). In the parts of Britain north of the Thames they are obscured by the action of the ice itself, which we shall now describe.

Glaciers are constantly, although very slowly, on the move, and they scrape up and carry along with them a vast quantity of earth, rock waste, stones and the like which is held in suspension in the ice. In addition, their top surface may be covered with blocks of rock of all sizes which have been detached by frost action from the valley sides and fallen on to the glacier. When the temperature rises the glacier starts melting and its nose stops moving forward; but the ice still flows on behind, and at the now stationary nose its load of rock and earth is piled up into a bank (a 'moraine') across

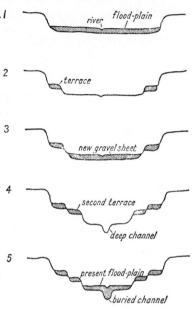

FIG. 2. The formation of terraces in the lower course of a river. The river alternately builds up layers of gravel (1, 3 and 5), and cuts through them again (2 and 4), following the rise and fall of the sea level during the climatic fluctuations of an Ice Age. (See Pl. 1, p. 37)

the end of the glacier (a terminal moraine). If the ice-front recedes, this debris will be spread back along the path of the glacier. Material at the sides is deposited in long lines, forming lateral moraines; if two glaciers meet and run alongside each other they form medial moraines. The terminal moraines can be seen across valleys, often containing a dammed-up lake, such as that at Tal-y-Llyn, Merioneth. Lateral moraines can be seen along the Yorkshire dales, sometimes, as in Nidderdale, complicated by hill-wash on top of them, earth which has come from the hillsides in different conditions.

Under many glaciers flowed a stream formed of melt-waters, which runs out from a hole or cave in the nose of the glacier; this carries a great deal of fine mud and pebbles, which may be deposited in a 'fan', and, as the nose recedes, in a long winding bank called an esker. There is a good example on the north Norfolk coast between Blakeney and Morston. The winding gravel ridges of central Ireland, although known as eskers, are really 'kames', having been laid down parallel to the ice-fronts and not at right angles to them. Roads are sometimes built on them.

If, instead of a terminal moraine, recession was so fast that a sheet of debris was deposited, this takes the form of a mixture of mud and stones called boulder clay: examples can be seen on the coast of north Wales and Yorkshire.

Incidentally, boulder clay shows by the provenance of the stones in it where the ice-sheet started from; the boulder-clay in north Wales contains stones from Scotland, that of Yorkshire from Scandinavia. Similarly, even quite large rocks may be carried many miles on the ice, and left stranded on a hillside (e.g. Ingleborough, Yorkshire); see p. 143. When the ice passed over a rock in its path, it might striate it (pl. 2, p. 33), or smooth it, leaving 'roches moutonnées'; these are very common in Scotland. Sometimes pockets of debris are deposited as rounded hillocks (ground moraines), which can often look like barrows (see p. 163); these morainic mounds called 'drumlins' are common in Yorkshire (Craven has many of them), the Vale of Eden, and south and central Scotland, where great tracts of country are dotted with them—often they are elongated, and all pointing one way, thus showing the direction of the ice (often a later glacier) which finally moulded them.

We are not concerned with other ice-effects, such as diversion of rivers, or valley formation; but mention may be made of the horizontal banks near Ben Nevis called the Parallel Roads of Glenroy (pl. 1, p. 32), which are beaches at different levels of a glacial lake. Two moraines important archaeologically are those, close together, across the Vale of York, at Escrick and York itself. These provided ridges of dry ground on which the marshes could be crossed, and formed part of the pre-historic route from north Lancashire to the Yorkshire coast, through the Aire gap and along Wharfedale.

Glacial deposits are important to the archaeologist, because they offered suitable soils for settlement by man, whose implements are found in them. Caution however is needed here, for two reasons; the pressures and stresses under which the rock was brought to its present resting-place may well have fractured it in a way very like human working; and, where implements are genuine, some of them may be rolled, that is, rubbed down by their travels and their redeposition in the moraine—such rolled pieces are not contemporary with the men who lived on the moraine after it was formed, and therefore cannot be dated so easily; they come from an earlier period, and need to be dated by other means. The ice, of course, sweeps up everything in its path, of whatever date, and mixes it all up in forming the latest moraine. (Material later than the moraine will be found on or near its surface— the earlier inside it.) Rolled stones can also be found in river beds, some of which may be genuine implements washed down into the river from the valley sides. Early man also settled round the shores of the glacial lakes, some of which have now dried up (as Ehenside Tarn, Cumberland; Lake Pickering, Yorkshire).

POST-GLACIAL PHASES

After the ice of phase III of the Last Glaciation finally receded to the highest lands of Scandinavia and the Alps, the climate of northern Europe gradually changed through various phases until it reached the point we are at now. Much research, principally by way of pollen analysis, has been done both on the Continent and in Britain, to establish a sequence of phases through which the climate passed. These phases had also their characteristic vegetation, and have deeply influenced the way of life of the inhabitants of Britain down to our own day.

Table 2

POST-GLACIAL CLIMATIC PHASES AND CULTURE-PERIODS

Date		*Phase* (flora)	*Culture-period*
12,000 BC	Ia	Oldest Dryas (called after the plant of that name, then predominant); tundra flora—pine and willow	Palaeolithic survivals
11,000	Ib	Bølling oscillation—warmer	
10,000	Ic	Older Dryas	
9000	II	Allerød oscillation—birch	
8850	III	Younger Dryas (these phases make up the Late Würm or Late Glacial)	
8300	IV	Pre-Boreal; gradual then rapid rise in temperature; birch dominating over pine—much herbaceous vegetation	Mesolithic
7600	V	Early Boreal; cold and dry—continental climate;	
7000		pine dominant. Hazel increasing at end of phase	
5500	VI	Late Boreal; warmer. Pine-hazel zone; more alder; oak and elm increase, and squeeze out hazel at the end	
3500	VIIa	Atlantic; warm and moist. Mixed forest (alder, oak, elm, lime)	Neolithic
1800	VIIb	Early Sub-Boreal	Bronze Age
1500	VII-VIII	Later Sub-Boreal	

Date		*Phase* (flora)	*Culture-period*
1000		transition period. Peat formation on moors	
600	VIII	Sub-Atlantic; sudden deterioration of climate—cool and wet. Blanket-peat; birch increases, and beech more prominent	Iron Age

These phases should not be thought of as violently fluctuating one from another; climatic changes are gradual. The main changes since the end of the Ice Age (as established by the work of H. H. Lamb and others) are:

Bølling warm phase, *c.* 12,000–11,500 BC

Allerød warm phase, *c.* 10,000–9000 BC

post-Allerød cold epoch, *c.* 8800–8200 BC, drop of summer temperature in N. England by 4°C

post-glacial climatic optimum; level highest from *c.* 5000–3000 BC, but the same level may have been reached many times between 6–7000 and 1000 BC

decline from 3000 BC—cool and wet low between *c.* 1000 and 500 BC (fall of about 2°)

in the Roman period the climate was similar to today's, but there was an improvement leading to a lesser optimum in the early Middle Ages, culminating between about AD 1000 and 1300 (vine-growing in southern England)

colder again, with the worst conditions ('the Little Ice Age' between about 1550 and 1700 (very bad in the 1590s, and starvation in Scotland in the 1690s)

improvement in 18th century—peak in 1730s, then sustained high levels—new optimum 1890–1930, climax in 1920s

decline since, sharply from 1940; summers wetter since 1950, winters dry from 1961.

The importance of climate for the life of man should certainly not be overlooked. The optimum conditions since the last ice age were during the early Neolithic. Some authorities think that we are in an interglacial now, and heading eventually for another ice age; certainly the mean summer temperature, which was 44° F in 16,000 BC, reached 65° about 6000 BC, and is now 61°, which indicates a significant trend.

CHAPTER 4

The Cultures of Britain

A brief description of the various peoples who have settled in Britain over the centuries, and of their cultures, may be helpful, not only in understanding references to their names and remains elsewhere in this book, but as a very brief background to fuller literature and to museums.

HUNTERS, FISHERS AND GATHERERS

The greater part of human history (from soon after two million years ago to c. 3000 BC) is occupied by the Stone Age, when man was not able to control his environment.

THE BEGINNINGS

When the phrase 'man the toolmaker' was taken literally, and a sudden evolution was not thought possible, the age of Man had to be measured by means of stone tools whose origins were sought back in the pre-Pleistocene period of geological time. Hence for many years, in fact until very recently indeed, the older archaeologists regarded as humanly made tools flaked stones now shown to be of natural origin. These were the 'eoliths' (dawn-stones), made famous in Britain by Benjamin Harrison of Ightham, Kent; the 'rostro-carinates' of the Red Crag of East Anglia; the flints of the Cromer foreshore; and several others, both here and abroad, including Belgium and France, and the so-called Kafuan of Africa. But humanly-struck flints have in general a lower angle of flaking (see p. 255–6) than stones flaked by nature, and these eoliths have been shown statistically (by Professor Barnes) to be natural; they were made either by the creep of frozen soils, or by the foundering caused by solution of underlying soil, or by whirlpools at the confluences of rivers, or by the movement of moraines, or of ice-packs or sheets (eoliths, red crag), or by wave- or river-action (Cromer and others); in the tropics yet other natural forces are at work. So, to the regret of some, eoliths have had to be abandoned, except as examples of what nature can do.

Recent evidence from Africa (Olduvai) shows that the first

authentic stone tools were made by man-apes of the *Australopithecus* type (which includes *Zinjanthropus*) and *Homo habilis*, which lived from about 1,800,000 to 800,000 years ago. No doubt these and other hominids were already using tools of wood, bone, horn, teeth, etc. which have perished; archaeology has so often to be content with only the imperishable part of man's equipment. These first stone tools, which in Africa are of the **early Oldowan** culture, are just pebbles or lumps of rock 'flaked by percussion to form crude chopping tools', as Dr Leakey describes them. The flaking is done in two directions along the chopping edge. These date from the early Pleistocene (the Villafranchian stage of the geologists), well before the early glaciation.

LOWER AND MIDDLE PALAEOLITHIC

The Lower and Middle Palaeolithic (to about 100,000 BC) is the period of primitive types of man, making crude implements from cores and flakes of flint and other stones. Man leads his life against a background of the Ice Age, alternate glaciations and mild periods.

The tools of this period develop into bifacial hand-axes (fig. 25, p. 260) (the Oldowan), used by the sub-man *Homo erectus*, who spread from Africa to Java, China and Europe.[1] The first tools in Europe are just these crude handaxes, of the culture once called Chellean, now **Abbevillian**, first recognised in the Somme terraces, but found in England also (e.g. at Caversham in the Thames valley). This culture dates from either just before or at some point inside the antepenultimate glaciation, some 500,000 to 450,000 years ago. Abbevillian axes were struck by hammer-stones or on anvil-stones, and have large, deep flaking.

The Abbevillian people seem to have been driven from Britain again by the second glaciation, and after a gap their place was taken, in the warmer second interglacial, 400,000 years ago, by the **Acheulians**, who brought with them a better-made and less crude type of handaxe, almond-shaped with shallow flake-scars, made with a bone or wood baton, or a soft hammerstone. The development to this type, and beyond, throughout the long life of the Acheulian culture, is continuous from the early pebble-choppers (fig. 25, p. 260) through the crude bifaces. In fact, if the pebbles were made by *Homo habilis*, and the bifaces by *Homo erectus*, the Acheulian axes must have been made by those of the succeeding 'generalised Neanderthal' men who afterwards developed into full Man, *Homo sapiens*. The others, those who specialised into *Homo neanderthalensis*, took to using tools based on flakes and not on cores (fig. 25, p. 260); it is interesting that this

[1] There is no space here to describe the evolution of man, but see *Books to Read* p. 336.

broad division begins very early—the *Homo erectus* men of China and Java used a few flake tools, and from this branch it looks as if the European flake cultures in part derive. At any rate, there are two broad culture-areas by the second interglacial, the Handaxe cultures to the south and west, the Flake cultures to the north and east. The old chopper idea survives in the flake cultures in a purer form, so the flake people, as might be expected if they are Neanderthals, are more primitive than the *Homo sapiens* stock.

The handaxe was used for cutting and scraping as well as chopping. Acheulian man must have had tools of other materials also, and killed animals by bolas, stones tied together with strings which caught round the animal's legs and slowed it up. The famous human remains from Swanscombe, Kent, which belonged to a man on the direct line of evolution to *Homo sapiens*, were associated with an Acheulian culture; he lived about 250,000 years ago. The handaxe grew in grace, developing from the ovoid, ovate (fig. 25, p. 260) and almond-shaped, to a pear-shaped and later to a pointed form (the Micoquian). The Acheulian culture lasted some 200,000 years, and went through seven different stages.

The earliest flake-culture people reached Britain, and brought with them the culture called **Clactonian**, after a site on the foreshore at Clacton (Essex), which was formerly on the banks of an early channel of the Thames. They arrived at the beginning of the second glaciation, 475-450,000 years ago, replacing the Abbevillians who were withdrawing to the south, away from the onset of the glaciation. During the second interglacial period they were partly supplanted by the incoming Acheulians, and thereafter both races lived side by side, and intermingled their cultures to a great extent. The Clactonian industry consists of rough choppers (fig. 25), like those of the early African (Oldowan), and later Indian (Soan); heavy scrapers and points of many kinds (fig. 25); it has no handaxes. These tools were made on anvilstones and have wide flaking-angles and prominent bulbs; the cortex is left on (fig. 23, p. 256). There are also core-tools, chipped all round and biconical. Many of the scrapers are hollow (i.e. with incurved cutting edge) as if for shaping wooden spears, of which a tip was found at Clacton. Bone tools, e.g. wedges, are also suspected.

In eastern Europe the Clactonian probably developed into the **Mousterian** (there is an intermediate mixed culture, the Tayacian, which does not concern us, but which was used partly by pre-*sapiens* man), which comes into the story later. Meanwhile, by the third glaciation, the dominant flake-culture of Britain was the **Levalloisian**. This is characterised by a very specialised form of flintwork, in which the core was prepared as a first process before the flakes were struck off from it and themselves made into tools. The whole prepared core (i.e. flaked all over, thus giving a ready-made back to the flake), is called a 'tortoise-core', from its appearance (fig. 25, p. 260); the flakes made from it will have, not a plain striking-platform as in the Clactonian, but a faceted one. The origin of this peculiar technique is obscure; it may have arisen in several industries, even in some Acheulian groups. The Levalloisian culture, indeed, may represent cross-fertilisation of ideas between Acheulian and Clactonian peoples, or may have been adopted by Acheulians to deal with the onset of cold, wet conditions at the time of the third glaciation. The Lower Thames terraces (Northfleet, Crayford, etc., in Kent) have produced classical settlements of this culture; it has not been found north of Welbeck (Notts).

Meanwhile, the Neanderthal type of man was also living in Europe, with his rather crude Mousterian culture, which evolved from the Clactonian, but with strong influences from the Acheulian and Levalloisian. The later, more advanced form of this culture was well-adapted to the cold tundra conditions of the fourth glaciation. These men lived in caves where they could, and worked skins for clothing and shelter. Their tools included discoidal cores, well-retouched flakes with plain butts, side-scrapers and triangular points. They lived by hunting, and became great experts in this, having a variety of food and bone tools and ornaments. Much evidence on their life was derived from the caves at Creswell (Derbyshire), where it is seen that the Mousterians in Britain just survived the second phase of the last (fourth) glaciation, and were then replaced, quite suddenly, some 50,000 years ago, by the true men, *Homo sapiens*, of the Upper Palaeolithic, who brought to Britain a much higher culture, and whose descendants we are.

The core peoples, Abbevillian and Acheulian, liked mild climates, and lived in Britain in the interglacials; they were vegetable and grub gatherers in the woodlands and scrub. The Clactonians were forest people, also in the mild periods, the Levalloisians and Mousterians were forced by cold to adapt themselves to hunting as a way of life, and lived in all climates. The details of their replacement by true men are obscure.

THE UPPER PALAEOLITHIC

In the Upper Palaeolithic (from c. 50,000 BC to c. 12,000 BC), during the last glaciation, true man (Homo sapiens) appeared, and developed a more complex way of life, with composite implements, art, religion and a more advanced social structure.

The replacement of the earlier peoples was so rapid and complete that we must postulate the immigration of new stocks from what is now the Continent, but of course was joined on in those days. These were true men, *Homo sapiens*, who could no doubt out-think, out-manoeuvre, out-invent and out-live the earlier peoples. This gulf of inventiveness, sensitiveness, conceptual thought, language, imagination and planning could never be bridged; the bewildered men of the lower species never had a chance of evolving into something higher. They retired in tiny groups into the forests, and died out, or were killed off.

Homo sapiens seems to have been cradled somewhere in south-west Asia, round the Caspian or on the plateau of Iran. From this region several cultures emerged, and streams of people moved westward into Europe. The first of these Upper Palaeolithic cultures, the Chatelperronian, reached France about 50,000 years ago; some of its features were inherited from the long Acheulian past, and no doubt *Homo sapiens* himself represents an evolutionary leap from Acheulian man of the Swanscombe type. The evidence of the new cultures comes mainly from the French caves, especially those of Périgord, which were occupied by a long succession of peoples for about 40,000 years. The sequence thus worked out, Chatelperronian, Aurignacian, Gravettian, Solutrean and Magdalenian (to which is to be added a northern European culture of post-glacial times, the Hamburgian, and other survivals like the Aterian and the Capsian of north Africa) is not all represented in Britain. This sequence differs from that current in pre-war archaeology, but its main lines are firmly based.

The great feature of the new culture was not only its variety of equipment, in wood, bone, antler, etc., as well as stone, but the technique of the stone tools themselves. These were now smaller than before, and made of blades of flint etc., not cores or flakes. This was a revolution. It enabled more delicate tools to be made, and more adapted to a variety of specialised tasks, such as the burin, a characteristic tool, with an edge intended for graving with, made by means of a 'step' taken off the side of the piece, of which more than 20 types were devised. This was a tool for making needles and awls to make heavy clothing needed for cold climates. Moreover, it meant the development of composite tools, blades mounted in wooden hafts to form knives, saws, and the like (fig. 25, p. 260). There were also finely worked points of different shapes. The earlier men did not disappear at once, for the Chatelperronians absorbed a few Mousterian ideas.

The next people to reach western Europe were the powerful Cro-Magnons, bringing their **Aurignacian** culture. They had bone and antler tools, pins, awls, points with cleft base for mounting on a shaft. They had the beginnings of religion, and their cave-art, painting and sculpture, is now famous. Language in the modern sense may now be assumed; so complex a culture would need speech to transmit it. A few families of Aurignacians found their way to Britain, and left traces at Paviland (Gower), and in the Vale of Clwyd.

Meanwhile, in the east of Europe, the **Gravettians** were growing and spreading, some remaining in eastern Europe and Asia, some coming west. Their culture has affinities with the earlier Chatelperronian; it too had a narrow pointed blade, and a few bone tool types. At a late stage of its development, about 20,000 years ago, a few Gravettians reached Britain, and in the caves of Derbyshire they succeeded the Mousterians, no doubt refugees from the relatively teeming new life in France. In Britain they evolved a distinctive culture, called the **Creswellian**, which is an adaptation to local conditions of the Gravettian way of life, a genuine British thing; this sort of process is indeed a feature of British history.

During this time, in France, the brilliant **Magdalenian** culture arrived, and was decorating its bone tools and painting its caves in great profusion. The Creswellians had a few contacts with the Magdalenians, and some objects of the latter culture were found in Creswellian Caves at Cheddar, Aveline's Hole, Creswell, Kent's Cavern, Pin Hole, and Victoria Cave (Settle, Yorks). Whether these represent visits of Magdalenians to Britain or just trade objects is not of course known, but it does at least mean that the Creswellians were not completely cut off from the larger life to the south of them. But the Creswellian is essentially a British culture, based solidly on Gravettian models, but evolved in isolation. Only a few works of art have been found in Britain, an engraved horse's head, three engravings from Mother Grundy's Parlour, three from Pin Hole; they represent fish, chevrons, and a masked man executing a ceremonial dance. The Creswellians lived by hunting bison, horse and in the last cold phase (Würm III) reindeer, with occasional rhinoceros and mammoth. Hyaena and cave-bears were common, and lion present. A few open-air sites are known, besides the caves, mostly along the Lincoln ridge. Solutrian culture, with its economy based on hunting the horse, and its very fine flint-work, is not known in Britain.

During this last phase of the last glaciation, a new cultural tendency shows itself, the reduction in size of the blade-tools. A few small blades occur in the earliest levels of the Creswellian, but not until the end of the period did they become common. Then they proliferated, and by the time the last ice had receded they had become the characteristic tool of the next phase of human culture, the mesolithic, which lasted from about 12,000 years ago until the coming of the neolithic farmers in the fourth millennium BC.

Before we leave the Palaeolithic, it may be of interest to reflect that the races of man found in the world today descend from the three or four human types of the upper Palaeolithic. It looks indeed as though *Homo sapiens* was always, from his first emergence, divided into different physical types, with no doubt mental and temperamental differences also. This may reflect slightly different, if parallel, cradles of origin or descent, but the real reasons are obscure. It has been arguably suggested that the Combe Capelle race was the first to reach western Europe, long-headed people, with Chatelperronian culture: the Aurignacians were of the tall Cro-Magnon race, the Gravettians of a central European type called Predmost. The Negroid Grimaldi people of the Mediterranean had a culture allied to Gravettian; the Magdalenians were of the somewhat eskimo-like Chancelade stock. The Creswellians were apparently a mixture, and tended to broad-headedness, as did the mesolithic peoples. It would not be correct to imagine the population of Britain in the upper Palaeolithic as numerous. Hunting people need great areas to live comfortably, and it has been calculated that there were probably not more than two or three hundred people in Britain in the winter months.

In the lower and middle palaeolithic periods the distribution of these people was almost confined to the lowland zone, and particularly to the gravel soils of the river terraces, which could provide not only man's food supply but dry places to live, with timber to make into shelters—caves are not common in Britain. Great numbers of Abbevillian and Acheulian artifacts have been found in the valley of the Thames and its tributaries, and in East Anglia; important sites are in north Kent, Stoke Newington (London), near Reading (in Oxfordshire), Farnham and Lingfield in Surrey, and Hoxne in Suffolk. The Middle Acheulian seems to be absent from the south-east of England; but other phases are well represented. The Clactonian is best known from the Thames valley, both in north Kent and along the Essex coast, where the river once ran, and in later phases in East Anglia; the Levalloisian again from the Thames gravels. The Mousterian is somewhat different; this is best represented in the caves, from Devon to the Mendips, south Wales, Derbyshire and Yorkshire. There are a few important rock shelters in the south-east such as Oldbury and near Tunbridge Wells (Kent).

Man at this period did not apparently penetrate the highland zone, although there would have been nothing to stop him in the milder phases. But we are in a field of some controversy here, and caution is needed in interpreting finds in the North. The material for implements in the highland zone is not flint, but local rocks of a kind which are hard yet can be worked reasonably easily into the traditional shapes—chert, quartzite, ash, rhyolite, etc. A handaxe from Huntow, Bridlington, and a flake from Chester represent wanderings round the edge of the highland zone. Within it, lower palaeolithic age has been claimed for chert flakes, choppers, bifaces, etc., from Nidderdale (Yorks); but the dale was filled with ice more than once, and flaked stones found in the moraines and hill-wash may be so caused by soil-movements; stones rolled along the river-bed may also be naturally shaped. But it must be admitted that a few of these stones look possible implements, and it may be a case where the Frenchman's remark applies: 'Man made one, God made ten thousand; God help the man who tries to find the one among the ten thousand!' Some of the Lake District valleys (e.g. Borrowdale) yield similar materials; in Scotland also a few apparent implements have been found, as also in the boulder-clays of the north-east coast of England, but natural forces could account for all these. So, with the possible but still very doubtful exception of Nidderdale, man did not penetrate the highland zone in the lower Palaeolithic. In the middle Palaeolithic he is found in north-east Derbyshire, south-east Yorkshire (and possibly also Eskdale), and perhaps north Wales, none of these sites suggesting more than border exploration from the lowlands.

With the upper Palaeolithic, man, with his better equipment, undoubtedly ranged more widely. The Aurignacians reached Derbyshire; the Creswellians are found in Yorkshire, where the later Nidderdale material is unquestionable. Other settlements were at Flamborough, Eskdale, the Humber district, Lincolnshire and Norfolk. However, a few finds in Scotland are not unambiguous. The Creswellian, in its evolved form, lasted until the last glacial phase, and by then had traits which are also found in the later mesolithic cultures. The gap between the receding of the last ice-sheets and the mesolithic is filled with 'epi-palaeolithic' cultures, survivals of the late glacial peoples using distinctive tools such as backed blades and tanged points (fig. 25, p. 261). These are found in several groups in northern Europe, and one site, an open one on Hengistbury Head, Hants, has now been found in England.

MESOLITHIC

After the last glaciation receded the climatic changes led to different hunting conditions, and the Mesolithic (c. 12,000 to c. 3000 BC) is characterised by very small flint implements and a variety of adaptations to a somewhat bleak way of life.

When the ice of the third phase of the last glaciation receded, the climate went through phases of successive improvement; at first, and for thousands of years, the vegetation was tundra, succeeded by scrub of hazel and alder, and later by woodlands of birch and pine. The great animals had gone, and man had to live on roots, berries, and smaller animals. The Creswellian culture gradually adapted itself to these new conditions, and the microlith, mounted on wooden shafts and hafts, became the standard tool. Composite saws could be made up of small blades set in wood and stuck in with resinous glue.

Recent researches have considerably altered the accepted pattern of the mesolithic settlement of Britain. Whether actual settlers came to this country from France or not, and it is likely that they did, to reinforce the survivors of the Creswellian way of life, the character of the mesolithic of all but the south-east and east of England shows affinities with the French mesolithic culture called **Sauveterrian**. This is a culture once considered as merely a stage of the culture called Tardenoisian, but now shown to be quite separate, just one of the many reactions to the new conditions. The Tardenoisian itself never reached Britain at all, and moreover is later than was once thought. The Sauveterrian uses the micro-burin technique (see p. 258) of producing geometric implements from a long blade or flake, like many mesolithic groups. Its main types are elongated triangles, narrow rods with battered edges, penknife forms, crescents, blunted points and trapezoids (fig. 25, p. 261); some of these are very small. In the British industry there are also convex scrapers and a few burins. From the 8th millennium BC this culture spread over the higher, more open, lands—the sites are on moors or sandy heaths, or near the sea, and were chosen for their freedom from the thick forest-cover, even at the height of the birch-woods of the Boreal climatic phase. They range from Cornwall and north Devon to East Anglia, the Fens and Lincolnshire; there are important sites in the Pennines (those near Huddersfield are well known), older than the wetter climate of the Atlantic phase, which began about 5000 BC. They reached Wales and the Isle of Man, the North-East coast, and southern and eastern Scotland. Some sites are sealed under peat of Atlantic age, others are on open surfaces, and no doubt many more are to be found.

During all this time the east of England was joined to the Continent, and the dwellers in the forests of the north European plain could move freely into this country, where they settled in the similar woodlands as far inland as the Chilterns. They brought with them the culture called **Maglemosian** (after a site in Denmark) which was adapted to life in the forests. One of the earliest of these settlements (of the pre-Boreal phase) has been excavated at Star Carr, near Scarborough, by Professor J. G. D. Clark, the authority on the European Mesolithic. This site revealed a very full picture of a way of life based on hunting and fishing; the dwelling-places were built on rafts of branches by a lakeside, and much wood was used for domestic purposes; rolls of birch-bark were found, out of which receptacles were made. The flint forms include blunted points, triangles, long trapezes and irregular crescents, but are not so narrow or so small as the Sauveterrian tools; also tranchet edges (see fig. 25, p. 261). Pronged antler fish-spears were used. Maglemosian sites ranged from Co. Durham to Holderness, where bone harpoons were found (they were also dredged up from the North Sea banks off Norfolk, when this was part of the dry land); most are in the south-east of England, from Hampshire to the Thames valley and Essex. Much information was gained from a site at Broxbourne, on the Lea. In the Boreal phase perhaps the most distinctive tool was the core-axe (fig. 27, p. 263), with its edge made by means of a transverse blow called a 'tranchet blow'; this is well adapted for grubbing roots or for cutting timber. When Britain was separated from the Continent about 5000 BC the forest people were isolated in this island, and developed a still heavier implement to cope with the ever-thickening woodlands of the Atlantic phase; this is the so-called Thames pick, an axe-adze made on a thick core, longer and narrower than the earlier type; it is sometimes as much as a foot long. With it is also found the flake-axe, which also has a tranchet edge. The type-site of this phase is Lower Halstow, Kent. An arrow-head with tranchet edge was also used.

In the south-east of England is found a culture hybrid between the Maglemosian and the Sauveterrian, called after the site at **Horsham**. Whether this is a genuine mixed community, or either of the major cultures influenced by the other, is not clear. The sites are mostly on the sandy heaths of Surrey and Hampshire, but occur on other soils also. The tools include the usual range of microliths, including core-scrapers or 'push-planes', a type of palaeolithic origin, and scrapers on wide blades (fig. 25, p. 261), but the characteristic 'Horsham point' occurs, a hollow-based triangle; and the Thames pick indicates the mixture of cultures. The sites are often very large, some of them producing up to 200,000 implements, micro-burins and waste flakes; the culture was isolated at sites at Horsham, Farnham (Surrey), and Selmeston (Sussex) but a large number have turned up on the Surrey greensands, into Hampshire (Oakhanger), and on into Dorset (Iwerne Minster). Huts, scooped out of the ground and roofed with branches, have been found at Farnham and Abinger (Surrey). W. F. Rankine, a pioneer of the exploration of this culture, has shown by the distribution of coloured flint and flint of known local origin, how the colonisation of the south of England proceeded. He has also shown that stone 'mace-heads' and perforated pebbles (fig. 27, p. 263), are characteristic of the Mesolithic of south-east England, and probably of the forest elements.

Another hybrid culture, this time between the late Creswellian and the forest tradition, is found in Galloway and Northern Ireland (the **Larnian**). This is late in the Mesolithic; and indeed, it now appears that, apart from one or two doubtful exceptions, man did not reach Scotland at all until about 3000 BC. The old description of the **Obanian** culture, based on hunting, and on fish and molluscs, as a movement of the mesolithic people called Azilian, from south-west Europe, no longer holds. For one thing, micro-burins are found on the Scottish sites, whereas they are quite absent from the Azilian. No doubt this culture was a local adaptation to its environment, but having its origin somewhere further south in Britain; similar groups occur in south-west Scotland (Shewalton, Ayrs.; near Kirkcudbright), in Yorkshire (Settle) and Co. Durham; and elongated pebbles, like scoops but probably fabricators, have been found in Wales and Cornwall. Harpoons with two rows of rather clumsy barbs are found in this group. The separation from the Continent not only imposed an insular development on the culture of the island, but kept out the late mesolithic broad blade and trapeze culture, which may be linked with the slow spread from the East of a pre-pottery Neolithic.

Table 3

PALAEOLITHIC AND MESOLITHIC CULTURES OF BRITAIN

(Symbols used: E = *Homo erectus*; N = Neanderthal Man; S = *Homo sapiens* (modern man); P = pebble tools; C = core tools; F = flake tools; B = blades and burins.)

Years ago	*Glacial stage*	*Culture and type of man**
c. 1,000,000	Early glaciation (Günz)	
		LOWER PALAEOLITHIC
c. 600,000	Antepenultimate interglacial	Clactonian I (P&F;E)
c. 400,000	Antepenultimate glaciation (Mindel)	Abbevillian (C&F;E)
c. 250,000	Penultimate interglacial	Acheulian I-IV (C; proto-N)
		Clactonian II
c. 150,000	Penultimate glaciation (Riss) phase I	Acheulian V (Tayacian)
		Clactonian (High Lodge)
		MIDDLE PALAEOLITHIC
	interstadial	Acheulian VI-VII (Micoquian)
		Levalloisian I-II (F;N)
	phase II	Levalloisian III-IV
c. 100,000	Last interglacial	Mousterian I-II (F;N)
c. 70,000	Last glaciation (Würm) phase I	Levalloisian VI
		UPPER PALAEOLITHIC
c. 40,000	interstadial	Aurignacian (B;S)
		Levalloisian VII
c. 30,000	phase II	Mousterian III (Pin Hole)
c. 25,000	interstadial	Creswellian (B;S)
c. 18,000-15,000	phase III	do

Date B.C.	*Climatic phase* (see Table 2)	MESOLITHIC
12,000	post-glacial	Creswellian survivors
8300	pre-boreal	Sauveterrian (early)
7600	boreal	Maglemosean
		Sauveterrian (late)
		Horsham
5500	Atlantic	Larnian
	(separation from Continent)	Obanian
by 4000		NEOLITHIC (see Table 4)

* *Australopithecus* and *Homo habilis*, using pebble tools, are not found in Britain.

FARMERS AND HERDSMEN

In the sections that follow new cultures in Britain are usually ascribed to invasions. But it should not be thought that these were all massive; some might be mere trickles or local intrusions. And many new objects or customs may be results of increasing wealth on the part of the native leaders rather than the replacement of those leaders by others from abroad. Culture contact is often more important than invasion, as is continuity of local development.

THE NEOLITHIC

The first farmers arrived from the Continent by 4000 BC, and introduced the basis for our civilisation, which has developed without a break ever since. Although metal was used in the Near East, the new people were on the fringes of civilization, and still used stone; hence their period is called the Neolithic (c. 4000 to 2400 BC). The aboriginal mesolithic peoples gradually adopted elements of the new way of life, and created secondary neolithic cultures. Collective burial in long barrows, and new types of stone tombs were introduced from Western Europe.

During all this time, when north-western Europe was still in a state of hunting and food-gathering savagery, a movement of quite revolutionary importance for human history was taking place in the Near East, beginning about 10,000 BC. Farming and stock-raising were greatly developed, and gradually urban centres arose where goods could be exchanged and mutual protection made easier. Intensive cereal-growing enabled man to settle in one place (particularly where the land was made fertile by an annual flood—in western Europe at first the farmer had to move on when the fertility of a patch was exhausted) instead of wandering over a wide area in search of his food. He can now have more material possessions, which can be kept in one place. The surplus of the farm, if any, can be sold for tools, equipment, and ornaments, which can now be made by specialists; finally, man must now co-operate with his neighbours all the time, because there are more and more of them as the food supply increases, and they are living ever closer together instead of just meeting rarely for a tribal gathering or some communal work. Town-life is a direct outcome of these trends, and is of far-reaching consequence. Its origins have been recently observed at such sites as Jericho to go back to the early 8th millennium BC. Gods, kings (their representatives on earth), priests, merchants and people live together within their walls, with their farms and market gardens round, a city-state with definite and often rigid social structure. From this grew rivalries and alliances, wars, nations and empires, throughout the Iranian plateau, the Fertile Crescent from Iran and Iraq to Syria (with Asia Minor), and though Palestine to Egypt.

The late Professor Childe distinguished two economic and social revolutions in the Near East—the Neolithic (the invention of farming) and the Urban (which included the establishment of a metallurgical industry—essential for progress, but needing a large surplus of wealth to maintain). These, in his view, had delayed and long-distance effects on the life and economy of Europe; so delayed in north-west Europe that although the first set off our Neolithic, yet the second created a copper and then a bronze age in the Mediterranean area while Britain was still in its Neolithic.

The development of all this is of course outside our scope, and should be read in Childe's works. What is of importance is his concept that all this new way of life in its barest outline and its minimum practice, gradually spread from the Near East into Europe, by slow stages, and by radiating zones of culture, each less civilised as the west was approached. It took over 5000 years for the first farmers to reach Britain in the course of their slow moves from one exhausted patch of soil to the next fresh one further on. Late in the fifth millenium (say 4300–4000 BC) families began to land on the south coast of England with a few belongings, seed, and animals, and worked along the rivers of Kent, Sussex and Hampshire on to the chalk hills which they could see from the shore. From those small beginnings, through many different peoples and cultures, was finally built up the Britain that we know today, in an unbroken line.

The influence of the Near Eastern civilisations was conveyed across Europe by three main routes, a southern along the Mediterranean to Iberia and round or across France to the south-west of Britain; northwards from Greece to the Danube valley and across to central and northern France, and so to southern England; and a third, through northern Europe to eastern England. All these were diluted or affected by the peoples they passed through, and all three streams met at different times in Britain, and combined in various ways to create new and distinctive culture-patterns.

Childe's theories, which incidentally have sometimes been interpreted more rigidly than he intended, have been outlined here because of their dominance of archaeological thinking over the past forty years. They have however been partially undermined by several crucial recent developments. One is the extended dating of the Neolithic and Bronze Ages which results from the new calibration of radiocarbon dates (described on page 290), which has far-reaching implications. Another is the discovery in south-eastern Europe of aspects of civilisation which are very early, and which may even antedate similar features in the Near East. A third is the new concept of the origins of agriculture and domestication (put forward by Higgs and Jarman in 1970). The symbiosis of man with animals and plants may go back to the hunter-gatherer stage. So there is no need to look for a beginning of agriculture in a particular area—it is part of the economic basis of human life everywhere. The Near East was merely the area on the edge of two climatic zones, where a synthesis of practices could take place, and a new integrated economy could rapidly develop and explosively expand.

So, although Childe's concept of diffusion of cultures from the Near East into Europe will certainly have to be greatly modified, no new or final pattern has yet been worked out, nor will be possible for some years to come.

One should not think of the old mesolithic inhabitants as disappearing when the new settlers arrived, as the Neanderthalers did at the coming of *Homo sapiens*. There was room for all, and the older stocks lived side by side with the farmers, many ultimately imitating them, some actually adopting the new way of life, some using their local knowledge and keeping up their wandering habits to become traders and pastoralists. The secondary neolithic cultures were evolved by the former mesolithic peoples as a response to the new situation and, of course on the Continent the cultures which reached us were also secondary to the original civilisation.

The first settlers came from northern France and from several places in Germany and the Low Countries as well, some perhaps even direct from Iberia: their culture is called **Windmill Hill**, after one of their settlements in Wiltshire. This is dominated by a 'causewayed camp' (see p. 100 and pl. 4) dated by carbon 14 to 2570 ± 150 BC, and already some 4–500 years later than the first settlements. It is not a fort, but an enclosure in which the cattle could be sheltered, and selectively slaughtered hrough the winter. Round it were scattered the plots of the community, who lived in rough timber and thatch huts, and who cultivated patches of ground with digging-sticks, growing primitive species of wheat and barley. They wore skins, and textiles; they had flint tools, including scrapers of many kinds, made mostly by making a working edge along one side of a rough flake, borers, knives, saws, and, distinctively, axes of flint, ground smooth and polished. This was an improvement on the earlier rough flaked axes, and proved tougher for felling trees to make houses, fences and the like. They also used axes of various kinds of stone traded to them by the aborigines, and imported some implements from Scandinavia. They mined flint (see p. 116).

Pottery was brought over with them, the first in this country; smooth pots shaped like leather bags, with round bottoms, often shoulders or 'carinations', and lugs for hanging them over the fire; some have simple designs incised on them. Various local varieties are found, such as Hembury (in the south-west), with flaring 'trumpet-lugs', Abingdon and East Anglian. Pottery spoons and 'plates' (covers for storage jars) reflect (as do the causewayed camps) similar things in France and the Rhineland. The dead were buried in earthen long barrows, a northern European idea (some of the pottery styles may have come from northern Europe also). See fig. 11, p. 152, and fig. 32, p. 271.

These people spread later as far as Lincolnshire and Yorkshire, along the dry chalk ridge which runs north-east from Wessex; there other local types of pottery are found, Grimston and Heslerton wares, and there may have been direct colonisation here also. The barrows of this area sometimes contain cremations; some, as do all in southern England, inhumations; burial was collective, not individual.

(The former conception of massive invasions accounting for new cultures is now being played down, and more continuity of local development (of pottery etc.) seen.)

Megalithic tombs. After the Windmill Hill people had settled down Britain was reached in the years from 3500–3000 BC, by representatives of the cultures building megalithic tombs, constructions of large stones and dry-stone walling. The origins of these may be sought in the eastern Mediterranean area; the idea of rock-cut tombs and stone chamber-tombs was taken to the west, where, in Malta, Iberia and southern France, distinctive types evolved; from these regions they spread to the rest of France, Britain and Scandinavia. There are various theories to account for their movements. They could have been brought to Britain by prospectors for metals (and many of the tombs are in metal-liferous areas), by colonists (most are in good farming districts), by mere purveyors of new kinds of tombs or, as Childe elaborated in his last book, *The Prehistory of European Society*, by missionaries of the religion of the Mother Goddess. These were hermits like the Celtic saints of later days, who would settle in a place with devout followers. They would be buried in a special kind of tomb, which thereafter would be the privileged burial-place of the chief's family, and perhaps the local shrine as well. But there are difficulties in all these theories and, on the new view forced on archaeologists by the extended C14 dating, there was no megalithic colonisation of Europe. The question now is (Glyn Daniel, 1970) 'what peoples built megalithic tombs in which places, and why?' Perhaps they were just renderings in stone of wooden houses for the dead, evolving in different areas, such as Brittany or Northern Europe. The fact remains that, by the time the tombs reached Britain, they fall into two main types, with a number of local variations. Details will be found in the Burial section (see p. 151 and fig. 12), but in outline the position is as follows.

Most of the tombs are in coastal areas on the west side of Britain or in Ireland; inland penetration took place in Ireland, the Cotswolds and as far as Wiltshire. A small group of another kind, near Maidstone in Kent, is best explained as a colony from Denmark or north Germany.

The western tombs fall into Passage Graves and Gallery Graves, with variants and hybrids. Passage Graves have a chamber, round, square or with side chambers, connected by a narrow passage to the outside of the usually round mound or cairn which covers it; Gallery Graves are long stone passages, sometimes divided into sections by transverse slabs, or with side chambers, generally under long mounds or cairns. In both cases the mounds are usually very much larger than the chambers, and indeed this is one of the features of these tombs; Childe calculated that some of the stone cairns on the bare moorlands of Caithness each contained enough stone to build five fair-sized parish churches, which gives an idea of the social effort involved in building them, and of the power of the megalithic religion. The main groups, further described on pages 155-7, are:

Severn-Cotswold, in south Wales, the Cotswolds, the Mendips, and the Wiltshire Downs. These are long trapezoidal mounds with a stone revetment and often an elaborate forecourt for ritual; the tomb chamber was a gallery, sometimes with side chambers or 'transepts' or a large rectangular chamber; some of these opened into the forecourt, in others the forecourt had a dummy entrance in it and the chambers were along the side of the mound. Windmill Hill pottery is found in these tombs, with Peterborough and Beaker secondary; they last till about 1700 BC. (See plates 4 and 5.)

Roughly contemporary, or even part of the same stream, are the **Clyde-Solway** and **Carlingford** groups (formerly regarded as a single **Clyde-Carlingford** group) in northern Ireland, south-west Scotland, Man and west Wales. These are mostly oval or wedge-shaped cairns containing long segmented galleries. In Scotland some have prominent façades and forecourts at one end, in Ireland all have them. A variant is the 'lobster-claw' type in Sligo, which has a central court, for ritual, enclosed by two thick encircling arms. Cremations and inhumations are found in these tombs. The pottery in these tombs is partly Lyles Hill ware, plain, round-based, shouldered pots rather like the Yorkshire Grimston type; partly Beacharra ware in Scotland, carinated ('keeled') bowls with channelled or cord decoration, based closely on wares of the south of France; and partly coarse flat-bottomed ware. There are other Irish gallery graves not in this group, coming direct from Brittany; and linked with these are the 'portal dolmens', round or rectangular chambers which may never have been covered by a mound.

The main passage grave culture is known as the **Boyne,** from its fine examples in that area. This has several groups in east and northern Ireland, from where it spread to west Wales (particularly Anglesey), and to the Hebrides, Cromarty and Orkney. These represent a settlement from west France or west Iberia in the late 3rd millennium BC; they lasted some 500 years, well into the Wessex Food Vessel periods (in whose areas the passage grave art is found), and one tomb, Lough-crew H, was apparently not built until the Iron Age. The Boyne tombs are classical passage graves, but with a variety of chamber-plan. They are under round mounds or cairns—some, like New Grange on the Boyne, and Maes Howe, Orkney, of great size. Some are grouped in cemeteries (e.g. Carrowkeel, Sligo). The mounds often have stone kerbs (see plate 5), and the chambers may be corbelled. Some of the stones have incised patterns of spirals and symbols representing the goddess. The pottery is Loughcrew ware, rough bowls with much comb ornament.

The **Clava** group on the Moray Firth represents an early settle-ment of passage graves, but has a few mixed forms as well. In the Hebrides, Orkney-Cromarty (including the great tomb of Midhowe), and Shetland there are hybrids between the two main classes. In Orkney the pottery is Unstan ware, with deep collars and incised lines.

The entrance-graves, where the chamber opens straight out on to the wide end of the mound, of the **Scilly-Tramore** group of south-east Ireland and south-west Cornwall, are a late settlement from Finistère (1500–1000 BC). Finally, on the Medway in Kent is a small isolated group of entrance graves with long mounds kerbed with large stones, which may (but this is still not universally accepted) be a colony from Northern Europe.

This somewhat formidable variety of tomb-types, which cannot be simplified beyond a certain point, was of course brought in by quite a small number of people, spread over a long time; although both long barrows and megalithic tombs should be seen as inherent features of the Western Neolithic Culture. But the tombs and the ideas behind them became part of the lives of the natives, from the Neolithic until well into the Bronze Age (it is indeed confusing to think of them as neolithic, when they were in use after 1400 BC in some places). They were the burial-places of the chiefs' families, and in many cases no doubt the tribal shrines as well, although the henges and circle monu-ments took this role before long. As usual, Britain absorbed and adapted the contribution of the incomers, who made a deep impression on British culture in many ways.

THE SECONDARY NEOLITHIC

The way of life of the neolithic farmers could not fail to make an im-pression on the primitive aborigines, who when the farmers arrived were still living like savages, gathering and hunting their food. Before long we find them imitating and interbreeding with the newcomers, making crude pottery, and finally settling down as farmers themselves, or using their knowledge of the country (and no doubt their ingrained habit of wandering about) to engage in trade of tools etc. So a range of equipment evolved reflecting the adaptation of the farmers' possessions to the native traditions, or a fertilisation of ideas. The flint types are the tranchet axes, the Thames picks, waisted scrapers or adzes (fig. 27, p. 263); petit-tranchet arrows, polished blades, discoidal knives, plano-convex knives (fig. 25, p. 261; these knives are also found later in the Food Vessel culture), sickles, leaf- and lozenge-shaped arrows (fig. 25), and perforated 'maces' (fig. 27, p. 263), which were perhaps weights for digging-sticks (also found in the late Mesolithic). The stone axe factories were run by these peoples, and the rough-outs traded all over the country. Secondary neolithic cultures are found in all parts, and have an influence on later cultures, especially in the highland zone. The main groups are:

Peterborough. This represents the old Forest people; it has two types of pottery, Ebbsfleet (rough ware with incised lines or circular depressions or pits made with the end of a stick), and Mortlake, Fengate (round bases, very thick sides, shoulders, hollow neck, and with lavish decoration made by cord, bird-bones, finger-nails or shells). Both types have been recently shown to have arisen from the Windmill Hill complex; the Ebbsfleet type is closely linked to Windmill Hill itself, and Mortlake and Fengate derive from it. Fish-spears and hunting equipment indicate that these people still practised some aspects of their old way of life, but they are now farmers also. A picture of this culture was given by the famous sites at Peterborough and Mortlake. In Lincolnshire and Derbyshire Peterborough people made tombs in the form of passage graves (a small distinct group) and large stone cists of northern European ancestry. All this shows the variety of backgrounds and influences in the people of Britain at this time.

Rinyo-Clacton. This culture is divided between the far north of Scotland (the stone village of Skara Brae, Orkney, belongs to it), and the south and east of England. Its pottery is deeply grooved, or incised with triangles, loops, lozenges, or with bands or moulding in relief; some pots also are coarse and plain, others are 'rusticated'—an ornamental roughening of the surface. Knobbed stone balls were used, perhaps as bola-weights, in Scotland. In the southern province these people seem to have invented the earlier, single-entrance, type of henge circle. This culture had a long survival in the North; it may represent a resurgence of mesolithic traditions, and may also contain a foreign element. See fig 32, p. 271.

The secondary neolithic people also built henges, and circles of pits (e.g. the first stage of Stonehenge), in which they buried their cremated dead in bags secured by bone or antler pins. Professor Piggott ascribed these to a **Dorchester** group.

In the Isle of Man is a local culture called **Ronaldsway,** with its own pots, axes and houses. In northern Ireland are the **Bann** culture with tanged flint points, leaf-shaped flint spearheads and very large stone axes; and **Sandhill** wares.

The secondary Neolithic is now appearing more complicated than it looked a few years ago—some secondary neolithic may be direct 'primary' immigration from northern Europe; and the primary Neolithic may contain mesolithic elements imported with it, as well as those acquired after arrival.

The great contribution of the secondary neolithic peoples seems to have been the idea of the circle, or at least its use, for sacred or ritual purposes. Their henges (see p. 137) were developed further by later people, and are peculiar to Britain. Many features of their cultures survived in the Food Vessel and Urn cultures of the North.

EARLY BRONZE AGE

The Beaker invasions of c. 2400 BC introduced the use of copper for tools and weapons, and single burials in round barrows, and the use of bronze soon followed. Native cultures developed, and the Wessex people created a brilliant civilisation based on Europe-wide trade, during which Stonehenge and Avebury reached their present form.

Early Bronze Age I. The formal Neolithic ended about 2500 BC when metal tools and ornaments were imported from Europe (made of copper from sulphide ores, with high arsenic content). Soon after, say 2400–2100 BC, the **Beaker** peoples arrived, bringing with them knowledge of metal-working, at first in copper, soon in full tin-bronze (see p. 117). They came in several waves from the Rhine area (see below), and take their name from their characteristic pots. These were of two main families, or mixtures of these: bell beakers, ultimately from Spain, and necked types from Holland and Germany. Their burial customs were also new to Britain, being the northern European practice of single burial under round barrows.

The old classifications of beakers into A, B and C, or into Professor Piggott's revised terminology of long-necked etc, are now seen to be inadequate, being based on the shape and taking little account of the variety of decoration. Dr. David Clarke has now (1970) published a corpus of the 1944 Beaker finds known in Britain, and with the aid of a computer, has analysed them afresh. His study has revealed a new pattern of beaker settlement, and is already accepted as a triumph of the application of computers to archaeology.

Over several centuries, no less than seven groups entered Britain. The first were a wave of two groups, the All Over Cord beakers and the European Bell beakers (arriving about 2400 BC from the Rhine delta); then came a second wave of five groups, the Wessex and Northern/Middle Rhine (from the area of Mainz and Coblenz, about 2200 BC); the Northern/North Rhine and the Barbed Wire groups, from the European coastal areas from the Rhine to Denmark (2100–2050—these latter influenced the formation of the East Anglian beakers); and finally (2100–2000) the Primary Northern/Dutch group, from the Veluwe in Holland. From mixtures of these groups, and influences from cultures already in Britain, three final British insular traditions emerged: the Southern British, roughly the beakers formerly called long-necked; the Northern British, the short-necked beakers; and the East Anglian, which remained localised.

Thus there are well-defined groups; they all appear to have lived mostly by stock-raising, but practised simple cultivation also. Settlements are rare, but there was still plenty of room for wandering bands of people, and the many barrows imply some degree of settlement. Textiles were made, and cloth dress was worn. The beaker ware itself, used probably for a barley drink, is well-fired, and fairly thin-walled (see pl. 17, p. 160).

Beakers are found in most parts of Britain, but mainly in the Lowland zone. The Bell beaker burials are accompanied by tanged bronze daggers, barbed and tanged flint arrowheads, and archers' wristguards or bracers of bone. The necked beakers are usually decorated with comb impressions in triangles or panels; their burials are contracted (crouched), with tanged and barbed flint arrowheads, battle axes (the standard weapon of northern Europe at this time), flint daggers, V-perforated buttons (fig. 3) in jet, shale etc, and riveted bronze knife-daggers.

The Beaker people took over the idea of henge monuments from the secondary neolithic groups, and developed them into the large double-entrance type. They had a hand in the rebuilding of Stonehenge (see p. 140), and Avebury and its avenue is one of their works. They must have been an important constituent of the rich and powerful Wessex culture which succeeded them in the south of England, and some of their social and religious organisation affected later cultures.

Early Bronze Age 2. The full Early Bronze Age (EBA 2) opens when all the preceding cultures had had time to settle down and generate a new British way of life, made easier by the now more frequent use of bronze for tools and weapons. There were two main cultural provinces, largely synchronous, from about 2000 to 1400 BC.

In the North the **'Food Vessel'** culture absorbed very obviously many of the traditions of the secondary neolithic and Beaker peoples, and produced a somewhat coarse pottery, with neck and shoulder, and much ornament in bands and panels, from which it takes its name. It buried its dead in round barrows, which are often very complex in structure; the 'ritual pit' was also inherited, and various circular features and interior mounds, etc. The burials are either contracted inhumations, or cremations, and are often in graves under the barrows, or in stone cists. Stones in the barrows and on the trade-routes were sometimes carved with the same type of religious symbols as are characteristic of the Boyne culture, whence the Food Vessel people got most of their bronze and gold, and no doubt much of their religion also. Even 'double-axe' carvings of ultimate Mediterranean origin are found, and the chalk cylinders of Folkton (Yorks ER), buried with a child, are covered with the 'face' of the goddess and other designs. Such carved stones, which also have the enigmatic 'cup and ring' markings, are frequent in Yorkshire, Northumberland and elsewhere in the North (see p. 223). The Food Vessel people were traders as well as farmers, and many exotic

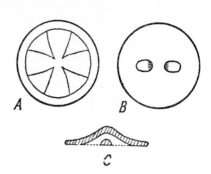

FIG. 3. Bronze Age V-bored button, showing A, top surface; B, under-surface; and C, the hole for the thread is in the shape of an inverted V

things, such as Irish halberds, and crescentic necklaces of jet, some times copied in gold, were used by them. The 'slug' flint knife is typical of their culture also. The Food Vessels themselves fall into four groups, the *Yorkshire*, a pot with wide mouth, constricted neck, wide shoulder, with one or more grooves round it, often interrupted by solid sections pierced for suspension, called stop-ridges—these pots are usually profusely decorated; the *Irish Bowl*, a low pot with bulging sides derived from the southern English A beakers; and the *Irish vase*, a triconical pot, i.e. with angular neck and shoulder profile. These last two types were in use in Ireland long after the Early Bronze Age had come to an end in England. There is much cross-influence between the three northern groups in Ulster and Scotland. The fourth type is the *southern English*, related to the Yorkshire type, but with less variety, and with a Rinyo-Clacton element where the Secondary Neolithic ancestry of the Yorkshire group is Peterborough. Some are very primitive indeed, even being built up in coils. They are largely contemporary with the Wessex culture, but are rare south of the Thames. Food Vessels are also common in Cornwall, and have local characteristics also found in the later Globular Urns (see p. 64).

In the south of England the chalk lands of **Wessex** became the home of a rich and powerful mercantile aristocracy, who traded as far as Greece, Iberia and the Baltic, and whose brilliance is the high-light of the Bronze Age in Britain. They reigned from about 2100 to about

1600, and were at their height in the 16th century BC, when Stonehenge was again remodelled (p. 140), and the Aegean daggers were carved on its stones. Silbury is one of their most astonishing monuments; this and the barrows must represent a vast expenditure of labour, and hint at the absolute power of these rulers, and at the social structure they head. The Wessex nobility seem to have come partly from Germany; much of their equipment has central European inspiration; links with Brittany also are certain, if obscure—perhaps it was partly a colonial outlet for younger sons. Their wealth was derived mainly from the metal trade, with the profits of which, and of a no doubt well-ordered agriculture, they could buy amber and gold, and foreign parade objects.

The Wessex culture dead were buried under barrows of various forms, the principal being the 'bell' and the 'disc' (see p. 160 and pl. 6). Bronze axes now have cast flanges for better hafting, and are no longer just flat; battle-axes of stone are used; several types of European pin; amber necklaces and cups; daggers with midribs and grooves. Pottery is oddly undistinguished, consisting of Urns related to secondary neolithic types and/or the Food Vessels; the only special types, and these have links with France, are the small vessels known as 'Aldbourne' or 'Grape' cups (fig. 33, p. 272). The segmented faience beads of Egyptian type found in many barrows, have now (1969) been shown to have been made in Britain; they were copied in stone etc. Foreign techniques also appear in the turned amber cups (e.g. the Hove Cup in the Brighton Museum), the Rillaton gold cup, pointillé ornament (patterns of gold studs on dagger-hafts etc.) and gold-bound amber discs, all of Aegean origin. Metal is now more plentiful, and hoards of tools or fragments, the property of merchants or travelling smiths, are found. The axe itself went through several stages until the final, more efficient, socketed form is reached in the Late Bronze Age (fig. 28, p. 265). Whetstone sceptres were used at the end of this culture-period; clothes were of leather, changing later to cloth.

The Wessex culture spread from the southern chalk country to south Wales, along the ridges to East Anglia, Lincolnshire and Yorkshire; a few outlying barrows occur in the south-west, and in Surrey. It is divided into two phases: Wessex I, using inhumation and tanged daggers with six rivets, as at Bush Barrow (to *c.* 1850 BC); and Wessex II, using cremation and ogival daggers with three rivets, as at Camerton and Snowshill. These phases may overlap, and may even be rather artificial.

MIDDLE BRONZE AGE

From 1500 to 1000 BC life in Britain settles down to an uneventful and not very brilliant aftermath of the Wessex and Food Vessel cultures. Cremation is now the universal custom. The pottery is coarse vessels of the Urn family, with overhanging rims, evolving into biconical collared and cordoned types; but several types existed together. Burials (ashes in these urns) are made under round barrows, or inserted in the sides of earlier barrows, or are arranged in groups (cemeteries or 'urnfields'). Pygmy vessels, some with openwork sides, some just miniature urns, for some ritual use, often accompanied the urns. In the North enlarged Food Vessels are found, and in Ireland also, as are encrusted urns, both survivals of earlier types. Many of these urn-types are long-lived. Settlements are still rare; there is one on Stockbridge Down, Hants. Metal types include the palstave, the rapier, and the British spearhead with looped socket. (See figs 29, 30, 33, 34.)

The distinctive, if uninspiring, aspect of the Middle Bronze Age has suggested to some a fresh incursion of immigrants from Europe, suddenly replacing the Early Bronze Age cultures. Even if this is true in part, a great deal of the earlier traditions survived.

The Middle Bronze Age has been divided into two phases, the first from just after 1500 BC, to about 1200, the second to 1050 or 1000, each had its own varieties of tools and weapons, and the second shows imports of northern European ornaments, which may indicate the arrival of new people. The highland zone and Ireland, which also had their own axe types, were affected by lowland Late Bronze influences before their Middle Bronze Age had finished. Even in the lowlands the Middle Bronze types lasted on so as to overlap the start of the Late Bronze Age as generally accepted.

LATE BRONZE AGE

From c. 1000 the Bronze Age was at its height, with a wide variety of implements, settled farming, and some new people from abroad.

The Late Bronze Age is marked by two things: the great increase, some tenfold, in availability (and no doubt of purchasirg power) of metal tools and of metalworking techniques (in LBA 1); and the introduction of the true plough (in LBA 2), which enabled more land to be farmed than was possible with the old digging-stick, more crops to be grown, and more people to live on the land. Marked advances of knowledge, and social development on the Continent, are responsible for this. The demands of the Cretan and Mycenaean worlds had stimulated the metal-producing areas of central Europe, and great activity resulted. By 1000 BC the effects of this were being felt in Britain.

The first phase (LBA 1), *c*. 1000 to 800 BC, is also marked by the advent of foreign types of metal-ware probably brought in by traders or travelling smiths; the new sword with leaf-shaped blade was of great importance, and a real advance over the MBA rapier (fig. 29, p. 267). Socketed axes meant better woodworking; riveted spearheads also arrived. The native spears gradually lost their loops.

The second phase (LBA 2), about 800 to 750 BC, is due, not merely to trade but to the advent of colonists from Holland and the Rhineland, the so-called Deverel-Rimbury people, who brought with them their distinctive globular and barrel-shaped pots; also some of the 'bucket' pots, though most of these are of earlier British origin (fig. 34, p. 274). These people were intensive farmers, and had a plough which could be drawn by oxen. They mostly cremated their dead and deposited them in urnfields, but a few single inhumations under barrows also occur. LBA 2 farms are widely spread, and in Wessex and the south-east, where the Deverel-Rimbury people settled, their remains can be seen in the form of farm and field boundaries, and various enclosures and circular huts (p. 102), e.g. Plumpton Plain 'A', Sussex.

A later influx of settlers brought new types still, and these are found from Sussex (e.g. Plumpton Plain 'B') to the North (Heathery Burn Cave, Co. Durham). The new types include winged axes (fig. 28, p. 265) of Alpine origin, and socketed axes with imitation wings; 'carps-tongue' swords from west France (fig. 29, p. 266); sickles; cauldrons and buckets of sheet bronze, copies of Greek and Italic pieces; horse equipment, which also gives proof of the use of carts.

The above account is on traditional lines, but recent research has enabled Professor Hawkes (in December 1960) to propose a new scheme for the Bronze Age in general. This begins by defining a Late Neolithic from 2000 to 1650/1600 BC, which includes the Beakers, and in its last phases is a Copper Age, full tin-bronze alloy being not yet known in Britain. The new scheme modifies the dating of the phases, and their subdivisions. Another important feature is to date the arrival of the Deverel-Rimbury earlier than was once thought, possibly from *c*. 1200 BC; at the same time leaf swords, northern European ornaments, certain types of palstaves, came in too, all overlapping with each other and with MBA survivals, to merge during the 10th century into the full Late Bronze Age.

The third phase (LBA 3), *c*. 750 to 650 BC, overlaps the earlier part of the Iron Age on the Continent (the Hallstatt phases there), and objects from this culture found their way to Britain (swords, razors, etc.). The

3. PERCHED BLOCKS. *Above*, natural, a glacial erratic. *Below*, artificial, the capstone of chamber tomb (Lanyon Quoit, Cornwall)

4. NEOLITHIC EARTHWORKS. *Above*, a causewayed camp, showing the gaps between sections of bank (Knap Hill, Wilts.). *Below*, a long barrow (Belas Knap, Glos.)

native LBA 2 cultures continued, but with a growing population, greater prosperity and settled life. With the better farming and metal techniques, Britain achieved a fair measure of wealth. A few fresh immigrants continued to arrive; new pottery (flat-rimmed) is found in Yorkshire, and newcomers are found in north-east Scotland (Old Keig).

EARLY IRON AGE

Iron was introduced from c. 700 BC by three waves of settlers from the Continent. These are:

> Iron Age A. 700–400 BC (*Hallstatt culture*)
> Iron Age B. 400–150 BC (*La Tène culture*)
> Iron Age C. 150 BC–AD 43 (*Belgae*)

The Hallstatt culture was essentially a continuation of the Late Bronze Age, but with iron implements. The La Tène culture reflected Greek influences, with superior social organization and a characteristic art-style. The Belgae were a vigorous military and trading people, already partly Romanized, bringing coins and wheel-made pottery.

It was only a matter of time before Britain accepted and absorbed the new metal, iron, for tools and weapons; it had begun to spread from western Asia by the end of the second millennium. Iron was even cheaper and more plentiful than bronze; its ores were common, and no complicated alloying was necessary; it became ultimately within the reach of everyone. So a wide variety of tools was devised for all purposes, and by the end of the period and during the Roman empire the tools of the carpenter and farmer were astonishingly similar, in number and variety, to those used until the present power age, indeed, to many of those still in use today.

Iron Age A. By the latter half of the eighth century BC (say 700) groups of people, already part of the iron-using culture known as Hallstatt in France and the Alps, came to Britain and brought their equipment with them. They landed along the coast from Wessex to Yorkshire, and soon spread inland. They lived in farms and small villages, and those at All Cannings Cross (Wilts.), Hengistbury Head (Hants.), Little Woodbury (Wilts.) and Scarborough (Yorks.) have yielded very full information on their way of life. They grew corn intensively and stored it on their farms in pits lined with matting, first parching the grain so that it would keep. When a pit became unusable for corn it was used for rubbish, and this too has provided much information. Little Woodbury, besides pits, had threshing floors, frames for drying corn and hay, and granary platforms for seed. The farmhouse was circular with a central rectangle of posts, probably containing the hearth, and was surrounded by a fence and outer ditch. Cattle and sheep were kept, and a few pigs—

as opposed to neolithic farming, where pigs were the most numerous; the increase of sheep implies less forest and more open pasture. Iron was worked locally in each community, not left as the preserve of a separate class of travelling smiths, as was metal in the Bronze Age.

The Iron Age A people also built hill-forts all over their settlement areas, mostly against the threat of the B people (see below)—banked and ditched enclosures into which the community could take refuge in times of trouble, and some of them permanent towns or villages. A few defensive enclosures indeed were built in the Bronze Age, but they were few compared with the rash of forts which now went up. The pottery was a coarse shouldered jar (fig. 35, p. 275), based on bronze buckets in shape. Early examples have finger-tip ornament: in Wessex a red haematite slip (see p. 272) was used as decoration also, perhaps to recall the burnish of the bronze 'model'. In Sussex and the upper Thames valley a jar with flaring rim was made. Textile equipment, loom-weights, spindle-whorls, weaving combs, are found; swan's-neck and ring-headed pins (fig. 31, p. 269), and brooches of safety-pin type, as well as a large variety of implements of bone and iron. A second stage of these cultures, called A2, can be distinguished by imports from abroad.

Iron Age B. While these people were settling in Britain, the Continent had already, under the influence of Greek contacts, attained a more advanced culture which is called La Tène, and a few objects of this culture (such as the safety-pins) had found their way to Britain. Folk-movements continued, and by the third century BC groups of immigrants began to reach Britain. At last we begin to emerge from the long, bewildering succession of nameless peoples, into the dawn of history, with references to individual tribes in the classical writers. States of a recognisable type are set up, with dynasties of kings. The language spoken was Celtic, ancestral to Welsh—although Indo-European tongues may have been spoken in Britain long before, perhaps even since Beaker times.

The immigrations of the three hundred years from *c.* 400 BC may be briefly summarised thus. Parts of tribes living in the Seine-Marne area of France (called 'Marnians') came to the south-east of England and east Yorkshire. Their chieftains (e.g. of the Parisi, the tribe that went to Yorkshire) were buried under barrows with their chariots and horse-trappings. Involuted (bent) brooches were used, but not very good pottery, rather like flower-pots (suggesting that the women, who were the potters in prehistory, were left behind in France). The Marnians in the south-east, however, did have a variety of pottery of continental types, which include shouldered bowls, pedestal-bases, and 'saucepans'. Later, by the first century BC, a Wealden culture had developed in this area, with foot-ring bowls (fig. 35, p. 275). While these people were settling down about the middle of the 2nd century (*c.* 150 BC), fresh groups arrived in Cornwall from Brittany and exploited the tin deposits. These people 'had pottery and brooches of Spanish origin, and built stone forts and villages (Chun, Chysauster, etc.); later they spread up the Bristol Channel, and worked the iron of the Forest of Dean. These and other non-Belgic peoples, from Hampshire and Wiltshire to the lower Severn, and along the Jurassic Way to Lincolnshire, used **Currency bars**, long thin strips of iron, with handles, shaped like swords or spits. These may be ingots, but were also meant for hoarding wealth. They seem to have been made at various places where iron ore deposits existed. They are also known in Germany, and may indeed have reached England from there by way of the Humber, late in the 2nd century BC, and continuing through most of the 1st century. To the east of these, in the Belgic area, are found various iron objects, including 'ploughshares' and double-pyramid ingots; although the former may have been used votively, these objects do not seem to be related to the currency bars.

The next recognisable influx was the flow of refugees from Caesar's conquest of Gaul in the 60s and 50s of the 1st century BC, although trade, bringing new pottery styles, had already been established between Britain and Gaul. The refugees came in small groups, with as many of their possessions as they could save, to various places in Britain. In the Somerset marshes they made 'crannogs' (artificial islands of stone and timber), on which the villages of Glastonbury and Meare were built. The villagers traded objects from all over England, and their pottery is of a high standard. The earlier forms are like those from Hengistbury Head (class B), pedestalled pots with cordoned ornaments; the later included bowls and jars with incised curvilinear patterns, ducks, etc. The lathe was used for turning wooden vessels and wheels. Weaving was a major industry; and the rotary quern (see fig. 37, p. 279) was used for corn-grinding instead of the older saddle quern. Perhaps the woodwork and the textiles were the sources of the villagers' prosperity. The arrival of refugees in south-east Britain (Sussex, Kent and Essex), using hollow-based bowls with curving patterns, is probably of this date also (see fig. 35, p. 275).

A third group was the Veneti, a maritime people of south Brittany, whom Caesar defeated at sea in 56 BC. The remnants of these sailed across to Britain, and had to carve a place for themselves among the by now closely-knit communities in Wessex and the south coast. They are said to have introduced sling warfare, but the multiplication of ramparts of some of the great hillforts, such as Maiden Castle (pl. 11), thought to have been caused to meet this technique, may actually have been begun earlier, and the sling warfare devised to overcome the now wider walls of the forts. In Wessex the local Iron Age A people absorbed the Veneti, and also new ideas in pottery such as the bead-rim (fig. 35, p. 275). Another group can be recognised in the Severn area.

Other groups went further away, to Scotland, and there built the characteristic brochs and wheelhouses of the Islands, Caithness, Sutherland and Orkney. These were fortified farms, and no doubt served as headquarters for piracy in the off-seasons. Their culture is a watered-down version of the 'South-Western B' of Glastonbury type. In central Scotland, from the Tay to the Moray Firth and to the west coast, are a series of forts built with stone ramparts laced with timber (Abernethy). These may also represent refugees from Gaul, as this principle of building is a continental idea. In south Scotland and Wales, small stone or earthern forts also date from this period and later. In the highland zone particularly there is much survival of older cultural traits, after the lowland zone has entered a new cultural phase. In the north of Scotland the neolithic way of life lasted until what was the Iron Age elsewhere. In south-east Scotland, the culture of the Votadini (p. 78), even in the Roman period, has been described as 'secondary Iron Age', implying that they were essentially living in Bronze Age conditions, but using as much of the Iron Age equipment as they could afford and absorb. In Yorkshire the same happens; beehive huts of Bronze Age type in the Pennines were in use until the Roman period, and Samian pottery has been found in them. The Iron A culture of the Vale of York, and the Brigantes generally, itself the expression of people still largely Bronze Age in tradition, was touched, but often only lightly, by the B culture of the Parisi of east Yorkshire. The mountain villages of north Wales, such as Tre'r Ceiri, essentially Iron Age in character, were fostered, if not actually set up, by the Romans, as centres for the federate tribes whose duty it was to repel the Irish raids. Ireland had a vigorous Iron Age of its own, which lived on undisturbed while Britain was in the Roman Empire, and which had a profound effect later on the life of Celtic Britain when the Romans left.

These groups should not be thought of as isolated from each other all the time; there was, as is to be expected, a good deal of intercourse and cross-fertilisation. Many of the Iron Age A cultures of southern England also took ideas from the Iron Age B peoples who came later, and mixed cultures resulted which are called AB. (If these then drew ideas from the Belgae they are ABC, as in the Weald.)

Iron Age C. During the first century BC Britain, particularly the south-east, became more and more Romanized, a process accelerated by the conquest of Gaul. A decisive factor in this was the advent of yet another people, the Belgae, a nation of mixed Celtic and Teutonic blood from north-east France and Belgium who come to Britain in several waves starting from the late 2nd century BC. The first group, from the Ardennes and Eifel region, settled in Kent, where cremation cemeteries such as

Aylesford are found. They spread across the Thames, and, as the Catuvellaunians, formed a state whose capital was at first at Wheathampstead, and later (when Caesar stormed it in 54 BC) at Prae Wood, St Albans; finally, about AD 10, at Colchester. Another people, the Atrebates, from Artois, landed in Wessex about 50 BC, and from there spread westwards to Devon and the Bristol Channel, north to Berkshire, and east to Sussex. The Belgae had a tendency to abandon the old hillforts, and build new sprawling towns near by on lower ground (such as Chichester, which superseded the Trundle), and this process was continued by the Romans.

The threefold division of the Iron Age cultures (A, B and C) was formulated by C. F. C. Hawkes in 1931, and was a great advance in simplification which has been used ever since, but elaborated, as knowledge grew, by the recognition of regional variants (e.g. South-Eastern B), representing different waves or immigrants and local admixtures of culture (e.g. AB). This proliferation of names, and the overlap of cultures in time, has led to growing confusion and lack of clarity, but with the fresh evidence that has come to light in the last few years, Professor Hawkes has proposed a new scheme of regional cultures, set against a fixed chronological framework: I. 1, c. 550–350 BC; I. 2, c. 350–150 BC; I. 3, to the beginnings of Romano-British culture, varying regionally from 43 to c. 80 AD. These periods are subdivided into phases, to cope with minor changes. The new evidence has also enabled the chronology of the three culture-phases to be lengthened; but the latest research (e.g. by McKie, 1970) suggests that these dates are still too low, and higher ones are used here.

The Belgae were vigorous, able people; they possessed the heavy plough with share to turn the soil, and thus were able to cultivate and settle sites in the valleys. So the pattern of settlement began to change, and to foreshadow that of the Saxons 500 years later. They had organised states, with kings and an aristocracy; they struck coins based on Greek models. (The Celtic coinage of Britain is mostly of Gallo-Belgic origin (from north-east France in the last centuries BC), except Armorican (Breton) influence round the coast, suggesting trade.) They imported Roman objects, and altogether had the highest standard of living in prehistoric Britain. Their pottery is now for the first time as a normal practice made on the wheel, and the bowls and jars of Wessex and the pedestal urns of the south-east of very high quality—the use of the potter's wheel implies the arrival of the specialist, as opposed to the domestic making of pottery. Metalwork was excellent, and wrought ironwork brought to a fine art. Lathe-turned woodwork and shale was used. Britain under the Belgae produced a surplus of corn, slaves, leather and other things, and trade with the Roman empire built up into very considerable levels. This is one of the reasons for the Roman conquest of AD 43; another being the threat to Rome on her flanks of an independent state willing to take in political refugees; a third being the subversive activities of the Celtic priesthood, the Druids, who had close links with their colleagues in Gaul. Add prestige, and desire to round off the frontier, and Claudius' main motives for the invasion were there; Caesar's expedition of 55 BC was a probe only, to test the conditions for a future conquest, to assess native strength and to show Roman power.

A word must be said about La Tène art in Britain, which is quite remarkable in its range and quality. Celtic art was derived from native (Hallstatt) geometric sources, with strong influence from Greek and Oriental styles, bringing stylised animal and plant motifs. It was the Parisi of east Yorkshire who brought this art into Britain in the 3rd century BC. With it they decorated iron and bronze objects of all kinds, shields, swords, mirrors, pottery. Enamelling was also used to enrich the flowing designs with bright inlaid (champlevé) pieces, red first, later other colours. Modelled iron masks and animals (boars, etc.) were also made, for staffs of office and on buckets, brazier-frames (once interpreted as fire-dogs), shields, helmets. This rich art, decorative and representational alike, was cut short by the Roman occupation, and swamped by the dull standardised products of the Empire (it was in any case weaker by the 1st century BC than it had been in the 3rd). It did not, however, utterly die, but survived in the highland zone, from where it returned after the Roman power waned in the 5th century, and forms part of the culture of Celtic and early Saxon England. Celtic religion was a varied and complex series of cults, of gods and goddesses of various origins, and of different functions, universal, national and local. Shrines were usually in the open air or in sacred groves; springs and holy wells had their healing divinities. A few temples of the more important gods were served by regular priests. Human sacrifice was resorted to in times of crisis; sacred lakes received votive offerings.

The Romans absorbed what fitted into their own complex structure, and suppressed the rest. Faint traditions got through, especially in the west and north, to enrich the Welsh heritage of post-Roman times. Ireland of course was never Romanized at all, even by the remote kind of contact which obtained in Wales and Scotland.

Table 4

NEOLITHIC, BRONZE AND IRON AGE CULTURES

c. 4300 BC Neolithic −3300	Windmill Hill: causewayed camps, long barrows Megalithic tombs
c. 3300 Late Neolithic	Secondary Neolithic Peterborough, Mortlake Rinyo-Clacton

c. 2400	Copper (Early Bronze I)	Beakers— round barrows
2000	Early Bronze II	Food Vessels: Southern, Yorkshire, Irish
		Wessex I
1800		Wessex II
1500	Middle Bronze I	Urns
1200	Middle Bronze II	Deverel-Rimbury
		Foreign metal types
1000	Late Bronze	Foreign metal types, expansion of farming
800	Late Bronze II	Bucket, globular urns
	Late Bronze III	Flat-rimmed pottery
700	Early Iron A	Hallstatt—storage pits
400	Early Iron B	La Tène
		Marnians
		Regional variants and mixtures
by 100	Early Iron C	Belgae I
75		Belgae II

TOWARDS A MODERN SOCIETY

THE ROMANS

In AD 43 Britain was brought into the Roman Empire, and a ready-made military and administrative structure, and a very high material and social standard, was imposed on the country. Britain shared in European history and life until the mid-5th century.

With the Roman conquest in AD 43 we enter the full light of history. Little of this will be mentioned here, except where essential to build up the background required for this book. Of course, Britain had always been affected by and concerned in what was happening in Gaul and elsewhere, but the nature of the evidence keeps these influences in general terms; now she suddenly shares in the life and history of the Roman world, entering a completely fresh phase, which lasted, or had echoes, over several hundred years.

After the initial campaigns in the south-east, the first five years were spent in consolidating the Roman hold over the lowlands; the armies halted on the line of the limestone ridge from Dorset to the Wolds, and the Fosse Way became a frontier. Professor Piggott has pointed out that the diet of the Roman armies was based largely on grain, and that they had to halt when they reached the limits of the area where grain was the staple crop. To penetrate the pastoral highland zone, with its economy based on sheep, cattle and horses, they had to organise corn supplies in their rear. Hence the very early draining of the Fens, so that bulk grain supplies could be obtained. The advance was in three prongs from London, which became at once the administrative and economic centre; north to Lincoln, west to Wroxeter and Gloucester, from which Wales could be contained. Roads were laid down by military engineers for rapid troop movement.

The next thirty years were spent in penetrating the highland zone, in order to make safe the lowlands, and permit them to develop peacefully and prosperously under civil administration. The legions at Lincoln, Wroxeter and Gloucester were therefore moved forward to York, Chester and Caerleon, and the frontier represented by these points became the effective limit of the civil zone.

During all this time the Romanization of the civil zone proceeded, and the face of the land underwent a remarkable change from the irregular and mostly insignificant prehistoric pattern of settlement to a ready-made, standardised, Mediterranean one. Towns, houses and institutions both social (like public baths) and political were set up with great rapidity and uniformity: the advantages of using them, apart from the impossibility of refusing to, went home to all classes of the native population, and the country settled down to be as Roman as it could. This the Romans encouraged, not only to make administration easier, but to distract the people from thoughts of rebellion or tribal feuds. In fact, tribal warfare did die out; the revolt of Boudicca (AD 61) was due to local Roman misgovernment which was not repeated.

This refers to the lowland, civil zone; the highlands never accepted the new regime, except in places superficially, and the old Celtic life went on in those areas.

The Romans found the country divided into little states, under native kings, and found it easier to build on this foundation rather than make an arbitrary break. They therefore adapted them into administrative units on the Roman pattern, called *civitates* or cantons. The kings and local nobles, where they were willing, and most were, continued to control the new divisions under Roman political and military supervision. On this native aristocracy was laid the burden of keeping local order, raising local taxes, and paying for public building, amenities and entertainment in the towns. The resulting mixed administration has been compared with that exercised by the British in the native states of India.

The new cantons, whose boundaries were mostly, but not always, those of the old kingdoms, were:

Cantiaci, Kent and east Surrey, capital Durovernum (Canterbury);
Regnenses, Sussex, west Surrey, east Hants, capital Noviómagus (Chichester);
Belgae, parts of Hants, Wilts and north Somerset, capital Venta (Winchester);

5. DOORWAYS OF MEGALITHIC TOMBS. *Above*, false portal set in drystone walling at Belas Knap. *Below*, entrance to a passage grave set in a stone kerb (Bryn Celli Ddu, Anglesey)

6. A GROUP OF BRONZE AGE BARROWS. *Above*, as they appear on the ground. *Below*, seen from the air (Lambourn Seven Barrows, Berks. — there are in fact about 40 in this group!)

FIG 4. Roman Britain

Durotriges, Dorset, east Devon, parts of Somerset, which had centres at Durnovaria (Dorchester) and Lindinis (Ilchester);

Dumnonii, Devon, west Somerset, Cornwall, capital Isca (Exeter);

Iceni, roughly Norfolk, north-west Suffolk, and the Fens, capital Venta (Caister St. Edmunds);

Trinovantes, most of Suffolk and north-east Essex, capital Camulo-dunum (Colchester), which was also a 'colonia', or place where retired veterans were granted land and civic rights, in return for which they could be called on to fight in emergencies;

Catuvellauni, the whole of the east Midlands down to the Thames, capital Verulamium (St. Albans);

Atrebates, Berks, parts of Hants and Wilts, capital Calleva (Silchester);

Dobunni, the Cotswolds and the lands on each side, capital Corinium (Cirencester)—this territory also had a colonia at Glevum (Gloucester);

Cornovii, the north-west Midlands, capital Viroconium (Wroxeter);

Coritani, north Midlands and Lincolnshire, capital Ratae (Leicester) and a colonia at Lindum (Lincoln);

Parisi, east Yorkshire, capital Petuaria (Brough);

Brigantes, roughly the rest of Yorkshire, capital Isurium (Aldborough)—this was not the whole of the lands of this great federation of tribes, but only that part within close control of the legionary fortress of Eburacum (York).

South Wales appears also to have had a similar organisation, the *Silures*, west of the Wye, and south Glamorgan, capital Venta (Caerwent);

Demetae, parts of Carmarthen, Cardigan, and Pembrokeshire, capital Moridunum (Carmarthen).

London had a special position; it was from the first the commercial centre of the province, and in later centuries performed many of the functions of an official capital, but the status of its municipal government was not commensurate.

Within this civil zone were a few small areas under direct Roman control: the Weald, for its iron, the Mendips, for the lead, the Forest of Dean (iron and coal), the Cornish tin district. All this zone developed a variety of industries, and many small towns and villages, too numerous to mention. As Romanization proceeded, and the zone forgot its tribal past, and prosperity became the rule, its history becomes uneventful; after the end of the first century the history of the province is largely that of the highland zone, and its reactions on the civil zone. The armies were increasingly on the northern and western frontiers. and troubled the rich lowlands little.

The cantonal capitals were all built to a pattern, centred round a forum, a market-place and ceremonial square, with a basilica, a large official building housing exchanges, shops and municipal offices, temples, theatres, baths, and the town houses of the local nobles and the merchants. The density of building was not always very high, and gardens or open land could occupy much of the space enclosed by the walls. Round the towns were the villas of the nobles, each surrounded by its dependent farms. Bath and Buxton were not cantonal capitals, but being spa towns were large enough to have the same characteristics.

The campaigns of the first century left lines of forts, large and small, in central and north Wales, the North of England and southern and east Scotland. The army consisted of heavily armed legions, supported by cavalry units, and by auxiliary troops drawn from all over the Empire and the tribes on the frontiers. In the later centuries the practice was to use the local inhabitants of the frontier regions to provide armed forces when required. All these troops, on discharge, tended to settle where they had been serving, and the population was accordingly variegated.

The military zone should not be thought of as completely un-romanized; at the gates of the forts, particularly between the Tees and Hadrian's Wall, were villages (*vici*) of long houses, 50 x 20 ft. These were under the control of the fort commander and were occupied by army families, traders, etc., who led a Romanized life in sharp contrast to that of the hundreds of native farms in this area.

The peoples of Scotland, particularly north of the Forth–Clyde line, were never brought under full control, and every so often, when pushed by lean years, and envy of the fat life of lowland Britain, would pour south and ravage what they could, usually assisted by the tribes of northern England and southern Scotland. This happened in 117–120, causing devastation as far as York, and the total loss of the Ninth legion, and inducing the Emperor Hadrian to come in person to re-organise the defences of the frontier; the result was the establishment of the Wall system, extended to Scotland by the next Emperor, Antoninus Pius. A similar disaster in the last years of the century led to the civil towns being walled.

The rising prosperity of the south was interrupted in the third century, when weak central authority, usurping emperors in Gaul, and the beginning of the barbarian raids which were to harass western Europe for centuries, all helped to reduce life in Britain to chaos. The south-east coasts of Britain were raided by Franks and Saxons from the middle of the century, and from about 275 the Irish began their raids on Wales which were to continue for two hundred years and more. In 287 Carausius, the admiral of the British fleet in the Channel, seized power, and tried to get things back into order. But he was murdered, and the central power was not restored until 296, when Constantius Chlorus was able to bring Britain back into the Empire. During the next few years the country was reorganised and a series of forts built along the south-east coasts against the Saxon raids; prosperity began again, and lasted for most of the fourth century. The province was divided into four, under the general control of the prefect of Gaul.

The fourth century saw the final development of the villa system (see p. 106), and of a vigorous rural life. The town defences were strengthened, but life in the towns went on under increasing difficulties. The cost of running the vast Empire had become astronomical, and the financial burden was passed on to the landed nobility and the rural and urban middle classes; to prevent evasion of taxes men were tied to their districts, and the standard of living became ever harder to maintain. For protection against extortion, small free men became dependent serfs, and the great estates dominated the countryside. The keys to the history of the 4th and 5th centuries are therefore the growing discontent of the peasantry, which sometimes flared into revolt, and the constant threat of attack from north, west and east. Christianity became the official religion in 312, but paganism went on in the countryside for another century. Pagan shrines and markets flourished, such as those at Woodeaton (Oxon) and Farley Heath (Surrey), and there was a pagan revival at the end of the century, as men lost faith in the new religion to cure man's ills (e.g. the great temple at Lydney).

British was still spoken in the countryside, though the upper class was bilingual and Roman in outlook; Latin was used by the officials, the army, the traders and the townspeople. The old Celtic culture had in fact never completely died, and Celtic influences reassert themselves by the end of the 4th century.

Trouble in the north brought Constans over in 343 to look to the defences, but in 367 a great inroad of Picts and Scots brought devastation far into the civil zone, helped by the peasants. Many villas and parts of towns were not rebuilt. From this time the central authority, owing to growing troubles abroad, weakened, and the power in Britain had to be assumed by the territorial nobles. The Welsh Emperor Magnus Maximus (383) is only a symptom of the growing but enforced independence of Britain. By the end of the 4th century native kings had emerged in the highland zone, often ruling states very similar to those of pre-Roman days. These kings regarded themselves as within the Roman tradition, and, with the great nobles inside the province, were an important factor later. When the break came with the central government, early in the 5th century, these nobles could carry on an essentially Roman way of life.

The break was due to the chaos on the continent due to barbarian raids and peasant revolts, which tied up all the available troops, including those in Britain.

SUB-ROMAN OR "DARK AGES"

When the Romans left (AD 410) Britain reverted to Celtic states with various degrees of Romanization.

In Britain also, in 407–9, there was a combination of Irish raids, Saxon attacks and a peasant revolt; the authorities appealed to Rome, but in 410 were told to look to themselves, although the Emperor had no intention of abandoning the province. Indeed, it looks as though contact was renewed from 417, when the revolt in Gaul was finally put down, until about 427, when the western Empire began to break up. A serious Saxon raid was defeated by St Germanus in 429. Verulamium was still in being as a town at this date.

During this time some damage was done to towns and villas, but life was not disrupted; the east coast signal stations, however, were destroyed. The Gaulish mints having ceased production, the rural markets used very small copies of Gaulish coins, called 'minimissimi'. The release from the burdens of central control actually led to a temporary prosperity, until the 440s. After then the villas cease, but for most of the century the nobles could lead a life of considerable comfort and culture. In some parts, indeed, such as east Wales, and the Severn valley, Roman life went on almost unchanged.

The middle of the century saw decisive crises. The practice had grown up, perhaps even as early as the late third century, of using the Saxons to protect the province against the even more destructive raids of the Irish, Picts and Scots; their friendly status is shown by Saxon graves in Roman cemeteries at York, for example. But as they increased in numbers, they could take advantage of the situation, and revolted to form their own kingdoms, such as Deira in Yorkshire, about 450, and in Kent by 455. The Welsh king Vortigern, who was supreme commander at this time, was therefore faced not only with Saxon revolts, but opposition from the magnates who objected to his policy. An appeal to Rome was made about 446, but without success. From then on trouble was continuous, as the barbarians poured in. Moreover, some of the anti-Vortigern party went to Brittany, where the peasants had decimated the nobles, to help to defeat the peasants and the raiders in Gaul; most of these colonists went from Wales and England.

Events drew to a head in the late 5th century. Hillforts, such as Cissbury, were refurbished, and some, such as Hamsterley (Co. Durham) built. Dykes, like Wansdyke, were laid down. The Saxons had a hold in the east, and no Roman town of any size (e.g. Norwich, Colchester) survived after about 450. Ambrosius, who succeeded Vortigern, got ready to fight, and his work was taken over with success by Arthur, the 'Dux Bellorum', an officer in command of a well-armed and highly mobile force of cavalry, which was just what was required[1]. He fought a series of battles, including one ('Badon', Badbury), about 520, which confined the Saxons to the eastern fringe[2] for another forty years. Arthur became a symbol of native resurgence, and attracted legends of the Celtic 'other-world' to him. Meanwhile trade and peace continued in the Celtic West, and imported pottery and glass is found in Wales and Ireland. Arthur also had to fight Celtic princes, and the lack of unity on the Roman side undid his work of preserving Roman

[1] Operating perhaps from the hillfort of South Cadbury (Som.), which may be the site of Camelot.

[2] The result of this was that some of the expanding Saxon population migrated back to Europe in the first half of the 6th century.

culture in Britain. Moreover, the very need to fight the Saxons helped to destroy Roman life in the old civil zone, from which alone a central government was possible. So the old culture had to be saved and handed on by the Celtic states, and the monastic cells of south Wales, themselves largely introduced from Gaul. Ireland, indeed, carried on the study of Greek during the 'dark ages', thus making a later renaissance possible. The old classical learning died out in confusion in the civil zone by the end of the 5th century, but Wales retained links with the Rhone region, and Ireland with Gaul. The Irish problem was not completely resolved; Cunedda and his people, the Votadini, from Northumberland and south-east Scotland, migrated to north Wales to keep them out about 450; but they settled south Wales, and their ogam inscriptions (see p. 225) are common there. Also in the mid-5th century, the Scotti from Ulster settled in Argyll. The movement to Brittany continued into the 6th century.

THE ANGLO-SAXONS

The Saxons, at first mercenaries and pirates, settled in earnest in the 6th century, and developed their own Germanic culture and social system. Invasions of Vikings (9th century) and Danes (10th century) complicated the political situation but enriched the cultures of England. Scotland, Wales and Cornwall remained Celtic.

The early Saxon raids were largely piratical, but by the late 5th century the Saxons were coming in by family groups, in a continuous stream, seeking land to settle and live peaceably on. By Arthur's time much of Wessex had been colonised, and after the interruption caused by his campaign (after say 550) Saxon kingdoms were formed. This is not the place to describe the course of the colonisation, the rise of Mercia, the merging of the two groups in Wessex, southern and Thames valley, and the gradual dominance of Wessex and the formation of an English nation. There was little difference between the Saxons, Angles and Frisians, all from north Germany and south Denmark, who formed the bulk of the settlers; the Jutes of the Isle of Wight and Kent were somewhat distinct in culture, and the latter had Frankish elements also. There was Swedish influence in East Anglia. Essentially the colonisation was of the lowland zone—the newcomers were lowland farmers—and the Celtic kingdoms beyond went on in their own way, often under warning not to interfere with the new order, as with those behind Offa's Dyke in Wales. But even in the lowlands the break was not total; an unknown, but not inconsiderable, number of Celts continued to live under the Saxons, not only as slaves or serfs. There are several Celtic names among the Saxon royal and noble families, and a large number of place-names, for instance, those of hills and rivers, still survive in the south of England. Some even of the boundaries of the new states,

FIG. 5. Saxon and Celtic kingdoms at the end of the sixth century. The Celts are underlined

like Kent and possibly Sussex, were very similar to the old ones. The old system of villas and land tenure disappeared by 500, and the former landowners were killed or went westwards, but many of the lower orders remained.

The Saxons introduced a new pattern of settlement (see p. 25), which had no need of the towns of Roman Britain, and very little of the roads. Thus most of the towns were abandoned for two or three centuries until their sites, usually good ones, were resettled. In the north the pattern is complicated; isolated communities of Britons survived in the Pennines, still speaking British, and the struggles between the Anglians and the Celtic states, like Elmet, lasted until well into the 7th century. Celtic influence was strong in Northumbria until the end of the 8th century (Sussex was a last stronghold, cut off by the Weald from Christian influences), and many traces in the form of place-names indicate the sites of shrines and the first farms of the settlers; Surrey, for instance, has a large number.

The people consisted of: (1) Kings or nobles and their war-bands of noble companions, whom they rewarded in lands. These became the basis of part of the later feudal, stratified, society; (2) Free peasants who worked the farms; (3) Slaves, owned by both nobles and peasants. This gave a structure not unlike that of Roman Britain, but with a different system of agriculture and tenure. The nobles lived richly in large halls, and were buried in great pagan barrows, often with heaps of gold and jewels; the peasants lived in squalid huts, with cemeteries of flat graves. Barrows were used until the early 7th century, and some, like Taplow, are very informative; the last was that of Sutton Hoo, about 625, a richly furnished cenotaph of a king buried elsewhere under Christian customs. By 600 the practice of depositing personal possessions of the dead in their graves was on the decline, and Christianity (brought by St Augustine's mission of 597) also set its face against grave-goods. Burials after this date are therefore much less informative about the people's way of life.

The Roman church had to counter the Celtic church of the old inhabitants, and finally an agreement was reached, at Whitby in 664, which gave supremacy to the Roman church, and set the religious pattern of the country until the Reformation, though Wales did not conform till 768. The Saxon sees, located by Theodore of Tarsus (669), were often at tribal capitals (Lichfield, Winchester, etc.), which enabled church and state to support each other.

We are not here concerned with the political history of Britain from the 6th to the 11th centuries. For our purpose it is enough to see the broad divisions of the country into cultural and racial blocks, as they took shape from the 5th century onwards. The Anglo-Saxons settled as far as the Tweed, reaching the Forth in the 7th century; the Humber divided the Northern from the Southern English, and the earthwork called the Roman Rig in South Yorkshire may be the formal boundary of Northumbria and Mercia. Scotland was shared by the Welsh kingdom of Strathclyde in the south-west, Manau Gododdin in the south-east, the Scots in Argyll, and the Picts to the north; the two latter united in the 10th century into one state. Manau Gododdin, the territory of the former Votadini (some of whom had gone to N Wales in the mid-5th century to combat the Irish infiltrations) was finally overcome by Northumbria in the late 6th century. The Scots, an Irish people, settled in Argyll in the mid-5th century, probably with the help of Strathclyde, who needed a buffer against the Picts. Strathclyde remained independent until the early 11th century. In the northern English area there were several small native states, such as Rheged in the north-west and Elmet in SW Yorkshire, and English supremacy in this area was not achieved until the late 6th century. Incidentally, the Roman Wall lost its meaning with Northumbria's extending beyond it to the Tweed.

The ten southern English kingdoms jostled each other, and equilibrium with the Celts was not reached until the late 6th century. The Fleam and Devil's Dykes across the Icknield Way possibly reflect incidents in this chequered story. Offa's Dyke (pl. 13, p. 136) was built to mark the boundary between Mercia and Wales in the late 8th century, and Cornwall remained independent till 838. The Irish, who raided Wales for centuries, got a foothold in SW Wales, and the kings of Dyfed were said to be related to those of Meath.

Scandinavians, mostly Norse, started to raid Britain in the late 8th century. They came by two routes, round the north of Scotland, where they founded earldoms from Sutherland to Shetland, to Dublin and Man, where they made kingdoms; and direct to the east coast of England —they sacked the great monastery of Lindisfarne in 793. Danes came to eastern England in large numbers, first as raiders then, in 865, in earnest to settle, founding a kingdom at York in 867 to 954 (settlers were still arriving in York throughout the 11th century). In spite of the efforts of Alfred, the Saxons had to recognise the whole of the eastern side of England, from Tees to Thames (as far west as the Lea) as under Danish control (the 'Danelaw').

Christianity did not reach the Norse parts of Scotland until 995.— Orkney and Shetland were under Norse rule until 1471, and Norse influence, in custom, life and language, was still strong into the 17th century, and has left many traces even today.

In the 10th century Norse-Irish, descendants of the Norse settlers in Dublin, occupied NW England and SW Scotland from the Wirral to the north shore of the Solway Firth. The place-names west of the Pennines therefore show Norse and Irish elements, which spilled over into the heads of some of the dales on the east side (e.g. Nidderdale). The linguistic and racial situation in these areas is complicated, having Welsh and Anglian elements also. The place-names and dialects of eastern England have equally strong Danish elements, such as the village names ending in 'by' and 'thorp' as against the 'tons' and 'hams' of the Saxon areas. Danish territorial divisions survive in the three ridings ('thirdings') of Yorkshire, and in those of Lindsey and Orkney.

By AD 1000 the pattern of shires, hundreds (or wapentakes in the north), and parishes, had been fixed, and this outlasted the next up-

heaval, the invasion of the Normans. The towns also were growing—
York by now had some 8,000 inhabitants.

In the south the English kingdoms, at first under Mercian pre-
dominance (8th century), came under the supremacy of Wessex in the
9th and 10th, but this made little difference culturally. After the Danish
invasions a mixed culture grew up in eastern and northern England,
which influenced the old Anglo-Saxon areas also. Anglo-Saxon
England reached impressive cultural heights in the 10th century. The
second period of Danish rule (11th century) had little lasting cultural
effect, except for certain art styles. The real break was with the Norman
conquest of 1066.

THE MIDDLE AGES

*The Normans (1066) accelerated the development of a mediaeval way
of life, and the country took its present stamp by the 13/14th century.*
Little need be said about the Normans, except that they brought Saxon
England into the West European culture-sphere, and away from the
Northern one. Their genius was for order, unity and good government.
For two hundred years after 1066 there was a great gulf between the
new aristocracy and the people, but in the end the nobles chose to be
English landowners and not French overlords. The feudal system continued to develop—after all, the Normans themselves were of northern
origin, and the fundamentals of their system went back to a common
source with that of the Saxons. The Norman genius was also expressed
in architecture. It has been said that they 'altered the face of England
in a way unequalled until the coming of canals and railways'. They
needed castles, churches, cathedrals and monasteries; and the sudden
organisation of the building trade and its supplies amounted to a
veritable industrial revolution. Saxon buildings, even royal halls, were
mostly wooden, and few of them stood up above the trees (exceptions
are great churches like Durham); the Normans at once made a mark on
the landscape, even with the earthen mottes (pl. 14, p. 137), but certainly
with the huge churches, castles and palaces which sprang up all over
the country. It was an old world in many ways, but a new beginning in
others, of a period of culture from which we have only been emerging
these last two hundred years.

The effects of these various settlements have been deep and long-
lasting. The character of the Celtic West—Wales and Cornwall—needs
no emphasising, but it is becoming increasingly recognised that the
regional flavours, in dialect, outlook and way of life, of the rest of
England are due to whether the area was strongly settled by Anglo-
Saxons, Jutes or Danes, and how much Celtic admixture there was.
For instance, the rich character of Yorkshire today is largely due to the

Scandinavian settlement, in contrast to that of Northumberland and Durham, which were Anglian areas.

THE MODERN AGE

The new scientific thought and religious freedom of the 16th century led to the elaboration of industry and commerce of a modern type (17th century). Technical advances, based on iron and steel, and powered machinery, took the Industrial Revolution to a new stage in the 18th century, and to its third, mass-production, stage in the 19th. The 20th is now trying to put this new house in order.

One of the results of this long history is *cultural overlap*, the survival of features of one age into the next. An example of this is a Tudor cottage with electric light, but this phenomenon is all round us, and is of the greatest interest to observe.

Table 5

SUMMARY OF DATES FROM THE ROMANS
TO THE PRESENT DAY

FIRST CENTURY	AD 43	Conquest by Claudius
Consolidation	47	Fosse Way frontier
	61	Revolt of Boudicca
	69–79	Advance to Wales and the north
	81–96	Towns built
SECOND CENTURY	119	Revolt in north
Prosperity	125	Hadrian's Wall
	140	Antonine Wall
	196	Disaster in the north
THIRD CENTURY	200–210	Town walls built
Mark-time	245	Pirate raids begin; anarchy
	287	Carausius Emperor in Britain
	296	Constantius: the new order. Coastal forts built
FOURTH CENTURY	367	Great raids on the lowlands
Prosperity	383–388	Magnus Maximus
FIFTH CENTURY	407–410	Revolts, raids, Britain alone
First half; Britain alone; rise of native states.	429	St. Germanus versus Pelagius and the Saxons
Second half; pagan Saxons invade.	445–450	Saxon revolts
SIXTH CENTURY	500	Arthur's victory
First half; still sub-Roman	530	Saxon settlement
Second half; pagan Saxons settle.	597	Augustine

SEVENTH CENTURY	664	Whitby
Christianity spreads		
Celtic v. Roman church		
EIGHTH CENTURY		
First Saxon culture		
NINTH CENTURY	850	Danes
First half: development		
Second half: the Danes		
TENTH CENTURY		
Mixed culture		
ELEVENTH CENTURY	1066	Normans
First half: second Danish power		
Second half: the Normans		
FOURTEENTH CENTURY	1350	The Black Death; deserted villages
FIFTEENTH CENTURY ⎫ SIXTEENTH CENTURY ⎭	1450–1550	Enclosure for sheep; more deserted villages
SEVENTEENTH CENTURY	1600–1700	Renaissance science; beginnings of industry (IR I) private enclosures
EIGHTEENTH CENTURY	1709	Coke-smelting of iron (Darby at Coalbrookdale)
	1720–1820	Horse-railways (IR II)
	1770	Steam Engines (Boulton and Watt)
	1770–1830	Canals
NINETEENTH CENTURY	1750–1820	Enclosure Acts; modern pattern of farms and villages
	1825–1850	Steam railways begin (IR III)
	1850–1900	Mass production; Victorian towns
TWENTIETH CENTURY	1900–1950	Electricity and internal combustion engine; nationalisation
	1950	Atomic science; new biology; plastics, electronics; new social pattern; welfare state; new methods in industry (IR IV)

Part II: Field Antiquities

CHAPTER I

Identifying Earthworks

The following list gives various types of earth or stone monument or feature which are likely to be met with. It cannot be exhaustive, but will help in reaching familiarity with the numerous possibilities. In the list:

- N = neolithic (4000–2400 BC)
- B = Bronze Age
- E = early (2400–1500 BC)
- M = middle (1500–1000 BC)
- L = late (1000–700 BC)
- I = Iron Age (700 BC–AD 50)
- R = Roman (AD 50–400)
- D = 'Dark Age' (AD 400–650)
- S = Anglo-Saxon (500–1100)
- *Med* = mediaeval (1100–1500)
- *Mod* = modern (1500 onwards)

The list falls into the following groups:

(a) Regular round or oval earth mounds (1–18)
(b) Irregular and other earth mounds (19–49)
(c) Continuous earth banks, terraces, etc., other than enclosures (50–88)
(d) Enclosures with earth banks (89–115)
(e) Ditches and hollows (116–164)
(f) Dry-stone enclosures and structures (165–182)
(g) Rocks and stone monuments (183–203)
(h) Soil and vegetation marks (204–211)
(i) Unclassified or in more than one category (212–218)

If you see . . .	*It could be . . .*	*For more detail see p. . . .*

(a) Regular round or oval earth mounds

1. Oval mound of earth or chalk, east end often higher and wider than the other (mostly some 100 × 30 ft. up to 300 × 100 ft., and 4-12 ft. high). Often ditches along sides — N long barrow — 151

2. Oval mound of earth or stones — N-B megalithic tomb — 154
3. Round mound of earth or stones — N-B megalithic tomb — 155
4. Round mound of earth, chalk or stones, usually with ditch close round, and sometimes low bank outside as well (up to 120 ft. across × some 5-20 ft. high). Often with depression in centre — B round (bowl) barrow (smaller ones often M or LB) — 159

5. Round mound of earth or chalk, ditch round separated from mound by flat platform — B bell barrow — 160

6. Small round mound with concentric ditch several feet away, and bank outside it — B disc barrow — 160

7. Low small round mound — S barrow — 162
8. Group of low round or oval mounds, 5-10 ft. across — S cemetery — 165
9. Round mound or platform with flat top, mostly about 5 ft. high and up to 100 ft. across, often with surrounding ditch

(a windmill-base sometimes has a cross-shaped depression on top) — B platform-barrow; unusual B barrow; S barrow; moot-hill; dancing-place; motte; base for post, beacon, gibbet, cross, windmill — 186

10. As 9, but with berm — Landscaping feature — 186
11. Conical mound, often with flat top — R barrow — 162
12. Conical mound with flat top and ditch round — Motte — 177

13. Conical or platform mound with banked enclosure attached — Civil War gun mount; motte and bailey — 179, 177

14. Row of round flat-topped mounds with depressions in centre — Waste mounds of *med* iron-pits — 122

15. Low convex mound with ditch and outer bank round it, mound filling all of central space — B saucer-barrow — 161

16. Low round mound, usually with ditch round — *Mod* tree-mound — 163

17. Rounded mounds, often oval, of stony earth, all sizes, and often in groups — Ground moraines ('drumlins') — 38

If you see . . .	*It could be . . .*	*For more detail see p. . . .*
18. Rounded mound in sandy country, no ditch	Stabilised dune	253

(b) Irregular and other earth mounds

19. Low mounds of chalky earth and flints.	Debris from N flint-working floor	116
20. Mounds of rock waste, conical or long, of different sizes, often covering large areas	Waste tips or slag heaps of mines or quarries	125
21. 'Ballast hills'	Dumps of ballast from coal-ships (Tyneside)	125
22. Clusters of small mounds	Coal tips, iron-working sites etc. (depending on composition of mounds)	119, 125
23. Low round or squarish mound, with broken pottery or tiles, etc.	Site of pottery kiln	125
24. Low squarish mound, strewn with burnt clay, some coated with glass, and fragments of glass waste. (Often in pairs, and may be in rectangular banked and ditched enclosure)	Glass kiln	127
25. Low squarish mound, with lumps of burnt clay, some coated with greenish smooth deposit	Remains of lime-kiln	126
26. Small mounds on roadsides, up to 2 ft. high × 5 ft. or so across	Dumps of stones, etc., for road repair	124
27. Oval ridges or mounds along railway line or canal	Spoil-heaps of cutting	240
28. Low oblong platforms, in groups, up to *c.* 3 ft. high	*Med* deserted village	113
29. Low irregular oblong platform	Deserted church or large house	114
30. Irregular oblong mounds, with stone, brick, timber; uneven ground, rank vegetation	Deserted house (*mod*)	114
31. Low, oblong mounds, often with transverse grooves on the top, and shallow ditch round	Pillow-mounds	235
32. Oblong platform with rim	Bowling green	206
33. Raised platform on bank of water-course	Old jetty or wharf	220
34. Extensive and irregular low platform of chalky soil	Dried-out mere	200
35. Rectangular earth platform projecting from bottom of a slope, and sometimes partly dug into the slope as well	Platform to keep house above flood-level	237
36. Rectangular platform cut into slope	Base for house	237

	If you see …	*It could be …*	*For more detail see p. …*

37. Mounds, low and rounded, or high and subconical — Ornamental 'mount' in garden — 215

38. Small oval mound with concrete structure inside — Ice-house; air raid shelter — 222

39. Low mound, various shapes — Plague-pit mound; grave of battle-dead — 236

40. Mound on intersection of old tracks or boundaries — *Med* (s) moot — 185

41. 'Hot cross bun' shaped mound — Obscure

42. Mounds on coast — Refuges for animals — 197

43. Short steep-sided banks in patterned clusters, usually with outer edge walled and or ditch — *Mod* fort — 179

44. Kidney or crescent-shaped mound, *c.* 3 ft. high, facing a stream, made of burnt material — Boiling mound (D) — 205

45. Platforms, irregular mounds — Disused golf-course, tees, greens, bunkers — 219

46. Bank in form of cross, sometimes in rectangular banked enclosure — ?R site of doubtful purpose; ? sheep enclosure — 207

47. Long narrow mound with tunnel inside, or, if disused, depression along top — Rabbit-refuge — 235

48. Short turf or earth wall in horseshoe or curve — Shooting-butt — 218

49. Small round turf structure, unroofed. *c.* 5 ft. across, with entrance gap — Shooting-butt — 218

(c) Continuous earth banks, terraces, etc., other than enclosures

50. Bank of stones and earth across a valley — Terminal moraine — 37

51. Dam across narrow valley — *Med* fish pond — 212

52. Bank across valley, with gap often at one side, and sometimes cinders or slag on lower side — Dam of hammer pond (the pond is sometimes still wet) — 121

53. Bank across valley, with narrow gap — Dam of ornamental pond — 122

54. Bank of stones and earth along the sides of a valley — Lateral moraine — 37

55. Bank of fine earth and small stones, winding — Esker or kame — 38

56. Continuous banks of silt, winding (show up also as dark centralline with lighter ones outside it) — Old river-course (rodham or roddon) — 200

57. Long flat steps along valley sides — Glacial terraces; old shore-lines of lake — 36, 38

7. STONE CIRCLES, where the religious and public functions of the tribe took place. *Above*, the normal rough type of natural boulders (Keswick). *Below*, architectural sophistication at Stonehenge, showing clear Mycenaean influence

8. STONE ROWS probably marked processional ways; AVENUES certainly did. *Above*, part of the great avenue at Avebury. *Below*, a small row (Trelleck, Mon.)

If you see . . .	*It could be . . .*	*For more detail see p. . . .*
58. Long horizontal banks on hillside	Caused by landslip	253
59. Long narrow parallel steps along hillside	Strip lynchets (cultivation terraces) (a few Belgic or R, most S or later)	112
60. Narrow parallel horizontal ledges on slope	Caused by soil-creep, not made by sheep or cattle (terracettes)	253
61. Long banks or terraces parallel to the sea	'Raised beaches' marking old sea levels	36
62. Continuous bank parallel to sea or river	Sea or river wall	196
63. Very long mound with side ditches (some 6 ft. high and up to hundreds of feet long)	N bank-barrow	153
64. Continuous bank with ditch on higher side (if on slope)	Defensive work (I-D)	182
65. Bank across neck or spur of land, with ditch on 'landward' side (sometimes several together)	I promontory fort or defensive work	169
66. Continuous bank, with ditch on either side, or in alternating stretches (sometimes enclosing an area, sometimes not)	Boundary of I or R ranch	184
67. Continuous bank and ditch, sometimes enclosing large area	*Med* deer-park or estate boundary	184
68. Low bank with ditch	*Mod* estate or enclosure boundary; field or plantation boundary	184
69. High bank with narrow walk along slope	*Med* estate boundary	182
70. Long banks, parallel or meeting at a point, sometimes with pits between	S animal-traps	184
71. Low flat continuous bank, often with ditch each side, up to *c.* 20 ft. apart	R road or by-way	131
72. Low continuous flat bank, ditch each side up to over 80 ft. apart	Major R road; turnpike or 'enclosure' road, with verges	132, 134
73. Continuous bank with flat top, and (sometimes) ballast on surface	Disused railway embankment	238
74. Broad green way between walls or hedges and ditches	Disused *med* road; drove road	133
75. Wide flat way, roughly level, with ballast (usually) on surface	Disused railway	238
76. Continuous flat terrace	Railway work	238

If you see . . .	*It could be . . .*	*For more detail see p. . . .*
77. Continuous terrace on hillside, level or sloping, sometimes with low outer rim	I or R terrace-way	130
78. Flat way straight up a slope	(wide) canal incline; (narrow) ropeway	195, 240
79. Twin raised banks, continuous	Disused canal	200
80. Narrow bank across marshy country (or former marsh)	Causewayed path	134
81. Ridges across field, *c.* 3 ft. wide, parallel	Plough-ridges	112
82. 'Ridge and furrow'—parallel ridges in field, *c.* 10 ft. across	*Med* cultivation strips	111
83. Low narrow ridge across field	Drain	
84. Ridging across lane	Caused by cattle	240
85. Single ridge across hill-road	For drainage	240
86. Semi-circular banked area on cliff-edge	I fort	
87. High steep-sided bank	Butt of shooting-range	181
88. High bank, often with ditch and trees	To ensure privacy	184

(d) Enclosures with earth banks

89. Earth bank in circle, up to *c.* 20 ft. high, with ditch inside or outside, and sometimes stone circle inside; one or two entrances (except Avebury, which has four)	Henge (EB)	136
90. Circular bank with ditch inside it	B ring-barrow	161
91. Circular bank, ditch outside	Ring-ditch, or earth circle; hut-circle (usually has gap); tree-ring	161
92. High bank, deep, often wet, ditch	Ring-motte (no gap, up to 200ft. diameter)	178
93. Enclosures of different shapes and sizes with low banks (round, oval, square, D, kite, etc.)	B, I, R farm enclosures	108
94. Bank, usually up to some 20 ft. high, with outside ditch and one or more gaps, enclosing space, usually roughly circular, of up to several acres	I hillfort (univallate) Norman fort	167, 177
95. Two or more concentric banks and ditches, often with subsidiary banks at the gaps, enclosing spaces, not always circular, and often larger than the forts at 94	I fort, multivallate	168
96. Banks and outer ditches enclosing very large areas of ground (hundreds of acres)	Belgic fortified town	106

If you see ...	*It could be ...*	*For more detail see p. ....*
97. Bank and ditch, enclosing playing-card-shaped area	R fort	171
98. Bank and outer ditch enclosing large area usually with stonework in bank	R town wall	173
99. Large hollow surrounded by high banks	R amphitheatre	185
100. High bank and outer ditch, enclosing oval, with gap	Norman fort	177
101. Banks with outer ditch, angular plan	*Mod* fort	179
102. Banks of stones and earth in small circles, etc.	I-D fortified farm	167
103. Low bank round house and garden	Plot boundary (*med*, *mod*)	115
104. Enclosures on coast, with banks 4-5 ft. high, and channels to sea	Saltings	197
105. Squarish areas ($\frac{1}{2}$-2 acres), delimited by very low banks	Celtic fields	102, 104
106. Banks enclosing meadows by a river	*Med* drainage	197
107. Shallow rectangular basin enclosed by 3 or 4 banks, in a valley, with channels to a stream; sometimes in series	Fishpond	212
108. Banked enclosure near stream, joined to it by channel	Millpond and race	233
109. Rectangular banked space with gap at one end only	Disused dock or canal basin	196
110. Rectangular banked space with gaps at each end	Disused lock	195
111. Low circular banks of burnt earth	Charcoal-burning site	206
112. Circular flat-topped bank, no ditch but entrance	May be site of rotary machine or horse-breaking ring	221
113. Round, oval or square enclosure with low banks, with outer ditch	Bee-garden	204
114. Small rectangular enclosure with 3 or 4 banks	*Med* pigstye	235
115. Enclosure with banks of turf 4 ft. high	Rabbit-warren	236

(e) Ditches and hollows

116. Shallow round hollows, up to *c.* 20 ft. across	Sites of B-D huts	101, 110
117. Round hollow	Cockpit	187
118. Small shallow hollows, round, in groups	I storage pits	
119. Shallow convex cavity with bank round it	B pond barrow	161
120. Round depression with bank and ditch round it	Games or baiting place	187
121. Small round hollow; banks round it	Gun post	180

If you see . . .	*It could be . . .*	*For more detail see p. . . .*
122. Shallow depression, on chalk, surrounded by low irregular mounds of chalky earth and flints.	Flint mine	116
123. Shallow depression with ring of stones round	Quarry pit for stone axe material	117
124. Round depressions, with irregular bank round	Pits for clay and ore extraction	119, 123
125. Round depression, with low irregular bank	Bell-pit	122
126. Round depression, sometimes with 'pushed-up' edges	Bomb-crater	180
127. Conical pit, no banks	Sink-hole or swallow hole	253
128. Depressions or pits in chalk country	Lime, marl or flint diggings	125
129. Irregular depressions or pits in sand or gravel, with steep sides (Pits etc. on heavy soils are often full of water)	Sand or gravel pits	124
130. Shallow depression	Dried-out pond or dew-pond	189
131. Round hollow with central platform	Cockpit	187
132. Oval depression with round bank and ditch inside	Cockpit	188
133. Small scooped depression, with blackened soil and broken pottery	Pottery kiln	123
134. Hollows on roadside	Sources of road-metal	124
135. Small pit or hollow	Remains of badger or rabbit trap	188, 236
136. Pit with ramp into it on one side	Saw-pit	244
137. Deep embanked pit	Spring-pond (may be R)	189
138. Shallow pit or trench	Open working for iron ore	119
139. Ring-grooves (shallow circular ditch)	I house	106
140. Ring-ditch (deeper than 139)	I house; B site of obscure purpose, probably mainly ritual or sepulchral	106, 161
141. Ditches enclosing a large circular area, interrupted, i.e. consisting of strings of oval trenches	N causewayed camp	100
142. Long parallel ditches, up to 3000 yds. long × 100 yds. wide	Cursus	136
143. Parallel grooves across field	Plough marking furrows	133, 284
144. V-sectioned gulleys straight down hillside, sometimes in groups	Erosion gulleys	253

If you see . . .	*It could be . . .*	*For more detail see p. . . .*
145. Gulleys in mountain, with low banks	Rock-slide	253
146. Continuous trench with flat bottom, in chalk or sand country, sometimes in groups	hollow way	129
147. Trench with flat bottom and bank on one or both sides, sometimes double (i.e. 3 banks, 2 trenches)	Cattle-way	182
148. Wide ditch, up to 20 ft. × 10 ft. deep, with vertical sides, usually enclosing square or oblong space	*Med* moat	178
149. Wide rectangular trench, *c.* 3 ft. deep, often with banks	Silage pit	211
150. Wide continuous trench with flat bottom and high banks	Disused canal	195
151. Continuous shallow depression	Disused canal	199
152. Continuous channels on level	Water-leet	190
153. Channel (dry) leading from a stream	Diversion channel for e.g. *med* glass-works	127
154. Channel diverting part of a stream	Fish-garth	212
155. Pool with channels to stream	For sheep-washing	245
156. Embanked channels leading from and back to a stream	For gold-washing	118
157. Pool cut at side of stream	For sheep-washing	245
158. Pond with dog-leg channels leading out of it, like spokes, each ending in a point at the landward end	Duck-decoy pond	217
159. Trenches and mounds beside them	Military practice works	180
160. Straight-sided trenching on moors	Peat cutting	
161. Ditch between garden and park, garden side sheer, park side sloping	Ha-ha	216
162. Short underground passage	Fogou	106
163. Long underground passage	Sewer; conduit access tunnel; refuge or escape tunnel	216
164. Tunnels into hillsides, with mounds of rock waste at entrance	Lead mine	119

(f) Dry-stone enclosures and structures

165. Irregular ring of stone wall (usually ruinous), often with hut-circles inside	I hillfort in highland zone	170
166. Irregular ring of stone wall, with masses fused together	I vitrified fort	170
167. Rectangular stone-walled enclosure, with remains of stone buildings inside, and often outside too (these latter now irregular stony mounds)	R fort (highland zone)	171

If you see . . .	*It could be . . .*	*For more detail see p. . . .*
168. Squarish stone huts, with roofed alleys between	N houses	100
169. Groups of stone huts with walls round	B-D villages	101
170. Round stone hut with beehive-shaped roof	B hut; *mod* hut, shed etc. of B type	101, 203
171. Small round dry-stone building, with one or two ditches and low banks round	Ring-fort	170
172. Small round stone building	Dun	170
173. Round stone tower, tapering slightly, up to 40 ft. high	Broch	105
174. Round stone house with radial divisions	Wheelhouse	103
175. Round house with rooms round a central space	Courtyard house	106
176. Galleried house	I wag	106
177. Small, irregular enclosures of stones	Corn plots; N huts	99
178. Dry-stone enclosures, of various shapes and sizes, sometimes composite	For sheep	244
179. Round or square walled enclosure, with entrance	Pound	237
180. Low stone walls in square	Pond	189
181. Dam of stones across stream	For sheep-washing	245
182. Stone platform, round or oblong	Peat-stool	235

(g) Rocks and stone monuments

183. Large isolated rock, rough and irregular in shape	Usually natural	143
184. Rounded, smooth rock	Roche moutonnée or rock-knob (glacial)	38
185. Large upright stone, usually elongated	B monolith; *mod*—set up for farming reasons	143
186. Tall thin standing stone, of regular cut and shape	Rubbing-stone	244
187. Round hollow on rock, smooth and deep, and often with undercut edges	Natural, water-made	223
188. Small shallow 'pecked' round depressions on rocks, *c.* 3 × 1 in. deep, often with circular grooves round them or connecting channels	B cup markings	223
189. Oval or round hollows on rock, 12-18 in. × 6 in. deep	Rock basins	243
190. Line of holes in rock	Feather holes	211
191. Vertical grooves on rock	Natural weathering	219
192. Grooves on rocks, not vertical or parallel, sometimes in groups	Sharpening-grooves	219

If you see . . .	*It could be . . .*	*For more detail see p. . . .*
193. Roughly parallel scratches on upper face of rock	Ice action	38
194. Row of large stones, sometimes twin, sometimes several in parallel	Stone avenues or rows	141
195. Circle of large stones, low or upright, usually a few ft. apart	B stone circle	142
196. Circle of stones, close together, with or without earth banked round it	Site of house, N to *med*	99
197. Large stones in heaps, or two or more covered by a horizontal stone	Remains of N-B chamber tomb	154
198. Cairn of stones on mountain	Barrow; mark	164
199. Group of small cairns	B-I cemetery	165
200. Heap of stones	Boundary mark; road metal; sighting mark; stones cleared from fields	101, 164
201. Lines of rocks like fallen walls visible at low tide	Actual submerged walls, natural boulders	198
202. Apparent ruins, of temples, abbeys, megalithic tombs, etc.	Follies	213
203. Steps beside rivers, in line of stream	Fish-weir	

(h) Soil and vegetation marks

204. Lines of darker, more vigorous vegetation	Ditch or deeply-dug soil —a small patch may be a pit or post-hole	283
205. Lines etc. of paler, poorer vegetation	Buried walls, structures, roads, etc.	284
206. Lines, patches, etc., of darker soil	Ditches or dug ground, (not always ancient); old watercourses, natural fissures in subsoil, etc.; differences in chemical or physical composition of soil	284
(e.g. a dark ring 40 ft. across may mark the ditch of a ploughed-out barrow)		
207. Patches, etc. of lighter soil	Mounds or banks (not always ancient), ploughed out	284
208. Parallel dark continuous lines with whitish soil between	Dried-out canal (slade)	200
209. Continuous line or strip of different soil or material	Filled-in ditch, tank-trap, etc.	133
210. Blackened patch of earth in field, or on edge of cliff, quarry, etc.	Hearth, various dates	101
211. Fungus or vegetation rings	Natural	285

If you see . . .	*It could be . . .*	*For more detail see p. . .*
(j) Unclassified, or in more than one category		
212. Patch of rough ground, with rank weeds, bricks, tiles, dressed stone etc.	Site of house, barn, etc. (R onwards)	114, 277
213. In coalfields, mounds, pits, ponds	Remains of coal-mining	125
214. Circular patch of iron slag	Site of smelting-hearth	120
215. Double hedgerow	*Med* or *mod* track; *med* boundary	182
216. Low turf walls, a few inches high, in pattern	Maze	229
217. Oval rings of low banks, multiple, broken into short lengths	Duck-breeding pond	217
218. A variety of mounds, pits, trenches and broken ground is caused by the exigencies of modern farming, some quite temporary, but none the less leaving their mark. Clamps or pies of roots or potatoes can be deceptive from a distance.		211

CHAPTER 2

Types of Field Antiquities: Fixtures

This section begins with several groups of major antiquities, many of them earthworks, and representing the main aspects of ancient life. The key to earthwork types on pp. 85-96 should be used freely in identifying them.

CAVES AND ROCK-SHELTERS

There is nothing in Britain like the great painted palaeolithic caves of Lascaux or Altamira; the cultures of the Ice Age did not have their centres of diffusion here. But the relatively few inhabitable caves in Britain were none the less used by man. The caves are mostly found in the limestone belts running across England from Devon to the Mendips, south and north-east Wales, Derbyshire and Yorkshire. Primitive people occupy only the mouths of caves and a short distance in, so rock-shelters, overhanging cliffs which could be made comfortable and weatherproof with screens of branches, were also used.

Remains of occupation of Mousterian men have been found at Kent's Cavern, near Torquay (Devon), in two deep shelters at Oldbury, Ightham (Kent), and at Pin Hole, Creswell Crags (Derbyshire). Pin Hole and its neighbour Mother Grundy's Parlour are classical sites for Britain; here was found a sequence of occupation, divided by layers of slabs fallen from the cave roof in the glacial phases of the last (Würm) glaciation, from Mousterian to the Gravettian which became the native Creswellian culture of Britain, and from then to the Mesolithic.

Aurignacians lived in Paviland Cave, Gower (Glamorgan), where a young man (known incorrectly as the 'red lady of Paviland') was buried with ornaments and the skull of an elephant, and covered with red ochre as a passport to immortality. Cae Gwyn, in the Vale of Clwyd (Denbighshire) was also occupied at this time. Other caves of the last glaciation are Wookey Hole, Aveline's Hole, Gough's Cave, and Soldier's Hole, all in the Mendips; and Victoria Cave, Settle (Yorks WR). This last, and the equally famous cave of Kirkdale, near Kirbymoorside, produced long series of animal bones of all the main Pleistocene types —hyena, elephants, hippopotamus, rhinoceros, lion, bear, and down to reindeer.

Caves were not only inhabited in the glacial periods. They were sought after as dwellings down to modern times. The mesolithic people of the Sauveterrian were particularly fond of rock-shelters, and many in the Pennines, such as Kilnsey and Great Almscliff (south of Harrogate) have yielded flints of this period. Even quite small clefts in rocks were used, as for instance that recently found near Stump Cross, Greenhow, near Pateley Bridge. One should not be led by the blackening due to fire on the overhang of a rock-shelter to assume that its occupation was prehistoric; these places are used today by farm-workers and vagrants, and digging below the fire-marks will not always produce ancient remains. Examples of caves used at different times are Ash Tree Cave, near Whitwell, Derbyshire (neolithic); Heathery Burn, Weardale (Late Bronze Age); Dog Holes, Warton, Lancs., Iron Age of Glastonbury type; King Arthur's Cave, palaeolithic, mesolithic and Bronze Age; Merlin's Cave (both these are near Ross, on the Wye), Bronze and Iron Ages; Wookey Hole was used in the Roman period.

At Waddon, Surrey, are four underground chambers, hollowed out of the rock and used as dwellings in the 1st centuries BC and AD. In the Middle Ages and later an overhanging cliff was often used as a snug back wall to a house, or a cliff was hollowed out for the purpose; such can be seen at the celebrated mediaeval inn at Nottingham, The Trip to Jerusalem. In Gracious Street, Knaresborough, are several 18th century houses similarly built. Knaresborough is unusually rich in inhabited caves; a mediaeval chapel (Our Lady of the Crag c. 1409), that occupied by Mother Shipton (15th century), the refuge of Eugene Aram (18th century), and 'The House in the Rock', also 18th century, a dwelling of several rooms cut out high up the cliff. Many caves have been enlarged, no doubt for occupation, such as the Giant's Cave on the Malvern Hills. The mediaeval chapel at Clifton, where a long passage in the limestone opens out high above the Avon Gorge, should be noted. Mediaeval **hermits** sometimes lived in caves; in some examples several rooms and a chapel have been hollowed out of the cliff—early ones are at Dale, Derbys., and Redstone Park, Stourport, Worcs., both possibly 12th century. The lore of caves should not be overlooked as possible clues to occupation—such as the legend of Arthur attached to a cave in the Cheviot, and countless stories of refuge taken in caves by heroes, robbers, patriots, religious groups. Caves and old mines have been used for storage and a variety of purposes, and these are often of interest, such as the flint mines at Chislehurst, Kent, and the very interesting 12/13th century clunch mine at Guildford (Racks Close), used as a mediaeval wine cellar by the Castle. Among the largest man-made caves are the Hell-Fire Caves at West Wycombe (c. 1750). Crosses, etc., were cut by mediaeval pilgrims on the walls of caves once inhabited by holy men or otherwise famous; e.g. St Ninian's near Whithorn (Wigs.); St Adrian's, Crail (Fife).

SETTLEMENTS, FARMS AND VILLAGES

PREHISTORIC HUTS AND FARMS

Palaeolithic man, being a nomadic hunter and food-gatherer, lived, in the milder climatic periods at least, in rough huts made of branches and roofed with skins or thatch, or simply behind windbreaks of similar materials. None of these has survived, and indeed their existence has to be deduced from a variety of evidence. But in the colder phases more complete protection was obtained by the use of caves and rock-shelters under overhanging cliffs, in front of which a sort of screen would be erected. Even these were only occupied occasionally and for short periods; the few human groups which roamed the country needed large areas to hunt over, and seemed not to have stayed long in any place; often they followed migrating herds of animals. But much of our knowledge of the life of palaeolithic times comes from the scanty remains left on the floor of the caves. (see p. 46)

Mesolithic man was still a nomad, and his settlements are almost equally primitive. Some were hollows scooped in the ground, and roofed with branches or turves; such were found at Farnham (Surrey), grouped round a spring; while at Abinger, not far away, one of these has been preserved. A site at Star Carr, Seamer, near Scarborough, had a platform of branches to keep it dry, and the remains included a most instructive variety of implements and utensils, and rolls of birch-bark from which small objects could be made. But most mesolithic people lived in open country, on moors in the Pennines and heaths in Surrey, Hampshire and most of the south of England, and although their flint implements turn up in large numbers, their huts do not; this applies also to the shore-dwelling peoples of west and south-west Scotland, and the river-folk of northern Ireland.

The neolithic farmers who arrived in the course of the third millennium BC lived in quite different conditions, being settled rural peasants, growing corn in little patches and keeping herds of cattle and pigs and flocks of sheep. Corn-plots of this period are rare, because the shallow scratching of the soil did not produce very marked lynchets (banks piled up at the bottom of a cultivated field on a slope, owing to the soil creeping down the hill when loosened, to the foot of the furrows), and in most places these have been ploughed out by later farming. But a few, small, irregular enclosures, associated with hut-circles (the banks or rings of stones marking the outer wall of a hut), can be seen in Devon and Cornwall—Carn Brea (this is a veritable village of some 60 huts); Trowlesworthy, White Ridge, Standon Down (Dartmoor); Rough Tor (Bodmin Moor)—and in Yorkshire. Rectangular houses were also built,

99

perhaps for chiefs; one was found at Haldon (Devon), and they can be deduced from the structures concealed in some of the long barrows of this period, which may be the burial-places of ruling families (e.g. Fussell's Lodge barrow, Wilts.).

A lakeside community with a different way of life (fishing and fowling) lived beside the now dry Ehenside Tarn in Cumberland; other waterside settlements are known in Scotland (e.g. Glenluce, Wigtownshire) and Ireland (Lough Gur, Co. Limerick), where there was a rectangular house. But the most distinctive feature of the primary neolithic farmers is the **causewayed camp** (pl. 4, p. 65), of which examples are scattered along the chalk and greensand hills of the south of England from Devon to Sussex. These are circular enclosures, usually with more than one concentric ring, consisting of a bank with external ditch; these are interrupted at frequent intervals by causeways across the ditch and corresponding gaps in the bank. Their purpose was not that of the later hill-forts, but was primarily to form a shelter into which the stock could be collected when need arose, and where those animals which could not be kept through the winter were slaughtered. The people lived in the shelter of the banks also, usually just inside the outer ring. One of these causewayed camps, that at Windmill Hill, near Avebury (Wilts.), has given its name to the primary neolithic culture of Britain. Others are at Hembury (Devon); Abingdon (Berks.); Whitehawk, the Trundle, Coombe Hill (on the South Downs in Sussex), and elsewhere. That at the Trundle is inside an Iron Age hill-fort. Causewayed ditches and enclosures have been detected from the air in the east Midlands, but their age and purpose is not yet known.

The secondary neolithic peoples were still partly mesolithic in living standards, and the only evidence for their houses is in the form of circular scooped huts roofed with branches. The exception is the northern branch of the Rinyo-Clacton culture (see p. 58), who have left in Orkney remains from which a fairly complete picture of their economy can be built up: at Skara Brae and at Rinyo are groups of squarish stone huts, connected by paved alleys, roofed over with slabs, and drained by channels under them. Wood being unobtainable, all the furniture, such as beds, dressers, cupboards and no doubt doors, were of stone slabs; there were cists in the floor to hold liquids (or shellfish), and all the surviving loose equipment is of imperishable materials like stone, bone, or pottery. This evidence, preserved under drifting sand, gives a rare and unexpected clue to what living conditions must have been like further south.

The Beaker people, and the Early Bronze Age, subsisted more by stock-breeding, and trade, and there was a good deal of nomadism; the absence of many remains of dwellings probably means that tents were used, although some people lived in the flimsy scooped type of hut, while it is also probable that some of the circular huts on Dartmoor

and in the north date from this time. Certainly during the Middle
Bronze Age the little corn-plots were used, but generally speaking there
is little clear evidence for the houses and farms of these long periods.

Most of the evidence comes from the highland zone. Devon, the
Pennines and north-east Yorkshire were colonised by the Urn-folk, who
pushed into poorer lands than their predecessors the Food Vessel people
did. At Grimspound on Dartmoor there are groups of round stone
houses with beehive roof and protecting wall (pl. 15); some ring-ditches
of southern England, such as on the Berkshire downs (e.g. Rams Hill),
may be similar farmsteads. The average internal diameter of the Dartmoor huts is about 17 ft. On the moors of NE Yorkshire are sites consisting of groups of shallow pits, of doubtful purpose but showing signs
of fire; a few small fields with stone walls, large numbers of small cairns,
forming cemeteries of humble folk whose bodies have disappeared (by
reason of the acid soil)—some may be merely the results of clearing a
field of stones, but most appear to be sepulchral; barrows where the
chiefs were buried, and sometimes a stone circle or enclosure with
standing stones in its walls; and the whole often on a ridge, protected by
dykes across the narrowest part. Spectacular examples are at Crown
End, Castleton; a well-known but rather decayed one on Danby Rigg,
and others in various parts of the North York Moors, such as Horn End,
Farndale. These appear to be settlements of the Urn culture of the
Middle Bronze Age.

At this point could be mentioned the possibility of finding **hearths**,
of various dates, by blackened patches in ploughed fields, or as horizontal streaks of black earth just below the surface at the edge of
quarries, streams, etc. Many sites have been found unexpectedly in
this way; quarry-edges also can reveal rubbish or storage pits, as deep
dark stains of earth descending from the edge, or the ditches of circles,
Roman roads and a variety of earthworks. The Roman iron-working
town of Ariconium (Weston-under-Penyard, Herefordshire), is visible
on the surface of the fields by the blackened patches representing the
smithy-hearths; Iron Age hearths and pits were seen in quarries at
Grafton, near Boroughbridge, and Clandon (Surrey) respectively.
Under a Food Vessel culture barrow, Green Howe, North Deighton
(Yorks. WR), was found a hearth of secondary neolithic date. All such
finds can produce important evidence in the form of pottery, metal
objects, etc., and in some cases the charcoal of the hearths can be made
to yield information on the local trees, and hence the climatic conditions
of the times. But to return to the Middle Bronze Age, little evidence in
all on the nature of the houses and farms of these centuries has survived,
although this may partly be due to a considerable degree of nomadic
methods of farming.

But before we go on to the Late Bronze Age, which has quite different
features, there is one source of information about the earlier phases of

the Bronze Age; the houses of the dead buried under barrows (as indeed occurs in the Neolithic also). In some cases it looks as if the dead person was buried in or near his house, which was then covered with a barrow, or a special 'dead-house' was built for him alone. These were probably typical houses of the times, but are now, of course, not to be seen. At Kemp Howe, Cowlam Farm, near Driffield (Yorks. ER), beneath a round barrow, was an oval trench 25 ft. long, 4½ ft. wide, and 6 ft. deep, approached by a sloping passage 11 ft. long; along the centre were 6 charred posts, and the filling of the trench showed the hut to have been roofed with timber covered with earth and stones. On the south side of the hut was a ledge, 6 ft. long and 10–12 in. high. This dates from the Neolithic, but the type no doubt remained in use in later periods. So, although a great many so-called 'pit-dwellings' have been discredited by later discoveries, there is no doubt that some houses were indeed sunk into the ground, perhaps for warmth.

For the Wessex culture, two barrows at Beaulieu (Hants.), covered the remains of houses some 5½ feet square, with timber-framed walls, and stout central posts supporting a ridged roof. To judge from the several sites which have revealed domestic remains inside circular banks and ditches (as at Playdon, near Rye, Sussex), the circular house, common later in the Iron Age, was in continuous use.

The Deverel-Rimbury immigrants from northern France in the Late Bronze Age brought with them an improved type of plough, an innovation which had profound effects on the economy of Britain, and determined the methods of farming for several centuries. This plough, the ard, did not turn the sod, but made a wide furrow; it could be drawn by oxen, and led to the formation of the so-called 'Celtic' fields, small, squarish plots from a half to two acres in size. These fields were square because ploughing was done along and across, to break up the soil thoroughly and so conserve moisture. All along the chalk hills from Sussex to Wiltshire and Dorset, groups of these fields, representing veritable farms, have been recognised, and a number of them are still visible. As however this type of farm persisted throughout the succeeding Iron Age and even the Roman period, it is not always easy to distinguish those dating from its first introduction. The classic site, established by excavation, is Plumpton Plain, near Brighton.

The lynchets, or low banks, which mark the outlines of the fields, straggle down the hillside in no regular pattern (pl. 20, p. 193); at the top is the site of the farmhouse and its associated enclosures. Other farms of this period show round and sub-rectangular enclosures, and sunken lanes between them; there are also rectilinear or oval enclosures with V-sectioned ditch and inner bank, like that on Boscombe Down, Wilts., with entrances, a type which was probably a stock-yard. This example appears to be connected with a cross-country ditch, probably a farm-boundary. The best group of Late Bronze Age enclosures of different types is on Marlborough (Ogbourne) Downs, Wilts.; others of the pastoral kind are to be found at Thickthorn, Dorset; Martin Down, Hants. Much evidence on the crops grown, and the way of life, has been recently excavated at the site at Itford Hill, near Lewes, Sussex. Plough-furrows have been found at Gwithian, Cornwall (EBA), and Albury, Surrey (LBA).

In the rest of the country the new methods of farming slowly spread, but not till the Iron Age, and the immigration of more continental peoples, did they become widespread. In the highland zone at this time the people went on using their scratch-ploughs and their little plots. There is little or no evidence for the houses, but by the Heathery Burn, near Stanhope, Co. Durham, a group of bronze-smiths lived in a cave, where a variety of their equipment and domestic refuse has been found. In Shetland, at Jarlshof, a group of stone houses, surrounded by a dry-stone wall, was occupied in different phases of building throughout the Bronze Age. The inhabitants lived on birds, fish and seals, and shellfish, like their predecessors at Skara Brae, but grew cereals as well, and kept cattle, whose manure they used on the corn-plots. Two or three houses were occupied at any one time, and in the Late Bronze Age the people were joined by a bronze-smith, a man from Ireland who set up his smithy with them. While he was there one of the houses was altered by the addition of an underground gallery or souterrain; it was then rebuilt on a circular plan, with a central hearth, a type which foreshadows the later wheelhouses of the Scottish Iron Age (a wheelhouse is a circular house with radial partitions like the spokes of a wheel). The whole community of houses at Jarlshof has now been restored by the Ministry of Works, and is one of the most interesting relics of its period in Britain (it also has a broch, wheelhouses, a Viking settlement, and a mediaeval laird's house).

The influx of people in the Early Iron Age, mostly spreading from the south, but some landing in Yorkshire, led to more land being occupied, and more intensive farming (spelt was added to the list of cereals grown). Throughout the Iron Age the same square Celtic fields were used, and now a great many may be seen, throughout the chalk and other light soils of southern Britain, and in many parts of the highland zone as well (pl. 20, p. 193). Farms were small, only a few acres, and consisted of round houses, timber-framed and thatched, often sur-rounded by a ditch and a palisade; the farm-yards contained pits for the storage of grain (parched with the help of hot stones which were once thought to be 'pot-boilers'), and used as rubbish tips when they got too sour to keep grain in. Corn was dried on racks, and stacked in frame-works of posts. The pits were for long thought to be 'pit-dwellings', but this misconception was finally cleared up by the excavation of a typical site of this kind, Little Woodbury, near Salisbury, by Dr Bersu in 1938–39.

The groups of fields, and sometimes the farm complex also, of this type of unit, can be seen in many places, and yet more are being revealed in air photographs. Good examples are those which can be seen on the slopes north of the great fort on the Caburn, near Lewes (Sussex), in which scores of storage pits and hut sites can be seen; along the South Downs, as at Park Brow; in Hampshire, where a large number in the Winchester district have been mapped (e.g. Worthy Down); in Wiltshire, where the chalk hills are rich in them (e.g. Fyfield Down); in Dorset, on the limestone, at St Aldhelm's Head; in the Mendip-Cotswold area, as at Bathampton Down and Clifton Down; and finally in Berkshire, where Mr D. N. Riley has plotted a large number, many revealed by air photography, north of the downs (pl. 15). These, which are mainly on the gravels, have besides storage pits, a variety of enclosures, circular or sub-rectangular ditches, larger oval, round or rectangular, D-shaped, and straight stretches of ditch; all these have farming uses, but without excavation their exact purpose, and in many cases their date, are obscure. They are very common in this district, particularly round Dorchester (Oxon) and Stanton Harcourt; but much remains to be discovered throughout central southern England. It should be remembered that the north-south lynchets of the fields are clearer than the others; odd pieces of pottery are more often to be found on the lynchets than in the fields themselves.

The various enclosures that formed part of the farms are often isolated now, and, as already said, their dates are not always known—this type of farming lasted for centuries. Several unusual ones exist, like the 'spectacles' at Pewsey Down (Wilts.) and elsewhere, which are round enclosures connected by a sunken way. Houses were round or rectangular, and their sites can often be detected on ploughed land by scatters of dark soil, burnt flints, bits of pottery; or, on grassland, by patches of lusher grass, often with mole-hills or rabbit-scrapes.

This Iron Age A culture was confined to the limited parts of England mentioned except for the colony at Scarborough. Elsewhere the economy was still of Late Bronze Age type, although Celtic fields are found in a few places further north. But, as Professor Piggott has recently shown, north-west of the Jurassic ridge the economy was basically pastoral, not based on corn-growing. In the north and west the small plots for hoe-cultivation were still used, and in addition there are large areas dyked off for cattle ranches, horses and sheep. North of the Tyne–Solway line there was still less grain grown. But in parts of the north Celtic fields are known, such as the well-known group at Grassington, in Wharfedale (Yorks. WR); others are at Ribblehead, and there are a few possible ones even as far as Northumberland (like the enigmatic lynchets along the Swinhope Burn, East Allendale). Dr Raistrick has mapped over 800 occupation sites (many with round stone huts like those in Grass Wood, Grassington) in Craven and NW Yorkshire

9. TYPES OF RELIGIOUS CARVING

Above, Bronze Age "cup-and-ring" marks (Roughting Linn, Northumberland). *Right*, a Celtic carving of a god (Iron Age) built into the wall of Copgrove Parish Church, Yorks WR, (13th century) showing the continuity of a sacred site from pagan times

10.   Iron Age chalk-cut figure, symbol of the Atrebates tribe (The Uffington White Horse, Berks.)

alone—these range from the Middle Bronze Age to AD 600. There are others at various places in the Pennines, and many circles which may have been stockaded enclosures (e.g. Hebden Moor and Kilnsey). Palisaded farms are also common on both sides of the Cheviot, in Northumberland and Roxburghshire (also in North Wales), and these have been described by Mr A. H. A. Hogg as 'secondary Iron Age', which well describes these communities of basically Bronze Age culture living in poor and marginal areas and having absorbed as much Iron Age culture as their way of life and resources would stand. Over 500 native settlements are known in Northumberland alone.

A few settlers at this time brought with them the idea of the continental pile dwelling, used for lakeside houses in west central Europe; in Britain they occur in Scotland (Loch Glashan, Argyll) and Wales (Llangorse Lake, near Brecon) but are commonest in Ireland, where crannogs, or artificial islands of stones and brushwood are found in swamps and small lakes; these were in use until the 17th century AD. In England there are remains of pile-dwellings on the Thames near Southchurch and Brentford, and in Yorkshire along the once marshy edge of what was Lake Pickering, now Ryedale, at Costa Beck, and at Ulrome in Holderness.

The Iron Age B peoples also had distinctive types of dwelling in the highland zone. In Scotland and the north of England stone hut-circles often cluster round the various types of fort, and there are fortified farms also which, being single households, should be mentioned in this section. Such are the small circular forts like those at Rahoy on Loch Teacuis (Argyll), 40 ft. across internally. The well-known and still somewhat enigmatic **brochs,** in the north and north-west mostly, date, or at least begin, in the last pre-Roman centuries, but continued in use into our era. Brochs are tall circular towers, each one dominating a seaward-facing valley or a small tract of country, and were evidently the strongholds of chiefs who lived by raiding as well as by farming. They have hollow walls, often containing stairs to upper floors; the ground-floor plan consists of a circular courtyard with small rooms or wooden 'flats' inside. The brochs are local adaptations of the small stone forts, which themselves grew out of the Iron Age hillfort tradition of the south. After earlier forms, they appear in Skye (e.g. Dun Liath), and from there spread to Orkney and Caithness, then to Shetland (where Mousa is the finest of all). They are the smallest in the west, and here often on rock-knolls; in the north-east they are often on flat ground. Wheelhouses developed from brochs, in Shetland. The broch culture is varied, and represents immigrants and influences from several Iron Age A and B cultures in England. (See also p. 68.)

Scotland also has several types of duns, from simple stone ring forts and promontory forts to chambered and galleried duns. Hundreds of these can be found in the west and north. There are various other local types of homestead: wags or galleried dwellings in the north (e.g. Forse, Caithness); double-walled round houses in the east and south-east; enclosed settlements of round stone huts; palisaded, platform and scooped settlements; ring-ditch and ring-groove houses.

The lake-villages of Glastonbury and Meare (Somerset) are too well known to need more than a reference. In Cornwall again there are distinctive types. Villages of irregular round or oval houses are found, with rooms arranged round a courtyard, rather like those at Jarlshof; each house has its little garden-plots, and Celtic fields surround the villages (Chysauster, near Lands End, is a good example, but over 20 are known in this district alone). Near this village is a fogou, or souter-rain, an underground refuge, house or store, and this is a characteristic Cornish type (there is a fine one at Carn Euny); it is also found in Scotland, associated there with wheelhouses. Hilltop villages like those in Cornwall are also found in Wales, and a good example, inhabited in the Roman period, is that at Tre'r Ceiri, Caernarvonshire.

The last immigrants of British prehistory, the Belgae, brought with them a heavy plough, with share to turn the sod, with which they were able to occupy heavier soils. This means that many, if not most, of their settlements are no longer visible, as they are on sites used later by the Romans and also by the Saxons. But the single farm (not the village) was still their normal unit; their houses were circular, with a few larger ones sub-rectangular. It is just possible that some of the strip-lynchets, characteristic of Saxon agriculture, date from this time, but doubt still remains on most of them; the only well-attested example is that on Twyford Down, near Winchester. Belgic towns were agglomerations of rather squalid huts, spread thinly over wide areas, as at Colchester and Selsey; at Prae Wood, above the Roman Verulamium (St Albans), a jumble of banks and ditches, not all of them Belgic, marks an important town, but is not very informative on the surface. There was another large, widely-spaced town at Wheathampstead (Herts.), and several small ones, such as Braughing (Herts.); but much excavation is neces-sary to elucidate the domestic life and economy of these people. The vast site of Stanwick (Yorks. NR) is exceptional in being a short-lived Brigantian place of refuge (in its final form owing much to Belgic ideas of fortifying a large area) in a campaign against the Romans. Apart from cases like this, and royal alliances, the Belgic settlement-area was broadly in the south-eastern part of England, although there is of course Belgic influence in other areas also.

ROMAN VILLAS

Romanization was beginning in this period, in the shape of coinage, growing foreign trade, and the increasing use of objects imported from

Gaul. But for most of the people this was a mere veneer, and left unaffected the houses and basic way of life, except in so far as the better farming methods could increase production and hence disposable wealth. That this wealth was very real for those concerned is indicated by a well-known passage in Strabo, who gave the exports of Belgic Britain as corn, cattle, gold, silver, iron, slaves and hunting dogs; in exchange the chief imports were ivory bracelets and necklaces, amber, glassware and pottery (some of it no doubt containing wine).

The Romans were in Britain for nearly 400 years from AD 43. South and east of a line roughly from the mouth of the Tees, along the Pennine foothills, round to Chester, south to Caerleon, and taking in south Wales to the coast of Carmarthenshire, the province was under civil rule; north and west of this line, as far as the Forth–Clyde level, was a military zone, governed directly from the forts (with oscillations in south Scotland); north of this the natives were free, except of what influences reached them. Again very roughly, the social-economic history of the civil zone may be outlined thus:

> 1st century (second half)—romanization
> 2nd century—peace and prosperity, consolidation
> 3rd century—decline
> 4th century—prosperity, development
> 5th century—disturbance, decline

One of the first signs that the country was settling down to the new regime was the building by merchants, richer farmers and the territorial nobility in the civil zone of houses in the Roman style. These villas, as these houses of urbanised, romanised gentry are called, were usually quite modest at first, consisting of a range of rooms connected by a veranda or corridor. Some have been shown actually to replace farms of the round Little Woodbury type, themselves succeeded by rectangular Belgic houses, as at Lockleys, near Welwyn, and Park Street, near St Albans (both Herts.); some, of course, are on new sites—mostly still on the lighter soils, but some on the lower lands. During the second century these villas were enlarged by the addition of wings at the ends of the main range, which was itself developed. The buildings themselves were usually half-timbered on stone footings, which in most cases is all that now remains.

Villas are distributed over the entire civil zone, and in certain areas, like that round the town of Ilchester, Somerset (Lindinis), are very abundant; but in others, such as the Fens and central Wessex, they are almost absent. This is probably due to the presence in those areas of vast Imperial estates, for the supply of corn or wool to the army. The economy of the villas was large-scale farming, entailing great open fields round the house and tenant farms of native type, with nucleated houses and Celtic fields, further away. During the fourth century some villas were rebuilt, and new ones built—the style now is that of a series of buildings, or ranges, round a courtyard. Some of these are very luxurious, with baths and elaborate mosaic floors. But all villas should not be thought of as having such amenities—over 600 villas are known, but only some 75 of these are luxurious. As one goes north into Yorkshire the villas get poorer. Some of the large later villas were adapted for industrial processes. Good villas to learn from are Chedworth (Glos.), Lullingstone (Kent), and the great and rich palace at Fishbourne (Sussex).

Several other villas can be seen, such as Brading (I.O.W.), and Bignor (Sussex); many have once been excavated, and remain in varying degrees of completeness as at Titsey (Surrey), and Well (Yorks. NR). Most are just sites, grassed over or even only known from air photographs; and more no doubt remain to be discovered, like that found accidentally at Ewhurst (Surrey) in 1957.

NATIVE FARMS

The native farms of the Roman period, not all of course even in the civil zone tied to the villas, need no description; they are difficult to distinguish from Iron Age ones, except for the objects to be found on them. And outside the civil zone the native life went on as before, except for the new settlements at the gates of the Roman forts, some of which, like York, became important towns. But before we leave the countryside, mention should be made of the variety of pastoral enclosures on the farms. These are of all shapes, as in the Iron Age, but a new type is found, shaped like a kite (e.g. Rockbourne Down, Cranborne Chase, Hants.). There are many enclosures on the chalk hills which may be of any date from the Bronze Age to the Middle Ages. There is a distinctive Romano-British type of enclosure with double ditches (e.g. a triangular one at Welney, Norfolk; a pentagon at South Damersham, Hants.). 'Long' Celtic fields are of this period.

A special kind of enclosure is known as the Highworth type, from examples at Highworth, Wilts. (also at Hannington); these are circles or 'playing-cards' with a bank outside the ditch, and no entrances. They are often in groups, one of which is a quatrefoil of four joined circles. Their purpose is still obscure, but they appear to be of Roman date.

A 4th century house recently excavated at Headley, Surrey, was built of timbers set in packings of stones.

A type of homestead or 'village', confined to north-west Wales (Anglesey, Caerns., west Merioneth), of which Din Lligwy in Anglesey is a striking example, is a group of round or squarish stone houses enclosed by a circular or oval wall. Most of these were in use in the Roman period, and some may be later.

The British Association has started (1964) an experiment at Broad Chalke (Wilts.) to investigate the properties of storage pits, lynchet formation, and ploughing methods. There is a plan for an experimental museum of ancient farming, crafts etc, at Butser Hill, Hants.

ROMAN TOWNS

A word should be said on towns, because they are a radically new feature of British life. As field antiquities they vary; some are concealed under modern towns, which emphasises the good selection of sites by the Romans, and in these cases only disjointed fragments will emerge from time to time as a building is pulled down or a street is widened. But some, like Verulamium, are beside, not under, their successor; some, like Silchester, are in remote fields, others still attached to the remains of Roman forts and the like. For the contents of Roman towns the reports and textbooks should be consulted; on few of their sites is there much to see now. They fall into the following classes: the *coloniae,* centres in which retired soldiers were granted land as a pension —these were Colchester, Lincoln and Gloucester (York was also a colonia, but as an honorific status); cantonal capitals, sometimes growing out of earlier settlements, sometimes on new sites chosen by the Romans, like Chichester or Aldborough; stations along the trunk roads, where horses could be changed and hotels kept (Braughing, Water Newton); villages at the gates of forts (a good idea of one of these can be got at Housesteads, on Hadrian's Wall); various centres such as Ariconium (Weston-under-Penyard, Herefordshire), where the iron of the Forest of Dean was handled. London and St Albans are special cases, and probably had a good deal of municipal independence and importance. Some projected towns, on road-junctions or native centres, like Old Sarum, never thrived even in the Roman period. But in general the pattern has worn suprisingly well.

Each town had its territory to feed it, sometimes an artificially created area as with the *coloniae,* usually the existing native canton or smaller unit (*pagus*). Even round the *coloniae,* however, the usual Roman land-divisions in straight-sided plots (centuriation), although to be expected, for some reason was not used in Britain; traces of such at Colchester, and in Sussex the countryside at Ripe, are not now accepted.

THE SAXONS

The balance of power in Britain shifted from Rome to local native centres a generation before the legions were finally withdrawn in 410, and during the 5th century Celtic states arose all over the country. But, at least in the civil zone, Roman life went on as far as possible, both in the towns (as at St Albans), and the villas, and the people still thought of themselves as Romans. This sub-Roman period, as it is now called, went on till the mid-6th century, by which time the Saxons had got a permanent hold over most of the lowland zone. In the highland zone the old native Iron Age continued, this time with no Roman influences, but with a growing and cultured Celtic Christianity to soften the implications of what used to be called the Dark Ages. The actual evidence for the way of life, except from literary sources, is however extremely scanty: in the lowland zone almost nothing which can confidently be ascribed to the 5th or 6th centuries; in the highland zone only a few settlements like those in Cornwall (e.g. Gwithian; Mawgan Porth is 9–11th century, but still 'Dark Age'). In the north and Scotland the old forms persisted, the stone farms and forts which go back to pre-Roman prototypes. Hut-circles can be seen, for instance, in the great hillfort on Yeavering Bell (Northumberland), and these are typical; the objects found in them are scanty and poor. Stone-hutted settlements, first fenced, then walled, north of Cheviot date from the 2nd, 3rd and 4th centuries.

Similarly, the succeeding period, that of the Anglo-Saxon settlements from the south coast up to the Forth, also has surprisingly little to show by way of houses. It now seems, from Mr Hope-Taylor's excavations of the Anglian palaces at Yeavering (7th century) (in sight of the hillfort just mentioned), that there were three kinds of houses—the kings and greater nobles lived in large rectangular halls such as those described in 'Beowulf' and other epics; the free farmers (the Saxons were essentially farmers) had smaller rectangular houses (it was the Anglians who introduced villages and rectangular houses into Scotland); the unfree serfs lived in small rounded hovels of appalling squalor. At Sutton Courtenay (Berks.) (5–6th century) more than 30 of these, squarish with rounded corners, were found; they were sunk 2 ft. into the ground, and had thatched roofs above low wattle and daub walls; these were probably industrial huts, for weaving, baking, etc. Others, also sunk into the ground, have been found at Canterbury; isolated huts are known from Selsey, Chichester, Thakenham (Sussex), Radley (Berks.), Farnham (Surrey), some of them early. St Neots (Hunts.), has some of the 9–10th century, but the list is quite short, and I do not know that they are visible today. Primitive as they were, huts of this type survived till quite recent times in remote parts; at Athelney (Somerset) there were huts in the 19th century with floors sunk in the ground, and walls of timber supporting a flat sloping roof with a hole to let out the smoke. These compare with Saxon huts from Bourton-on-the-Water (Glos.), equally sunk but with a ridge roof. However, not all Anglo-Saxon houses were squalid hovels; rectangular timber houses have recently been excavated at Maxey, near Peterborough.

Some houses were protected from hostile animals or humans by fences, or by banks and ditches, as Bede says of St Cuthbert's hermitage

on the Inner Farne. Long rectangular Viking houses, well seen at
Jarlshof (Shetland), are now being found as far south as Yorkshire.

But if the Anglo-Saxon period is poor in houses, it is the beginning
of the system of farming which lasted all through the Middle Ages,
and most of the villages founded then still exist. This offers a rich and
to a large extent only recently realised field for exploration.

MEDIAEVAL VILLAGES AND FARMS

The Saxons were village-dwellers, and introduced them wherever they
settled; in the Midlands villages are almost the only pattern till the 18th-
19th centuries, and they are frequent even in the Celtic West, but here
and in the north the pattern is mixed, isolated farms still being dotted
about between the villages. The villages always had open fields, two or
sometimes three or four, with an area of waste which was gradually
encroached on as the population expanded. This was cleared by fire,
axe and grazing, just as in the Neolithic. The open fields were cultivated
in strips, bundled together into furlongs, which were in turn grouped
in the fields for rotation. The fields needed a nucleated village to work
them, not only for social life and protection, but to provide a pool of
labour for the plough, the autumn slaughter of the beasts, the mainten-
ance of fences, ditches, clearing of scrub, etc.; this was a complete
revolution in the national life. Most villages were made up of houses
with crofts attached, along a street or round a green, with back lanes
behind the houses, and a local road system tied to the needs of the fields.
The varieties of village pattern make an interesting study; the green type
may be seen at Finchingfield (Essex), the street at Long Melford
(Suffolk), the scattered at Middle Barton (Oxon). Chinnor (Oxon) is
built in a square with the church outside it, Piercebridge (Co. Durham)
is a 'square' village inside a Roman fort. Hutton-le-Hole (Yorks. NR)
shows one side of a street village (with a winding stream between the
two sides) complete with crofts and back lane, behind which is a farm
occupying what is still called Westfield. The list of examples could be
extended indefinitely. Some greens were built over quite early; in
Lincolnshire some villages are rectangular, being built round a furlong,
and since filled in and expanded. Most of the present villages were in
existence by Domesday (1086), but the pattern of fields was not complete until the 13th century.

The furlongs varied in size and situation on account of natural
factors; the strips represent the families who cleared the furlong, and
are not always straight. The standard size is a quarter to a third of an
acre, mostly the latter, 220 by $5\frac{1}{2}$ yds. The strips were ploughed as
separate units, which built them up in ridges; in many places they are
separated by balks, narrow grassy boundary banks or paths, but most

boundaries are furrows. Some balks, as at Laxton, are between furlongs, as access-ways. Later ploughing may level off the soil, leaving the balks standing above the general level. The remains of the strips show most often as '*ridge and furrow*', which can still be seen where former arable is now pasture (pl. 21, p. 200); more remain on heavy soils—they are rare in East Anglia and the chalk lands, but common in the Midlands, the Welsh borders and the coastal part of Yorkshire, Durham and Northumberland. They are also rare in areas of late-surviving woodland, such as Essex, the Chilterns, Arden and the Weald; but patient observation can reveal many unrecorded examples, often largely obliterated by later ploughing, as at Shalford, Surrey. The oldest are nearest to the old village centres, the youngest further out. A series of fine examples can be seen from the train along the two main lines from London to Birmingham, especially between Leighton Buzzard and Rugby, and from Princes Risborough to Leamington. The furlongs are also visible here, with their strips running different ways. Some ridge and furrow is far from known mediaeval settlement, and may be earlier or later. Many indeed of the surviving remains, whether mediaeval in origin or not, may be 19th century.

In contrast to these mediaeval strips are the 18th and 19th century ridges, representing a special kind of ploughing; these are smaller and narrower than the strips (like long parallel waves), and once seen, cannot be mistaken for them.

On the slopes the heavy plough produced horizontal terraces or strip-lynchets; flights of four or five of these are not uncommon, and can be well seen at Bishopstone North (Wilts.) and in Wharfedale. Many seem to have been made deliberately, as terraces, and some have access ramps. Some in Wessex may be Roman terraces for vine-growing, but most are mediaeval, and some were in use as late as the 18th century (e.g. near Calne, Wilts.). Early 19th century cultivation-terraces in Northumberland, on poor land, can resemble much older lynchets (pl. 20, p. 193).

Survivals of the open fields still exist in a few places, e.g. Laxton (Notts.). Here, however, the strips have been rearranged and exchanged, so as to produce compact holdings; only a few unaffected strips still remain. On the Isle of Portland (Dorset) strips are in cultivation, but the original pattern has been altered by later building and quarries; these are on a steep slope, and lynchets have formed. Braunton Great Field (Devon) (pl. 21) again has been consolidated and partly enclosed, 85 owners 'within living memory' having been reduced to 12 by 1954. In other places the once open fields have remained sufficiently unchanged to give a good idea of what the mediaeval landscape was like; such is the country round Cholsey (Berks.). Other open fields survive at Axholme (Lincs.), West Runton (Norfolk) and Westcote (Glos.).

Kent, although it once had open fields, developed square fields in the Middle Ages by reason of the type of ploughing used there. In Devon the open fields were also enclosed in the 13th to 14th centuries. In wild parts of the west and north farms were created by way of scattered clearings with earth banks round small fields—in rocky areas the banks wound round large rocks. In the south-west at least, as W. G. Hoskins has shown, many farms and hamlets are on the sites of Iron Age or Romano-British farms. For instance, the field-pattern at Babeny, Dartmoor, is very like a Celtic field system. In Cornwall the same thing appears at Bosigran (Zennor); probably the 'megalithic' stone walls, once built, were not removed by later settlers. Occupation of some of these farms may have been continuous, but others may have been deserted and not reoccupied until the Middle Ages.

DESERTED VILLAGES

Interesting though it is, the history of living villages and towns, their siting, shape and growth, is outside the scope of this book; reference should be made in particular to the works of W. G. Hoskins and M. W. Beresford, who have dealt with most of the problems in this field. We must however look here at the deserted villages, the causes of which are outlined on p. 26. A few were abandoned before 1300 (Grenstein, Norfolk); and some in the 14th century (Flotmanby, Yorks.; Tusmore, Oxon, due to the Black Death, which hit the Midlands worst of all, but affected eastern England also). But the main period of desertion was between 1450 and 1550, when sheep-farming grossly expanded, enclosing arable for pasture and creating large spaces inside curving hedges (these vast pastures were themselves cut up into smaller fields later, but many 100-acre fields still remain in the Midlands). Examples of villages deserted at this time are Burston and Quarrendon (Bucks.); Cowlam (Yorks. ER), where the village-plan is shown in crop-marks; there are over twenty on the Yorkshire Wolds, including the important examples (because scientifically investigated) of Wharram Percy, Towthorpe and Cottam—these were not reploughed, like much of the Wolds, because of their stone foundations just below the surface. Thereafter a few villages were abandoned, largely by private agreement or Act, and some in the interests of landscaping or creating parks (Middleton near Pickering is one of the former, and Harewood near Leeds, moved outside the then new park, of the latter). At Westonbirt, near Tetbury, Glos., the village was moved because the landowner did not wish to see villagers; the church remained in the grounds of the house, but was connected to the new, hidden village, by an artificial sunken way! The model village at Milton Abbas, Dorset (1787) replaced a decayed market town.

Deserted villages show usually as a group of low platforms, the shallow troughs between them representing the roads and the little lanes between and behind the cottages; larger mounds represent the church, the manor house and the mill. A windmill mound and fishponds can often be seen as well. (pl. 23, p. 216).

Little remains of the villages deserted in the 'clearances' of Sutherland (1810–20), but the low banks of the croft enclosure walls (Rossal, Strathnaver).

It is not only villages that have been deserted. In the Pennines, Wales and Scotland many cottages and farms stand empty and are falling into decay; in Scotland this is partly due to emigration, in Yorkshire to the decay of the cottage weaving industry. In some cases a shell remains, in which the detail of past methods of building construction can be made out, in others only a grassy mound is left. Another cause of the desertion of cottages is the increasing mechanisation of farming, which can lead to the employment of fewer men. A few large houses isolated from villages, such as monastic granges, have also been abandoned. Many moats are to be found in the fields, which once surrounded 15th century farmhouses. The sites of deserted houses in mountain country are often marked by a tree or two in what was the garden, as well as by uneven ground and rank vegetation. The 'black houses' of the Hebrides and the W Highlands have low stone or peat walls and are thatched; when ruined they settle down into oval mounds with a hollow in the top. Old or ruined houses in Wales, the Pennines, and Scotland often reveal early methods of building or plan, such as cruck frameworks (inward-curving beams), or 'long houses' built to house family and animals under the same roof. Upturned boats are converted for use as sheds on the Northumberland coast.

A deserted church may be quite a small mound, but is of course usually in a recognisable churchyard (Townhead, near Kirkcudbright: St Mary's, Yarrow, Selkirkshire). But sometimes even the churchyard is missing—and there may not, in the case of a private chapel, have been one, but only a few family graves in a plot of consecrated ground not now delimited (Henderland, Yarrow).

The 18th and 19th century enclosures laid down the present pattern of squarish 5 to 10 acre fields, new roads and farmhouses, but under this pattern can still be seen the banks of the earlier fields. In the wooded hills called the Chantries near Guildford is a complete pattern of fieldbanks and sunken ways, with an enclosure probably related, which date from before the trees were planted in the late 18th century, and this sort of thing can be seen all over the country; much work remains to be done in mapping and studying such remains. The sometimes obscure pattern of old fields, roads, houses, etc., can often be elucidated by reference to local history and records. The latter can also help in locating now abandoned mines, canals, industries, etc., whose remains may still be visible if sought.

A note on garden walls: Plate 32 shows an occupied dwelling in the sandy wastes of south-west Hampshire. The photograph was taken in 1956.

The shed forming the dwelling is protected on one side by a windbreak of stout branches, and the whole is surrounded by a wall of turf, cut from the surrounding land. If the shed and windbreak were to be taken away, all that would be left would be a crumbling turf wall with a gap in it. Excavation inside this would find, if anything, objects of mid-20th century date, or perhaps a little earlier, among the postholes, which would only increase the puzzle.

It is indeed not always easy to tell the age or purpose of many enclosures or ruined walls which one sees; as this example shows, the most primitive is not always the earliest.

Earth banks round cottage gardens, as, e.g. at Shamley Green, Surrey, are similar in origin; not, as in Northumberland, defensive.

QUARRIES, MINES AND INDUSTRIES

FLINT MINES

The coming of the neolithic farmers led to a demand for good flint for implements; surface flint is not the best material, and it was found that better flint came from seams of nodules in the chalk of the downs, some of which of course must have been discovered by outcrops, others during the work of digging the ditches of the causewayed camps. The seams were reached by sinking pits from the surface; this was then widened at the bottom to get at the flints in the seam, and in some cases galleries were tunnelled along the seam, radiating from the pit-shaft as in figure 6. When a mine was exhausted or had become dangerous it was filled in from the spoil-heaps at the top, and a new one opened; so flint-mines show on the surface by a shallow depression surrounded by low mounds. The shafts were dug by antler picks or levers, and were lit by oil lamps; shrines were sometimes erected to encourage the abundance of flint. The mines are concentrated mostly on the South Downs behind Worthing, where there are extensive remains at Cissbury, Blackpatch, Findon and Harrow Hill; in this area the mines cover acres, and the ground and mounds are strewn with waste products. There are a few further west, such as Stoke Down, Sussex, and Easton Down, Hants., but they are rare in the great chalk area of central Wessex, where they might have been expected; perhaps some are yet to be found. Flint mines are beginning to be suspected on the North Downs, but few have been explored. At East Horsley (Surrey) a group was recently noticed, but on excavation proved to be neolithic working floors of surface or near-surface flint, the spoil-heaps of which had attracted mediaeval flint seekers (for building) who had sunk mine-shafts close by; but this is unusual. On the Norfolk–Suffolk border near Brandon (where there is still a small flint-knapping industry for gun-flints) is the important group of Grime's Graves; here two shafts with galleries are

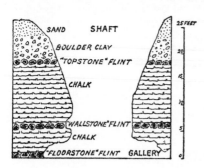

FIG. 6. Neolithic flint mine, showing the seams of flint in the chalk rock, and the shaft and galleries by which the good flint was exploited

maintained by the Ministry of Works, and are well worth a visit. The flint mines were begun by the Windmill Hill people, with some help from the secondary neolithic people, but went on into the Bronze Age, when they were taken over by Beaker people. Grimes Graves are later than the Sussex mines.

STONE QUARRIES

The products of the mines were usually in the form of rough-out axes, which were finished off by the purchaser. Meanwhile the demand for axes was also being met by stone from the highland zone, which was quarried and traded by secondary neolithic people. The products of these factories found their way to all parts of the lowlands, and the long-distance trade so revealed at this period is impressive. The actual quarries or outcrops which produced these stone axes are not in all cases still visible, and some have been determined by petrological methods only. But several of the sources are exactly known, and can be seen. Greenstone was obtained from Cornwall (Penzance region, Trenow, Balstone Down); spotted dolerite (blue stone or preselite) from the Prescelly Hills in Pembrokeshire (Carn Meini)—this was not only used for axes, but in large blocks for barrows and monuments such as Stonehenge; augite-granophyre from Graig Lwyd near Penmaenmawr in North Wales was very popular, and factory sites here can be seen over a wide area. A very important source is the group near Great Langdale in the Lake District (Stake Pass, Pike of Stickle), producing the grey-green Borrowdale ash, a fine-grained stone very suitable for axes; Northern Ireland yielded porcellanite from Tievebulliagh near Cushendall (Antrim) and Rathlin Island; rock from Ailsa Craig was also used, and recently a new source has been found at Killin, Perthshire; picrite from Cwm Mawr, Corndon (Shropshire) is distributed in the west Midlands. In addition to all these (and many other rocks were used, the origin of some of which still has to be found) axes were imported from Brittany.

At Mynydd Rhiw (Caerns.) three stony ring banks, previously thought to be later huts, were recently shown to consist of debris surrounding quarry pits for stone axe material.

METAL WORKINGS

Copper. When flint got short in the later Neolithic other stones were pressed into service, and it was found that certain of them had curious properties, and, when heated, produced another substance which could be shaped. (Metal-working had started in the Near East, and took a long time to reach Britain.) Native copper contains many other substances as natural impurities, such as arsenic, antimony, cobalt, bismuth and lead, which gave different results in terms of brittleness and wearing power. The ores of copper were soon recognised, and the first to be used were the oxides, which needed only simple smelting. But these were soon worked out, and few of their locations in Ireland and Scotland can now be traced (e.g. Leadhills, the Ochils, Crinan, in Scotland). By the late Bronze Age men had to turn to the sulphide ores, which involve a more complicated process of roasting. Incidentally, bronze was discovered by way of certain copper ores which contained tin as an impurity; its value was realised, and finally the standard 90 per cent copper to 10 per cent tin alloy was evolved. Sulphide ores were worked in the south-east of Ireland in the late Bronze Age, and in the Roman period in Wales (Parys Mine, Amlwch, Anglesey, which remained in use throughout the Middle Ages; Great Orme, Llandudno; and Llanymynech, Montgomeryshire).

Tin. The prehistoric bronze industry depended on two not very common metals, copper and tin. Tin came exclusively from Cornwall, where it has been mined to the present day. The earliest datable working is at Redmore near St Austell, which is Iron Age; there must have been a large number. Four sites are known to be of Roman date: Boscarne on the Bodmin moors, Carnon in Feock, Treloy in St Columb Major, and Carnanton in Mawgan in Pyder. The industry slumped after the 1st century AD. The spoil-heaps of later workings are a familiar sight in, for instance, the Bodmin Moor area. Tin was later mined on Dartmoor, where remains of the mines and of the smelting-furnaces ('blowing-houses') can be seen, e.g. at Henglake.

Gold was used quite extensively in the Bronze Age by the wealthy magnates of Ireland, who produced most of it, and of Wessex, who bought it. It was obtained by washing in the rivers of Co. Wicklow and elsewhere in Ireland, and most of the sources cannot therefore now be traced, being long since worked out. Sites in Scotland are known at Leadhills, Helmsdale and elsewhere. The gold used in the Iron Age and the Roman period was mostly got by mining, and the main source was Dolaucothy, Carmarthenshire, where the deposits were worked till recent years (some of those near Dolgellau still are). An interesting more recent site is at Glengaber, a tributary burn of the Megget Water (Selkirkshire); here, for a mile or so along the burn, can be seen the embanked channels through which the burn was diverted for washing the gravel; these workings are of uncertain date, but fall between the 17th and the 19th century.

Lead was a major product of Britain in the Roman period. It was used by itself, and also contained silver as an impurity, which could be separated from it by the cupellation process. In the Iron Age it was got in the Mendips and Yorkshire. In the Roman period the mines were still largely in native hands, but under official Roman supervision, no doubt because of the silver. Pigs of lead have been found in Yorkshire and Derbyshire bearing the stamp EX ARG, which means 'from the silver (i.e. lead) mines'. Two methods of winning were in use, the adit or 'level' which consisted of shafts driven into the hillside following the vein, and 'hushing', washing-out, in which water under pressure was used to separate the ore from the rock down a steep slope on the surface. The mines at Greenhow Hill, near Pateley Bridge (Yorks. WR), of which some levels may be pre-Roman, used this method. These mines, and those in western Shropshire (Linley, More), may have been under direct military control. Other centres were in Flintshire (Talargoch), and in the Mendips (Charterhouse and Priddy). The lead mining of the north of England was a major industry in the 17th and 18th centuries, and extensive remains can still be seen in the shape of spoil-heaps and old galleries (e.g. near Allenheads, Northumberland), and where these work an ancient lode, as at Greenhow, it is not easy to distinguish the Roman workings. 18th century leets for ore-washing and drainage (Hebden, Yorks.) can still be seen, as can smelt-mills (Malham, Yorks.), or chimneys at the ends of long flues from the smelting furnaces (Swaledale).

Other metals used by the Romans, e.g., zinc, had to be imported.

Iron was made by the direct process, that is in simple ovens to smelt the ore, from the Iron Age, c. 550 BC, till the end of the 15th century, and even up to about 1540 in some places. Blast-furnaces, where a forced draught is made by bellows, reached this country just after 1490. Coke was used instead of charcoal as a heating agent from 1709; The commercial production of the steam engine from 1775 inaugurated the modern phase. This is the broad pattern, but the details are somewhat complex, and worth close study.

Various ores were used in the Iron Age; haematite in Glamorgan and Weardale; magnetite at All Cannings Cross; siliceous ironstone (carstone) in West Sussex and at Hascombe (Surrey)—although here it might be said that the iron pans of the Greensand, although plentiful, do not appear to have been used on any appreciable scale, in later times; clay ironstones in the Weald; bog iron in Shetland and Ireland. The ores were got by grubbing and pitting, probably in open pits. These were shaped like pudding-basins, not like the later bell-pits (see p. 122); they show as round depressions. The furnace was a shallow pit. Open workings were sometimes used; like the ditch along the south side of the fort at Urswick Stone Walls, Furness, Lancs. The earliest is the Round Pond, near Kestor Rock, Chagford, Devon (c. 400 BC). Others are Chelms Coombe Cave, near Cheddar, 3rd century BC; Chun

Castle, Cornwall, early 3rd century; Rowberry Warren, Som., 2nd century; Saxonbury, near Frant, Sussex, 2nd–1st century; Ridge Hill, near East Grinstead; Loanhead of Daviot, Aberdeenshire; Wiltrow, Shetland.

The Romans worked some 13 or 14 sites in the Weald, including several of Iron Age origin, and opened up the district near Hastings (see below). They also went to the Forest of Dean area, the Midlands (Worcestershire; Rockingham Forest); Cheshire and Lancashire; and Lincolnshire (Thealby). Furnaces were of varied patterns. Remains of Roman workings, low mounds and depressions, can be seen at the Scowles, Bream, near Coleford, and in Lydney Park (both Glos.). Anglian monasteries in Northumbria worked iron. The Normans disrupted the industry, but it recovered, and the Cistercians in the North, e.g. Byland and Fountains, developed it. The depressions called 'pit dwellings' on some maps of Nidderdale are the remains of monastic iron workings (Blayshaw Crags, near Ramsgill). By the late 13th century iron was being made in the Dean and Wye area, in south-west Yorkshire, in Cleveland and Pickering Forest, in Scotland, the Midlands and the Weald. Water-power for driving the hammers came into use by about 1200, and the industry survived a slump in the 14th century. The introduction of the blast furnace from the Continent, by 1490 or so, was a revolution, and caused a great boom in the Weald and expansion in south Wales, Shropshire, and the north-east; the boom reached Ireland, the north-west and Scotland only in the 17th century. In Furness there was a bloomery as late as 1709, when the industry took its second step forward, the use of coke.

The Wealden iron industry is a compact example of an early key industry, and can be studied on the ground. The full history and technique are outside our scope, and can be read in W. H. Straker's book. The industry depended on the belt of iron-bearing clays in the Weald. the plentiful timber for charcoal-making, and the many streams for power. The earlier method, the direct or bloomery, yielded a small quantity of wrought iron, often impure or steely, which could be forged at once into implements, etc.; it was hammered out to a solid mass called a bloom, and later extended into bars. This beating expelled the cinder which was embedded in the iron, and which itself contained much unextracted iron—in the Forest of Dean old cinder was used as ore in the later blast furnaces, but in the Weald it was mostly used for road-making (including Stane Street itself). Few remains exist of the circular hearths used in this process, but slag can be found which can be distinguished from that left by the blast-furnaces, being rich in iron (see p. 122). About 100 sites are known, mostly in East Sussex; in most of them the cinder has been spread by ploughing or removed, and the hearth is not traceable. They lingered on as domestic industries until the 17th century. Roman examples are at Maresfield, Crowhurst, Battle,

11. IRON AGE FORT (Maiden Castle, Dorset). *Above*, aerial view from the west. *Below*, detail of the ramparts

12. ROMAN MILITARY WORKS. *Above*, Housesteads, a fort on Hadrian's Wall, and traces of its attendant village on its southern side. (See Fig. 14 for plan of Roman forts). *Below*, the Vallum and its ditches with a modern road (*left*) following the line of the Wall

Westfield and Forest Row, and possible Iron Age ones at Playden, Bardown, Saxonbury, Dry Hill. Saxon bloomeries existed near East Grinstead, and mediaeval ones at Roffey, near Horsham, and Tudeley, near Tonbridge.

The new methods permitted furnaces to be permanently built of stone, and then higher and larger; they were fed from the top. Although they consumed much fuel, these furnaces produced much greater quantities of iron with less effort. The greater heat caused some of the ore to become fluid and not plastic, and this 'cast-iron', at first a waste product, had to be heated and hammered to produce bar. By 1500 furnaces were in use at Buxted, Hartfield and Newbridge, and by the late 16th century 7,000 men were employed in the Weald area alone. Cannon were first cast at Buxted in 1543, and the industry depended largely on armaments, and fluctuated somewhat with the demand for them. By 1574 complaints were being made that such vast quantities of timber were being consumed by the iron industry that shipbuilding, also vital to the country, might be endangered. About 115 works then existed.

During the 17th century the industry moved north, where there was ironstone as well as wood. The Quakers, not wishing to make armaments, went into the domestic ironware market, and became immensely prosperous; they built up huge industrial groups in Wales, the Midlands, Furness, and Yorkshire, and their organisation enabled them to experiment with new methods. Hence Abraham Darby, at Coalbrookdale, perfected in 1709 the use of coke for firing, and made the industry independent of wood; he developed the steam engine, thus stimulating deep mining, and used wagon-ways, with iron rails, in his works. His old furnace, redesigned for the making of the Iron Bridge (1777–9, p. 243), has been restored as a commemorative monument.

But we have digressed from the Weald. In its own line, armaments, it was defeated by the Carron works getting the contract for naval guns in 1769; the first half of the 18th century was abnormally dry, and fuel costs rose; other factors, such as competition of other industries for labour, combined to kill it, and the last forge, Ashburnham, closed in 1820. The relics of the industry centre round the **hammerponds**. The narrow valleys of the Weald were dammed to provide water to work a mill, which at first may only have worked a hammer to crush ore for the older process, but later worked the bellows for the blast-furnaces. The dams (bays) are of clay; the overflow or spillway is at one side, with sluices for controlling the flow; in later mills these were of stone or brick, often stepped to prevent a fall of water sufficient to undermine the bay. The water was led to the wheel by oak 'shoots' (Ashburnham). In some cases chains of ponds were made along a valley, to add to the water supply. The larger streams, liable to flooding, were not dammed, but tapped by means of a leet to a pond at the works (Bibleham; Etchingham). Silting was a problem, and some bays had to be heightened (Warren Furnace). Not all the ponds in the Weald are hammer-ponds; some are ornamental lakes in parks (Crabbett; Wadhurst). Most of the hammer-ponds are now drained, but can usually be easily recognised. The furnaces were just below the bay; none remains—the materials were re-used when the works closed. Fragments of a shed to protect the bellows and the casting floor can sometimes be seen. The forges were sometimes worked from the same pond as the furnaces, but more often were some way down the stream, or even several miles away. The sites, even when the ponds have gone, can be identified by the presence of *cinder* (bloomeries) or *slag* (blast-furnaces); cinder contains about half iron oxide and a third silica—it is in shapeless masses, with striations, or little globular excrescences; colour mostly blue-black or rusty. Slag has a high proportion of silica, and looks like bottle-glass (mostly black, olive, grey-green, rusty brown), with bubbles; it is very brittle.

The ore, mostly clay ironstone or ragstone, was mined by **bell-pits,** about 6 ft. across at the top, and wider at the bottom, and rarely more than 20 ft. deep. Large numbers of these exist in wooded country, partly filled up with spoil, and the depressions often full of water. The charcoal was often burnt on the iron sites, and traces of burning can be found. Minepits can be seen at Witley, and in St Leonard's Forest, and trenches at Weybridge. Lanes took the products away, and can still be seen, metalled with cinder or slag. Loading-places exist at Pevensey Sluice and Chilthurst Bridge. Sites are often advertised by field names, such as Forge Meadow. Good examples of hammer-ponds can be seen at Worth (Kent) and Godstone (Surrey), a series of three; Cowden, Kent, with slag and sandstone quarry; Ridge Hill, near East Grinstead, Iron Age and Roman bloomery, with large slag heap, and hearths; Withyham; Eridge; Steel Cross, Crowborough, mounds and pits; Robertsbridge Abbey Forge, Salehurst; Crowhurst Park, Roman, with blackened soil, mine sites; Fernhurst; Imbhams, near Haslemere, sluiceway; St Leonards Forest, two very large ponds.

Finally, there is an unusual series of mediaeval (late 12th century onwards) iron mines at Bentley Grange, Elmley (Yorks. WR) —round mounds, 6 ft. high, flat-topped, in rows; these are the waste piled round the pit-openings—the shafts have collapsed, leaving little hollows in the mounds, each filled by a bush or tree. These mounds overlie ridge and furrow, which must date from at least the 12th century.

POTTERIES AND TILERIES

These were only built on a domestic scale until just before the Roman period. Then both became important industries, having a steady market to supply. The clay was dug and made up on the spot, so the potteries are mostly where the right clay is to be found. The remains are the mounds and depressions of the clay-getting, and sometimes small blackened dips for the kilns. Isolated potteries and tileries are scattered widely over the civil zone, but in some areas they are concentrated; such are Alice Holt Forest, near Farnham (just inside Hampshire), where hundreds of mounds can be seen; the New Forest (Linwood and Ashley Rails); east Yorkshire (Crambeck; Throlam; Norton; Knapton); Castor and many sites near Sibson and Water Newton (Hunts.) Both updraught and horizontal types were used.

These sites are littered with pieces of pot: a surprising variety can often be picked up. Tileries are similar; these were sometimes, as at Ashtead, Surrey, worked from a large house. At Ewhurst, Surrey, are bell-pits some of which may have been dug for tile clay (some perhaps for iron) —Roman tileries exist near by, and mediaeval ones too. Many mediaeval clay-pits show as small ponds, but they are not easy to identify unless wasters or kiln-remains can be found. Place-names may be helpful, such as Kiln Wood and the like. The great heaps of spoil from the kaolin workings on the Cornish moors are a special manifestation of this industry, although modern brickfields run them close. Kilns for brick and tile making were common on large estates, and a few survive—at Nettlebed, Oxon, is a handsome one of the Burgundy-bottle shape seen in large numbers in Staffordshire.

BUILDING STONE

The Romans got their building stone from many sources, not always possible to relate to remains of quarries. In many cases too later workings have obliterated the Roman ones. Important quarries existed on the oolite near Bath, and on the sandstone between Bath and Bristol; stone was also quarried in the Isle of Wight. Roman quarries exist at Chilmark, Wilts.; near Swindon; Ham Hill, Somerset. The rocks of the East Midlands were also used; rag from Barnack and Stanion, Northants; 'slates', thick oolite slabs, from Collyweston, Easton and Kirkby; marble from Alwalton. Marble also came from Purbeck, Dorset. Some of this stone found its way to buildings and town walls a long distance away, but of course the Romans used local stones when good and convenient; an excellent example of this at Aldborough (Yorks. WR) where, just outside the town wall, is a deep and large Roman quarry from which was got the stone to build the town; this quarry was 'embellished' in the 18th century by the addition of niches filled with statuary, which give it a very strange air. Querns needed a hard sandstone, and from the Iron Age throughout the Roman period this was got partly from the Pen Pits near Wincanton, Somerset; it also came from the neighbourhood of Hunsbury, Northants, and from several small pits near Faringdon, Berks., and from the greensand in Surrey at Farnham and Godstone. At Wharncliffe (Yorks. WR) is a quarry where unfinished millstones can be seen.

The shale of Kimmeridge, Dorset, was quarried in the Iron Age and by the Romans, and was used for furniture, floor-tiles, armlets and other small objects.

Mediaeval stone quarries are easier to identify, being usually larger. The marble of Purbeck and Corfe was sought after, and quarries exist at Downshay Farm and Afflington. The oolite near Bath was fully exploited, an industry which built so many towns and houses, and which created the vast mines at Corsham and elsewhere. 12th century quarries are known at Box; while at Taynton, near Burford, Oxon, mediaeval (11th century on) and later quarries have produced a large area of jumbled heaps of waste. Headington stone was used from the 15th century; clunch, a hard chalk, came from Totternhoe, on the Chilterns; there were quarries also at Chilmark, Wilts. (whence came the stone of Salisbury Cathedral) and Wheatley (Oxon). Stonesfield (Oxon) 'slates' were used; they were worked by hammer-splitting from the 13th to the 16th century, and by 'frost-splitting' from then on; tips can still be seen there. Collyweston 'slates' were used extensively, but in the south, those from near Horsham. Barnack rag was much used, and the mediaeval workings have produced an area of grassy mounds known expressively as the 'hills and holes' (pl. 28), some of which may go back to the Romans; the rag was worked out in the 15th century, but another stone from Barnack was used later. The Nottingham alabaster-carvers were supplied from quarries at Chellaston, Derbyshire, and elsewhere. A small mediaeval quarry can be seen at Compton (Surrey), typical of many still remaining.

Many other quarrying industries have left traces; alum in north-east Yorkshire, salt in Cheshire (Northwich and Middlewich), from Roman times; (for marine saltings see p. 197); fullers earth at Nutfield (Surrey); clay for brick-making, etc. Jet from the shore near Whitby was used from the Early Bronze Age, but was collected, not mined. Sand and gravel have left the familiar scars, often filled with water, in the Thames valley and elsewhere.

Stone and flints were quarried not only for building, but for road-making and repairing. On the chalk hills, for instance at Chinnor in the Chilterns, hollows and hummocks can be seen where flint was extracted. On the roadsides also, small mounds, a foot or two high and a few feet across, are the grassed-over remains of dumps of stones or gravel for repairing or remetalling the road, and not fully used up. The hollows from which the material was dug, if local, can often be seen near by. The local landowner was often responsible for the upkeep of the roads on his land.

A special type of roadstone quarry is the following of an outcrop or dyke of rock across country; this leaves a long continuous trench, which can be misleading (example on Sleights Moor, Yorks.).

Many types of holes in the ground were once mistakenly called 'pit-dwellings', such as diggings for lime or marl, or for road-metal.

COAL AND SLATE

Coal was used by the Romans, but probably from outcrops only; the great abbeys in the North began mining, and although most of these are overwhelmed by modern workings, some are still traceable. Coal produced a typical and blighted landscape in the North by the mid-19th century, and much of this still remains, in the form of waste-tips, disused pits, derelict canals, and 'flashes', pools due to subsidence. Old coal-pits and air-shafts, with spoil-heaps or lips round them, are dotted over the Yorkshire moors. The filling-in of a mine-pit or air-shaft can result in a circular mound or bank. The 'ballast hills' on Tyneside were formed by colliers dumping their ballast on the river banks.

In the Forest of Dean the commoners have the right to mine the local coal. These 'Free Miners', working mostly by simple methods in family units, have filled certain areas of the Forest with their waste tips, much smaller of course than those of the deep mines; these tips can be seen in profusion round Coleford and Bream.

The slate workings of North Wales (Blaenau Ffestiniog, Corris, Bethesda, etc.) are impressive, and the stone quarries of the Eifl and near Portmadoc are altering the mountain faces. The landscape of the Midlands and North has also been affected in recent years by opencast mining of coal and ironstone; e.g. the 'hills and holes' of ironstone workings are a conspicuous feature near Kettering and Corby.

MARL AND LIME

Marl is decayed chalky soil from the surface layers, and was much used in the 18th and 19th centuries for spreading on the land. Lime was used largely for making mortar. The marl (and certain clays in some places, e.g. the Wirral) was totally removed, and the pits still remain, sometimes filled with water. Good examples can be seen near Guildford, on Pewley Downs and on the Roughs near Newlands Corner. Lime was not always quarried, as it is today; from possibly Roman times it was got by vertical shafts, sometimes 100 ft. deep, opening out at the bottom into galleries like flint mines. They give rise on the surface, when filled in, or partly so, to the hollows and pot-holes known as 'dene-holes' in the chalk country. They were once thought to be underground dwellings, or even towns, but date mostly from the 18th and early 19th centuries (although those at Little Thurrock and Orsett, Essex, may be older). The best-known are those representing shafts into Chislehurst Caves, Kent; these caves, which have as much as 22 miles of galleries, began as chalk workings, but were extended and developed as 'invasion shelters' during the Napoleonic wars. The galleries bear fanciful names such as the 'chapel', but these have accrued as part of the commercial exploitation of the caves as a showplace. A good example of a small clunch-mine, with galleries and shaft, is at Racks Close, Guildford (13th century). Lime-burning was done in kilns, and remains of these can be found in many places, sometimes near farmhouses or in woods, or in rows in old walls or low cliffs (Ewhurst, Surrey).

Limekilns were usually operated on the farms where the lime was needed, not where the chalk or limestone was dug—it being cheaper to cart the chalk than fuel and water—thus in Surrey, they are on the Weald clays and on the greensands, not on the chalk Downs. Kilns in the Orkney farmhouses were for corn-drying.

Lime-burning was carried out round the coasts throughout the 18th and 19th centuries, the stone often being quarried locally, and the produce shipped away. Remains of stone limekilns are still common, circular buildings some ten feet high and the same in diameter, with a central space in which the stone was burnt, and usually two furnace-apertures, one on each side, triangular openings 6 ft. or so high and the same deep, with holes into the central space to extract the lime. Four remain at Solva (Pembs.) out of a flourishing industry; good examples exist in this area at Brynhenllan and Parrog (a joined pair on the quay), and at Gwbert and Mwnt (Cards.). The most spectacular are the three on the quay at Beadnell, Northumberland; lime had been made and shipped from there at least by 1747, but one of the present kilns was not built till after 1789, when the harbour was constructed (probably 1798), and two not till about 1801; they were in use until at least 1841. Pits were normally used for the extraction of marl, but limestone was usually quarried. Limeworks contain plant for crushing the chalk etc. and kilns for burning it; circular banks at Merstham (Surrey) represent a plant (pond and mixer) for making large quantities of mortar or cement.

GLASS WORKS

Glass was not used in Britain before Roman times, but was then imported in great quantity and variety, both as vessels and as window-glass. But little seems to have been made in Britain; furnaces such as Castor, Northants, and Wilderspool near Warrington are rare. Glass remained in use in Saxon times, but again little was made here; a works is known at Glastonbury. More no doubt await discovery. A flourishing industry was however introduced from Normandy by 1226, beginning at Chiddingfold, Surrey, and remained till 1618 in the Weald. It was all plain (i.e. greenish-white) glass—coloured glass was imported until the late 16th century, when it was made in the Weald. In the mid-16th century demand for glass increased, and the industry was greatly expanded, by Lorrainers in 1567 (Alfold), and Normans in 1572 (Wisborough Green), making glass of better quality but by the same basic processes (using potash from burnt wood or bracken—fougère). The Lorrainers made window glass by the cylinder or 'muff' process, the Normans by the 'crown' method, and vessels of all kinds were also made. But vast quantities of wood were needed (for fuel and ash), for which glass had to compete with iron and building, and the makers soon went elsewhere, to Hampshire (Buckholt), Gloucestershire (Wood-chester, Newent, Newnham-on-Severn—where blocks of glass are built into walls), Staffordshire (Bishops Wood; and in Bagots Park and Cannock Chase many glasshouses have recently come to light), etc. Meanwhile Venetian-type 'crystal' (soda-glass) was being made in London, and soon prospered. In 1611 coal-firing was invented, and monopolies were set up; the industry settled in the great glass centres, such as London, Newcastle-upon-Tyne, Stourbridge (where the best clay for crucibles came from), Bristol, etc., and the old Forest glass went out. In 1674 flint (lead) glass was patented, and the quality again improved.

Mediaeval furnaces were rectangular, with straight central flues and sieges on each side (with small round separate subsidiary ovens); 'late' Forest furnaces could be composite, with linked or radiating chambers; 'Venetian' furnaces were round and tiered; and modern 'cones' were developed to use coal.

The main Wealden sites are round Chiddingfold, (particularly Vann Copse, Hazelbridge Hanger and Chaleshurst); Alfold (Sidney Wood); Ewhurst (Somersbury Wood); Loxwood; Wisborough Green (Malham Ashfold); Kirdford (Hog Copse, Glasshouse Copse); Petworth Park. Sites are also known near Horsham, Reigate, Carshalton, and at Graffham near Pulborough, and more are still being discovered. The determining factors are wood and water; siliceous whitish sand, and clay for crucibles and firebricks need not be local. The sites are to be recognised by: one or two round or oblong mounds representing the ruins of the two types of furnace, which are often within a rectangular banked and ditched enclosure; a pond or pond-bank, with sometimes a channel diverting water from a stream; and often a hollow-way (the access road). The furnaces were usually built at or near the top of a steep hanger, so as to catch all possible draught. Glass refuse will clinch the nature of the site. This takes the form of 'cullet' (broken glass for mixing in); frit and scum in lumps; broken crucibles, some-times containing traces of glass; drips and fragments of glass. Earlier glass is light milky-green; from 1550–1620 it is deeper blue-green, translucent, smooth and polished. Weathering can produce iridescence or blackish decay. Glass from Roman sites is often iridescent. Soda and flint glass is generally clear. Bricks and pieces of clay, coated on one side with glass, and often burnt, which are from the kiln floor on which glass has dripped, also indicate a site.

Since 1965, several important new finds have been made. At Alfold (Surrey) a furnace with two square chambers, a type new to England, was built, about 1550, for annealing crown glass sheets; at Rosedale and Hutton-le-Hole (Yorkshire NR) winged furnaces are associated with cylinder glass (late 16th century). And in Lancashire (Denton, and near Ormskirk) early 17th century furnaces, fired with coal, have come to light. Much is now being learnt about movements of the glass industry, and about the types of glass made in the different kinds of furnace.

Other industries have left their mark on the landscape, and local observa-tion will reveal these. One interesting landscape effect on a large scale is the extensive beechwoods on the southern Chilterns, which were planted for the chair industry of High Wycombe in the 18th century, and for firewood for London in earlier centuries.

There are many other industrial sites worth finding and recording, and in many cases preserving; the rate of destruction is high, and there is often no time to be lost. Some of these, in addition to those mentioned above and elsewhere, are: old cotton, etc., mills, including early iron-framed buildings of the 1790s onwards; early blast furnaces; shipyards, slipways, docks, etc.; small domestic workshops. The relation of in-dustrial buildings to contemporary houses, in structure and siting, should be borne in mind. Industrial archaeology is now becoming deservedly popular and well-organised (see books, p. 338).

ROADS

PREHISTORIC

Settled farming in the neolithic period no doubt brought with it the need for regular paths between farm and pasture, between farms, or for longer distances to tribal meeting-places, or even right across country for trade; but there is no direct evidence on the point. It is not precisely known how the products of the axe-factories of Cumberland, for instance, reached Wessex, whether by being passed from hand to hand in short stretches, or carried by a trader for the hundreds of miles of wild country. Of course rivers were used, as was a coastal trade in small boats, but in addition there must have been tracks along the ridges or from landmark to landmark. Definite evidence comes from the Bronze Age, where trade-routes have been distinguished by finds of objects along them, as for instance that from the mouth of the Ribble through the Aire gap along the Wharfe ridges ('Rombalds Way'), across the Vale of York by one of the morainic gravel stretches at York or Escrick to the Wolds and the coast.

From this time on, and reaching a full development in the Iron Age, the trackways along the ridges were in use. Some of these are well known, like the Icknield Way at the foot of the Chilterns, the 'Jurassic Way' along the long ridge from Lincolnshire to Dorset, the 'Pilgrims Way' on the North Downs, and shorter ones like the Ridgeways of Dorset (one converted into a Roman road). These are now represented by footpaths or bridle roads, but once were less well defined. Some, like the 'Pilgrims Way', were doubled by another track at the foot of the ridge, for use in seasons when the hilltop track was impassable; on steep slopes, too, the original path would tend to get rutted and difficult, and would be duplicated and then multiplied at that point. In sandy country a track on a slope could become a deep cleft with wear and running water, and some of these too are doubled; there are parallel groups of such hollow ways on the slopes of Blackheath (Surrey). At Arncliffe (Yorks. WR) multiple tracks and vertical strip-fields have been confusingly deepened by surface drainage.

Hollow ways, as on the greensand belt of Surrey, mostly have mediaeval or recent origins, although some may be older; some of the lanes here (as near Shere and Albury), are twenty feet deep, between veritable cliffs of sandstone, carved out by traffic and water, and in part cut down to ease the gradients. Duplication on a large scale is exemplified by the Icknield Way in its Berkshire section. This track ran from Norfolk to Wiltshire, first along the foot of the Chilterns to the Thames, which it crosses at Streatley; thence it continues through Berkshire in two main parts—the Ridgeway (which also has a branch crossing the Thames at Pangbourne), and a lower route on the Greensand at their foot (just like the Pilgrims Way and its companion ridgeway along the North Downs). Branches may have crossed the Thames at other places (e.g. at South Stoke), and a major arm (the Roman Port Way) crossed at Wallingford and joined the Icknield at Wantage.

Where such tracks descend the scarp of the downs, they were levelled off, probably by the Romans, into terraceways, with the outer side built up into a low bank (e.g. Firle, Sussex). Some Roman ways up scarps are zig-zagged. Hollow ways with a bank on both sides can be found on the South Downs crossing a ridge from one valley to another; these seem to have been for the passage of cattle between pastures without being seen. Iron Age farms, marked by groups of Celtic fields, usually have access lanes from farmhouse to fields, which can often be seen where the system of lynchets is clear (Itford, Sussex; Little Woodbury, Wilts.).

An attempt was made by Mr Hippisley Cox to construct a map of prehistoric trackways in Britain, but this must be used with caution, as many of his suggestions cannot be proved. Even greater caution is needed with the ingenious proposals of Mr Alfred Watkins (in *The Old Straight Track*), who deduced the existence of straight stretches of track at all periods from prehistoric to mediaeval from the apparent fact of alignments, across country, of 'sighting-points' in the form of barrows on hilltops, large rocks, forts, even church towers. This can be taken too far, although obviously primitive man would have used prominent marks to guide him through the wilds; no doubt church towers were used for this also (at a later date), as were beacons on hills and towers (e.g. Hadley, Middx.; All Saints, Pavement, York). But early tracks were not straight. Theories based on lines of 'marking-stones' across country, such as that which links boulders of pudding-stone from Hertfordshire to East Anglia, also need caution. Bronze Age tracks indeed may sometimes be deduced by rows of barrows or isolated standing stones, but generalisations should be avoided in this matter.

ROMAN

However adequate the pre-Roman system of tracks may have been for the purposes of the many and varied Celtic states, the Romans needed at once a very different means of communication; a planned network of hard roads, passable in all weathers by troops and officials, and linking all the important centres of population and military operations. From the outset of the conquest the military engineers laid down such a system, from the south-east coast to London, from London to the cantonal capitals and the legionary fortresses, and, diagonally across England, from Lincoln to Exeter, following the old Fosse Way. Here the Romans had to halt their advance while they worked out how they were going to take the next steps into the highland zone, a halt also necessary because that was the end of the corn-country on which their armies could live without adaptation, and the beginning of the cattle and horse areas in which supplies of food had to be carefully organised. When this problem had been overcome, partly by increasing the area under corn in the occupied parts, the roads pushed on again into Wales, the North and Scotland. Up to Caerleon, Chester and York, they were in civil cantons; but beyond that was essentially military country, dotted with frequent forts, rarely quite at rest, a buffer and frontier zone between barbarism and the peacefully developing, prosperous and romanized province to the south-east. The Ordnance Survey map of Roman Britain will make it easy to visualise this pattern.

In addition to the great new main roads, there were a large number of branch and subsidiary roads, linking villas and centres of industry to the main roads; examples have been recognised in the Weald, serving the ironworks there, and enabling the iron to reach London, Chichester, Silchester and other towns. The natives outside the towns continued very largely to use the old tracks along the ridges, and much of the farm-pattern of Celtic type throughout the Roman period is related to these tracks.

Roman roads were usually laid out in straight stretches between prominent points, often several miles apart; they were not however straight over long distances, and sometimes not straight at all, particularly when the Roman roads followed the lines of older tracks. Hilly country could involve cuttings, and marshy places were crossed on embankments or causeways of piles and timber; e.g. the Roman road east of Wellington (Salop) is laid on oak logs. Timber trackways were built before the Romans, and many Iron Age examples are known. Recent C14 investigation of those which cross the Somerset levels (e.g. Meare and Shapwick Heaths), and at Fordy (Cambs.), Brigg (Lincs.) and Pilling (Lancs.) has been able to date them to the years round 600 BC; they were necessitated by the flooding caused by the deterioration of the climate at this time. The roadway was made in layers mixed with earth, usually large stones at the bottom of an excavated bed, then smaller stones, then a surface layer of gravel, flints, or other local material; this would be supported by kerbs or stones at the sides, and pegs to fix the metalling at intervals inside it. In the north, e.g. over the Pennines, the road was paved with slabs, but this is not usual in the south. There was also a V-shaped ditch on each side, firstly for marking-out, then for drainage (fig. 7). The whole road was normally about 22 Roman feet wide (see p. 175) between the ditches, and the metalled way rose in a camber; banking would be necessary on slopes.

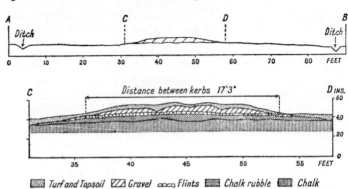

FIG. 7. Cross-sections of a Roman road, showing its two ditches and
details of its construction

The low bank of a Roman road, and sometimes the ditches also, can
be seen crossing open country or in woodland. A major road was often
84 ft. wide between ditches, having grass verges for horsemen. Tracing
a road should be done with a large-scale map, and Mr Margary's
surveys will be found useful; alignments of recorded Roman finds are
always suggestive, as are disjointed lengths of lane, parish boundary,
etc., on the map. Once an actual piece of road has been sighted, it can
often be followed for long distances. Sometimes, as has happened also
to Hadrian's Wall, the hard structure has been found convenient as the
base for a later road, which of course conceals completely the original
one (see pl. 12, p. 129). There are many surviving stretches, some of them
preserved by local bodies; Stane Street is visible at several places
between Dorking and Chichester (e.g. near Box Hill); Watling Street
leaves the south gate of Verulamium and crosses a field as a faint bank;
the local road through the Forest of Dean is preserved near Blackpool
Bridge; the road over Blackstone Edge east of Manchester is visible in
places with its large stone blocks. Many main roads are on the line of
Roman ones; e.g. the 20-mile stretch north of Lincoln, and those both
sides of Cirencester. Most counties have examples or possibilities; it is
interesting, and can be useful, to study closely a small area, and work out
in it the local branch roads. Some of the major ones also have obscurities
which an amateur could unravel. Surviving visible roads are not usually
complete, but the present stony layer may be the foundation; only
excavation of an untouched stretch can reveal the original construction,
which varied very widely.

Corn, etc., stacks built on the dry, firm foundations provided by a
Roman road can give a clue to its presence and line.

Caution is needed over wide trenches, such as war-time tank-traps, filled in with flints or gravel; these can look surprisingly like Roman roads when running straight across open country. Among the many other things which can look like Roman roads are mediaeval strips, in certain conditions, where one strip is isolated; its bank and the two hollow paths along its sides can then be deceptive. Ploughing is sometimes done with the aid of marking furrows, a few yards apart across the field. There are deep and prominent, and can be confusing, although their number and regularity is the key.

MEDIAEVAL

The Roman roads stood untouched and mostly unrepaired for centuries, and decayed all through the Saxon period and the Middle Ages; not till the 17th century were new roads built which made communications as easy, after 1300 years, as they had been in the 4th. The Saxons used the Roman roads to penetrate the country, but not much more; their villages were usually well off them. Saxon roads, and indeed mediaeval ones as well, were mostly of local importance only—connecting villages to farms or fields, as outlets for quarries, and the like. The lane along the foot of the scarp of the South Downs, from Alfriston to Firle, is not really a continuous road, but a series of short stretches joining a line of Saxon manors to each other. There were also the roads from town to town, or village to market, abbey or castle. This network grew during the Middle Ages, and the Roman roads were mostly forgotten, except for a few main routes. Mediaeval roads, and their modern representatives, are zig-zag or winding, due to following the boundaries of the furlongs or bundles of strips in the open fields, or, in Kent and the highland zone, the small farms and irregular fields; the former can be seen in the Midlands, the latter in Monmouth and Hereford, for example. A road or track might, in these centuries, wander or be multiplied (as in the prehistoric periods), over a wet or steep patch of hillside, or common or wood (Beacon Hill, Bulford, Wilts.).

In the Middle Ages ways were developed for special purposes. The Salt Ways of the west Midlands may have used earlier tracks, but that from Droitwich to Princes Risborough, for the transport of salt from the royal mines to a manor entitled to be supplied from this source, is probably of mediaeval origin. Drove roads, for the movement of cattle and sheep, usually do follow old tracks (e.g. the Icknield Way and the West Ridge leading to Newbury; the Drift, on the borders of Leicestershire and Lincolnshire; there was a well-developed system in Scotland[1] and in the Border country, such as Clennell Street, from Alwinton over Coquetdale (this has barrows along it), and the Crakemuir Road, from

[1] Converging on Falkirk.

Eskdalemuir to Newstead, Roman). These show today, unless they are covered by a modern road, either as tracks or as broad ways between widely-spaced parallel walls (as south of Peebles over Kirkhope Law). Other special ways are the corpse-roads from a village to a distant church in a large parish, such as Danby (Yorks. NR) and Eardisley, Hereford-shire. Adjacent valleys in mountain country were often joined by a road 'over the mountain', often still occasionally used, although now a track or path only.

Shifts of population, decay of villages, or replacement by a new road, may strand a mediaeval road, and turn it into a green lane in the fields; there is a network of these in west Essex, and one near Woodstock. Some of these green lanes, however, are boundaries, others remains of drove roads. Stranded lanes may sometimes be seen embedded in towns, such as Cross Lanes in Guildford; the winding Marylebone Lane in London is a built-up example of this (it winds because it follows the course of the Tyburn).

ENCLOSURE

The parliamentary enclosures of the 18th and 19th centuries produced a system of new roads for the newly-made farms; these are straighter and often narrower than the older roads, and usually have hedges and ditches. The turnpikes of the early 18th century are very wide between the hedges, and have grass verges. Many are on new lines, e.g. in Lancashire between new towns, but some follow Roman routes, as Telford's road from London to Holyhead. Roads are often in pairs along valleys, on each side of the river (as in Weardale); here one only may become a major road, the other remain an unchanged lane. Cause-ways are of course frequent in the Fens, and some carry modern lanes, as at Stuntney, and Aldreth (Cambs.), 11th–12th century. At Kellaways (Wilts.) is a path carried on 64 arches (late 15th century).

Paved paths are an alternative to causeways where a track or pack-horse road crosses soft ground. One from Crowhurst Place (Surrey) to the church, one mile, was laid down in 1631; that between Ripley and Clint (Yorks. WR) is probably 18th century; the five ancient paths which meet at Okewood church (Surrey) are paved across the church-yard. At West Grinstead (Sussex) is a paved path on a causeway. The well-known Roman Steps, in Merioneth (through the pass between the Rhinogs called Bwlch Tyddiad), although certainly not Roman, seems to be on a mediaeval packhorse track from Harlech to Bala. The paving-stones may be 18th century, but may also date from when the path was first used, between 1300 (when Harlech Castle was built), and 1350 (the Black Death, after which labour, and travelling, was scarce).

Packhorse trails can be seen beside modern paths in N Wales, as from Dolwyddelan to Penmachno (Caerns.). Mules' Stepway, Exeter, is a pack-path from the harbour to the old town. Bewdley is an example of a transit port (on the Severn) at the end of packhorse routes.

Roads, as do parish boundaries, sometimes make sudden deviations, as though avoiding an obstacle which is no longer there; it is an interesting exercise to try to find out what these obstacles were, by search on the ground and in old records—they may be ploughed-out barrows, or buildings.

CIRCLES, CROSSES, HOLY PLACES

If shrines existed in Britain before the Neolithic none has survived, and the question must be left open. From the Neolithic onward there is a variety of sacred sites, and some of them are among the most prominent ancient monuments.

Shetland has two very odd buildings of megalithic type, which may be temples; one is Stanydale, a complex of chambers reminiscent of the temples of Malta; but this may after all be a chief's house, or a communal building such as a 'club' house for young men. The other is at Yuxie, Whalsay, which has a circular paved court and a passage leading to a circular chamber with an inner chamber beyond; a façade and horns reminds one of certain types of megalithic tomb. These sites, so local, are not yet cleared up. It is however certain that the forecourts of megalithic tombs were used as local shrines.

Many shrines of this period must have been humbler and temporary, like the places in the flint mines (Cissbury, Sussex; Grime's Graves, Norfolk) where rough statuettes were prayed to for a good harvest of flint.

CURSŪS

A class of still enigmatic neolithic monuments are the cursūs (Latin plural of cursus). These are long parallel banks with outside ditches, with squared or curved ends, running across country often for long distances. The Greater cursus at Stonehenge, which is contemporary with the first phase of that monument, is over 3000 yards long and up to 110 yards wide. There is a smaller one north-west of it. The longest is the Dorset cursus, from Thickthorn Down by Gussage Hill to near Woodyates, nearly 6¼ miles. One was recently found underlying the henge at Thornborough (Yorks. NR). They are known in the Midlands and East Anglia as well. At first sight cursūs look like processional ways, but this is not easy to show unless it is known what was the significance of both ends; they may equally have been for racing or funeral games.

HENGES

A spectacular legacy of the neolithic peoples is the idea of the circle as a ceremonial structure. A special class of these is the henge, which derives from the causewayed camps, and whose idea may lead on to the hillforts. This is a stone circle, or in certain cases wood, enclosed in

13. *Above*, a linear defensive earthwork (Offa's Dyke). *Below*, a sunken trackway descending a hill in Sussex

14. A small Nuxman matta and broiler spotte on the Welsh Marches.

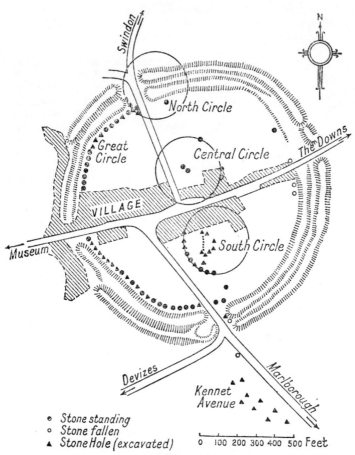

FIG. 8. Plan of Avebury

earthen banks with one or more entrances. Those with one entrance (Class I) seem to be the original invention of the secondary neolithic peoples in Britain—henges are not known abroad. Those with two or more entrances (Class II) are an elaboration of these developed by the Beaker people, apparently mostly by the A Beaker people. A sub-class of Class I has ditch outside the bank, and ritual pits (e.g. the first phase at Stonehenge—see below); another related group is the circular settings of wooden posts, some of them perhaps once roofed, like Woodhenge, near Stonehenge; the Sanctuary on Overton Hill, near Avebury;

Arminghall near Norwich. Examples of Class I are Gorsey Bigbury, near Charterhouse-on-Mendip; and the four circles at Priddy (Som.). They are rare in the north and Scotland (Balfarg, Fife).

Class II henges are often large and impressive. They are well spread over the country, and some are very large. Durrington Walls, near Amesbury, with ditch and outer banks, is 1720 ft. from east to west; one of the circles at Knowlton, Dorset, has a church inside it, thus showing continuity of its sanctity; Maumbury Rings at Dorchester, Dorset, was converted into a Roman theatre. Other good examples are Eggardon (Dorset), Arbor Low (Derbyshire), Penrith (Cumberland), and Brodgar and Stenness in Orkney. A sub-class of Class II has two (or more) concentric ditches with a bank on the berm between them; such are the rows of three at Thornborough and Hutton Moor, north-west of Ripon (Yorkshire). and one at Dorchester (Oxon). The henge at Yanwath, Westmorland, has an 18th century earth platform inside it. There is a group of very large henges in Wiltshire and Dorset (Durrington Walls, Marden, and Mount Pleasant, all excavated recently), which have wooden circular shrines inside them; the primary pottery was Grooved ware. Avebury also belongs to this class.

Avebury. One of the greatest henges is Avebury (Wilts.) (fig. 8). This consists of a huge bank and inner ditch, with four entrances, enclosing a stone circle round the ditch, with inside it two smaller circles and a 'setting' at the north entrance. From the south entrance runs an avenue of stones, leading to the Sanctuary on Overton Hill; there were once other avenues and stones, and Silbury Hill must also be thought of with Avebury. The first phase of the monument was probably three stone circles in a row, with an avenue to the Sanctuary, all secondary neolithic or B Beaker (c. 1700 BC). In the second phase—A Beaker (c. 1600-1500 BC)—the outer stone circle and earth bank and ditch were built, destroying the northern of the three smaller circles, and altering the line of the avenue, whose northern part dates from phase two. The circle as we now see it is a colossal work; it encloses 28 acres, and most of the modern village is inside it. The diameter of the circle is 1400 ft. and the bank, from the floor of the ditch, was once 55 ft. high. The avenue consists of pairs of stones, each about 50 ft. apart transversely and 80 ft. apart longitudinally; the pairs alternate between tall thin stones and broad, lozenge-shaped ones, representing the male and female principle respectively. The whole complex—and much has been lost, although what is left is admirably cared for by the Ministry of Works—is one of the great monuments of Britain, and every effort should be made to see it. Incidentally, Avebury gave evidence of the splitting of stones by heating them and dashing cold water on them. (See also p. 165.)

Stonehenge is perhaps the best-known single ancient monument in the British Isles, but perhaps also one of the (popularly) least under-

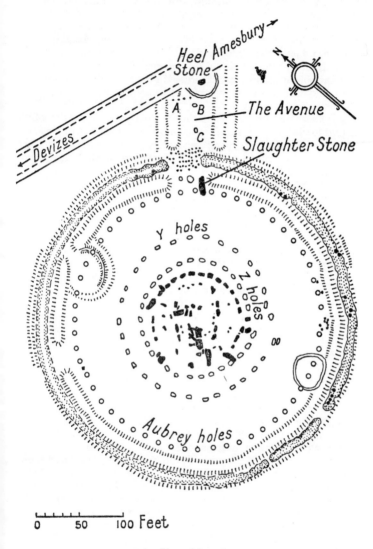

FIG. 9. Plan of Stonehenge

stood. It is admittedly complicated, being a sort of cathedral, in use for many centuries and altered and rebuilt several times in different styles, as cathedrals often are. But the excavations of the last few years, mainly by Professor Piggott and Mr (now Professor) Atkinson, have revealed and publicised the history of the monument, and cleared away a lot of the obscurities which had made ill-founded speculation possible. That some of the ceremonies performed in it were solar or astronomical is not impossible, but its connection with the Druids is a popular misconception.

Stonehenge gets its name from the old English word 'henge', which referred to the 'hanging' stones of the inner horseshoe of trilithons, the lintels of which appear to 'hang' in the air on the tops of the uprights. Stonehenge is in many ways the supreme example of the henge monuments, and can be regarded as the epitome of the prehistoric sacred circle. A brief summary of its history may help in unravelling it; it is not at all easy to understand at first sight (fig. 9, above).

> *Phase I.* 1900–1700 BC (Secondary Neolithic). Stonehenge began as a circle of pits, the Aubrey holes, called after the 17th century antiquary who discovered them. These pits had some kind of ritual purpose such as communicating with the spirits of the earth; some of them contain cremations tied up in bags with bone pins. They never held posts, as was once thought. This circle of holes was surrounded by a bank and ditch, defining a sacred area. The Heel Stone, and stones D and E, also date from this phase, as does a timber structure ('gateway') A. There was probably a timber building in the centre of this circle. (Grooved ware was found at the base of the ditch, and the radio-carbon dating of charcoal from Aubrey hole 32 was 1848 BC ± 275 years.)
>
> *Phase II.* 1700–1600 BC (Beaker period). The bluestones were transported from the Prescelly Mountains, Pembrokeshire (where they had formed part of an earlier sacred circle), and erected in a double circle. The east end of the ditch was filled in to widen the causeway. The Heel Stone ditch was dug and filled in again. The Avenue was built. Stones D and E and the timber structure A (from phase I) were dismantled. Stones B and C were possibly put up in this phase. (Beaker ware and bluestone chips occurred above the primary silting of the ditch.)
>
> *Phase IIIa. c.* 1500 BC (Wessex culture). The double circle of bluestones (phase II) was dismantled. The sarsen stones were transported from near Marlborough, and erected into the trilithons, circle, Station Stones and the Slaughter Stone and its companions. Carvings of daggers, like those from Shaft Grave V at Mycenae, were executed on some of the sarsens. (Wessex type barrows near by may be the graves of the chiefs connected with this work, and who were able to command the immense labour involved.)

Phase IIIb. 1500–1400 BC (Wessex culture). Tooling and erection of the stones of the dressed bluestone setting (i.e. the bluestones dismantled from the Phase II monument were reshaped and re-used in a different manner). The Y and Z holes dug and abandoned (this may mean a grandiose scheme dropped owing to change of plan, lack of resources, etc.).

Phase IIIc. c. 1400 BC (Wessex culture). The bluestone setting (phase, IIIb) was dismantled. These and the remaining bluestones, left over from the phase II scheme, were re-erected in the present circle and horseshoe.

Stonehenge has now reached its present form, subject to the attacks of time and some deliberate destruction, partly during the Roman period, partly in the Middle Ages (a scatter of chips in Y and Z holes match the scatter of Roman pottery on the site—these chips are later than the grave at hole Y9. Was there a 'symbolic' scatter of chips all over the site, to indicate a ritual destruction of the shrine, and the cessation of its religious significance?) If Stonehenge *was* used by the Druids, this would have given the Romans ample excuse for destroying it; the mediaeval church also had its struggle to wage with a recrudescence of the 'old religion'; the great prehistoric temple of Avebury was deliberately damaged at this time.

In 1958 the Ministry of Works re-erected, using the most advanced techniques, a few stones which had fallen down in 1797. Complete restoration would be neither desirable nor indeed possible. In May 1959 a radio-carbon determination was made of antler picks or levers found in connection with a ramp dug for the erection of the Great Trilithon; this gave a date of 3670 years ago, $\pm$ 150, that is, between 1860 and 1560 BC, which accords with the date of 1600 to 1550 ascribed to the trilithons by other methods.

STONE CIRCLES

With a different distribution from the henges, the stone circles are among the commonest monuments of the highland zone, where most of them are. The idea might derive from the stone kerb round some collective tombs, although in Wales, Professor Grimes noted that their distribution pattern does not coincide with that of the tombs. The answer is probably complex; some of the circles were made by Beaker people, but some may be earlier and some later; the Druid's Circle, Penmaenmawr (Caerns.) contained central Food Vessel burials, so was sepulchral. Stone circles have no ditches, and are usually on rocky ground. They vary in size from a few feet to some 400; the size of stones also varies. Some are near barrows, many associated with stone rows or avenues (and therefore probably are secondary neolithic). Some are in groups—the great monument of Stanton Drew (Som.) consists of a Great Circle 368 ft. across, with an avenue leading from it; north-east of this is a small circle and avenue; south of it another small circle. West of the latter is a group of large stones arranged in a close horse-shoe and called the Cove; it must have had some ritual purpose, but what is not clear. There is another cove at Avebury, in the central inner circle. The Bleasdale circle (Lancs.) had an eccentric wooden circle inside it, probably a shrine. There are some 700 stone circles extant, and the largest are not always the most impressive; a very good idea of them can be got from perfect small ones such as Yockenthwaite in Wharfedale, Yorkshire; or the Loupin' Stanes, Eskdalemuir, Dumfriesshire.

A special class is that of the **recumbent stone circles** of Aberdeen-shire, where there are over seventy, and Banff and Kincardineshire. These are circles in which two tall ones flank a gap across which lies prostrate another monolith; the stones diminish in size from these two round to the other side. Cup-marks are often carved on the three great stones. In the centre is a cairn or ring of boulders, kerbed with stones. These complex structures have an affinity to the Beauly group of pas-sage graves, although made by Beaker people. The recumbent stone appears to have the function of ritually closing the circle at the end of its purposive life. (Old Keig; Loanhead of Daviot; Kirkton of Bourtie.)

Not all apparent stone circles are really such; one at Bught Rigg, Selkirkshire, may be the remains of farm-buildings. Some embanked stone circles in N Wales are settlements, not ritual circles (see p. 108). But the ring-bank circles of Derbyshire, associated with cairns, may be ritual.

MONOLITHS

Linked to the same religious background of the Bronze Age are stone monoliths, large standing stones which may be memorials, or statues of a deity. The maps of moorland areas will show large numbers of these; they are sometimes in walls or hedgerows and sometimes free-standing in fields or on the moors. Their sanctity is shown by the stone in the churchyard at Rudston, near Scarborough. Standing stones occur in rows, and there are many such on Dartmoor and the Bodmin Moors. The finest stones are the Devil's Arrows, Boroughbridge (Yorks. WR), three of which survive out of perhaps five; they are deeply grooved by weathering, but the largest still stands 22 ft. high. Sometimes the different forms of stone monument are found together, on a site of great sanctity, such as Cerrig Duon, Brecknockshire, where there is a circle, with a menhir (monolith) and an avenue associated with it. A large stone set upright in a field is not always a prehistoric monolith—At Birstwith (Yorks.) one has been propped up to get it out of the way of the plough, this being easier than shifting it. Some marked ways.

Caution is necessary in respect of monoliths. Traditions have grown up round many natural stones, usually glacial erratics, or hard blocks left when the softer material of a hilltop has been weathered away. Names like Druid's Altar, Devil's Kitchen, etc., attached to rocks should be regarded with suspicion; few of these are prehistoric monuments. They are frequent on exposed moors, such as Brimham Rocks, near Ripon; rocks along the Crimple valley near Spofforth (Yorks. WR); the Cheesewring on Bodmin Moor; many on Dartmoor. 'Rocking stones' are natural, and many weathered rocks are in queer shapes, and look like objects or animals. The 'Roman Altar' at Tremadoc (Caerns.) is a natural rocky knoll. The vertical fluting often seen, even on genuine monoliths, is the result of weathering.

Sarsens, stones foreign to their districts, such as the sandstone blocks which are a familiar sight on the chalk downs of Wiltshire (and there called 'Grey Wethers'), are probably the remains of once overlying strata.

EARTH CIRCLES

In the lowland zone, although stone circles do exist, the earth circle is found. This is part of the ring-ditch problem mentioned on p. 161; some however are ritual circles. They are often associated with barrows, and many have been revealed from the air in Berkshire and Oxfordshire, and the east Midlands. Stone and earth circles may be incorporated in later work. The stackyard wall at Castiles, Laverton, near Ripon, is partly made out of a stone circle. Many churchyards are circular, and some may be survivals of prehistoric sacred circles; some originally circular have been added to or altered, but the point is worth investigation. Some churches are associated in folklore with a circle, and this may represent a situation where the founder of the church had to compete with an ancient sanctuary, and resolve the problem so caused. (Penn, Bucks., may be one of these.) At Botany Hill, near Farnham, Surrey, is an earthwork having a low bank outside a circular ditch; the central area has a bank round it also; it is not clear whether this is domestic, agricultural, sepulchral or 'ritual'. Old churches on isolated or prominent hilltops often perpetuate ancient sacred sites; when dedicated to certain saints known to have taken over from the gods of such sites, such as Michael and Catherine, this is very likely indeed. Examples at West Wycombe, St Martha's and St Catherine's, near Guildford; St Michael's Mount (Cornwall). Churches are sometimes built on ancient mounds, such as Holkham (Norfolk). In Wales and Cornwall Celtic cemeteries and timber (later stone) chapels often precede churches.

The Iron Age peoples, although there is evidence that they used some of the circles and henges for their cults, preferred natural places like *groves*—in fact one derivation of the word 'druid' is the priest of the oak trees. But by the nature of things the location of these groves is not known; the ancient yew-wood at Kingley Vale, under the southern scarp of Bow Hill, Sussex, has been taken to be a Celtic grove, but this must be plausibility only. The great woodland sanctuary in south Scotland, Medionemeton, is also unlocated.

Some earth circles in the highland zone enclose cremation cemeteries.

SACRED LAKES

Sacred lakes and pools are better attested. The cult of water-deities was wide-spread among all the Celtic peoples, for whom they represented the forces of nature; both personal and tribal prosperity depended on their goodwill. So many rivers, springs and lakes acquired a sanctity which had a very long life, in the case of holy wells right into the present day. Sacred lakes are identified by the votive offerings found in them, or by the traditions attached to them; the varied collection of Iron Age objects, including fine works of art, found at Llyn Cerrig Bach, Anglesey, puts this in the former category; the strange stories and properties of the Silent Pool, Albury, Surrey, justify its status as a sacred lake. Legends about lakes are always significant, and carry the presumption of sanctity; so Lochmaben, Dumfriesshire; Mathern Pill, near Chepstow (Mon.); the village pond at Ewelme, Oxon. Rivers too are often sacred; an altar to Verbeia, the goddess of the Wharfe, of Roman date, was found at Ilkley. Shrines were often set up at the source of a river.

HOLY WELLS

A large class of centres of the cult of water-deities are the holy wells; the 'holiness' of many of these, in the negative sense that it would be better not to defile them, is still active. Some too are still credited with properties of healing or granting wishes. Many must have dried up, or been filled in or forgotten, but most counties have some, and many have a large number. The more 'live' ones carry names, often of Christian saints; and because many of the pre-Christian spring-deities were feminine, a high proportion of Christian dedications are to female saints, as Anne, Agnes, Helen, Catherine, Our Lady. Others are called after historical or legendary personages (Talbot, Robin Hood), or various things (Borage Well, Ripon), Healing wells were invoked by the gift of a metal object or a rag torn from clothing, ribbon, tape, etc.; or just by putting the hand in—the object being to place yourself, by substitution, in the beneficent power of the spirit of the spring.

Examples are St Bede's, Jarrow (children—pins); St Helen's, Thorp Arch, Yorks. (rag); Fergan, Banff (for skin diseases); St Dwynwen's, Anglesey (love-sickness); St Cynhafel's, Denbighshire (warts). Wishing-wells cover a variety of subjects, such as Sefton, Lancs. (fidelity, date of marriage); St Keyne, Cornwall (fertility); Mother Shipton's, Knaresborough (anything—this is still in very active use); St Elian's, Denbighshire (cursing). Water-worship can be traced in the use as baptismal wells of St Chad's, Lichfield; St Milburga's, Much Wenlock. Some of the more potent wells had to be secured to Christianity by the building of a church over or by them; such are St Winifred's, Holywell, Flints., covered by a 15th century chapel; Holybourne, Alton, Hants.; St Helen's, Kirkby Overblow, near Harrogate; St Brides, London. Some wells are natural wet hollows or springs (some piped or tapped), others have more or less elaborate stone or brick structures over them. Few of these are older than the 18th century in their present form, but some may have replaced earlier structures. Good examples are St Anne's, Trelleck, Mon.; St Anthony's, near Flaxley, Glos.; both these have basins, Trelleck with steps down to the water, and seats round it, Flaxley a basin, rebuilt during this century, into which pins are still thrown. There is a rather surprising 20th century 'shrine' over a well at Dunsfold, Surrey (1953). St Edward's Well, Sutton, near Guildford, with a Victorian brick edging, covered with a large stone, was re-dedicated in 1959. Some wells are on roadsides, as St Chad's, Lastingham (Yorks. NR). The many St Helen's wells in Yorkshire arises from a confusion between the Christian Helen, mother of Constantine, and Elen, a Celtic goddess of armies and roads; many of her wells, such as that at Thorp Arch, were on Roman roads, and there are Roman roads in Wales called Sarnau Elen (or Sarn Helen).

There are hundreds of holy wells in Britain, and they need modern study. Those of Wales have recently received it, but the English ones are poorly covered; the best-known work is that of R. S. Hope, 1893, who listed 67 wells in Yorkshire, 40 in Cornwall, 36 in Shropshire, 35 in Northumberland, 30 in Staffordshire, 26 in Cumberland, 24 in Derbyshire, and only a few each in other counties. But these figures are certainly inadequate.

Several county surveys of holy wells, particularly in the west of England, have been published in recent years, but these necessarily deal only with small numbers. The survey of Wales made by Mr Francis Jones enables more general conclusions to be drawn. Mr Jones deals with no less than 1179 wells, of which 236 are in Pembrokeshire and

180 in Glamorgan (but even these figures are incomplete). Of these wells, 437 have saints' names, 369 are healing wells, 66 are associated with chapels, feasts, etc., 62 with megaliths, 53 are pin wells, and 10 rag—the categories in many cases overlap. Well-names are often very informative; in addition to the 437 with saint-names, 104 are named after secular people (but some of these may be otherwise obscure holy men), 32 have occupational names, such as blacksmith, perhaps after people who lived near by, 93 are adjectival, 25 are called after trees, 61 after animals and birds, and the other 125 are topographical.

Very good wells still survive in Wales; St Beuno's at Clynnog Fawr, Caerns., has a square basin with stone seats and alcoves round it; perhaps the best of all, for it gives a genuine glimpse into the life of such a well in its heyday, is St Cybi's at Llangybi, Caerns. This has a square basin with stone seating and five niches in the walls; behind this is a smaller basin, next to a cottage, called a bath-house, perhaps for a custodian as well; to it are paved paths, and nearby is a latrine. All this was built in 1750, but similar if less permanent buildings can be assumed for many wells in use in mediaeval times, and even earlier. St Non's well, near St David's, recently restored, has a stone canopy over it, and in front are the remains of a walled forecourt; the fields in which stand this well and St Non's chapel are dotted with ancient standing stones, which may, if they relate to the well, indicate its great antiquity as a sacred site.

Scotland has over 600 wells, many with female dedication.

TEMPLES

The spirits of the wells are part of the ancient earth-religion which goes back at least to the Neolithic; the male sky-gods brought over by the Celts were worshipped partly in temples in the accepted sense, which accordingly begin in the Iron Age. Wooden temples were found at Frilford, Berks., and Heath Row (London Airport), preceding later stone foundations. The Celtic type, brought from the west Alpine homeland of the Celts, were standardised by Roman times into a very distinctive form. It consisted of a square chamber or *cella*, in which were the cult-statue and altar; this was surrounded by a veranda (*porticus*), used for personal memorials and for meditation and teaching; the building was enclosed in a sacred garden or *temenos*, which sometimes, as at Farley Heath, Surrey, was bounded by a polygonal wall. Celtic temples of this type are fairly widespread in south and southeast England; most of them are merely sites, but a good impression of their layout can be got at Farley Heath and at Maiden Castle, Dorset, where there is a priest's house as well. A circular type is also known.

Temples of the classical type, an oblong building with pillared and pedimented portico, existed in most of the larger towns. Two have been traced at St Albans, and the foundations of the temple of Claudius lie below Colchester Castle. The most impressive remains are those of the late 4th century temple of Nodens at Lydney, Glos. Mithraea, temples of the oriental god Mithras, worshipped by soldiers and merchants, are to be sought in the towns and in the military zones; that found a few years ago in the City of London is still fresh in public memory; the best to see is that at Carrawburgh, on Hadrian's Wall. These buildings are quite small, with very narrow nave and side aisles, and rounded apse to house the altar and statuary group of Mithras killing the bull. Local shrines range from simple altars sometimes enclosed in small boxlike buildings, and often inside a wall (Gosbecks Farm and Sheepen, Colchester), springs with statue and simple roof (Chedworth, Glos.; Coventina's Well, Carrawburgh), to small buildings and nave and apse (Benwell, Northumberland). Forts had their regimental chapels. The Roman practice of naturalising native gods, if they could be fitted in, led to a wide variety of altars and local shrines, in town and country.

At Chester (Edgar Park) a niche and statue of Minerva, or a Celtic goddess assimilated to her, perhaps Deva, was carved on the face of a Roman quarry.

At Stone-by-Faversham (Kent) a Roman mausoleum or martyrium was incorporated into a church.

Christian churches of Roman date are rare, but no doubt many await discovery. One of the basilica type, an oblong with a round apse, was found at Silchester, and also at Caerwent. At the villa at Lullingstone, Kent, an upper room was adapted to a chapel. Saxon and Scandinavian sanctuaries have not survived, except in place-names and traditions, e.g. hills called Harrow (holy), and places like Thursley (Thor's enclosure) and Wednesbury (Woden's stronghold).

This section might also mention the cells and chapels of Celtic saints or hermits such as at Beachley, Glos.; or St Non's, south of St David's. A fine example is the oratory at Gallarus, Co. Kerry. Some are beehive, some, as at Tintagel, square. (See also p. 136.)

Keills are small square oratories; there were 200 in the Isle of Man —Maughold churchyard has four.

CROSSES

These are the commonest Christian field antiquities of which there is still a wide variety (fig. 10). The Celtic 'high cross', as at Iona, was based on the menhir idea, ornamented in Christian fashion, but still in its designs looking back to Iron Age ideas from Ireland, Wales, Strathclyde, and the Pictish symbol-stones. This British Christian tradition was merged increasingly after AD 600 with the new Roman

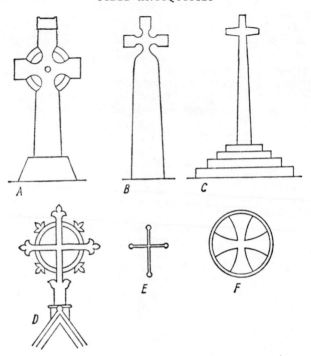

FIG. 10. Types of crosses: A, Celtic and B, Saxon (both richly decorated with carving); C, mediaeval village or market cross; D, gable cross on a church roof; E, cross incised in church door-post against the powers of evil; F, consecration cross, incised or painted on a church wall

churchmanship brought in by Augustine, but even after Whitby (664) when Rome became supreme, the Celtic elements lived on. The Northumbrian renaissance (late 7th and 8th centuries) produced tall graceful crosses such as Ruthwell (Dumfriesshire), 675–685, with figure-subjects and vine-scrolls with bird-reliefs; a little later, Bewcastle (Cumberland) has linear patterns, and abstract interlacings. Runes (Scandinavian script) appear at this time. In the 8th century the Celtic fret patterns are common—Hexham; Aberlady (Haddington). Carolingian influences affect England from the late 8th to the late 9th centuries, in the shape of naturalistic vines and figures, as at Otley, Easby (Yorks. NR, but now in the V and A museum), and Rothbury (at Newcastle).

The Anglo-Danish period (late 9th century to 1066) found a lively profusion of barbaric art, with jointed ribbon animals, and interlace (as at Gloucester and Collingham, Yorks.), which was affected and altered by the incoming Danish styles. The first product of this fusion was the Jellinge style, with 'great beasts' (lions, etc.), and ribbon animals (Levisham and a group in north Yorkshire are good examples). Gosforth (Cumberland) shows Manx or Irish influence. In Wessex at this time (late 10th century) a more naturalistic style, of Romanesque background, is seen (Bradford on Avon; Deerhurst; Colerne). In south Yorkshire and the north Midlands in the early 11th century appear representational art such as hogbacks (houses of the dead), as at Dewsbury, and survivals of Anglo-Saxon cross-types (Leeds; Shelford, Notts). The next main style was the Ringerike, in the first half of the 11th century, which has foliage—long twisted leaves—added to the animals of both great beast and ribbon types. The old cross from St Paul's, London (now at the Guildhall), is a fine example. Other foreign influences, such as Byzantine, are now seen in church carvings. After the Norman conquest, to the mid-12th century, the Urnes style reverts to ribbon animals (Jevington, Sussex), and subtle, rounded, flowing lines (Cong). Meanwhile the great period of the Celtic high crosses, still essentially Western, but some with runes and Scandinavian devices, is the 10th to the 12th century (Iona; Louth; Kells; Monasterboice).

Crosses decorated in these rich styles are very common in the North. In northern England and Scotland they tend to tall shafts and small heads; in the north Midlands to round shafts; in north Yorkshire there are local styles. In Ireland and the highland zone the wheel-head is normal after the 10th century. Wales also is very rich, having some 400 crosses, mostly in the west, and particularly Pembrokeshire, most of them 9th or 10th century. Cornwall has many, and other carved Christian stones.

In the Middle Ages standing crosses were set up in every suitable place, at cross-roads, on roadsides, in villages and market-places, in churchyards, on village greens, as boundary-stones, or as marks to guide the traveller; some also are memorials. They were used to preach at, to transact business by, for public proclamations. Later mediaeval crosses usually have plain shafts, and sometimes decorated heads; the base was usually circular and stepped. There are still fine examples to be seen all over the country, although many have been weathered down, or damaged in the Reformation and the Civil War. So many are now just old steps with modern crosses (Shere, Surrey), or mere stumps (How Caple and Llanwarne churchyards, and Madley Village, all Herefordshire). Good examples are: preaching crosses, Black Friars, Hereford; Ampney Crucis, Glos.; churchyard, Dorchester, Oxon, head restored; Somerby, Lincs.: village, Lydney, Glos.; Eastbury and Lambourn, Berks.; market, Winchester, of pavilion type, Chichester, Malmesbury

(Wilts.), Swaffham and Wymondham (Norfolk). In Scotland the mercat crosses fulfilled many functions—there are good ones at Melrose and Kirkcudbright (not in original position). Memorial crosses are at Otterburn, Northumberland, battle and death of Douglas; Boroughbridge, Yorks., battle; the series where the body of Queen Eleanor rested on its way to Westminster (original ones at Geddington; Hardingstone near Northampton; Waltham Cross, Herts.). Penitents' crosses had knee-spaces on the steps to allow people to pray round their foot (Ripley, Yorks. WR). Wayside crosses are still common, even in the lowlands—in the moorlands they have the function of marking a road in winter; they are sometimes just tall stones on which a cross has been carved; some of these, especially at the edges of abbey lands, may be boundary marks (e.g. near Pateley Bridge, and in north-east Yorkshire, on Byland Abbey land). The North York Moors have a very interesting series of wayside crosses, of different shapes and quite rough; White Cross or Fat Betty, south of Castleton, is just a square stone with a little round cross-head on top. Some crosses have been stranded by a change in their original surroundings—Lacon Cross, Sawley (Yorks. WR) is now in a field. Sanctuary crosses were set up where roads ran into areas of ecclesiastical liberties, such as Ripon; eight crosses once stood round the city, of which Sharow remains; but some of these may have been really boundary marks.

Crosses were also incised high up on church walls, as consecration marks (Pyrford, Surrey); and on door jambs, to keep evil spirits out of the church (Crondall, Hants., and Shere, Surrey, have good examples) —these are sometimes referred to as crusaders' or pilgrims' crosses, but the former explanation is more likely. At Wrotham, Kent, one of these is carved on an external passage wall. Evil spirits were also kept away from churches by means of stone crosses at the gable-ends (Castle Acre, Norfolk; Boxgrove, Sussex; Washburn, Worcs.); fantastic animals and monsters were also used as gargoyles, but may have had this other function also—Southwell Minster is very rich in animals on the roof. Animals also protected barns, as at Highleadon, Glos. Another device for protection, Irish in origin, was the grotesque female figure, the Sheila-na-gig, of which a good example is carved on the south side of the apse at Kilpeck, Hereford. Grave-slab, processional and crosses used inside churches are outside our scope. Celtic crosses are found in west Scotland, carved on rocks. They date from the 8th century and earlier; their arms have triangular ends (and see p. 225).

BURIAL

The mystery of death, and the treatment of the dead, has occupied man's thought and ingenuity since palaeolithic times, and in certain periods, such as the neolithic and Bronze ages, a great deal of social effort was devoted to it. Burials therefore loom large in archaeology, and much of the available evidence for the life and customs of past peoples is derived from their graves. Grave-mounds, or barrows, are also by far the most plentiful pre-Roman remains in this country, and as such a good starting-place for field study. The best introductions and companions to these are the works of Glyn Daniel for megalithic tombs and L. V. Grinsell and P. Ashbee for earthen long and round barrows.

LONG BARROWS

Burials of the palaeolithic and mesolithic periods are so rare as to be practically non-existent. The first regular and visible burials are the long barrows introduced by the neolithic farmers (c.4000—2000 BC; see pp. 53 to 82 for the general background to the various tomb-types dealt with in this section). There has been a good deal of discussion as to the true origin and nature of these tombs. In fact, as in so many cases, the truth may be complex. Some of the barrows, and even the idea itself, may have been brought from northern Europe, whence some of the settlers came; but some may have come from Brittany. Many think that the shape and layout of the interior, and the fact that many of them are built of chalk blocks, not of earth, suggest that rather than being a separate type of barrow, they are merely megalithic tombs adapted to the materials available in the lowland zone. Certainly Windmill Hill farmers built both types of tomb, some of the rites are similar, and the contents of both are often identical. Perhaps two origins can be made out, both using a long mound, and therefore not easy to distinguish without excavation and analysis.

Long barrows are mounds of earth or lumps of chalk mostly from about 100 to 300 ft. long, and from 30 to 100 ft. wide. They are usually wider and higher at one end—this is normally at the east—and this end contains the interments. The height is from 4 to 12 ft. (fig. 11, below). The mound was often once revetted by wooden posts or turf, and there was sometimes a wooden forecourt or façade. Most of them had a ditch along each of the long sides, and sometimes joining up in a curve or horseshoe (fig. 11). There are about 200 surviving long barrows, distributed on the chalk hills, mostly in Wessex, but also on the South and North Downs, along the Chilterns to East Anglia, and in Lincolnshire and East Yorkshire. They represent the burial-places of tribal chiefly families or other notables—they cover 'collective' burials—and there is one on every block of downs in parts of the chalk country.

Internally these barrows reflect a rather curious ritual. Some have the remains of post structures inside them, which, taken with the conditions of the skeletons, suggest that the barrow itself is only the last stage of a process. First an open space was set aside and fenced off as a 'mortuary enclosure'; the dead were laid out at one end, sometimes on a low platform. 'Long mortuary enclosures', with causewayed ditch round a post or turf enclosure with entrance passage, have been recognised as neolithic features; some have been found under long

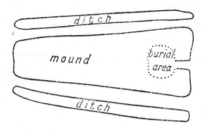

FIG. 11. Plan of a long barrow

barrows (Wor Barrow), some free (Normanton). The enclosure was apparently used for a considerable time, for later bodies were added until it was decided to close the space. This was done with ceremonial, including often a feast. At Skendleby (Lincs.) a forecourt could be the place of ceremonies; here also there were eight bodies, and eight wooden posts, presumably representing them, were erected. Finally a mound was piled over the whole enclosure, and this is what we see as the barrow. In some Yorkshire barrows the bodies were laid along a trench, which seems to have been covered by a long wooden shelter; in others the central feature of the barrow was a house, either one specially built for the dead (a mortuary house), or actually the house of the dead man himself, dedicated to him and so not available for the living. At Fussell's Lodge barrow (Wilts.) the barrow may have been caused by the collapse of the house; Mr Paul Ashbee's recent excavations showed that there was a long wedge-shaped 'house', the walls represented by a line of timber, but filled in with chalk dug from two deep parallel ditches. The dead were exposed elsewhere, and their bones laid in heaps at the porch end of the house; these were covered with a cairn of flints, and the 'house' filled in. When the timbers rotted away the earth filling would naturally collapse and spread out over them, finishing up as a long mound of earth. Houses of this kind, rect-

15. *Above*, soil-marks from the air. The circles mark the ditches of ploughed-out Bronze Age barrows, the rectangles (*centre* and *left*) the enclosures of an Iron Age farm (Eynsham, Oxon.). On the rocky soils of the Highland zone, buildings were of stone and without ditches: *below*, a Bronze Age hut at Grimspound, Dartmoor

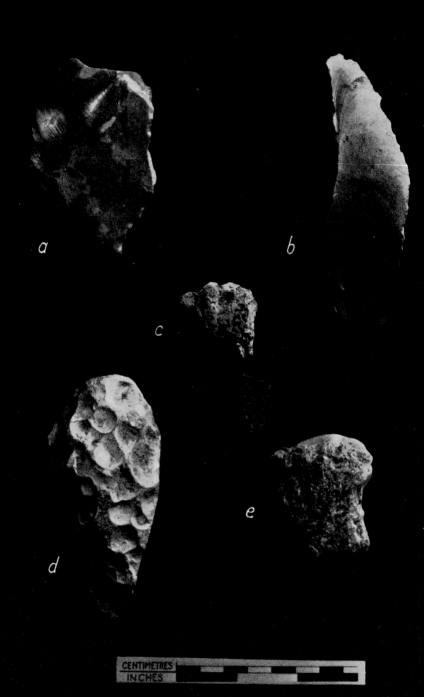

a

b

c

d

e

CENTIMETRES
INCHES

angular or trapezoidal, with post or stone walls, are known in N. Germany and Poland, and it may be that influence or actual people from those parts are included in the Windmill Hill population of Britain. At all events two broad types of long barrows can be distinguished from the nature of their internal construction (fig. 11, above).

Long barrows contain an average of six bodies, of all ages and both sexes; one at Thickthorn (Dorset) appeared to have been a cenotaph. In Yorkshire, on the fringe of the long barrow country, some cover stone cists, and some 'pit-dwellings', which may be partial rock-cut tombs. But the contents of barrows are not predictable; we shall see with round barrows that prehistoric burial rites were marked by great fluidity and variety, as though personal ideas of what was fitting were allowed free play.

There is an unusual type of neolithic long barrow, distinguished by inordinate length, and called a **bank barrow**; there is one inside Maiden Castle (Dorset) a third of a mile long, which had a mutilated body at one end; two others in Dorset, to where they are almost confined, are at Martins Down, Long Bredy, 645 ft. long and 6 ft. high, with berm and side-ditches, and a less well preserved one at Broadmayne. Small, often pear-shaped long barrows are found associated with round barrows (e.g. at Woodyates, Wilts.), and contain cremations —they are probably later than the large neolithic barrows covering unburnt burials.

The best areas to see long barrows are the Marlborough Downs, south of Avebury; around Stonehenge; Cranborne Chase and the hills south-west of this; and between Dorchester and Bridport; but there is a series along the Sussex Downs, mostly not such fine barrows as in Wessex. (The largest are Hunter's Burgh, Wilmington Hill; and Bevis', Bavere's or Solomon's Thumb, Up Marden, near Compton.) Particularly fine examples are: Fairmile Down (Tidcombe); the group of six at Tilshead; Pertwood Down; those in the Winterbourne Stoke, Lake and Normanton groups; Gussage Hill; Bokerley (an alignment of five); Wor Barrow, Handley Down; Pimperne, near Tarrant Hinton.

---

16. SURFACE FEATURES OF FLINT. A flint shows the different influences which have produced its surface

(a) the surface of a *struck flake*, with point of percussion, bulb, flake-scar and ripples (see p. 255 and fig. 23).

(b) A *natural fracture*, caused by frost. These have a dull surface, flat or gently undulating.

(c) *effects of heat:* the surface is crazed with tiny cracks, like some Chinese pottery. This is a pot-boiler (see p. 262).

(d) surface *pitted by frost*, with shallow depressions where tiny 'pot-lids' have been forced off.

(e) *crushing:* the result of using flint as a hammer.

MEGALITHIC TOMBS

Megalithic tombs have been broadly described on pp. 55 to 57; here only a few details are necessary. The general principle is quite different from that of the long barrows; here the mound is not just the final covering of a ritual area in which the dead have been laid—these are tombs, chambers for the dead, which necessitates the mound and its chambers being built first, and all of a piece. The shape of the mound and of the chambers varies, and the material depends on what is locally available. The burials are again collective, sometimes perhaps reserved to a class, sometimes certainly for a family—at Lanhill (Wilts.) several generations, recognisable by their common physical characteristics, were buried in the same tomb. A feature of this sort of burial is that only the last skeleton is found intact and orderly; the others are heaps of bones pushed aside to make room for the last. This does not really indicate any lack of respect; but merely that the soul was only thought to inhabit the body while flesh remained—when this had disappeared the soul had gone too, and it was then safe to move the bones. After each burial the tomb was closed and ritually sealed, by ceremonies held in front of it, or in the forecourt, when there was one. It looks as if megalithic tombs acted as temples for the people who built them. Evidence has been found of dancing in front of tombs; and many have ritual pits, with remains of feasts, and traces of fire. Unfortunately the ritual of barrows cannot be certainly reconstructed, and may indeed have not been constant or standard from place to place. Symbols of the goddess of fertility and death, round whom the neolithic religion revolved, are often carved on the stones of the chamber or the forecourt.

There are between 1,500 and 2,000 megalithic tombs surviving in the British Isles; some 250 in England and Wales, about 350 in Scotland, and over 1,000 in Ireland. The distribution is essentially in the highland zone, but there are a few strays in the long barrow area in Wessex (e.g. the magnificent East and West Kennet barrows near Avebury), and the isolated group in Kent. The size range is similar to that of the long barrows; this often means a vast pile of stones, in many cases over 15,000 tons, with a chamber and passage a few feet long at one end. Effort on this scale, repeated all over the highland zone, shows the power of the religion which caused the tombs to be raised; proportionally, it is not unlike that needed to build the pyramids of Egypt. Most of these tombs are in a ruinous condition, and the layout of the chambers is not always clear; in many cases too the cairn has been used for later building, or for walls, or the mound, if of earth, has weathered away. In these cases all that will be left is the chamber and passage, or a jumble of great stones in disorder representing them. (Isolated chambers are often called 'dolmens'—'cromlechs' in Wales.) But some are still intact, and can actually be entered, and the spirit of their age experienced. (See plates 2, p. 33, and 5, p. 72.)

The Severn–Cotswold group has some 65 pear-shaped cairns (originally straight-sided) in south Wales, from Gower to the Black Mountains, and in the Cotswolds and Mendips, with outliers in north Wiltshire and Berkshire. The cairns are limited by dry-stone walls, and there is a shallow forecourt at the wide end, into which the chamber usually opens. The latter is normally a 'transepted gallery', a passage with little rooms or transepts opening off it (Notgrove, Glos.); but many have just irregular chambers opening off the forecourt (Tinkinswood, Glam.). Some have round chambers entered by means of narrow passages opening out of the sides of the mound, and these have a 'false portal' on the forecourt (Belas Knap, pl. 5, p. 72). Arthur's Stone, Dorstone, Herefordshire, has a passage with a right-angled turn. At Wayland's Smithy, Berks., the wide end is straight, not indented into a forecourt. Other variants exist, but perhaps the most instructive to visit are West Kennet, near Avebury (the largest in England and Wales); Hetty Pegler's Tump, Uley, Glos.; and Belas Knap (pl. 4, p. 65).

The Clyde–Solway and Carlingford groups, in northern Ireland and south-west Scotland, with outliers in Man and west Wales (Pentre Ifan, Pembs.), have a similar range of variants to the Severn–Cotswold group, but here the chamber is normally a 'segmented gallery', a passage divided into sections by transverse slabs. The forecourts are more pronounced, most being semi-circular, except in the 'lobster-claw' group in Ireland, where they are round or oval, enclosed inside the barrow by arms of stone-work. Good examples from the 30 odd in Scotland are Carn Ban, Arran; Cairn Holy, Galloway: and of the 360 or so in Ireland (some 120 horned cairns and over 240 court-cairns), Ballyalton; Clady Halliday; Browndod, Antrim; Crevykeel, Sligo. A few tombs in the southern Pennines may also belong to this group, perhaps at second-hand (the Bridestones, Congleton, Cheshire; Minninglow, Ballidon, Derbyshire).

There are some 400 gallery graves in southern Ireland of separate origin from the northern horned cairns. These comprise a northern group of wedge-shaped galleries such as Dunteige and Moylisha, and a southern group such as Labbacallee (Cork).

The other type of megalithic tomb, the passage graves, contains some of the finest prehistoric monuments of Britain. The pure Iberian form, with passage leading to a corbelled stone chamber, often with side chambers forming a cruciform plan, the whole under a sometimes very large round cairn, is seen in the Boyne culture-province of Ireland, with outliers in north Wales. The classical example is New Grange (Meath). This is an enormous round mound 45 ft. high and 265 ft. across, containing a passage 62 ft. long leading to a fine corbelled

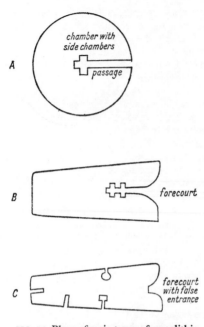

FIG. 12. Plans of main types of megalithic tombs. A, passage grave in round barrow; B, gallery grave in long barrow; C, Severn-Cotswold gallery grave with side chambers

chamber 20 ft. high. Along the Boyne river there are groups of passage graves of this type, in cemeteries, as also further west at Loughcrew (Meath) and Carrowkeel (Sligo) — the latter has 14 tombs, while Carrowmore, not far away, has about 60. The great Boyne tombs are often richly carved with symbols of the goddess and other religious matter. They have a kerb or peristalith which sometimes curves in at the entrance to form a small forecourt. Isolated stones and pits had a ritual purpose. These features are also seen in the colonies of this culture, Bryn Celli Ddu (pl. 5, p. 72) and Barclodiad y Gawres, in Anglesey; there is an outlier at Liverpool (the Calderstones). Another movement reached as far north as Orkney, where the great tomb of Maes Howe is one of the finest monuments in Britain, although a good deal smaller than New Grange. The passage here is 36 ft. long, the mound 115 ft. across; the chamber plan is squared, not curved.

Another passage grave group is the Clava, on the south side of the Moray Firth, about 30 tombs of early form but with variants (Beauly; Achnachree). Caithness and Orkney have a group of some 100 cairns with passages 'stalled' by slabs projecting from the walls. Variants exist, both of chamber and shape of mound. Eday and Rousay have good examples. Shetland has a group of heel-shaped cairns.

The entrance graves of Cornwall, Scilly, Wales and south-east Ireland, with chambers opening through a portal with no passage, are a separate group. Finally, the small group of half a dozen or so near Aylesford, Kent, are a form of entrance grave coming not, like these, from Brittany, but from north Germany. They have massive chambers and elongated mounds (now gone) surrounded by a kerb of large stones. The best-known example is Kit's Coty House (chamber only), but the most complete and informative is Coldrum. The megalithic tomb at Park Place, Wargrave (Berks.), although genuine, was brought from Jersey and re-erected here in 1783.

Secondary neolithic burials were often cremations tied up in bags and deposited in pits, so they are not visible as field antiquities. A circle of such pits forms the earliest phase of Stonhenge.

Stone tombs now seem to be versions of wooden houses of or for the dead.

ROUND BARROWS

We come now to the most numerous of all field monuments, the round barrows (pl. 6, p. 73 and fig. 13, p. 158), the standard tomb of the Bronze Age (c. 1800–550 BC). There are somewhere between 10,000 and 20,000 of these, that is, an average of more than one for every parish in the country (this is not of course to say that every parish has one). There were once probably as many more, but destruction by farming, quarrying and building has been continuous, and unhappily is still going on. These barrows are by no means merely featureless mounds of earth; there is extraordinary variety in their contents and structure, and no more than a very brief survey of them can be given. As with the earthen 'unchambered' long barrows, the round barrows are not tombs as such, but only the final coverings of a sacred area, where the dead are laid, and where the ritual is carried on.

Beaker burials are contracted, that is, the body is flexed in the position of sleep, or, less likely, of the pre-natal state; they are accompanied by equipment such as food and drink in pots, weapons and tools, to help them in the next life. These tools are sometimes broken, either to release their spirits, or to save the living from the risk of using the property of the dead. Sometimes they are given a boat as well, in which to make the journey. Mortuary houses are known (such as Beaulieu, Hants.), which may be the dead man's own house, in which he is left until it falls down over him, when the barrow is erected. But Beaker burials are simple compared to the elaborate rituals of the full Early Bronze Age, Wessex and Food Vessel. Considerable complexity also continues during the Middle Bronze Age, but ritual is simpler in the Late Bronze and Iron Ages. Cremation comes in with the Food Vessels, but inhumation is used as well. Generally speaking, a circular area, anything up to 120 ft. across, was marked out, usually by a ditch or a circle of stakes, or stones (ditches are absent on rocky soils in the highland zone). Here the dead was laid, sometimes on a platform of stones or wood, where the body could disintegrate. Sometimes the primary burial is in a grave at the centre of the circle, but quite often it is laid on the natural surface (Childe has pointed out that pastoral people do not like digging!), or in a stone cist. Sometimes it is placed on a little conical mound of earth,

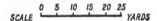

SCALE 0 5 10 15 20 25 YARDS

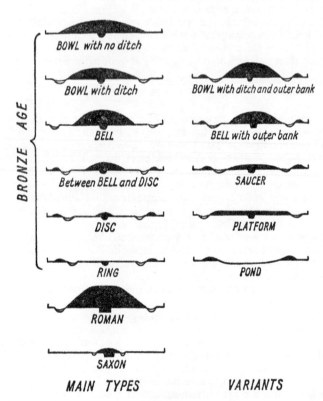

BRONZE AGE

BOWL with no ditch

BOWL with ditch

BOWL with ditch and outer bank

BELL

BELL with outer bank

Between BELL and DISC

SAUCER

DISC

PLATFORM

RING

POND

ROMAN

SAXON

MAIN TYPES

VARIANTS

FIG. 13. Types of round barrow

sometimes under a small cairn. The body can be tied up, weighted with stones, or mutilated. There is evidence that in some cases the body was kept elsewhere until the time was ripe for it to be brought to the sacred circle. Although the normal rite in the Bronze Age is single burial, as opposed to collective, this is not universal, and many barrows have several burials all primary; of course, these may not all have died at the same time—the circle seems to have been kept open for considerable periods. When the time had come, and the body or bodies had been variously disposed of in the circle (often the same barrow has a variety of methods of disposal), the sealing rites were held; these included

feasts, fire, pits possibly for libations to the spirits in the earth. Finally
the whole area was covered with a mound; this could be fenced or
revetted, often leaving a gap, usually on the south-east, where the
original entrance of the circle had been.

Some mounds were sloping or flat-topped for other rites to be held on
them. A post was sometimes erected on the mound which may have
been carved as a memorial or an image. The ceremonies often included
the use of white stones, as symbols of immortality, or white sand or
clay, spread over or round the body, and sometimes brought from long
distances; gypsum, also white, has been detected on the banks of the
henge monument at Thornborough (Yorks. NR), also with a ritual
meaning. The mound itself was not always simple; it could be built in
layers of different soils, or have an inner mound of turf; it was sometimes
added to for later burials. It could be surrounded by a kerb of stones.
Later burials could be inserted in the sides of the mound, which retained its sanctity for a long time, or laid round its foot. Iron Age and
Saxon burials are found as secondaries in Food Vessel barrows.

Middle Bronze Age burials were usually cremations in urns, usually
in a small pit in the centre of the barrow, closed with a flat stone. Urns
are frequently secondary in barrows, and are often inverted, for what
reason is not clear. Stone circles are found in Urn barrows, and inner
cairns or mounds. Mortuary houses were still used. In the Late Bronze
Age urn-cemeteries are the rule, and these are not apparent on the
surface. Barrows and pits are still in use in remote parts. Generally,
barrows decline in size throughout the Bronze Age, until in the Iron
Age, covering a single inhumation, they are quite small, except for the
great chariot burials of the Marnians in East Yorkshire. Cemeteries
gradually supersede barrows, and are normal from the 7th century AD.

Reports of modern excavations of barrows show their astonishing
variety and interest. One of the first to realise this was Canon William
Greenwell, who dug nearly 300 barrows in Yorkshire and elsewhere.
It is a very valuable exercise indeed to work through his accounts of
them (in *British Barrows* [1877] and *Archaeologia 52* [1891]), and try
to construct plans and sections, to scale on squared paper, of some of
the more complex ones. This will give the feel of the subject very
vividly.

By far the majority of round barrows are of the simple 'bowl' form,
like an inverted pudding-basin. They cover the whole of the Bronze and
Iron Ages. They vary from about 15 ft. across to over 100, and can be
20 or so ft. high. The earlier ones are surrounded by a ditch, except in
places where the soil does not permit this; in these cases the mound
was made of earth scraped off the surrounding land. The ditch was
once up to 4 or 5 ft. deep, and 10 ft. wide (in the case of a large barrow)
but has of course silted up, and now is only a foot or so deep; sometimes
there is a low bank outside the ditch as well. The profile can vary as well

as the size. Green Howe, N. Deighton (Yorks. WR), has one side sloping less steeply than the other. Barrows are sited on open stretches of country (moors or commons), or on hilltops; if the latter they may be slightly below the actual top, on what is called the 'false crest', so that when seen from the settlement lower down the slope they are on the skyline. Round barrows are so common that there is not much point in giving examples; most areas contain a few, and certain regions, such as the chalk hills of Wessex, from Dorset to Berkshire, and the moorlands of north-east Yorkshire, are dotted with hundreds. Wessex alone has nearly 4,000.

The Wessex culture-period is characterised by special forms of barrow.

The most spectacular are the **bell-barrows**, which have a deep ditch, sometimes with an external bank; the mound, often large, is separated from the ditch by a berm or flat platform of varying width. A few have Beaker inhumations, but most are the tombs of cremated Wessex chiefs, some accompanied by rich grave-goods, including gold and amber. They centre in Wessex, and radiate from there to Sussex, Surrey, East Anglia and the South-West. Good examples can be seen at Normanton (Wilts.) and near Stonehenge; West Cranmore (Som.); a fine one stands just north of Maiden Castle (Dorset). At Monkton Down, Sussex, are six large ones in a row (The Devil's Jumps). The same ditch can enclose more than one mound, and at Elstead (Surrey) is an example with three.

Disc-barrows are made on the same principle as bell-barrows, but have the central mound reduced to very small proportions, sometimes scarcely visible. Instead of tools and weapons, these usually contain jewellery, ornaments, sewing implements and domestic pottery, and it has been assumed that they are the graves of Wessex culture women. Like bell-barrows, discs can be composite, or may overlap with another

---

17. THE TEXTURE OF POTTERY (A). The variety of pottery is too vast to be fully illustrated, but a few examples can be given. Neolithic and Bronze Age pottery is generally coarse, friable and loose-textured, being fired at too low a temperature to harden it properly. The features pointed out with each example are characteristic of their type, but should not be taken as exclusive:
(a) *Neolithic A* (Windmill Hill), smooth plain ware.
(b) *Secondary Neolithic* (Peterborough), thick and coarse, with patterns made with sticks, bones, etc.
(c) *Secondary Neolithic* (Rinyo-Clacton 'grooved ware'), thick, with deeply incised line ornament.
(d) and (e) *Early Bronze Age* (Beaker), thinner and often rather harder, with fine incised or impressed decoration (comb, fingernail, etc.).
(f) *Middle Bronze Age* (Urn), coarse, often 'corky'.
(g) *Late Bronze Age* (Deverel-Rimbury), rough and gritty.

CENTIMETRES
INCHES

barrow or earthwork; the ditch is occasionally oval. Their distribution is the same as the bell-barrows. Good examples are at Upwey (Dorset), Grafton (Wilts.)—overlapping; Oakley Down (Dorset)—various forms. Variants of the disc type are **saucer-barrows**, which have a low mound covering the whole circle inside the ditch and outer bank; and **pond-barrows**, which are shallow cavities enclosed by a bank, sometimes with a causeway on the east side. Recent work on a pond barrow at Snail Down (Wilts.), suggests that it (and other pond barrows) was a fenced and banked enclosure, probably for the exposure of corpses subsequently cremated and buried elsewhere. Some, however, were the tops of Bronze Age shafts, as at Wilsford (Wilts).

Grinsell has estimated that the numbers of these types in Wessex are: bell, 245; disc, 149; saucer, 63; pond, 53; many have been ploughed out, but these proportions are probably right, and these special types remain relatively rare (against 3,650 bowl barrows).

There are also **ring-barrows**, discs with no central mound at all, and **ring-ditches**, where the bank is inside the ditch, but which have in some cases been proved to contain central burials. Some however may never have been barrows, and their purpose is obscure. It is however possible that most of them once contained burials, which have disappeared owing to the acidity of the soil (this may apply to the earth circles on St Martha's Hill, Guildford, Surrey), or to other causes. They have no gap or entrance, so are unlikely to be hut circles or farm enclosures (although this is not an infallible test); some could be **tree-rings** (banks with external ditch to protect an ornamental clump of trees from damage by animals—usually 18th or 19th century)— these can be barrow size, but also quite large, as one in Stoke Park, Guildford, about 60–70 yards across). Incidentally, some barrows are surmounted by a clump of trees, and if there is a bank round them it may be a tree-ring, not an original feature. But ring-ditches not obviously barrows can usually be taken as Bronze Age ritual circles. They are found all over the country, and air photography is constantly revealing more, including those ploughed out. Work is needed on this problem.

---

18. THE TEXTURE OF POTTERY (B). Iron age and Roman pottery is better made and fired. The wheel was used from Belgic times.

(a) *Early Iron Age A*, still rather thick and coarse.

(b) *Early Iron Age B*, finer, often with bead rim and incised decoration.

(c) *Early Iron Age C*, hard burnished ware, with bead rim.

(d) *Roman* (Samian), very hard, with moulded decoration.

(e) *Roman* (New Forest), part of a 'poppy-head' pot with deep undulations. Fine, thin ware.

(f) *Roman* (Castor), hard, thin, with 'barbotine' (raised slip) decoration.

(g) *Roman* (Coarse), thick and rougher.

A form special to the Late Bronze and Iron Ages is the **platform-barrow,** a low platform up to 5 ft. high, often lower, with usually a ditch round it (Tyting, Surrey). They are still somewhat obscure archaeologically. A special type of barrow enclosure is the **square ditch.** These are of Marnian origin, and are found in east Yorkshire (although most of them are hardly visible now).

Roman barrows are conical, with steep sides and often flat tops, perhaps to take a memorial stone or post. Only about 100 are known or suspected, the best being in Kent (Holborough Knob), Essex (The Mount, Lexden; the Bartlow Hills, Ashdon), Cambs. and Herts. (Six Hills, Stevenage); others occur to the west and north of this area, as far north as Hovingham near Malton (Yorks. NR). Alignments are common along Roman roads. A roman barrow on Mersea Island, Essex, covered a brick tomb. But look round Roman towns.

The Saxons of the pagan period (up to, say, AD 650) buried their chiefs in barrows, either very large, and often flat-topped (Taplow) or quite small (Whitmoor Common, Worplesdon, Surrey). One of the last, but not the least, was the great mound at Sutton Hoo, near Woodbridge, Suffolk, which contained a boat (brilliantly excavated by C. W. Phillips from the impress of its timbers and nails in the sandy soil), with rich furniture, weapons and jewellery, some indicating long-distance connections (e.g. a Swedish helmet and Byzantine silver). This was a cenotaph, of c. AD 625, representing the pagan tomb of a Christian king buried elsewhere. There are some sixty primary burials of Scandinavians (early 10th century) under barrows, many in or with ships. Most are in Scotland, but three are recorded in Yorkshire—including Camphill, Bedale and Northallerton—and one in the Isle of Man, at Ballateare, Jurby. Most of these covered inhumations, except the two last. Danish burials of the late 19th century all seem to be secondary in earlier barrows.

Mention of **Silbury** (near Avebury, Wilts.) may be made here. This stupendous mound is the largest artificial hill in Europe; it is on a natural knoll of chalk, but is mostly artificial. It is 125-130 ft. high, about 550 ft. across at the base, 100 ft. at the flat top, and covers about 5½ acres. There is a low flat platform in the middle of the flat top. The re-excavation in 1968-70 by Professor Atkinson has revealed a central turf barrow, surmounted by a 'pyramid', built in a series of small mounds, with internal retaining walls to hold it firm. This was a special monument, whose significance and inspiration is still not understood; many possibilities are open, and it may well be connected with Avebury. The C14 dating of the barrow was 2145±95 BC, which may represent a true date of some 2400 BC, or roughly contemporary with some of the pyramids of Egypt.

Barrows are often found in groups, which can be all of one type, but sometimes of several types together. These are excellent places to see and compare the various forms. Some contain long barrows, and presumably were gathered round them because of their existing sanctity. Good groups are: Lambourn Seven Barrows (pl. 6, p. 73), some 40 of many types; Snail Down, Tidworth, about 30, mostly bowls; Silk Hill, near Amesbury; Winterbourne Crossroads, near Stonehenge —this latter is the finest group in Wiltshire, containing fine examples of almost all types; Woodyates, Cranborne Chase, Dorset; Iping Common, near Midhurst, Sussex. Small groups of two or three are common. Alignments are also met, sometimes along a prehistoric track (e.g. Overton Hill, near Avebury) or on the edge of the old fields.

Most barrows have shallow depressions on their tops. In the rare cases where they have never been excavated, this may represent the collapse of some internal structure, such as a cist. But unfortunately it usually means excavation by unscientific hands. The Victorians 'opened' thousands of barrows in this way, often several in a day, to extract the central burial with its grave-goods; they quite ignored the possibility of a complex structure inside the mound, and of the evidence they were destroying. Many are ruined, but many would repay re-excavation on modern lines. Many barrows were dug into, or stones overturned, to get at the gold popularly supposed to have been buried under them.

An unknown, but very large, number of barrows has been ploughed out or otherwise destroyed. Many of Greenwell's most important barrows have gone in this way, and now in parts of the Yorkshire Wolds one sees only small mounds sheltering under the hedgerows. But their traces can still be seen, in proper conditions, from the air, and often on the ground too, showing up as circles or horseshoes of lighter soil, or as crop-marks. Several, for instance, can be seen from the northern rampart of Maiden Castle. Some of these traces could be confused at first sight with vegetation ('fairy') rings, or with the places where farmers' heaps of lime, phosphates, etc., have once been dumped. Ploughed-out barrows should be recorded and investigated (pl. 15).

It is possible to mistake a small, lumpy, rounded moraine, in once-glaciated areas, for a barrow. Some apparent bowl-barrows may really be bell-barrows, the mound having slipped down over the berm and altered the original shape. On sandy soil, barrows can slump out of shape quite markedly, e.g. at Sutton Hoo.

Barrows have been used for many purposes: with flattened tops, for moot-hills or dancing-places (see p. 186); as bases for windmills, gibbets, beacons, guide-posts; as boundary marks (e.g. Five Lords' Burgh, Sussex, where manors meet). Incidentally some mounds on boundaries are not barrows, but just mounds of earth; they cannot always be distinguished from barrows externally. Ornamental mounds on which trees were planted in 18th century parks are sometimes very hard to distinguish from small barrows (e.g. those in Ribston Park, near Harrogate, shown as tumuli on former editions of the OS maps).

Sheeans, or fairy mounds, in Scotland, next to churchyards, were where souls could await the resurrection of their bodies buried nearby (Carnock, Fife); their origins and later uses were various.

Barrows have always been recognised as sacred sites, and a copious lore has grown up round them, to which the best introduction is in L. V. Grinsell's *Ancient Burial-mounds of England* (2nd edition 1953). The lore may be divided into names and customs, and much has still to be recovered, classified and studied; this is a good field for an amateur willing to get a working background of folklore science. In any case the names and lore should be recorded. Names were given to barrows by Saxon and mediaeval people, and represent their ideas on the nature and purpose of the mounds, the real origin of which was unknown. Some are ascribed to giants or 'little people', common conceptions for earlier peoples—as Giant's Grave or Elf Howe. The oddly named Obtrusch Rook, Farndale (Yorks. NR), means the cairn of Hob, a form of Puck; similarly there are Robin Hood's Butts. Some refer to heroes or known invaders, fictionally of course—Wayland's Smithy, Dane's Graves, Lilla Howe, Arthur's Stone; some to gods, as Norns' Tump, Thundersbarrow (i.e. Thor's), the Devil's Jumps. Some are descriptive, such as Green Howe, some are called after local villages, as Duggleby Howe. Some are connected to battles, as Warriors' Grave, some with various characters, as Hetty Pegler's Tump. There is much lore also, some of it stories of supernatural events at barrows, some of it customs such as games played on or round the barrow on certain days (the great Hove barrow, no longer extant, is one of these). There is no need here to multiply instances, but the field is very wide and of great interest.

CAIRNS AND OTHER BURIALS

Cairns, if not barrows, can be either boundary marks (a 'pile of stones' is marked on the OS map on the West Clandon–East Clandon (Surrey) boundary); memorials, each stone added by passers-by on the site of a violent death, to lay the ghost; a similar idea produces the cairns on the tops of mountains, where it is the spirit of the wild that needs protecting against (many mountain cairns are sepulchral); to commemorate a historical event, e.g. a battle, or the landing of Prince Charles Edward; sighting-marks for laying out tracks, etc.—these can be ancient; or heaps of stones removed by farmers from the surface of fields.

A special type of Roman burial-place is the 'cartwheel' mausoleum, usually an octagonal brick building; they are rare in Britain, but probable examples are at Holmstreet Farm, near Pulborough, Sussex, at Nettleton Shrub, near Bath, and Wickwood, West Kington, Wilts. A very low oblong mound near Uffington White Horse (Berks.), was found to contain 46 skeletons of the 4th century AD.

Roman walled cemeteries are also rare, only 13 being known, of which eight are in Kent, and the rest in Essex, Cambs. and Herts. They consist of enclosures, usually rectangular but sometimes square or round, of different areas, some covering 1000 sq. ft. Inside were tombs, and sometimes a tower, mausoleum or statue. Most are now destroyed or covered in, but examples can be seen at Harpenden, Herts., square, with round footings inside; Keston, Kent (War Banks), a circular and a square enclosure, visible now only as mounds.

Burials in cists (boxes of stone slabs) are common in stone areas from the Middle Bronze Age onwards, often with no covering mound. In parts of the North, in the late Bronze Age and particularly the Iron Age, large cemeteries, presumably for people not entitled to barrow burial, were made, each body covered with a small cairn of earth and stones. That on Danby Rigg (Yorks. NR) has over 800 such cairns; at Struntry Cark, Goathland, is an oval clearing surrounded by the stone removed from it, and containing 25 small cairns. The Late Bronze Age urnfields, and the cemeteries of flat graves of the Iron Age and the Anglo-Saxons, cannot normally be seen on the surface; they are usually discovered during farming, building or quarrying operations.

Roman cemeteries were along the roads outside the towns or forts—they contain coffins of stone, lead or gypsum—sometimes cists of tiles were made. Tombstones are rare, but still possible (their inscriptions are an important source of information on the life of the province and army—they should be studied in the museums and the literature). Late Bronze Age and Roman cremations in urns can turn up anywhere, representing people buried on their farms, or even under the house floor, as can isolated burials of all periods. For instance, in 1850 the body of a Romano-Briton was found well-preserved in peat on Grewelthorpe Moor (Yorks. WR); it was tanned and dried, and clothed in a green cloak, a scarlet garment, yellow stockings and leather sandals—an extraordinary glimpse of the past.

A special class is that of sacrificial burials, in sacred circles, in front of barrows, under walls (a spectacular foreign example is the famous Tollund man, hanged and deposited in a sacred lake or bog in Denmark). Accidental death is represented by the 14th century barber-surgeon crushed by the fall of a stone in the circle at Avebury which he was trying to overturn, no doubt on religious grounds; his purse and scissors were found with his bones.

Some Anglo-Saxon cemeteries, mostly in the south-east, are clusters of low circular grave-mounds, 5 to 10 ft. across, not always easy to see (examples in Greenwich Park, London; Farthing Downs, Coulsdon, Surrey; Derringstone Downs, Kent). Grave-goods practically cease after the conversion of the Anglo-Saxons to Christianity in the 7th century, and thereafter graves become less informative (although coins, mugs of beer and joints of meat still occasionally accompany burials in remote districts). Tombstones in the modern sense, except inside churches, were not used until after the Reformation.

Mediaeval charnel-houses, like the bone-filled crypts at Hythe, Kent, and St Bride's, London, are outside our scope, but there is an odd case at Ripon, where a morainic hill (looking like a motte), Ailsey Hill, contains burials on its slopes, some of which may represent reburials of bones resulting from periodical clearances of the Minster charnel-house.

Unbaptised children in Ireland are buried in enclosures called *cillini*, which are stone-walled areas resembling ring-forts, and often containing the remains of a church or monastic cell. Some are actually former ring-forts, given by their lords to a Celtic missionary, and since used for burial purposes.

Isolated and unexplained burials frequently turn up along old roads, and may be of any age.

Funeral cairns were built in Scotland where coffin-bearers could rest their burdens on the way to a distant church or graveyard (e.g. Glen Laxdale, near Tarbert, Harris).

MILITARY WORKS

HILLFORTS

A high proportion of the visible antiquities of Britain are military works, and among them the hillforts are both conspicuous and familiar. They are essentially an Iron Age phenomenon; the immigrant farmers in the 6th century BC mostly lived on undefended sites, whether farms or hilltop villages (such as the first settlement on the Caburn (near Lewes)), but a few sites of this phase are defended by a rampart of earth, following the contour of the hill-top, with a ditch outside it of V-section in the Late Bronze Age manner, and a simple entrance (Figsbury, near Salisbury). It is possible that some of these simple forts actually date from the end of the Late Bronze Age, like the semicircular one on the edge of the cliff at Eston Nab (Yorks. NR), of which there are similar examples in Yorkshire, and a few in Scotland, such as (possibly) the little one at the foot of the Grey Mare's Tail waterfall in Moffatdale (Dumfriesshire); but it is probably better to think of forts generally as Iron Age.

The earliest forts were no doubt built against the original inhabitants as well as for local inter-tribal defence; but they became common in the 3rd century, when scores were built to meet the threat caused by the invasion of the Iron Age B peoples. Right across southern England forts sprang up on the hilltops, or on plateaux, still usually with one bank and ditch, but now with more complicated entrances, of several forms of curving passages between banks, to force the enemy to slow down at the gate, which was seen as a weak point. Farmsteads, such as Little Woodbury, were given a ditch and palisaded bank at this time, and this was no doubt the origin of many of the forts; the light defence was developed into a strongly-ringed place and finally into a full-scale fort (which is of course not usually on a hilltop, but a slope or plateau). The larger ones may have either enclosed the hilltop villages, or have been refuges for all the local people—a tribe or clan—in times of sudden scare. For not all of them appear to have been inhabited, at least for long.

During Iron Age B, hillforts became a more regular feature of life; it was once thought that they were all tribal towns, and that for instance the blocks of downland in Sussex, each with its fort (Cissbury, etc.), were each the home of the tribe whose refuge the forts were. So indeed it was in one sense; but it is possible also to regard at least the smaller forts as comparable to the smaller mediaeval castles—strongholds of nobles, used as much for aggression as for the defence of their peoples. This concept I find very helpful and illuminating in explaining the large number of small forts which abound. For instance, the fort on

Puttenham Common, Surrey, is too strong for an ordinary farm, but not in the same class as the large hilltop forts like Hascombe or Holmbury.

The construction of the early forts can be sensed at Ladle Hill (Hants.), which was left unfinished, with irregular mounds of chalk left lying inside the bank, waiting to be built in; the topsoil from the ditch was put on one side, and the ramparts based on blocks of chalk dug from deeper levels. Several forts, like Hollingbury (Sussex), Wimbledon (London), Yarnbury (Wilts.), and the first Maiden Castle, had their ramparts built up in timber frames, with a protected walk along the top, and filled with rubble and earth; the whole wall was set back a little from its ditch by a narrow platform or berm, and was backed by a sloping ramp. This type is based on a Continental '(Preist') model, but is not the same as the later Gallic forts.

Many forts were enlarged or strengthened in Iron Age B, from *c.* 300 BC to the Roman conquest. Walls were often doubled or trebled (pl. 11, p. 128), and this reflects a development of techniques of warfare, with, for instance, the introduction of the sling (for which mounds of ammunition, sling-stones, were found at Maiden Castle). The ramparts are further apart on gentle slopes (Badbury Rings) than on steep slopes (Hod Hill). It should not however be assumed that it was the use of slings which led to the multiplication of ramparts; indeed, it may have been the other way about. On a steep slope the best way to build a rampart would have been by means of a quarry ditch inside, with the upcast thrown outward; the wall so produced would be heightened outside by way of another ditch outside it, whose upcast would also be thrown outside, thus producing two ramparts. This method could then be easily developed, and with it the methods of warfare to cope with it. A good example of this is Scratchbury (Wilts.).

A further fillip to massive fort-building was given by the arrival of refugees from Caesar's wars in Gaul (e.g. the Veneti of Brittany after their defeat in 56 BC). Finally, the Belgae adapted forts to Roman methods of warfare by altering the shape of the ditches; those at Caburn and Oldbury (Kent), for instance, have flat bottoms (see below). Belgic forts also are sometimes no longer on hilltops, but down the slope (Stockton, Dorset). These are not to be confused with the 'hill-slope forts' of the south-west and south Wales, which are a local Iron Age type (e.g. Dane's Hill, Worcs.)—a few of these are possibly to be recognised elsewhere, like that at Goose Hill on the eastern slope of Bow Hill (Sussex).

The survey of hillforts carried out in connection with the Ordnance Survey Iron Age map now in preparation, records 1,386 fortified sites in the area of the south sheet (south of Scarborough). Of these 793 cover less than three acres; 600 are true hillforts, but only 166 of these have been excavated in any way. There are almost none in East York-shire, Lincolnshire and East Anglia, the area of the chariot-burials of

Iron Age B. The chief areas of multivallation are the south-west (west of the Exe) and Wessex; in the south-west this feature is often original, in Wessex usually secondary—a rebuilding and enlargement of an earlier single-rampart fort. In the south-east are the Oldbury I and II type forts (see below), and in the highland zone several distinctive types. The pattern in the south-east of England is distinctive, and has recently been worked out as: c. 300 BC, forts along the chalk hills built by the Iron Age A2 people against the incoming B people; often timber-laced (Hollingbury type): c. 100 BC, forts in the Weald and on the greensand built by the AB people against the first Belgic invaders or a second wave of B people; these are hastily built with earth banks of 'dump' construction and simple V-section ditches (Oldbury I type—these include the series along the northern greensand ridges, such as Holmbury I, Hascombe I, Anstiebury (all Surrey), and others such as High Rocks and Squerries I (Kent), Hammer Wood, Philpotts, Dry Hill and the inner ramparts of the Caburn (all Sussex): c. AD 25, the Belgae got possession of some of these forts, and enlarged and re-fortified them, with stone-faced ramparts and wide flat-bottomed ditches (Oldbury II type—the second phase of several of the forts named above is of this type (e.g. Hascombe II); it was once thought that the Oldbury II type was built against the Romans, but this is now considered unlikely, with the possible exception of the later stages of the Caburn.

Another widespread type of fort, running throughout the Iron Age, and possibly also used in the Late Bronze Age, is the promontory fort, where a spur of hill is cut off by a rampart and ditch across the neck; a good example is at Danby Rigg (Yorks. NR), and just west of the Caburn. Along the south-west coasts there are cliff-castles, promontory forts built by the Gaulish refugees. Ireland too has cliff-castles, such as Dun Aongusa on Aran.

The Romans stormed and destroyed some of the major hillforts, such as Maiden Castle, leaving their inhabitants to trickle down to new towns established in the plains below; many were just abandoned as the Pax Romana made them unnecessary and out of keeping with the Roman way of life—but some of the Celtic nobles must have preferred their freedom, even with its squalor. In the highland zone the forts continued in use, and were even occupied after the Romans left (e.g. Yeavering Bell, Northumberland). In the military zone the forts were generally slighted, rather than just being abandoned; the people of, say, Ingleborough in the Pennines and Eildon in Selkirkshire, were brought down or closely watched.

The downward movement from the hillforts had begun before the Roman invasion, and in some cases may have been made by way of a Belgic town; as for instance from the Trundle to the Belgic town at Selsey, and later to the new Roman town at Chichester, Noviomagus, 'the new town in the plain'. Belgic towns were scattered over considerable stretches of country, surrounded by a rampart of great length, which included farmlands as well as civic centres; Colchester is a good case. That at Stanwick (Yorks. NR)—not Belgic, but of similar type, and possibly laid out with the help of Belgic refugees—was a refuge for that part of the Brigantes who fought a last stand against the Romans; the walls here are 4½ miles long, enclosing nearly 700 acres.

The Iron Age forts of the highland zone are of several types. Of Hallstatt tradition, from the Rhineland, but of 3rd and 2nd century date, are the timber-laced walls of 'Preist' type, which had inner and outer vertical posts tied with transverse timbers, and stone facing walls, with a core of earth and stones; these walls carried platforms. The 'Avaricum' type, from Gaul, was built of transverse and longitudinal timbers in alternate layers, bolted together, but with no verticals; each course was separated by earth and facing stones; ditches were not important in this type. They date from the 1st century BC. Of the latter type are the 'Abernethy' forts in the Tay valley, built by a movement from England in the 1st century BC. It should be said that if such a fort was set on fire, the burning of the timbers would create spaces inside the stonework which could cause a draught enough to raise the heat to a point where the stones would be fused together in shapeless masses. The result is called a 'vitrified fort'; they are common in coastal and western districts of Scotland. A 'gallic' fort is one with nailed timber constructions arranged horizontally—only one is known in Britain, Burghead (Morayshire). A few forts were built with timber frames well down in England, such as Almondbury, near Huddersfield, and Wincobank, near Sheffield; the former began as a Preist-type fort and was finally rebuilt in Avaricum style—both were probably built against the Roman invasion. There are other groups in Cheshire and the Welsh marches.

In north and north-west Scotland at this time the Iron Age B peoples built the brochs, round stone towers with several floors, each defending a valley or small area of country, and each occupied by a farmer who no doubt also lived partly by raiding. Over 400 can be traced, including 145 in Caithness (e.g. three near Keiss), and 78 in Orkney. Fine examples can be seen at Midhowe, Rousay, and Mousa, Shetland. In Arran, Bute, Argyll, SW Scotland and the Western Isles are small forts called duns, built of dry-stone walling, some on hilltops or promontories, some circular on lower ground (Rahoy); these were occupied throughout and after the Roman period, and some may have been built in the Dark Ages by the Irish invaders of Argyll. In the Pictish area in east Scotland the forts are either oval with heavy walls, simple ring-forts, or citadels surrounded by earthworks. 'Ridge-top' forts are found in SE Scotland (e.g. Bell Hill, Selkirkshire); also nuclear forts. Small castles similar to the brochs are common in Cornwall. These are called ring-forts, since they have one or two ditches and low banks piled against the central stone structure. Chun and Castle-an-Dinas, both protecting stone-built villages, are typical. Ireland has a large number of small forts, with or without earth banks, the raths and cashels, which were occupied throughout the first millennium AD, and even later in some cases (bank and ditch-types, platform types, and round stone enclosures with houses inside). A very fine example is Staigue Fort, Co. Kerry. Here the hilltop villages of north Wales should be mentioned, such as Tre'r Ceiri, Caernarvonshire, which is protected by a stone wall; the Romans probably permitted the Welsh natives to live in these places, in return for auxiliary service. Some hillforts in the west of Ireland, and one in Wales (Pen-y-Gaer, Llanbedr-y-Cennin, Caerns.) are protected by *chevaux-de-frise* of pointed stones.

Hillforts are a study in themselves, and their great variety and their fine sites make them a good subject for amateur field-work, especially in relation to the field-systems by which their inhabitants lived, and on which more knowledge is needed. Many are called 'camps' on some maps.

ROMAN FORTS

Roman forts are very different in spirit from the prehistoric series. They are no longer sprawling and irregular, following the contours and adapting themselves to the ground, but are planned on uniform lines, and built by military engineers. Few Roman remains give a clearer picture of the Roman mentality and its power. There were several types; legionary fortresses, auxiliary forts, practice and campaign camps, Saxon Shore forts. The legionary fortresses, exemplified at Caerleon, can cover over 50 acres; they usually began with earthen ramparts, but during the second century were rebuilt in stone. The form was rectangular, with rounded corners (like a playing card) with gates in the middle of the sides, connected by roads. Inside were buildings, usually wooden, and therefore of which only the foundations now remain; a head-quarters building, a commander's house, barracks, stores, chapel, kitchens, sick-bays, latrines, etc. (fig. 14, below). Most of the larger forts are on this general pattern, and most sizeable towns also, being often laid out in the early days of the province by military engineers. The internal buildings were later reconstructed in stone, and at Caerleon a representative area can be seen. The auxiliary forts, mostly in the highland zone, were designed for more mobile, less heavily-armed, native troops; they usually have earth, clay or timber ramparts, and are also rectangular, with wooden internal buildings. Some, like Manchester, were rebuilt in stone. They are much smaller, often under ten acres. Many can be seen in the Pennines (Slack;

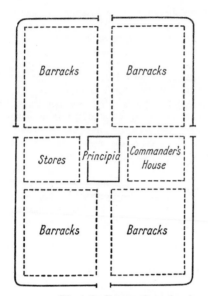

Ilkley), and in Scotland Campaign camps, such as those built during the march into Scotland (Ardoch; Inchtuthill), are similar to these, but if the legions were involved, larger. One or two forts occupied for a long time, were left in Scotland, such as Newstead on the Eildons, to watch the less friendly native tribes; in this territory also are the temporary camps at Oakwood, of which type there are many. Marching and practice camps can be seen at Chew Green (Northumberland), and Cawthorn (Yorks. NR); at Wodenlaw (Rox.) there are Roman practice siege-works round a native fort. Recent air surveys of the highland zone have revealed a large number of Roman

FIG. 14. Plan of a Roman fort, showing the typical 'playing-card' shape, and the roads and buildings inside

camps, well up into the east of Scotland (Pass of Grange, Banffshire, is the northernmost so far) and it is now becoming possible to reconstruct the history of the initial campaigns and the vicissitudes of the long occupation and struggles in the frontier regions.

Back on the east and south coasts of England, in the civil zone, the Romans built a series of forts, to defend the 'Saxon Shore' against raiders, from the late third century onward. These are magnificent works, having the flavour of town defences of the Constantinian type, with turrets and bastions. They run from Brancaster (Norfolk) to Portchester, which remains one of the most impressive Roman buildings in the country; inside it is a fair-sized Norman castle and a priory, while the adjacent harbour was used in Roman and mediaeval times, and no doubt earlier. Pevensey is also a good example; similar forts were built (e.g. Cardiff) against the Irish pirates who were raiding Wales. Further north, along the east coast, a line of signal stations was built to give warning to inland forts like Malton of the approach of raiders. Such are to be seen at Goldsborough, Ravenscar and Huntercliff in Yorkshire; they were also built in Cumberland, and inland in the Wall area and in Scotland (e.g. Mains Rigg, Over Denton, Perthshire).

Police posts on lonely roads are similar, like that at Maiden Castle on Stainmore. These were small square towers, often protected by a bank and ditch which was either round (Scarborough), or square with rounded corners (Perthshire).

ROMAN TOWN WALLS

Roman town walls were apparently normally of earth with a deep ditch outside, in the early days of the province (Silchester; Verulamium); they were moreover built on the fort pattern of a rectangle with rounded corners. Comparison of town plans will show that those towns which did not grow much retained this shape (except for suburban development outside the walls), throughout their history (e.g. Aldborough, Yorks.). The defences were rebuilt in stone around AD 200 in most cases (earlier at Aldborough), and the plan was often then altered to fit the new shape of the town, which by then had become irregular (e.g. Wroxeter, Cirencester). The earth bank was at this stage cut back, and a wall built into its outer side. These walls were sometimes, as at Verulamium, built partly to satisfy civic pride, but also, no doubt, because of the troubles in the north at this time; in some cases the walls were built by military engineers on their return from securing the northern defences after 211. In the case of London a fort was built outside the open city as a result of the native revolt of 61; this was near St Giles, Cripplegate. When the walls were built they were joined to this fort, which accounts for the sudden sharp turn of the wall at the north-west corner, a fact not realised until the recent excavations in the City. In the mid-fourth century the walls, in most cases neglected, were renovated, and strengthened in the current style, by the addition of bastions along the sides. Examples can be seen at Verulamium, and in the Multangular Tower at York. The old ditch had to be filled in in places to provide foundations for the bastions, and a new ditch was dug further out, not V-sectioned like the old one but wide and shallow: this also reflected a new method of warfare, using catapults from the bastions. The lower parts of the London wall, with bastions, can be seen in many places (Fore Street, etc.), surmounted by mediaeval work.

HADRIAN'S WALL

The greatest Roman military work in Britain, and one which perhaps gives the clearest picture of the nature of the military occupation and its problems, is Hadrian's Wall. The Romans had no formal frontier in the north at first; they consolidated their positions progressively from south to north with the aid of military roads and a scatter of forts, so

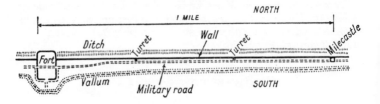

FIG. 15. Hadrian's Wall, Schematic plan and cross-section

that by the end of the 1st century the province of Britain consisted of peaceful country with towns and farms, on Roman lines, as far as Yorkshire (excluding Wales and the south-west). Beyond that was a zone held down directly by the army, centred on the great legionary fortresses, York, Chester, Caerleon, with outposted forts manned by auxiliaries from all over the Empire. In the north this land was once part of the powerful native confederation of Brigantia, which stretched from Trent to Tees; beyond it were other tribes in alliance or at least relations with the Brigantes, such as the Selgovae in South-east Scotland. Beyond them still, the obscure and independent tribes of the Highlands.

As the province settled down to a life of increasing stability and prosperity, these inhabitants of the military zone and beyond, deprived of the benefits of Roman civil life, made inroads from time to time on the richer lands, partly from envy, partly discontent, partly land-hunger. Sometimes these raids were concerted between the tribes, and assumed the dangerous proportions of full invasions. In 117–119 such a disaster overtook the loosely-garrisoned north, and struck into the civil south; the 9th legion, based on York, met with a still unknown catastrophe, and disappeared from history—its remnants, if any, being redrafted to other units.

The new emperor, Hadrian, an administrator of genius, visited Britain to consider what should be done to safeguard the province. On the analogy of the other frontiers in barbarian lands, such as central Europe, north Africa, he decided to create a formal frontier line, behind which defence could be more easily consolidated, and which would not only delay the Scottish tribes long enough to enable the army to prepare for their coming, but would separate the Brigantes from their friends in the north.

The governor Agricola (77–84) had already built a road, the Stanegate, to link his forts at Carlisle and Corbridge, and this line, across the narrowest part of Britain, was chosen by Hadrian for his new frontier; its military advantages were decisive. Hadrian, or the governor, Aulus Platorius Nepos, planned a vast multiple work, of which the parts and sequence are:

1. The barrier was, as first planned, 76 Roman miles[1] long, from Pons Aelius (Newcastle), along the northern hills of the Tyne and Irthing valleys to the Solway below the lowest ford (Bowness). The eastern 45 miles (from the Irthing) were a wall of stone, ten Roman feet wide (as planned—part was finished 8 feet wide) and about 16 feet high to the rampart walk; the western 31 miles a rampart of turf, 20 feet wide at the base and about 12 feet high.

2. This barrier was accompanied, where the ground dictated it, by a great ditch on the north side; it had fortlets, or milecastles, built on to the wall, every Roman mile, with two turrets between them. Patrolling was thus a simple matter, and all could be kept under continuous observation. These works were aimed at preventing infiltration by small parties or unauthorised travellers.

3. Defence against regular attacks was a different problem. To cope with this each milecastle had a wide sally-port, to enable the garrisons to issue against the enemy and pin them back against the wall, from which they could be dealt with. This meant keeping the garrison on the wall itself, not behind it as at first intended, and this change of plan occurred while the wall was still being built. So 16 forts were gradually built, covering all main lines of approach; the wall itself was extended eastwards along the north bank of the Tyne to Wallsend, another four miles.

4. Once this was done the whole work was sealed off from its hinterland, or vice versa, on the south side, by a strip or *limes* of cleared land, 'bordered by mounds and made into a formidable obstacle by a deep flat-bottomed ditch running along its axis', as Professor Richmond puts it—the Vallum.

5. A road was laid between the Vallum and the Wall.

6. The western half, the turf stretch, could then be replaced by a stone wall; this was begun during the building of the forts, when the wall from the North Tyne to five miles west of the Irthing was built at a thickness of eight feet. This was finally extended to the Solway.

7. The west flank of the system was protected along the Cumberland shore by milefortlets and towers, like those on the Wall, but with

[1] All measurements in this section (pp. 175-6) are in Roman feet and miles. The Roman foot is shorter than ours (on average 11.65 inches; it varies slightly from site to site). A Roman pace was 5 R. feet and 1,000 paces a Roman mile. A Roman mile is thus approximately 1,620 yards.

no connecting barrier. The Cumbrian approaches also were covered by forts like Bewcastle, Netherby and Birrens. These seem to be in the original plan.

8. The fort at Corbridge, which before the Wall protected the Tyne crossing, was transformed into a great base store, a few miles behind the Wall.

This great work was built between 122 and 128 or 130. It provoked immediate response in the form of pressure from the north, and had to be kept vigilantly guarded. This pressure could only be reduced, and men freed for service elsewhere, if southern Scotland were occupied; the emperor Antoninus Pius conceived the idea of another Wall between the Forth and the Clyde. This new barrier consisted of a high and steep wall of turf, along which were forts, smaller and closer spaced than those on Hadrian's Wall. There were no milecastles or turrets. This wall ran from Bridgeness on the Forth to Old Kilpatrick on the Clyde, 36½ miles; it had a V-shaped ditch on the north side, and a military way on the south. It was however strategically weaker than Hadrian's, needing outlying forts and garrisons at both ends. But it enabled Hadrian's Wall to be thrown open, and its garrisons to be reduced. The revolt of 155–8 changed the situation; land on both sides of Hadrian's Wall was held with difficulty, and rebuilding and reinforcements were needed. So Hadrian's Wall became more important again, and changes north of it were frequently made. The great invasion of 196 led to the abandonment of the Antonine Wall, after 54 years, and the rebuilding of the gravely damaged Hadrian's Wall, which remained the northern frontier thenceforward, until its final loss in 383, when it was not re-garrisoned.

The Wall forts (excluding Carvoran, which lies back, and was part of the older, Stanegate, system) were from 2 to 8 miles apart, depending on the terrain. A smaller type of 3–3½ acres housed 500 infantry, a larger type of 5–5½ acres was for 1,000 infantry or 500 cavalry. The complete garrison of the Wall was about 8,000 men. Each fort had a wall 5 feet thick, and was of the usual shape. They usually lay north and south across the wall, but a few, e.g. Housesteads, were parallel to it on the south side. The milecastles were about 75 by 60 feet, the turrets about 20 feet square; the road was about 16 feet wide; the ditch was V-sectioned, 27 feet wide, 9 feet deep, its inner edge about 20 feet from the wall. The Wall was built by the three legions then in Britain, assisted by Britons, and by units of auxiliaries. Each unit built a section, and its commander put up an inscribed stone to mark the completion; a century would have 50 yards to build.

Temples, shrines (e.g. the Mithraeum at Carrawburgh), baths and houses gradually appeared in the shelter of the Wall, and villages round the forts. The impact which the Wall makes on the modern visitor is profound; the best places to see it are Housesteads (pl. 12), and a mile or two on either side where it runs along the edge of the whin sill crags;

Chesters, where it crosses the North Tyne, and the base store at Corbridge. There are good museums at these places, and also at Newcastle University and at Tullie House, Carlisle.

The end of the Roman period, and the *sub-Roman* (and the post-Roman beyond, in the Highlands), gave rise to linear earthworks (see p. 182); native states arose, and native forts of many types were used.

Some of the old forts were used in defence against the *Saxons*, and some of the great dykes were built for this purpose. The Saxons themselves have left surprisingly few military works, and most of their local forts, or burghs, cannot be traced. Traces of the banks of that at Shoebury still exist, also at Lewes and at Hastings; the town ramparts of Wallingford may be Saxon. The Danish raids of the 9th century led the Saxons to build forts, or to adapt earlier works; such are an Iron Age fort at Witham (Essex), and a promontory fort at Burpham (Sussex). The circular fort at Warham St Mary, Norfolk, which contained objects of the 2nd century AD, may have been used and adapted by the Danes round AD 1000. Clearly there is room for field-work here. A unique type of defence was excavated at the Anglian royal town at Yeavering (Northumberland), but cannot be seen on the ground; this was a wooden wall, supported by two rows of posts set in a trench; a gateway (the wall was penannular) was flanked by two towers.

MOTTES

The Norman invasion led to the rapid building of earth castles, called mottes, all over the country; there are hundreds of them, and they are particularly numerous along the Welsh border. They are the bases of the mobile bands of cavalry, with archers, which were the Norman military units. Mottes are usually conical mounds of earth, with flat top, surrounded by a ditch; the mound may be high or low, or crater-shaped —it may 'improve' a natural knoll. Attached to it normally is a banked and palisaded enclosure, the bailey; this can have various shapes, and different relations with the mound, sometimes touching it, sometimes enclosing it. The top of the motte was ringed with a stout palisade, with a platform on the inner side; wooden steps led up one side. Inside this was a square wooden tower, used for storage of weapons, as a watchtower, a firing-post and a refuge; the bailey was for horses and food-storage. Mottes are illustrated in the contemporary Bayeux tapestry, and the superstructure proved by Mr B. Hope-Taylor's excavations at the mid-12th century motte at Abinger, Surrey. In some places there are two mottes near each other, and these, if not belonging to two separate manors (as at Kirkbymoorside, Yorks.) represent siege-works or resiting. The larger mottes with stone buildings like Guildford or Clifford's Tower, York (13th century), are better described as *castle-*

mounds. The motte and bailey idea evolved in England after the Norman Conquest, succeeding the earlier Norman earth ringworks, and preceding the stone castles. A motte is called a tump on the Welsh border, and a tomen in Wales (pl. 14, p. 137). Note the peles and bastles of the Scottish border.

Mottes are a very common feature of mediaeval towns and villages, and examples are unnecessary. But some mottes are not always recognised as such, and can indeed be mistaken, if not very high or if rounded off, for large barrows; some also are the subject of misleading local beliefs, such as the fine motte called Howe Hill, at North Deighton (Yorks. WR), long thought to be a burial mound for some of the dead of Marston Moor, and only recently proved to be a motte; in this case there are near-by mounds which represent associated buildings. A specialised form of motte and bailey is where the motte is low, more of a platform than a cone, with or without an encircling bank. Many of the Herefordshire 'tumps' are low platforms. Sometimes there is a large area with only a simple bank and a ditch round it (a ringwork); in these cases the earthwork can look very like a prehistoric fort, and only excavation could show when it was built (Caesar's Camp at Folkestone is an example). A ring-motte, such as The Crump, Berden, Essex, consists of a bank with outside ditch (sometimes wet), enclosing a flat circular space; the bank has no gap in it. A type recently discovered, from the air, shows only as a system of ditches, a circular one with an enclosure attached; any banks must have been very low.

A unique Norman fortification is Littledean Camp (Glos.), which consists of a very high and thick bank in an oval, with external ditch—part of this bank supports a motte (late 11th-early 12th century). At Farnham (Surrey) is a rare motte built up *pari passu* with a tower inside it (later surrounded by the present keep wall); Ascot Doilly (Oxon) has the same feature.

A few temporary camps, or siege castles, of the Norman period are known; such as the earthwork on Rackham Hill, Sussex (Siege of Arundel, 1102), and a camp on a fenland 'island' near where the Alderbrook joins the Ouse (Siege of Hereward the Wake at Ely by William I).

Castles usually had a village, or a town, crowding close to them for protection. A very interesting variant of this is where the village itself was enclosed in a bank running off from the bailey bank of the castle, so that the whole forms one defensive complex; a fine example of this is Pleshey (Essex). At Lee (Bucks.) a village enclosure includes two churches. Town walls of the Middle Ages are outside our scope.

MOATS

Besides being a feature of mediaeval castles, moats were frequently dug round houses of the later Middle Ages, not always for genuine defensive purposes, but sometimes as a symbolic survival of a certain prestige. Essex and Suffolk are particularly rich in them. They are usually about 10 ft. deep and 20 wide; they have vertical sides, which were originally often lined with wood or brick or stone. The defensive type were continuous, and crossed by a bridge (Ightham Mote, Kent), but the symbolic, and normally later, kind, have an earthen causeway left across one side. Most are square or oblong but not all; that at Broughton Hall, Send, Surrey, encloses an L-shaped space. There may be a low bank on the outside of the moat, but a few have one inside. When the house has vanished and the moat dry and ploughed down they may be mistaken for Roman camps, but the deciding factor is the situation, often low-lying and wet. Roman camps always had the ditch outside the bank, and were never deliberately built in wet ground.

LATER MILITARY WORKS

Little earthwork seems to have survived from the later mediaeval wars; a few forts were built in the 15th and 16th centuries (e.g. Southsea). The Armada scare in 1588 provoked the building of some defences; and these can be seen at Tilbury (Essex) and inside the Roman fort at Pevensey (Sussex). Town walls of this period, such as the fine set at Berwick-on-Tweed, are outside our scope. The Civil Wars left more marks; many castles and houses were put into a state of defence, and several new works were built. These were of earth, sometimes revetted with stone. Not many have survived, but they can be distinguished by their angular bastions and sharp corners. The defences of London have gone, but small sections remain of those of Bristol and Carmarthen. Several forts are to be seen round Newark (Notts.), the best being The Queen's Sconce; others are in Devon (Dartmouth) and Hunts. (Earith and Horsey Hill). At Basing House (Hants.) are three bastions of siegeworks; at Quarrendon (Bucks.) are trenches and gun-posts; the latter are low earthworks with a ditch round all four sides, but a bank only on three (also at Skipton, Yorks.; and Cornbury Park, Oxon). One of the earthwork forts on Lansdown Hill, Bath, may be of this date; and some prehistoric forts, etc., were used by the rival armies, such as Oliver's Battery, near Winchester, an early Romano-British enclosure re-used by Cromwell in 1645.

The next crop of military works is that of the Napoleonic War; the invasion scare caused the south-east coasts to be defended by a line of Martello Towers, circular brick buildings which can still be seen in holiday resorts, sometimes diverted far from their original purpose. 103 were built from Seaford (Sussex) to Aldborough (Suffolk), of which some 45 still exist; and there is a similar tower in Leith harbour. The Admiralty built a series of signal stations to get messages rapidly from

Portsmouth and Deal to London, and many of these survive; they are houses with flat roofs, sited on prominent hills, on which a semaphore was mounted. Examples are Semaphore House at Guildford and Telegraph Hill near Claygate (Surrey). Tilbury Fort (West Tilbury), Essex) is one of a series of forts along both sides of the Thames estuary. It grew out of a Henry VIII blockhouse, one of several; was altered in the Armada scare of 1588; redesigned in the late 17th century, with angle-bastions, outworks and two moats; altered again at the end of the 18th century. It was finally rebuilt in the 1860s, by which time bastions had been replaced generally by a polygonal plan. (Henry VIII's block-house had been removed before this.) In the 1890s concrete gun-positions were inserted. Tilbury thus reflects all the major theories and periods of fort-building since the early 16th century. Other Thames forts of the 1860s survive, such as Coalhouse (East Tilbury), still used, and Shornmead (Kent), ruined. The 1860s also produced the forts known as Palmerston's Follies, such as those round Portsmouth.

Another series of military works must be mentioned, the forts along the North Downs. In 1888 a scheme for the defence of London was drawn up, against an invasion prospect not very apparent now, and this included a defence line from Guildford to the Darent, then to the Thames at Dartford, and on the north bank to North Weald in Essex. This line was to consist of entrenched positions which were in fact never dug; but a series of thirteen storehouses to support them was actually built (from about 1895–7), and these can still be traced. Some of them are in private hands, and are worth a visit. They are not strictly forts, but were commonly called such from the beginning; they consist of massive earth banks, surrounded by a moat faced with concrete. There are two at Guildford (Henley Grove and Pewley Hill), and others at Boxhill, Betchworth, Reigate, Westerham, Farningham, and else-where.

Militia exercises in the 19th century produced mounds and trenches, and those on Farley Heath, Surrey, for long confused the elucidation of the Celtic temple site there. The last two wars have also left many similar traces, particularly on the soft soils of south-east England. Practice trenches of the 1914–18 war; gun-posts, and tank-traps of the last war, can still be found, and they can still confuse. Practice diggings are of course still made. From the air, the parks and commons of south London are in places dotted with the earth-scars of such works. Tank-runs on moors and commons can be useful to the archaeologists, in breaking the surface and exposing a flint implement; many important mesolithic sites, in (e.g.) Hampshire and Yorkshire, have been dis-covered by this means. Craters of practice bombs (1914–18) and real bombs (1939–45) are often seen, and when old and worn down can be taken for hut circles and the like. (Linear tank-traps and tank-runs can sometimes be taken for ancient tracks.) Some long ditches in open country, such as downland, were cut to prevent the landing of aircraft. Craters can also be caused by meteorites, ice-meteorites, or lightning-strikes.

The butts of rifle ranges sometimes take the form of long straight banks of earth (e.g. Puttenham Common, Surrey). Magazines are usually protected by earth banks, but these are not often seen without the central buildings.

LINEAR EARTHWORKS

There are a large number of stretches of bank and ditch, sometimes with two banks, particularly on the lighter soils of England, but in most other parts also. They may be classified in two sections, those built for farming purposes or as boundaries, and the defensive ones.

Wessex is particularly rich in the farming type; most of them date from the Late Bronze or Early Iron Ages, but a few may be of Roman date. The purpose can often be determined by the relation of the bank to the ditch; when the bank is sometimes on one side of the ditch, sometimes on the other, whichever was easiest to build, then the work is a boundary. When the bank is always on the higher side of the ditch, the work is defensive, against the people approaching up the slope. Ditches with a bank on each side are usually cattle-ways, to enable animals to cross land without damaging crops on either side, and also sometimes without being seen; a few of these have two protected ways, with three banks, for traffic in both directions. There are several of these on the South Downs in Sussex, and a good example on Wingreen Hill, west of Salisbury (across the Ox Drove—field systems can be seen near by). The banks and ditches in these cases are about 4 yards wide. Linear earthworks can be from a hundred yards or so to several miles long. Examples of pre-Roman works are Grim's Ditch (Berks.), Quarley Hill Tilshead (Wilts.). Much more knowledge is needed before the ranches which these earthworks represent can be fully understood and mapped, and this is a field for amateur work. Lines of pits, found particularly on the east Midland gravels, are the quarries for Iron Age boundary banks.

Saxon and mediaeval ditches are also common. They also consist of boundaries of various kinds; deer-parks were often enclosed in this way, like those at Highclere (Berks.), and Hall Park, Walton (Yorks. WR). Some mediaeval estate boundaries in the south-west take the form of a high bank with a narrow lane or walk half-way up the slope along one side; these sometimes pass into the ditch and bank type (e.g. Somerton, Somerset). Many double hedgerows are boundaries, not tracks. Parish and shire boundaries often follow linear earthworks (e.g. Gryme's Dyke, Lexden, Essex), or are marked by an ordinary farm ditch (e.g. at Guildford, Surrey, on the former boundary of the parishes of Stoke and Worplesdon). Parish boundaries are often farm boundaries too. Old boundaries can thus afford clues to something even earlier. The age of a hedge can be assessed roughly: if there is only one species of tree or shrub in any thirty-yard stretch, the hedge is up to 100 years old; if two species, 200, and so on.

Unexpected and unexplained kinks, bulges or deviations in boundaries should be carefully investigated; parish boundaries were mostly fixed by Domesday, and a kink implies that some building or thing was in the way or had to be included in a particular side of the line—a

Roman building, perhaps, or a barrow. An example of this is at Chilworth, Surrey, where the mystery has not yet been solved.

A few shire boundaries are of bank and ditch form; one, a cross-valley type, has recently been found at Westerham, on the Kent-Surrey border. The great sub-Roman or Saxon dykes are not always easy to classify as between boundaries and defensive; but most are military, even when, like Offa's Dyke, they served both purposes.

Offa's Dyke (pl. 13, p. 136) is the most impressive of the military linear earthworks, and in many ways typical of them all; it was built by Offa, king of Mercia, in the 8th century, as a boundary between his kingdom and the Welsh. It faces Wales, that is, its ditch is on the Welsh side. It runs from the north coast near Prestatyn to the Severn by Chepstow (actually Tidenham, Glos.), where it can be well seen; the best parts are between Presteigne and Montgomery. It has the at first sight puzzling feature of being discontinuous, and some of the broken stretches appear to have little point; but the explanation is that when it was built the dyke ran across open country only; it was not needed, so not built, across marshes, or through dense forest, or thorn thicket, which were impenetrable. Some of these features have now changed, leaving the ends of the stretches of dyke no longer resting on these natural obstacles.

Not many dykes are as well attested historically as Offa's, but most of them conform to much the same pattern. Many are still undated, but it looks as if most of them were made in late Roman or post-Roman times. A few are earlier, like the series of linear ditches across the Ickneild Way in the southern Chilterns, which are Iron Age territorial boundaries. That at Aberford (Yorks. WR), was built to halt the Roman advance to the north. Wessex has some fine examples, such as Bokerley Dyke, built in several stages, probably at first (*c.* AD 330) to protect grazing grounds, later as a bulwark against raiders into Dorset in the late 4th century, finally against the Saxon advance. Wansdyke is in two parts, one in NE Somerset, one along the north edge of the Wessex downs; this was aimed at containing the Saxons in their push to the south-west.

There are innumerable others, long and short, like the Grim's Ditches of Berks. and the Chilterns; the Fleem Dyke and Devil's Dyke in Cambridgeshire, barring the Ickneild Way; the Beech Bottom Dyke (Herts.), which may have been built as a barrier across a traffic-route rather than a tribal defence (this is Belgic, and has a V-sectioned ditch); some which control Roman roads, when the Saxons were using them to advance along, or indeed in wars of Celt against Celt. The exact situation is rarely known, and few of the wars or threats which caused dykes and forts to be built are quite clear to us. In Scotland also there are extensive dykes; the Catrail or Picts' Work, in Selkirk and Roxburgh, is several miles long, and is of Dark Age date. Perhaps the latest dyke is the Scots' Dyke, built after the agreement of 1552 to define the west end of the Border; this has a bank between two ditches.

The banks and ditches of promontory forts have been dealt with on page 169, but mention must be made here of the class of cross-dykes on ridges, as in the Cheviot and Teviot areas and the similar cross-spur dykes in Sussex. These seem not to be the same as the hollow cattleways mentioned above, but may well be prehistoric boundaries. Spectacular examples such as the (Iron Age) Double Dykes across the landward end of Hengistbury Head (Hants.), are no doubt both defensive and boundary at the same time; these are on low ground, which is unusual.

There are a large number of still enigmatic linear earthworks and enclosures in the eastern half of Yorkshire. Many of those on the Wolds are probably connected with the great ranches and horse-breeding stations of the Iron Age and Roman periods; some of the enclosures have double or triple banks (Aldro; Calais Wold, etc.). Huggate Dykes are a remarkable group of five parallel banks across a ridge; works of this kind may have been built to stop the advance of the chariot-using Parisi (Iron Age), but may after all be pastoral. Argam Dyke, five miles long with three banks, may be pastoral or defensive, but the Danes' Dyke, across the Flamborough headland, is most likely defensive. The dyke systems on the moors north of the Pickering-Scarborough road are quite different. Here there are several sets of long banks, either parallel or meeting in a point or a narrow gap; some (Givendale Head, Allerston) have pits at intervals between the banks. The Scamridge Dykes, Ebberston, are only the most celebrated of many. These systems are in the Anglian royal deer-park, and they may well be for driving animals for slaughter, either at the ends of the runs, or by means of the pits. On Levisham Moor is a system with enclosures attached to it, which could have been for driving animals into along the long dykes. Some parishes, like Hutton Buscel, are full of earthworks of various kinds.

A very minor form of linear earthwork is the bank and ditch thrown up to delimit some of the 18th and 19th century enclosures or as field or estate boundaries; these were often planted with hedges or trees. The treeless remains of these can be seen crossing fields when the pattern has been changed. They are often best preserved in woodland, or where little or no ploughing has been done, e.g. along the track from Farley Heath to Albury (Surrey).

Linear earthworks have also been built by recluses to protect their privacy, as at Great Canfield, Essex, where a bank 50 yards long and 7 or 8 ft. high, with a wet ditch, was thrown up by a hermit at the end of the 19th century. At Amersham recently a bank 200 yards long with trees and a fence was erected to separate Beel House from a new school. Ditches have even been dug to keep gypsies off commons.

Banks dividing crofts along the contours, were for containing the flow of water down the slope.

THEATRES, MOOTS, ETC.

AMPHITHEATRES

Many Roman towns in Britain had amphitheatres for public games and spectacles. Most of these were close outside the walls of the town; they had excavated arenas, the earth from which was piled up to form the banks on which the seating was laid. Some took advantage of natural slopes. Most places had simple earthen ones, and some may still await discovery; that at Chichester (now built over), was only recognised in 1935. At Aldborough (Yorks. WR) the mounds and hollows of Studforth Hill may be an amphitheatre, and not a motte, but this has never been conclusively determined. The well-known and imposing amphitheatre at Dorchester, Dorset (Maumbury Rings), was an Early Bronze Age henge adapted by the Romans; it was used again in the Civil War for the siege of Dorchester, and the artillery platforms made then in the banks can still be seen. Amphitheatres vary of course in size; that at Caerleon (Mon.) has an arena 200 by 150 ft., and could seat about 6,000 people; its banks were faced with stone, and the arena itself was limited by low stone walls cemented over. At the other end of the scale is the little oval one at the mining town of Charterhouse-on-Mendip (Som.).

Only four theatres are known in Roman Britain, at St Albans, Colchester, Canterbury and Brough, the last recorded in an inscription only, but others may well exist. Only that at St Albans is anything like complete, but this gives a very clear picture of the sophisticated building, on a classical (Greek) model, which a major town was able to support. It is an open circular building with tiers of seats, a central space for dancing and spectacles, and a stage with dressing-rooms, etc., abutting on to this.

Mediaeval plays were performed in churches or public places, and in the 16th and 17th centuries halls of houses or castles were used; but now also special theatres were built, such as those in Southwark (the Globe, etc.), long since disappeared. But a few open-air theatres were built in this period, like the 17th century one at Crowhurst (Surrey). In a garden at Weybridge (Surrey) there is a mound on which performances were given to an audience seated in front of it; this is associated with Fanny Kemble and Mrs Siddons (late 18th century).

MOOTS

It will be convenient to deal with moots at this point. Meeting-places where tribal business could be conducted, as well as festivals held, would be needed at all periods. In primitive communities a distinction between secular and religious matters was not always clear, and tribal meetings doubtless took place at 'sacred' sites such as the henge monuments. Many sacred places were however natural grooves, hills, etc., hence it is not always possible to identify them. But a long folklore tradition attached to a site, particularly if doubled by physical remains such as barrows or circles, establishes a probability. St Martha's Hill near Guildford, with Bronze Age earth circles and dancing on Good Friday until quite recent years, is such a sacred hill, where secular as well as religious ceremonies were no doubt held as far back as the Bronze Age. But the positive evidence dates from post-Roman times. The early Saxons held folk-moots, which gave a basis for the later hundred-moots, meetings of a group of parishes every four weeks, from which appeal could be made to the less frequent shire-moots.

Hundred-moots were held at some convenient or conspicuous spot. Sometimes this was on cross-roads or where parish boundaries met; Nassaborough hundred meeting place (Northants.) is where three parishes meet, and also on the crossing of King Street and another Roman road—this is recorded in the 10th century. Rosemary Hill, Blackheath (Surrey) is also on the intersection of boundaries and local tracks. Sometimes moots were held in ancient hillforts (Badbury Rings and Eggardon, Dorset), or at prominent trees or stones, or wooden posts (Maidstone, Brixton, stones; Whitstable, a post; Copthorne (Surrey), a tree). Often a natural hill was chosen, as Claro Hill, Allerton Mauleverer (Yorks. WR), which is a morainic knoll; Spellow Hill, near Boroughbridge; or Swanborough (Sussex). Barrows were frequently used, and sometimes had their tops flattened to seat the chief men; Cuckhamsley (Berks.); Mutlow, Wendens Ambo (Essex). A variant of this was to raise a flat mound specially for the purpose; these are usually lower and wider than barrows. A Moot-lowe near Alsop Dale in Derbyshire is four feet high and 20 yards across: in Weston Wood, Albury (Surrey) was until lately a large flat mound with a berm, which may be an 18th century landscaping feature, but with the added interest of being associated with a tradition of dancing at certain festivals. There is indeed strong probability that popular ceremonies and festivals were held at the same place as moots. At Kings Caple (Herefordshire) is a flat mound with a bank or rim of earth round its top, known to have been a dancing-ground (this village also has a sun-dial, mounting-steps and a square dovecote).

FLAT MOUNDS

In the highland zone flat mounds are also found; at Stirling the Mote-hill was also used for games; that at Hamilton is motte-like; the famous

Tynwald Hill in the Isle of Man is in four steps, and a flat top 6 ft. across. It should be borne in mind that flat-topped mounds can be many things—a motte, a moothill or a dancing place; some barrows have flat tops (Gilling, Yorks. NR), apart from the type called platform-barrows; some were made to support posts or beacons for guidance through forests or wild country, as perhaps a mound near Woking; some had a wayside cross on them, some a gibbet (e.g. Gallows Hill, Inveraray, Argyll), while a windmill mound is not always distinguishable from these. Silbury has a flat circular platform on its top. Two exceptional meeting-places are the great complex at Tara, Eire, where was the stone on which the High Kings were crowned; and the most unusual wedge-shaped building, excavated at the Anglian royal town at Yeavering, Northumberland, which was a sort of segment of a theatre with the tiers of seats facing the 'chairman', presumably the king himself; this arrangement may await discovery elsewhere.

There is scope for field-work here, and the picture is still not complete. The folk-traditions need fuller study, and new evidence can still be collected from village people, which can throw light on the uses to which the various mounds, etc., were put; place names and boundaries should be carefully followed up.

A few dried-out ponds have been used as village meeting or games-places, even in pre-Roman times (Park Brow and Falmer, Sussex; Woodcuts, Dorset). In Cornwall 'rounds' were built in the Middle Ages, depressed rings with earth bank and ditch round them, on which tiers of stone seats were put (Perran; St Just); a few also exist in Wales (Llanidan).

BULL-RINGS AND COCKPITS

Most sports took place on open sites, or at traditional spots, which cannot now be recognised unless recorded, but some needed special constructions. Among these were bull- and bear-baiting and cock-fighting.

Bull-rings are commemorated in many towns by street-names (e.g. Birmingham and Wakefield), but few have survived. At Northallerton the site of one is preserved in the market place. The name is also given to the iron rings set in a stone or post, to which the animal was tethered for baiting. Some of these have been preserved, as at Snitterton (Derbyshire), Cellarhead (Staffs.), Brading (IOW), Horsham (Sussex), and Loppington (Salop); the famous one at Eyam (Derbys.) is covered over. A bull-pit, to keep the animals in when not being baited, is at Buckland Dinham (Som.).

Cockpits were either hollows in the ground (usually covered by a house), or on the tops of low mounds; there are some in Wales—

Aberavon; Llandwrog (Caernarvonshire); of two on the Boverton estate, near Llantwit Major (Glam.), one is walled. One with a sunk circle surrounded by a raised bank is at Embsay, near Skipton (Yorks. WR). A special type is that on Chislehurst Common (Kent), which is an oval pond-like depression some $4\frac{1}{2}$ ft. deep and 125 ft. long, with a circular space inside marked by a shallow bank and ditch. The famous bull-ring, bear-pits, cockpits, etc., of London and Southwark have not survived.

Badgers were usually hunted with dogs, but they were baited as well, and a pit for this purpose survives at Ipsden, Oxon. Pits were also used by farmers to catch badgers, about 5 ft. deep and 4 ft. long, narrowed at the top and bottom, and wider in the middle.

WATER SUPPLY

PONDS

Primitive man of course had to rely on natural sources such as springs, streams and ponds for his water, and evidence of artificial supply before the Iron Age is very doubtful. The first device seems to have been the pond, and some farm and village ponds may have a long history. Most villages are on new sites, but a few appear to be on pre-Saxon sites (those on hilltops, for instance); Ashmore, in Cranborne Chase, is built round an embanked pond which may be Iron Age or Romano-British—here the church is on the edge of the village, and so later than its foundation; Buttermere, Wilts., has a similar pond. But most farm and village ponds are unlikely to be older than Saxon or mediaeval. The date of **dewponds** is obscure, but some of them may be Iron Age, although most are modern; they were carefully made with beds of straw and puddled clay, with a layer of loose flints above that, and banks of chalk; they are found mainly on the chalk uplands (e.g. Orna Mere, Alton Priors, Wilts., at least 9th century). The well-known example near the hill-fort of Chanctonbury Ring (Sussex), made in 1874, was damaged in the last war. **Spring-ponds** were dug in Roman times down to the water-table, and show now as deep embanked pits; a good one is on the Everley and Pewsey boundary (Wilts.). A few other ponds of presumed Roman date survive, such as the Skemp Pond on Farley Heath (Surrey). In former mediaeval open-field country, particularly in dry areas, small ponds can be found in the fields among the ridge and furrow of the old strips and furlongs. These are not modern ponds to water animals at pasture, but lie in field corners and can often be shown to cut through the remains of mediaeval ploughing. The pre-enclosure ponds were along the balks (the access-ways between the strips): they were used for watering the plough-animals, and some may have been a source of marl and clay as well. Square farmyard ponds with dry-stone walled banks are a feature of south-west Wales. Streams were sometimes widened to make small ponds.

WELLS

Prehistoric wells and shafts are known, some of them ritual. Wells were used by the Romans, and can be seen on the sites of their villas (Colliton Park, Dorchester, Dorset), although some, like Chedworth, had springs, often protected by a shrine to the local water-nymph or goddess. Wells and pumps were a feature of village greens or streets, and were usually the only, communal, water-supply (e.g. Bamburgh, Northumberland). Abbeys, castles and great houses had them also, and a fine example is that in the cloisters at Fountains Abbey. Wells, cisterns and pumps were often protected from the weather, for the convenience of their users, by wooden, brick or stone shelters; examples are the pump-shelters at Honingham and East Tuddenham, Norfolk, and the elaborate one at Abinger, Surrey: the Tudor pump or well-houses at Long Melford, Suffolk, and Little Walsingham, Norfolk; the 17th century ones at Abbot's Hospital, Guildford, and at Charterhouse, London. A few conduit-houses, over cisterns on a pipe-line, survive, as at Coombe, Surrey (16th century), and Rye, Sussex. A long conduit, as well as having cistern-houses, was divided into sections, for repair purposes, and the joints, with stop-cocks, etc., were protected by small buildings called 'tamkins'. One of these, on the pipe-line to Hampton Court (1516) survives on Coombe Wood golf course, near Kingston-upon-Thames.

The ornamental pavilions over wells or springs at spas should not be overlooked, such as those over Tewit and St John's Wells, Harrogate (1842). A pump in an urban setting (surmounted by a street-lamp) can be seen in Bedford Row, London, WC1. There is a signpost combined with a pump at Dorking, Surrey.

TOWN SUPPLIES

Piped water supplies were a Roman introduction; some towns had very elaborate systems. Lincoln had a complete series, not only of sewers and drains, but an aqueduct fed from springs tapped by pumps; the main was of tile pipes jacketed in concrete. Other towns had gravity supplies in underground timber pipes with iron collars at the joins (Silchester, Caerwent, Caister by Norwich). An open leet or water-course (a contour canal), was used at Dorchester (Dorset), several miles long; this can still be well seen at Fordington Bottom. Wroxeter had lead and timber pipelines sufficient for private houses as well as the public buildings. These things are not ordinarily visible, having mostly been discovered in excavations, but a few short stretches of Roman leet can be seen on sites such as forts on the Wall, and lead piping, still in use, at Bath. Similar courses can be seen in mediaeval castles, abbeys, etc. Lead piping was in frequent use in the 16th century (e.g. Hampton Court) and later.

Wooden water pipes were a standard method of supply for towns in the 17th and 18th centuries, and may still frequently be seen exposed when streets are taken up. The earliest were laid down by the New River company c. 1610 (this company laid some 400 miles in all). Most are of elm, and vary in length from about 5 ft. to as much as 42 ft., but a length of 10 or 12 ft. is common; the bore is about 5 or 7 in. They were often fitted by their tapered end into the larger end of the next pipe without collars. They continued to be laid until about 1810. These pipes are to be found not only in the Georgian parts of London, but in towns all over the country. Similar pipes occur in houses before 1600, and were also used in mines and quarries.

The maze of passages beneath Exeter was made for the city's mediaeval water supply.

A very interesting example of a large-scale water-supply system is the New River, a canal built in the early 17th century (1609–13) to bring fresh water into London. London was expanding beyond the capacity of its wells to keep supplied; the water-table was falling, and the Thames and Lea becoming less suitable (unfiltered) for domestic use. Sir Hugh Myddelton, against opposition, cut a canal 10 ft. wide and 4 ft. deep for 38¾ miles from springs at Chadwell and Amwell (Herts.) to Islington (London). This New River has since been enlarged, and reservoirs added, but its course is very largely as Myddelton planned it, except for some shortening. It now ends at Green Lanes; it can be seen at many points, and in London conveniently where it crosses Seven Sisters Road, and, disused and partly dry, in Clissold Park, Stoke Newington.

TROUGHS, FOUNTAINS AND CISTERNS

Watering-troughs for horses, farm stock and dogs can still be seen on farms, but not so often now in streets (and if so usually Victorian). Farm troughs are mostly of rough stone, and of indeterminate age, but some may be 18th century or even earlier. Hooded troughs exist in Yorkshire (e.g. Old Hall Farm, Silsden), but the purpose of the stone hood is unknown. Troughs and drinking-fountains were set up in Liverpool and then London from the 1850's, and few fountains are earlier than this. In 1746 the Corporation of London erected a pump in Lamb's Conduit Street (WC1); the inscription which was set up over this pump is now built into the wall of a new building.

Cisterns of lead or stone can be found at old houses (a fine stone one is at Low Hall, Appletreewick, Yorks. WR).

A feature of Harwich (Essex) are the 'rainbacks'—water-storage pits underneath old houses and yards.

CANALS AND MARSHES

CANALS

Canals followed the turnpikes as the transport system of the earlier phases of the Industrial Revolution, but they were seriously affected by the changed conditions of the latter half of the 19th century. Their present situation and possible future do not of course come into this book, but a new era seems to be dawning (1967).

The size of boats used on the early navigations varied with the depth and width of the rivers and the traffic carried, and this affected the size of the canals, which were usually built to take a particular local traffic, and in any case had differing types of country to run through. For hilly country, and to save building costs and water, many canals were built to take boats of about 30 tons, with locks only 7 ft. wide. This variation of size hampered the canals when they had to compete with the railways. and was one of the causes of their decline; frequent transhipment was uneconomic, and rebuilding was out of the question. The result is an incomplete system of relatively short lengths of various width and depth. The largest are the main canalised rivers (Severn, Trent, Weaver) and certain canals taking sea-going ships (**Manchester Ship Canal, Gloucester and Berkeley, Caledonian, Crinan**); next comes the bulk of the river navigations, and most canals north of the Trent and the **Trent and Mersey Canal**, with locks at least 12 ft. wide; after these are the 'narrow' canals, with 7 ft. locks, which run in a band from SE to NW England (the **Oxford**, etc.); finally, the tub-boat canals, now derelict, in Shropshire and the south-west, had boats 18–21 ft. long and about 5 ft. wide, usually working in trains and being raised to higher levels by inclined planes instead of locks. There was once a fifth class, the mine canals of the early days, such as the **Duke of Bridgewater's** at Worsley, which had 42 miles underground.

---

19. THE TEXTURE OF POTTERY (C). Mediaeval pottery is often rather thick and coarse; it may be thickly glazed in green, brown or yellow, or may have painted or incised decoration. Stoneware is very hard indeed.

(*a*) *14th century*, part of the base of a jug, showing thumb-pit ornament.

(*b*) *14th century*, the handle of the same jug, slashed to prevent distortion in firing.

(*c*) and (*d*) *14th century*, glazed ware.

(*e*) and (*f*) *16-17th century*. Salt-glazed stoneware. The neck of a jug, showing the 'mask' ornament, representing Cardinal Bellarmine.

a

b

c

d

e

f

CENTIMETRES
INCHES

20. EARLY FIELDS. *Above*, the rectangular pattern of "Celtic Fields", (Iron Age and Roman periods) (Fyfield Down, Wilts.). *Below*, "strip-lynchets", cultivation-terraces on the side of a hill. They are usually Anglo-Saxon or Mediaeval (Bishopstone north, Wilts.)

The navigations and canals were designed to serve (and indeed they deeply influenced it also) the pattern of trade of the years 1700–1850 (only two are later than this); this trade was the movement of coal and raw materials in industrial areas, and coal, limestone, and road and building materials and farm produce in rural areas. The **Leeds and Liverpool** still carries coal from the Yorkshire pits to canal-side mills in the Aire valley; but in general this pattern has been broken. Modern canal traffic is in quite short hauls. But in 1840 the 4,250 miles of canal (of which about half are still open) and the 22,000 miles of turnpike road formed a coherent system, with a few tramroads and railways, and the coasting trade. The railway boom, which reached its height about 1845, eventually brought about the dislocation and final disruption of this balanced system.

The first canal in Britain was the **Fossdyke**, built by the Romans; it runs from Torksey on the Trent to Lincoln, was restored in 1121, improved in 1782 and 1840, and is still in use (the Roman Car Dyke is also still in use as a land drain in the Fens). The next was the **Exeter Canal** (1566), from Countess Wear to Exeter, extended to near Topsham in 1677, enlarged and lengthened to Turf in 1820–30. Most rivers were navigable, but shipping was hindered by the frequent mills; boats had to pass through a movable section of a weir at each mill, and after the Civil War growing trade caused many rivers to be 'improved'. Locks were built to control the current. By the middle of the 18th century many smaller rivers had been so treated, and there were 1,200 miles of river passable for barges.

The industrial revolution greatly increased this demand; in 1759 the Duke of Bridgewater obtained an Act to build a canal from his coalmines at Worsley to Manchester. This was carried out by James Brindley (by 1761), who even got the canal over the Irwell by means of an aqueduct. This canal was extended to Runcorn on the Mersey. Brindley was much in demand by other canal promoters, and from 1761 to 1772 he planned, surveyed and partly built a network of canals linking Trent and Mersey; the **Coventry and Oxford**, linking the Grand Trunk with the Thames; and others. About this time the **Forth and Clyde** canal was built and the Thames was linked to the Severn via Stroud. The mania was in full swing by 1792, and lasted till 1810; many towns subscribed to bring them into the system by branch canals, and more longer ones were cut—the **Kennet and Avon**, the **Wilts. and Berks., The Grand Junction** (London to Braunston, with links with Leicester and the Trent, and with Birmingham), two from Lancashire to Yorkshire. Passenger boats were run as well as freight; e.g. on the **Lancaster** and the **Glasgow, Paisley and Ardrossan**, and to Chester races as early as 1776. After a long gap the **Manchester Ship Canal** was built in 1894. A Government enquiry in 1906 produced a valuable report (not implemented), but decay went on; in

1947 the British Transport Commission took over most waterways, with certain exceptions, including the Manchester Ship Canal, the River Thames, the Yorkshire Ouse, the Nene and Great Ouse system, and the waterways of East Anglia.

The first canals were based on existing rivers, with branches, by-passes or links. The latter, which cross a watershed (e.g. Thames to Severn), have many locks, and a reservoir and pumping-station at the top. Others are cross-country (**Grand Junction**), following a fairly direct line; some join an industrial region with a port (S Wales). Later, canals became straighter, and embankments, cuttings, tunnels, or aqueducts were needed (the **Shropshire Union** is a good example of this). The **Leeds and Liverpool** is a contour canal; the **Oxford Canal** was converted from a contour to a straight canal in 1829–34, and the old curves can still be seen. Similarly, a navigation, such as the **Wey** (to Guildford 1653, to Godalming 1762), was based on cutting across the bends of the river, as well as on dredging and controlling what part of the river itself could be used. A 17th century canal, with 12 locks and independent water-supply, from near Stamford on the Welland to Market Deeping ($8\frac{1}{2}$ miles), was rediscovered in 1958.

Subsidence produced problems, and many northern canals have their banks raised and strengthened at weak points. Towpaths were not used in early navigations (where men hauled the barges), but all canals (which used horses) have them. Horses are still used for example on the River Lea and the **Birmingham and Fazeley** canal. Distance posts at $\frac{1}{2}$ mile intervals can be seen on many canals. Basins and loading-points had to be specially built, and Stourport is an example of a whole town created for the canals; many wharves can be seen, some disused, some in remote villages. At junctions, e.g. Braunston, a toll-house and warehouse can be seen as well. Lockhouses are often of distinctive type on a particular canal, such as the 'cottages' (*c.* 1770) on the **Staffs. and Worcs.,** the round houses on the **Thames and Severn,** and the classical bridge-houses on the **Gloucester and Berkeley.** Inns grew up for the canal workers (e.g. the Navigation Tavern at Mirfield, Yorks. WR).

Bridges also can be characteristic and individual, not only road or accommodation bridges, but towpath crossings (roving bridges). Wooden bridges occur, and some swing or lift bridges; on the **Stratford on Avon** canal the roving bridges have a slit across them to take the towrope without unhitching it. Tunnels had to be built on some canals; their course above ground is often marked by a line of spoil-heaps, deposited above the tunnel from shafts. Standedge (5,415 yards long) on the **Huddersfield Narrow** canal, and Sapperton (3,817 yards) on the **Thames and Severn,** are now disused; Strood (3,909 yards) on the **Thames and Medway,** is now used by the railway; the longest in use is the Blisworth (3,056 yards) on the **Grand Union**; Harecastle New (2,926 yards) on the **Trent and Mersey** is accompanied by

Brindley's old narrow tunnel, now disused. When a tunnel had no towpath, boats had to be poled along by pressing against the roof or sides (the marks are still there), or 'legged' through, by men lying on the top of the boat, or on planks at its sides.

Aqueducts were needed in some places, the greatest being Telford's masterpiece at Pontcysyllte over the Dee (**Shropshire Union**); those at Chirk, Marple and near Bradford-on-Avon are also noteworthy, and there are many smaller ones of interest, including Telford's early iron one at Longdon-on-Tern (Staffs.), made of Coalbrookdale iron.

Canals are part of the water and drainage system of the country, and feeders and outlets are necessary. Differences of level are overcome by locks ('pound'-locks, superseding the 'flash'-locks at the weirs); most of these are of brick or stone, but at Beeston on the **Shropshire Union** is one of cast-iron, with a bed of sand. Some have turf banks, and timber framing (**Kennet and Avon**). Design of gates varies. Sometimes flights of locks had to be built, and spectacular examples can be seen at Devizes (**Kennet and Avon**), with 29 locks, and Tardebigge (**Worcs. and Birmingham**), with 30. Where the locks adjoin, with common gates, they are known as staircases or risers (Bingley, on the **Leeds and Liverpool**, has two groups of these; and Northgate, Chester). Inclined planes were built in a few places, where boats could be hauled up a slope to a higher level (Morwellham, **Tavistock Canal**, 237 ft.; Hobbacott Down, **Bude Canal**; The Hay, Coalport). Vertical lifts were also used, and one is still in use at Anderton, on the Weaver.

It is a good plan to explore a stretch of live canal, then to trace a disused one. An accessible example of the first is the **Regent's Canal** in London (1820). In the short stretch from Paddington to Camden Town can be seen: a tunnel (Maida Hill, with poling scars); cuttings, basins and branches; 'winding holes' for turning; Macclesfield Bridge in Regent's Park is a product of the Coalbrookdale Ironworks—it was blown up by accident, and the doric iron columns were replaced with their best surviving sides outwards; grooves worn by towropes can be seen on bridges, parapets and walls (some canals have iron strips, rollers or wheels on these places); horse-ramps along the towpath, so that horses which had fallen in could walk along in the water until they reached a ramp and could regain the towpath.

A clearly-traced disused canal is the **Wey and Arun** (1816, abandoned 1868). This leaves the Wey by the factories at Shalford south of Guildford, and runs 18½ miles to Newbridge. Its course, and some of its 23 locks, can be seen either as an empty, but very damp, wide ditch (e.g. at Birtley, near Bramley, where from a track just east of the railway a wet section also begins; also across Run Common); or as rough and weedy, but still full of water (Birtley, and between Cranleigh and Loxwood).

The folk-art of the old narrow boats is worth a mention—hand-painted sides, deck-houses, buckets, etc., with 'roses and castles'. Standardisation has nearly killed these, but a few can still be found. Incidentally, the word 'navvy' recalls the men who dug the 18th century navigations.

A related matter to canals is the isolated **dock** often for handling a particular commodity; a fine example is that at Bullo Pill, on the Severn near Newnham (Glos.), built in the early 19th century for shipping coal from the Forest of Dean. That next to Battersea Church, London, is mediaeval in origin.

There is a fine wooden **crane** on the riverside at Guildford (Surrey), worked by a treadmill.

MARSHES AND SEA-WALLS

Many, if not most of our rivers, particularly in the lowland zone, are still liable to flood, and this was a major factor in determining where men with only primitive equipment could live. Moreover, the water-table has been steadily falling, partly owing to drainage and partly to increased population, but before it did the problem for primitive man was even more insoluble. The waterlogged areas also harboured liver-fluke and foot-rot; fortunately for early man, lighter soils were also the best grazing areas. The Romans and Saxons tackled the problem, but the position then became complicated by the slow sinking of south-east England; even faster sinking of the Thames estuary has caused the mean sea-level at London Bridge to be 12 ft. above what it was in Roman times.

Taking the Thames at London as an example, although the Romans built a wall to contain the river, by mediaeval times the south bank was a vast sprawling marsh; Southwark was criss-crossed by drainage ditches, and even on the north bank, the sites of the water-gates of the great houses, well back against the terrace on which the Strand runs, show how much land the 19th century embankment has reclaimed. Until well into the 19th century also the low-lying parts of the south bank could be used for little except market gardens (much of Bermondsey is below sea-level).

The Roman works included the reclamation of part of the Fens, so that corn could be grown to feed the armies stationed in the North; the Car Dyke is part of this work, but many of the smaller dykes must be of Roman origin (see below). Traces of sea-wall (earthen embankments) have been found along the Essex coast, at Barking, Dagenham and Foulness, and in the West also (e.g. at Llantwit Major, Glam.). In Kent, the Rhee Wall on Romney Marsh is probably Roman; reclamation south and west of it began in 774, and most of the area was 'inned' by 1479, but not completed till 1661. The Somerset levels, where trackways and platforms of timber had been laid over the marshes in Neolithic and Late Bronze Age times, may also have had Roman works; the drains, or 'Rhines', there are at least mediaeval.

Serious reclamation was carried out by the Saxons and Scandinavians before the Norman Conquest in the above areas, and also in Holderness and parts of Devon. In the Fens and Lincolnshire the 'Roman Bank' was built, and a row of villages grew up on the dry edge; a similar line was that along the Sea Dyke from Tetney to Saltfleet. Many of these banks now carry roads, which wind along the old marsh-line. More reclamation in the 12th and 13th centuries led to new 'colony' villages, and new cultivated land, out in front of the parent villages along the new coast-line. The later (17th century) works in the Fens are in straight lines. The Essex coast from the Thames northward was progressively embanked from the 12th century; in 1531 'levels' or local authorities were set up to maintain the sea-walls, of which there are now some 300 miles. By the 17th century a bank had been built along the south side of the Thames from Southwark to Greenwich; Canvey Island was reclaimed at this time.

Inland too, drainage was carried out along the rivers, particularly by large landowners such as the monasteries. A good example of this, on a small scale, is the system of banks enclosing meadows along the Crimple Beck at Spofforth (Yorks.), made by the priory.

It has recently been established that the Broads of East Anglia are not natural lakes, but water-filled peat-cuttings. Rise of water-levels in the 14–15th century flooded what had been a major local industry. The islands in Barton Broad are the remains of balks between the peat-pits. The same events led to the embanking of the rivers which run beside (but not through) the Broads, by banks called 'ronds'.

Some mounds on the coast of Sheppey (Kent) have been recognised as having been made in the Middle Ages as refuges for cattle and sheep against tidal flooding.

SALTINGS

The traditional industry of the sea-marshes is salt-making, and many remains of saltings can be seen. The salt was extracted from the sea-water by making shallow enclosures, with banks 4–5 ft. high, and collecting channels, which were filled by the sea. The process of evaporation was assisted by the heat from charcoal or turf fires; the black patches left by these fires, and the heaps of burnt clay and ash, are features of saltings. The Red Hills of the Essex coast, long mysterious, are the fire-reddened heaps of Romano-British saltings. As each ground became silted up with mud, new ones had to be embanked nearer the sea, and the old ones became pasture, which also absorbed much of the burnt

matter. But in some places the whole system can be made out (Marsh
Chapel, Lincs.; and in Essex and Kent). The curving enclosure banks
and the blackened patches can be seen not only on the coast, but up to
15 miles inland where the sea has receded (Bicker Haven, Lincs.).
The salt-producing area of Cheshire used a different method (mining
of rock-salt), and maritime saltings are now relics only, found in Lancs.,
Lincs., Essex and Kent principally. Roman saltings were at Colchester
and on the Blackwater near Maldon; mediaeval pans were concentrated,
in Essex, north of the Blackwater (Bradwell, the Soken), with an outlier
on a tidal river at Wanstead. At Seasalter, near Whitstable (Kent), long
oval mounds of clay represent the breached remains of a mediaeval
sea-wall, used for a time as a salting. There are few elsewhere, such as
Exceat, at the mouth of the Cuckmere (Sussex).

SITES SUBMERGED BY THE SEA

The sea level round the British coasts has been rising since the last ice
age at a slightly faster rate than the land. This, coupled with the slow
downward tilting of the land south of the line Liverpool–Hull, has
resulted in encroachment of the sea round the coasts of Wales, south
and east England, and has given rise to legends of sunken cities as well
as actual losses of land and towns.

Wales. Here the losses are mostly of land only, but legends are persistent. Llys Helig, located between the Great Orme and Anglesey, and
Pentre'r Gwaelod in Cardigan Bay, are not actual towns and palaces,
but the lines of stones visible at low tides are really natural deposits
of boulders once contained in boulder clays and washed clear by the
sea, in an encroachment during the late Bronze and Early Iron Ages.
'Sunken towns' legends are widespread, and have become attached to
lakes as well as the coast (e.g. Llangorse Lake, Brecknock). But a
reverse movement has also occurred—Harlech was a port on the coast
till the 15th century, but is now behind a sea-marsh.

Cornwall. A large island has sunk, and its hills have become the Scilly
group; stone walls of farms now submerged between these islands can
still be seen at low water. This territory has been wrongly associated
with the land of Lyonesse in the Arthurian cycle of legends. The encroachment took place apparently in the Middle Ages. Related movements submerged land, including forests and ancient monuments, in
Cornwall itself, and in Jersey and Brittany.

South Coast. Here the encroachment has in places been very violent,
and the Saxon town of Selsey is now under the sea. The Seven Sisters

are receding at a rate of 18 in. a year, and the sea level is rising by 6 in. in 100 years. But the position is complicated, partly because of currents and the configuration of the coast, and in some places (Sheppey, Thanet, Dungeness area, Pevensey area) the sea has actually receded. Winchelsea, a flourishing mediaeval seaport, was gradually left high and dry, and by the mid-16th century had ceased to be a port; it is now over a mile inland. Its neighbour Rye had lost most of its traffic by the silting of the river by the early 17th century; Tenterden, some ten miles inland behind Rye, was a port in the 15th century, but was completely stranded by the 17th.

East Coast. Here again most of Dunwich (Suffolk) has been lost, and the sea is still advancing, involving costly works along the Norfolk, Suffolk, and Essex coasts. Lincolnshire and Holderness have also been affected. There have been prehistoric movements also on the East Coast, such as the 'Lyonesse' transgression (an encroachment of sea on the land) along the Essex coast in the Early Bronze Age, which was so rapid that it divides two closely following peoples, B Beakers being below it (i.e. before) and A Beakers above (after), a situation also found in the Fens. In the Yarmouth area of Norfolk and Suffolk the sequence is transgression of the sea over the land in Iron Age and Roman times; land-emergence in Saxon times to the 12th century, with a disastrous flood in 1287; land-submergence again, rapidly till the 17th century, more slowly since.

Scotland. The Culbin Sands (Morayshire) were laid down in a great storm in 1694, overwhelming a tract of fertile land. In Caithness, Orkney and Shetland there are no raised beaches, as in the rest of Scotland; in these parts the history has in fact been one of subsidence instead of elevation.

THE FENS

The situation in the Fens is so complicated that a separate note on them is necessary. The Fens are the low-lying lands which prolong the Wash inland as far as Peterborough. They are made up of clays and silts deposited by marine transgressions. In the north and west, roughly between the Welland and the Nene, these still form the soil; in the south and east, from Nene to Ouse, they are overlaid by thick layers of peat due to changes of relative land and sea levels, and land-subsidence, since the Iron Age, which caused the rivers to slow up and flood the land, leaving it waterlogged and choked with vegetation. The silt fens were reclaimed early, in Roman and Anglo-Saxon times, the peat fens not until the 17th century. (A piece of undrained natural fen can be seen at Wicken Fen, preserved by the National Trust.) Drainage and other factors have caused the peat to shrink, which it is still doing. It is alkaline, with only a few acid patches, unlike the strongly acid peat of the Pennines, formed in different conditions. The peat fens have recently been studied by Mr A. K. Astbury, who has thrown much new light on the succession of waterways and drains in this area.

Old watercourses are of several kinds: a dried-out canal, known as a **slade**, shows as parallel dark lines with whitish soil between—the banks carried peat, and show dark, the course is chalky. A Roman example (probably) is at Stretham, and there is one from Reach to Upware. Old canals can also show as **shallow depressions** running across country (e.g. Colne Dyke). the pre-Roman courses of Ouse and Nene have been altered by cuts, some Roman, some 17th century (like the Bedford Rivers); some of the original courses dried up in the 17th century—they show as **twin raised banks**, often followed by parish boundaries (Doddington). **Silt banks**, otherwise known as roddons, or rodhams, are caused by tidal action depositing silt up slow rivers; they show as a dark central line (the river course) with two lighter ones (the banks). Where rivers are wide there are two of these banks, joining into one upstream. They formed in the Iron Age and Roman period, due to land subsidence. They carry two Romano-British villages (Welney, occupied 1st–3rd centuries, then abandoned in late 3rd century, then reoccupied in the 4th—it has a triangular enclosure with double ditches) and two Roman roads; the mediaeval village of Benwick, on the West Water; drove roads, modern farms and houses. At Rodham Farm is a rodham 8 ft high and 70 yards wide, along a Roman channel. The old course of the Little Ouse runs 5 miles from Littleport to Old Decoy Farm; the Prickwillow Ouse east of Ely, a mediaeval cut in Caudle Fen, has two banks—the village of Prickwillow is built on this rodham. **Old meres**, with chalky soil, due to their vegetation, stand out as platforms of soil above the shrunken peat (Willingham); Grunty Fen was a Bronze Age sacred lake, and has yielded votive deposits.

All the towns are on 'islands' in the peat, except the two villages on rodhams; some islands carry only a single farmstead. Peat wastage has by now lowered the surface to Roman or even pre-Roman levels. **Roads** have therefore had to be built up, or have stood out of the shrinking peat (Akeman Street). Faggot causeways were laid in the Bronze Age (Wicken promontory, at New Fordy Farm—this is 20 ft. wide, with 8 ft. piles a yard apart, topped with 6 in. of gravel and fascines). Roman roads (near Castor to Denver, Cambridge to Denver, and perhaps Ely–Soham–Colchester) used levees where possible, but where they crossed the peat they were laid on oak trunks and branches with stones—the metalling was wattles with gravel or gypsum. Mediaeval causeways were laid to abbeys, and to the island on which Ely stands (Aldreth, early 12th century; Stuntney, 12th century; Hill Row)

21. MEDIAEVAL FIELDS. *Above*, unfenced cultivation-strips in open fields (Braunton, Devon). *Below*, "Ridge and furrow", bundles or "furlongs" of cultivation-strips in former open fields (Soulbury, Bucks.)

22. 14th century Lighthouse (St. Catherine's Oratory, Isle of Wight).
A brazier shone through the apertures — the system in use until the 18th
century

As for the Fen **waterways**, all but a few miles of each river is artificial. The origin of half the artificial waterways of the southern Fen is unknown, and dating is difficult. Some are undoubtedly Roman; the Car Dyke runs from the Cam at Waterbeach, via sections of river and dyke to Peterborough, then to the Witham at Lincoln, a distance of 73 miles. This is probably a transport canal, begun in the first century, for the movement of corn to Lincoln; it was then extended by means of the Foss Dyke and the Trent to York, when the military centre shifted north. Other Roman dykes are assumed at Lark Slade, Reach Slade, and at Rodham Farm; the Colne Dyke may be part of the Car Dyke system. March Cut and Soham Lode may be Roman also. Cnut's Dyke is of uncertain age, but certainly pre-Norman (Saxon canals are known, such as the ¾ mile cut through a bend of the Thames at Old Windsor). Conquest Lode is a boundary, and at least early 11th century. Several were cut in the Middle Ages, such as Monks Lode (late 12th century), and Old Podyke, 1223; Ely Cut may be monastic. Moreton's Leam is 15th century. Then followed the great drainage effort of the 17th century. The Old Bedford River was cut in 1630 (River Delph); the New Bedford in 1650, to straighten the Ouse and drain the loop. This drainage led to peat wastage, and the use of windmills, which lowered the peat by ¼ in. a year; finally, steam and diesel pumps were used, with an effect of 4 in. a year, to lift water into the now raised rivers. River banks had to be raised to maintain their levels, and these are now up to 20 ft. above the fen surface.

The land-sea levels are relatively the same now as in Roman times; the land rose until c. AD 700, then sank to its present level. The Fens were higher and drier in Roman times, for the ends of Roman roads are now submerged in the Wash. The so-called Roman Banks are a Saxon sea-wall, now 11–12 ft. high; the land sank 8 ft. from Roman to Norman times.

SITES RE-USED

It is not uncommon to find a site which was so well chosen for its purpose (or for another), that a later culture has appropriated it. A few examples will demonstrate this:

The Trundle (Goodwood, Sussex), consists of a neolithic causewayed stock-enclosure later surrounded by an Iron Age hillfort.

Jarlshof (Shetland) has a Bronze Age village succeeded by an Iron Age one, a broch, and mediaeval houses. Torwoodlee (Selkirkshire) has a broch and a hillfort on the same site.

Bronze Age sacred sites, such as the circles at Knowlton (Dorset), which has a church inside it, and the monolith in Rudston (Yorks.

NR) churchyard, indicate continuity of sacred sites, and quite a number of these are known. Similarly, holy wells, which in some cases can be shown to go back to the Iron Age, have been in continuous use.

The great fort of Maiden Castle, Dorset (pl. 11, p. 128), has a very long barrow and a small Roman shrine inside it. The fort of Hod Hill (Dorset) has a Roman fort in one corner. The Saxons re-used and possibly built up the Iron Age fort at Witham (Essex), and the promontory fort at Burpham (Sussex). Old Sarum, with its Norman castle and cathedral, began as an Iron Age fort, and continued as a Roman and Saxon village. Similarly, the fort of Castell Dinas, in the Black Mountains, magnificently sited on a hill blocking a valley, is occupied by a mediaeval castle. The Roman Saxon Shore fortress of Portchester, not only contains a castle, but a priory as well, and is one of the most instructive ruins in the country. The Norman bailey at Thetford (Norfolk) probably uses the banks of an Iron Age fort.

Many towns have continuous histories from Roman times, such as London and York, and some, like Colchester and St Albans, from Belgic times with slight changes of site. But these do not really come within our scope. Examples of these and other combinations could be multiplied.

ODDS AND ENDS

These are a miscellaneous collection of minor objects with little, if any, relation to each other or to the major groups on pp. 97-202, or which are otherwise difficult to classify. The headings are alphabetical, but the index should be used to find objects which have no heading of their own.

Animals' doors etc. (see also sheep-creeps, p. 210). On the same principle as sheep-creeps are dog-doors, holes cut in the bottom of a door through which a dog can get without having to open the whole door (Scow Hall, Fewston, Yorks. WR). (Dog-gates on staircases are outside our scope.)

At the post-mill at Saxtead Green, Suffolk, is a little door, in the main door, for the miller's cats; this consists of a hole cut in the door, in front of which swings a flattened wooden disc, which can be pushed aside by the cats.

A deer-jump at Woburn consists of sloping laddered planks on a gate, which the deer can negotiate one way only.

Ash houses are small buildings for the storage of wood-ash taken from the fire-places of farmhouses for use as fertiliser on the fields (18th century). One at Thorn Farm, near Moretonhampstead, Devon, is a low circular stone hut with a conical roof. Some dovecotes were adapted for ash storage.

Barns. Irregular patches of rough soil or vegetation in the corners of fields may be the sites of barns, etc.

Beehive Huts. Stone huts, of beehive shape, often corbelled, were inhabited in the Bronze Age, and are still used in the highland zone (e.g. Moylgrove, Pembs.) as tool etc., store-houses. Some are of considerable age, and the principle is ancient (they are very common in central and southern France). A fine group is at Skellig Michael, Co. Kerry. On Holy Isle, Western Scotland, is one ascribed to St Columba. There are round corbelled stone pigstyes in West Wales.

In Ireland some beehive huts were heated, for sweating away aches and pains ('sweat houses').

Drystone-walled storage cells roofed with growing turf are a feature of some Scottish islands; there are hundreds on Hirta, in the St Kilda group. As well as for storing crops, etc., they are used as shelters by the sheep. They are called *cleitean*, or in the singular *cleit*.

Bee-keeping. Honey was an important crop in the Middle Ages, for sweetening, before sugar was used, and for making mead, and bees were kept in some parts of England on a commercial scale.

Bee-gardens are consequently found in these areas, like that at Ibsley Common (New Forest), and in Cranborne Chase. These were circular, oval or square banks of turf, in which several hives could be kept. They were from 30 to 50 ft. across, with banks 2 to 3 ft. high, and a ditch outside the bank. They were in use until the mid-19th century. When decayed however they can easily be mistaken for small enclosures of different origin and purpose (although many of the latter are very obscure); and many enclosures marked Bee-garden on the early Ordnance maps were probably not made as such, but used for bees later in their history. Such are those at Holt Heath (Dorset), a small mediaeval square enclosure with entrance, 86 by 92 ft., of uncertain purpose; and Chobham Common (Surrey), possibly a small Iron Age fort.

Bee-boles. In the 15th century and later, bees were kept by most large houses, and bee-boles came widely into use (pl. 27, p. 256). These were niches in garden or house walls, about 4 ft. from the ground, and from 9 to 30 in. deep (usually 14 to 21 in.); Tudor examples are often shallow. They had pointed or rounded heads, and some had shelves enabling two or more hives to be kept in them. They are found singly or in rows; Abbot's Hospital, Guildford (*c.* 1620), has six out of what was probably originally a row of twelve (pl. 27, p. 256). A few are in chimney stacks. They are common in the wetter parts of England (Yorkshire, Lancashire, the Lakes, Devon), to protect the hives, but are found in all parts; about 300 are known. Kent, for example, has several early ones (Roydon Hall; Quebec House, Westerham; Wrotham Water). Those in stone country are mostly 17th century.

Not all holes in walls were made to shelter beehives, but this is likely if there is a local tradition of beekeeping; if the recesses face south or south-east, and are sheltered; if they are of the right size, and are arranged in groups or rows, in a garden or orchard wall. Some have been converted to other uses (e.g. for tools or braziers to keep fruit-trees warm) after being made and once used for bees. But some, particularly single recesses, or those facing north or west, were built to house hens, rabbits or garden tools; for farm-tools, milk-vessels, etc. (often near a back door or barn entrance); for braziers in an orchard wall; even, as at East Riddlesden Hall, Keighley, for housing falcons. In ecclesiastical buildings recesses near a door may be for holy water stoups or statues of saints; and some are quite obscure, and may have been merely ornamental (e.g. Canterbury Cathedral; Eynsford Castle, Kent, *c.* 1100; Richmond House, Charing, Kent, 4 to 5 in. deep).

Alcoves in old walls may have been intended for seats, but some are hearths for keeping warm fruit-trees trained on the wall. In this case the wall may have channels inside it to convey the hot air, or is hollow; but this is by no means always so. A low arch at the base of a wall is sometimes built to accommodate the root of a tree growing close against it, and can look enigmatic when the root is no longer there.

Bee-houses. Bee-hives were also, for a time in the 18th and 19th centuries, kept in bee-houses, which look like small pigeon-houses. They were not however a success, and died out. Typical examples are at Eynsford (1770) and Arnold Hill, Leeds (1870) (both Kent), and there is a famous one at Appleby Castle, Westmorland (Lady Anne's Bee-house).

Boats are occasionally found in rivers or old watercourses. Thus, Bronze Age and Iron Age boats have come from the Humber and its tributaries, and Roman ships turn up in London. They were also used for burial, symbolically, such as under a barrow at West Tanfield (Yorks.), or in the great ship-grave at Sutton Hoo. Some barrows have settings in them in the shape of ships, and some Viking houses are in this form too. The first boats were of skin (from which the coracles descend), or dugout from logs. Frame boats with carvel (smooth) planking reached us from the Mediterranean area, and with clinker (overlapping) planks from Northern Europe. Local types can still be seen of very long ancestry, e.g. Norfolk cobles, Shetland double-enders.

Coracles may be regarded as field antiquities in view of their primitive construction, which continues a prehistoric tradition. They are baskets of split withies, covered formerly with skin, but now with tarred canvas. They are still in use on the Teifi, in south Wales[1]; those of Cenarth are tourist attractions, but at Cilgerran they are still used for fishing. The curraghs of the west coast of Ireland (e.g. Kerry, the Arans) are equally primitive, but of a different shape, longer than the Welsh boats (like a long box with one pointed end, rather than like a trug). They are capable of standing surprising seas and of carrying a heavy and varied cargo.

Boiling-mounds are kidney- or crescent-shaped mounds about 3 ft. high, usually near a stream and facing it. The inside curve of the mound encloses a hearth, and the mound itself is made of burnt stones and charcoal, which are also scattered round about. They were probably communal cooking-places, and post-Roman. They are frequent in N Wales; there are several in Llanfairfechan parish, e.g. south-west of Camarnaint and south and south-west of Moelfre.

Boose stones, slotted bases for wooden partitions of cattle stalls, have usually now been replaced by concrete, and can still be found round the farms. Some are 17th century; common in Yorkshire.

[1] and a somewhat different form on the Towy.

Bowling-greens are sometimes met with in old or deserted gardens, or at manor-house or castle sites. They appear as raised platforms of grass-covered earth, oblong, with a lip or rim of earth round the edge. There is an early Tudor green at Melcombe Bingham, Dorset (which also has a 15th century dovecote).

Carts and farm equipment. The shapes and local styles of farm carts are of considerable antiquity, and worth study. This applies to other carts and horse-drawn vehicles (e.g. milk-floats, gipsy caravans, etc.), as well as to other things like gates and gate-fastenings, stiles, implements, tools and bygones, but details cannot be given here.

Cattle-railings. When cattle were kept in towns, or driven through the streets to slaughter-houses, railings were erected on the kerbs to keep them off the pavements (e.g. Reading and Harrogate had some until a few years ago). Most of these have been removed, but it is possible that a few may still exist.

Charcoal-burning. Charcoal was made in large quantities for smelting and domestic use from at least Roman times. Mediaeval records show that the process was to scoop out a shallow circle ('pan') in the ground, 20 to 30 ft. across; within this was stacked the wood, in 3 ft. lengths, round a central post, and packed with smaller pieces. The post was removed, and the whole heap was covered with turf, loam or clay in which holes were made for draught. When the wood was converted into charcoal by firing the heap, the burnt earth covering was moved aside, and the charcoal raked out. The remains of the earth cover should be visible in forest country, e.g. the Weald, or Epping Forest, as low circular banks of burnt earth, but are very elusive. Some 20 to 30 have been traced near Flaxley, in the Forest of Dean (Glos.), each circle about 8 yards across. Modern ones tend to be smaller (12 to 16 ft. across) and are about 18 in. deep.

Charcoal-burners' huts were very primitive, and the late Hazzledine Warren was able to elucidate problems of prehistoric houses by a study of those in Epping Forest.

Charms. Little circles of small stones, sometimes with a central stone, set over the door or window of an old house, are charms to keep evil spirits out of the house. They are commonest in the highland zone (e.g. on a cottage at Rhiw, Caerns.); but a similar practice is that found in Surrey and Sussex, where the chips of ironstone inserted in the mortar of walls, between the stones, had originally the same function (e.g. Dunsfold Church, Surrey). Portable charms, e.g. acorns, holed stones, arrows, axes, etc., are still carried or hung in farm buildings.

Cross-banks. Low raised cross-banks of earth are enigmatic; there is a well-known example at Hanwell, near Cheddar (Somerset), where, inside the hillfort, is a cross 2 ft. high with arms 4 ft. broad, enclosed in a rectangular bank with an entrance. This type was once thought to be the emplacement of a Roman surveying post for land measurement or division, but this is not now accepted; it is not a windmill mound either, and its purpose is so far obscure. The base of the great Roman monument (if this is what it is) at Richborough (Kent) is in the shape of a cross. A few also occur under Bronze Age barrows in Yorkshire (e.g. Helperthorpe, ER), but again their purpose is unknown. In Wessex there exist banked enclosures in the form of a square containing a cross, and these may be for sheep (Uffculme, Devon; Brow Down, Dorset).

Discs of Stone. The game of road-bowls was popular in the Pennines in the 19th century. It was played with discs of stone, averaging 3 in. diameter by $1\frac{1}{2}$ in. thick. These are often found, and some 50 were recently ploughed up together at Haworth. Other possible uses of stone discs are for throwing sports, or for hunting, even in prehistoric times. Some may be lids.

Dovecotes. Pigeons were kept by the Romans, mostly for the table, but for carrying also, in round pigeon-houses, but evidence for such in Britain seems to be lacking. Dovecotes appear in England in Norman times.

The problem until the late 18th century (when rootcrops were grown) was to get fresh meat during the winter, when most of the livestock had to be killed off because it could not be fed. Pigeons provided both eggs and meat, and most estates kept numbers of them[1]. In the mid-17th century there are said to have been 26,000 dovecotes in England, each housing from 500 to 1,000 pairs of birds. The vast quantities of grain eaten by these birds was also a factor in the decline of the system. Only the lord of a manor was allowed by law to have a dovecote, in order to restrict the numbers; they are therefore to be looked for normally only next to old manor houses or in manor or monastic farms.

The type introduced by the Normans was massive and circular, with low-domed vaulted roof, with a hole in it to admit not only the pigeons, but light and air. Nest-holes covered the walls. Later, a framework of timbers, revolving round a central post, supported a ladder by which the highest nests could be reached (this device, called a 'potence', is well seen at Bisham Abbey (Berks.), opposite Marlow). The circular tower type was gradually replaced by other shapes, mostly square, oblong or octagonal. Windows in the walls were introduced, or as dormers in the roof; access holes could be in the walls, singly or in rows. Mat-

[1] Pigeon dung was also valued as manure, and for making saltpetre for gunpowder.

erials of dovecotes vary, but are usually local—stone, brick or half-timber. Walls are thinner in 18th century dovecotes, and doors larger from the 17th century.

Pigeon-holes are also found in gables of houses or farm-buildings (pigeon-lofts), or even in porches or chimney-stacks; they can occur in churches. The holes in the tower of Cranleigh church (Surrey), although resembling pigeon-holes and used by birds, are scaffolding holes. Hawks or falcons were sometimes kept in cotes.

Square or oblong openings spaced out in walls of farm buildings are not pigeon-holes but airholes.

Most parts of the country still have good examples, and sometimes nearly every village in a small area has one; for instance, in Northumberland there is a square brick 18th century specimen at Embleton, a round one at Bamburgh, one at Belford, and one at Haggerston. A few representative examples are: Garway (Herefordshire), stone, circular, 1326, with entrance in roof, L-shaped holes and bathing-basin; Bollitree Farm, Weston (Herefords.), rectangular, with iron rat-guards; Melcombe Bingham (Dorset), round, 15th century; Henley Hall, Ludlow (Shropshire), octagonal, potence, holes with left turn (unusual); Elmley Lovett (Worcs.), brick, square, but with potence, and alighting-ledges; Bretforton (Worcs.) once had six, still has three, one mediaeval, one 17th, one 18th century. Garsington (Oxon) has two square ones, 17/18th century. At Maxstoke (Warwicks.) an upper room in the castle gatehouse was fitted with nests in the 16th century; Warmington (Northants.) has the nest-holes built out from the wall on a wooden framework plastered over; Notley Abbey, Long Crendon (Bucks.), has projecting inner walls to carry more nests (it has between 4,000 and 5,000). Nest holes can be seen in the church towers at Sarnesfield (Herefords.) and Llanwarne (late 14th century, in ruins); Collingbourne Ducis (Wilts.) and Monk Bretton (Yorks.); at Elkstone (Glos.); at Marlborough a room over the chancel was adapted for nests; there are some in a mill at Manor Farm, Upper Swell (Glos.). At Corby (Cumb.) is a cote in the form of a Doric temple, with potence (1813); the Halifax district has several 'pigeon-hoils' in gables and porches. At Llanthony (Mon.) is a circular one 7 ft. below ground level, with a beehive roof (once perhaps covered with earth); domed roofs are also found in Pembrokeshire and the south-west of England. At Bucklandtout-Saints (Devon), a thatched cote was adapted as a game-larder, and at Stoke Rivers (Devon) a cote was converted for bees. At Wisbech (Cambs.) is a cast-iron cote with two boxes, set in a bricked-up window space of Queen Anne date. There are many cotes in the south-west (called culveries), and in some parts of the Midlands.

The Scottish 'doocots' (met with also just on the English side of the border) are usually round or oblong; some have two compartments, perhaps to avoid disturbing the birds too much, or to foil thieves; nest-boxes are usually rectangular, not L-shaped. Of the oblong types Nether Liberton, near Edinburgh (with lean-to roof) is typical; of the circular or beehive, Gilmerton (Haddington); and of the circular with sloping roof, Phantassie, Preston Kirk (Haddington).

Dry-stone Walls. Stone walls without mortar are familiar sights in the stone regions of Britain, where they either replace the hedges of the lowland areas, or divide the sheep runs across the moors. Many of them are ancient; but all give a curiously distinctive character to the countryside, and their making is still a live art.

Dry-stone walling was used by the neolithic builders of the chambered tombs, and several of these have forecourt walls, or chamber and passage walls, in this technique (e.g. Belas Knap, Glos.). What continuity there was, if any, is uncertain, but dry-stone walls appear again in the Early Iron Age (there are some in Yorkshire); some of the 'megalithic' walls in Cornwall, e.g. in Zennor parish, may be original Iron Age farm enclosure and field walls, which incidentally means that some of the present farms occupy pre-Roman sites—walls once built are in practice rarely moved. In the North and Scotland the technique was widely used in Iron Age, Romano-British and Dark Age structures, such as forts, brochs, wheelhouses and the like, and for fields and farm enclosures, e.g. Torwoodlee Broch, near Galashiels, and Iron Age farms at Malham, Grassington, etc. (Yorks. WR). See pl. 25, p. 224.

But the present pattern is mainly due, like that of the hedges of the lowland zone, to the replanning of agriculture during the 18th and 19th century enclosures, before which there was not much fencing at all, except on some of the great village fields. In Scotland dry-stone diking seems to have begun in Kirkcudbright about 1710, and spread rapidly all over the country. The best and tallest dykes were estate boundaries, and there seems to be a high standard of work after 1840. In the north of England, particularly the Lakes and Northumberland, and in Wales, stone walls had been in use before this, and the later enclosures added little to them. In the Yorkshire Pennines the pattern is one of irregular and roughly-built walls on the lower slopes, enclosing small areas, and representing the farms of the settlers of the 16th century and earlier; higher up are larger enclosures, due to agreements between owners to enclose more land, perhaps part of the waste (16th and 17th centuries); above these still are the great common sheep-runs on the high moors, fenced under the Enclosure Acts with walls of good quality. The average life of a wall is about 200 years. See plates 25 and 26.

There are astonishing lengths of stone walls—some 7,000 miles in Kirkcudbright alone. They are made either by collecting stones from the neighbouring land, or by quarrying from near-by outcrops and boulders. A typical wall might be about 4 ft. 6 in. high; it rests on a base of small flat stones in a shallow trench, and is slightly narrower than the base: the wall is then built up, with an inward batter, of larger stones on each side and a packing or hearting of small ones between. At about 2 ft. above ground level is a throughband of large flat stones laid horizontally right across the wall, and sometimes projecting from it; above this the wall continues narrower. A cover band or top of flat stones surmounts this, and the wall is finished off with a coping of stones laid vertically or slanting along the top of the wall. There are many variants of this general pattern; certain regions, like Cornwall and the Cotswolds, produce flatter stones than the Pennines or Scotland, which affects the building and appearance of the wall. In Derbyshire there are often three rows of throughbands; in Ireland the top may be castellated, or, as in Selkirk and Roxburgh, the top may have a layer of turf instead of a coping. The Galloway hedge has thorns set through the wall into the slope the other side, which will grow up through the wall and make it impervious to sheep; these dykes, as also march dykes, are up to 6 ft. high. In Devon and Cornwall stone hedges occur, topped with turf or quickset. A locked top has thin slabs inserted at intervals, for strength.

'Consumption' dykes were made as wide as was necessary to use up all the stones on very stony land; the West Dyke at Kingswell (Aberdeenshire), is 5½ ft. high, 27 ft. wide at the top, with a path of flat stones on it, and 500 yards long; it may be older than 1780.

In the Pennines the walls in the millstone grit areas are usually more irregular than those in the limestone, owing to the nature of the rock; the difference is very distinctive. Cotswold walls are made of thin stones, laid lengthwise into the walls, and have copings or 'combers', rough squarish stones. In Galway and Clare walls are often rows of large boulders topped with smaller stones with unfilled interstices. **Turf walls** are often used in Wales, the Isle of Man and the Yorkshire Wolds.

Up a slope the stones of a wall are laid horizontally, not parallel to the slope; 'heads' ('cheeks' in Scotland) are placed at intervals, on which the wall can lean; coping stones are stronger if leaning upward.

Sheep-creeps, square openings, are made through the base of the walls. These should not be confused with the much smaller drainage-holes. Cow-creeps are sheep-creeps between two wall-heads, with detachable stones above the lintel of the creep (pl. 27, p. 256).

In Cornwall, at Pendeen in Penwith, there are very massive walls, one of them 17 ft. 6 in. wide, which formed part of an Iron Age settlement. In one of these there is a fogou, or underground storehouse, which is built up into the wall to about 3 ft.; in this and another wall there are 'aumbries' or low cupboards at ground level; in a third there is a storage pit set vertically in the wall, opening at the top—this is a variant of the pits in the ground on Iron Age A farms like Little Woodbury, in which grain was kept (see p. 65). These are fairly recent discoveries, and throw new light on the use and buildings of walls in this period.

In SW Wales (and occasionally also in Lleyn) banks are often faced with drystone walling set vertically, and some walls also are finished in this manner, and in herringbone. A fine example is the wall round the churchyard at Mwnt, Cards.; the seawall at Parrog, Pembs., is in this technique. In these areas the stone walls are built up with earth and topped with turf, which form banks of great permanence.

In N Wales **slate fences,** made of pointed slabs of slate set on end and tied together, are still seen. They date from the 19th century (e.g. Corris, Merioneth.; and in the Bangor area). Note the inevitable use of local stone in walls, which gives them distinctive character; north of Harlech, for instance, the walls are of flat stones, south of it round and lumpy, as the native rock changes from the Caernarvonshire shales and slates to the grits of Ardudwy. Some walls in NW Wales are made of very large stones.

Mention should also be made of the flagstone hedges of Caithness, and, although not of stone, the reed fences of East Anglia, as using local material (e.g. Iken churchyard, Suffolk).

Enigmas and Farm Works. There will probably always remain a few enigmas which cannot be cleared up, odd mounds, banks or ditches for which no purpose can be suggested. Excavation may solve some of these, but soil conditions do not always allow conclusiveness. If in doubt it is a good plan to ask the farmer; he will sometimes know the explanation, which can be surprising; some earth works are the result of quite casual and temporary incidents in the life of the farm. Some represent more permanent works, such as ponds and silage pits, which when disused may just be scoops, shallow pits or wide trenches, often with banks of up-cast soil.

There are many earthworks whose purpose is still unknown. Such is the semi-circular bank at Llyn Gwyn (Radnor), or the reaves of Dartmoor, parallel stone banks in groups (e.g. Widecombe).

There are the remains of timber beams laid across the bed of the river Arun, at Grungewick, near Loxwood, Sussex, at intervals of about 10 ft. I do not know the explanation of this.

Lynchets can be formed over, or caused by, walls or fences on slopes, and can be puzzlingly wrongly placed for ancient fields or terraces.

Feather-holes. At Cottingley Woods, Bingley (Yorks. WR), at Ghyllwood Drive, is a rock with a line of 'feather-holes' made for the insertion of wedges to split the rock for use as a building stone. Somewhat similar holes, e.g. in stones in old churches, etc., were made to take the prongs of a lifting tackle, or 'lewis'.

A Ferryman's Seat can be seen in the wall at Bear Gardens, Bankside. London, SE1.

Fishponds (or 'stews') are another feature of mediaeval life, like dovecotes, arising largely from the difficulty of getting fresh meat in the winter. Many villages, as well as manors and monasteries, had them, and kept a variety of fish in them, including eels, as well as crayfish. They were not always close by the house or village, but might be anywhere on its territory, according to the whereabouts of a suitable stream or spring (pl. 23, p. 216).

They are often mistaken for moats, but are really quite unlike. The pond was either made like a hammer pond, if the valley was steep-sided enough, by damming the stream; or by excavating a shallow rectangular basin with three or four banks, two parallel to the stream, the others across it. The banks were high enough to maintain a pond of moderate depth with a gentle flow of water through it (rather on the principle of a watercress bed); the stream had to be a small one—a large one might flood, break away the bank and sweep away the fish. The banks might be faced or strengthened with stone, and there would be a sluice to cope with swellings of the stream (a complete example is the garden of St Cross Hospital, Winchester). Fishponds may occur in sets, a main pond having subsidiary ponds for breeding linked to it, or there may be several main ponds for different sorts of fish. Quite complicated arrays of banks and enclosures may therefore be found (fishponds are of course now usually dry).

Chains of ponds can often be traced by deserted village sites, e.g. Wormleighton, Warwickshire; or at Harrington, Northants., where there are two ponds, supply channels, and a relief channel for surplus water outside the banks of the ponds. Fountains Abbey has some good examples at its farm at High Morker, $\frac{1}{2}$ mile from the abbey; there are two (still wet) at Chilworth Manor, near Guildford, on a hillside, and a possible third; and two on Epsom Common (both Surrey). On larger streams fishing was sometimes done by **fish-garths**, artificial channels diverting part of the river, and fished with nets hung from stakes. Stake and poke-net fishing is still done on the Solway.

Follies and Garden Features. Follies are architectural erections without functional intention. They are characteristic of the rich 18th century landowners, who were not in general afraid of the bizarre; they fit in too with the mentality that could alter a landscape on a large scale to make a park which was a purely artificial creation. The Renaissance rediscovery of the classical world had let loose a flood of ideas, and the Grand Tour enabled impressionable young men to see for themselves. But what they actually saw was mostly ruins of ancient buildings. Added to this, the 18th century had discovered the romantic charm of 'gothick'. The result of all this was the building, by all who could afford it, of architectural follies and artificial ruins. The impulse which created these things has passed, and they are now fossils, and as such come within our scope. In any case it would be a pity if they did not; England is crammed with oddities, and cannot be fully understood unless they are considered and appreciated.

Follies. Architectural follies actually go back to 1595 in this country, when Sir Thomas Tresham built Rushton Lodge and the unfinished Lyveden New House (Northants.) to symbolise his views on the Passion. Freston Tower (Suffolk), *c.* 1595, and Eyre's Folly (Wilts.), early 17th century, are other early examples.

The architectural soon merged into the ruin; moreover the dividing line between a folly and a legitimate building is not easy to draw. The following illustrations will necessarily bring out these confusions. Stowe has a Temple of Modern Virtue (a ruin), as opposed to a Temple of Ancient Virtue (not a ruin); the 'bridge' at Kenwood is a façade only; a lodge at Mereworth Castle (Kent) is in the form of a Roman triumphal arch; the most magnificent triumphal arch is 'The Gates of Jerusalem' at Shugborough Park (1763). Tombs lend themselves to this treatment; pyramids were popular, as at Castle Howard, Farley Mount (Hants.), and St Ives (Cornwall); Dashwood's Mausoleum at West Wycombe may perhaps be included in this class. The Sugarloaf, Dallington (Sussex) was built to honour a bet. Cottages, cowsheds and hermitages were built as ruins, with carefully placed cracks and well-trained ivy; façades are frequent, and whole villages could be 'picturesque'; the 'ferme ornée' at The Leasowes, Shenstone, is of this type, as is the 3-sided 'Gothic' church tower added to the front of a group of cottages at Tattingstone (Suffolk), to improve the squire's view. Whole houses may be considered follies, as Brighton Pavilion, and Fonthill (no longer extant). Sham castles are not uncommon, as at Mow Cop (Cheshire); Allen's Sham Castle at Bath is not strictly perhaps a folly—it was built to try out an architectural principle, afterwards used at his house at Prior Park. At Scotney Castle (Kent) the 17th century part was deliberately 'ruined' when the new house was built. In Abingdon Abbey gardens is a building in the 'gothic' style, made of stones from St Helen's Church. At Virginia Water is a temple built of genuine stones from Leptis Magna (1826). Leith Hill Tower (1765) was built to raise the sightseer from the hill (965 ft. high) to 1000 ft. Mixtures of styles did not deter the folly-builder; by Colchester Castle is an imitation Roman temple combined with a sham gothic ruin. Yorke's Folly, perched on the edge of Guy's Cliff, Nidderdale (Yorks. WR), was built to relieve unemployment; it was intended as a picturesque ruin, but its exposed position has produced what might be called secondary ruination. The unfinished Colosseum overlooking Oban harbour is well known; the fragmentary copy of the Parthenon on Calton Hill, Edinburgh, is not a folly as such—it was projected as a memorial to the Scottish dead of the Napoleonic wars, but funds ran out and it had to be abandoned.

Follies went on being built till the 19th century; Wainhouse Folly, Halifax, 282 ft. high, dates from 1871–4, and Lord Berners built a tower at Faringdon (Berks.) not long before the war (1935). Some follies have been engulfed by urban development; Perrott's Tower (c. 1760) is now well inside Birmingham; while at Stamford Hill, N London, a tower of 'rustic' brick, once in the grounds of Craven House, now stands among the back gardens of suburban houses and blocks of flats.

Two other types of folly are the summer-house or 'hermitage' built against standing tree-trunks (Halberton, Devon); and a roughly pyramidal stone 'hut' over 12 ft. high with a seat in an embrasure— Jossy's Pike, Thorn Moor, near Kirkby Lonsdale, Westmorland (late 19th century).

Some follies aim at reproducing prehistoric remains, such as the remarkable Druids' Temple at Ilton, Masham (Yorks. NR), and the apparent passage-grave at Tibradden, near Dublin.

Before we somewhat regretfully leave follies, one of the most incredible is worth mention—the planting of dead trees in Kensington Gardens in the early 18th century, for the effect.

Grottoes are a kind of folly, or at least a very eccentric sort of pavilion. They are essentially artificial caves, and sometimes therefore are real caves adapted, sometimes wholly or partly underground, and occasionally just buildings above ground. The grotto at Margate (18th century) has rooms and passages, and is encrusted with shells in decorative and symbolic design; Goodwood has one built by the Duchess of Richmond and her daughters with their own hands in 1740, and adorned with shells. That at Fonthill (Beckford's house, 1796–1807) had a paid hermit living in it, as did many others; some have baths included in them (Downton). Pope's grotto at Twickenham was used as a study. A large number still exist, of which other notable examples are at Liverpool (a private work-relief project of c. 1820), Welbeck (Notts.), Wanstead (Essex), Moor Park (Surrey), and West Wycombe Bucks.).

Belvederes. With these general classes of buildings may be linked the belvederes, gazebos, pavilions, and 'temples' of the 18th century parks. These are sometimes gothic, but usually charming little buildings in the classical style. Unlike follies, they had a functional purpose, as quiet retreats, picnic-places, summer-houses or just ornaments. Most 18th century parks had one, and some several. Stowe and Studley Royal have a large number, of all shapes and sizes, and very lovely and impressive they are. The Temple of the Four Winds at Castle Howard is a larger example. Circular temples at viewpoints, open all round, are common (Clandon), A special kind of Belvedere was the *gazebo*, which was situated to command a view of a road, so that the ladies of the house could pass the time watching the traffic (e.g. North Stainley, near Ripon, Yorks.).

Mounts. Belvederes were sometimes built on artificial mounds, called mounts, particularly in flat country, but mounts occur frequently by themselves, as purely ornamental features. They are sometimes low and rounded, sometimes high and rounded, or sub-conical. They can therefore be mistaken, particularly if derelict, for barrows or even for mottes. They sometimes, but by no means always, had steps or a spiral path leading to the pavilion on top, if there was one.

A good example of the high kind is in the garden of New College, Oxford. They range from the 16th to the 19th centuries. The low rockeries at the corners of Russell Square, London, WC1, are the remains of four early 19th century mounts. There is a delightful very low rounded mount in the middle of the Circus at Bath; the Circus was originally, when laid out, paved, and the mount was added in the early 19th century, with the great plane trees which stand round it. Another accessible example is in Kew gardens.

Vistas and avenues. Other methods of getting a view were the hole in a hedge through which a prospect or a temple could be seen as in a picture-frame (Studley Royal has one of the latter); and the vista, which was a space in trees through which a distant object could be seen, like the remarkable set converging on to Rievaulx Abbey (Yorks.). The avenue is another landscaping device, enhancing the view of a house as one approached it from the gates (that at Traquair, Peeblesshire, might be mentioned out of hundreds). The trees of some avenues were planted on low banks, and parallel banks may therefore sometimes be the remains of a vanished avenue. Also the walk among the trees, at the end of which was often a seat or statue. Incidentally, do not miss the narrow avenues along paths from lychgates to churches, of which good examples are those at Crondall (Hants.) and Hatfield Broad Oak (Essex). Fine avenues survive along roads, as north of Kingston Lacy (Dorset) and south of Wilton (Wilts.). Trees were sometimes arranged in purposeful clumps or copses, not only for scenic effect, but to represent something; as at Blenheim, where the copses represent the line-up of the troops before the battle; and at Douthwaite Hall, near Kirkbymoorside (Yorks. NR), which has clumps of trees shaped like ships all sailing towards the hill from which they can best be seen (the whim of an Admiral). See also p. 237.

Ornamental lakes should be mentioned, as human intervention in the landscape; there are fine ones at many places, e.g. Blenheim (Oxon),

Castle Howard (Yorks. NR), Holkham (Norfolk) and Sheffield Park (Sussex). Wanstead Park (Essex) has a magnificent **canal**, and Studley Royal (Yorks. WR) a whole collection of pieces of water of different shapes. These lakes were usually made by damming a stream, and the site of a dry one can be detected by the broken dam still remaining. The earth removed in making an ornamental pond can be used to make mounts, 'scenery', etc., as in Battersea Park, London.

Terraces. A feature of many formal gardens on slopes is terracing, and this may be decisive, archaeologically speaking, for identifying the garden on the site of a deserted manor house. So, the garden of the former late mediaeval manor house at Brearton, near Knaresborough (Yorks. WR), appears among the other low mounds which represent the house, its moat and fishponds. At Harrington (Northants.) are five long, broad terraces descending the slope, with traces of paths or steps joining them; below these, at the lowest level, is a rectangular sunken garden or lawn. Similar features exist at Holdenby (Northants.), the Tudor seat of Sir Christopher Hatton. The place of such terraces in an actual garden can be well seen at Albury (Surrey), where Evelyn's terrace (late 17th century), under a steep hillside, is nearly ¼ mile long; Studley Royal also has elaborate terracing round the central canal.

Ha-has. To prevent cattle and deer straying out of the park into the garden, the ha-ha was devised. This is a low wall with a slope down to its foot on the park side; the effect is that of a ditch invisible from the garden side. Most great houses with grounds laid out since the early 16th century have them, and a good early example is at Lacock Abbey (Wilts.). There is a small ha-ha round the Gray monument at Stoke Poges (Bucks.), to prevent it being damaged by animals but to obviate also the need for railings, which was another object of the ha-ha.

Secret Passages. In this section we might also include 'secret passages', some of which were built as whims, and may be classed as follies (like the series of rooms and passages built underground at Welbeck (Notts.) by the 5th Duke of Portland (mid-19th century)). Others have other explanations. There are indeed persistent legends of the existence of passages linking old houses with monasteries or churches (e.g. from St Martha's Church, near Guildford, to the former old house and chapel of Tyting ½ mile away, down a steep hillside in soft sand); some are said to be for getting persecuted priests and recusants away from hiding-holes (16th and 17th centuries); to get contraband from secluded coves or desolate but exposed beaches to secret storehouses; and for many disreputable if romantic purposes. Few of these stories can be substantiated; most of the passages just never existed. In some cases there is a natural fissure in the ground into which animals or men may

23. *Above*, a deserted mediaeval village, surrounded by its fields (top of picture). The houses show as low platforms between the lanes (Ingarsby, Leicestershire). *Below*, a group of mediaeval fishponds, long trenches running into a channel (Kirkstead Abbey, Leicestershire)

24. WALLING (A). Roman bricks or tiles, incorporated in the flint wall of a mediaeval church (Moorfield, Essex)

have fallen, to give rise to the legend (St Guthlac's Priory, Hereford);
or, as in the case of Llanthony, the monastery sewer. But some passages
are said to run for distances which rule them out of rational considera-
tion (e.g. from the 'Roman Well' at Ipsden (Oxon) to Wallingford,
four miles in hilly country); and some are said to run under rivers and
other obstacles. The author of *The Old Straight Track*, A. Watkins,
had an ingenious theory to account for these, which cannot itself be
proved; such a legend might represent the imaginary direct line between
two prominent points linked by a track overground, but which cannot
be seen from each other because of an intervening hill, e.g. Danebury
to Quarley camps (Hants.), four miles apart. But there are no doubt
many different explanations of these passages, some equally psycho-
logical. Actually most underground passages, where they exist, seem
to have been sewers, or for water-supply; a few appear to have been
made genuinely as escape passages from castles, houses, etc. Some
castles have them, e.g. Dover, and these are probably mediaeval (those
at St Andrew's are a mine and counter-mine (1546); some are 16th or
17th century, as those at Shrewsbury (St Chad's and Dogpole). Studley
Royal (near Ripon), has a carriage road reaching a higher level by means
of a **tunnel.**

Fowling. This pursuit uses mostly devices like nets, snares, etc., but
there are a few cases of earthwork.

Duckponds. One type is the protected 'duckpond', to prevent disturbance
to nesting birds; 'The Ringlets' on Hutton Moor, near Ripon (Yorks.
NR) consists of eight oval rings of banks, broken into short lengths. It
can be taken for a maze at first sight; it was built about 1770 as a breeding-
place for wild-fowl, and the idea was to cut off, by wet spaces between
the banks, the nesting-place, which was on a low mound in the
centre.

Decoy-ponds. Wild birds, mostly duck, were caught up to the Middle
Ages in nets of varying complexity, often supported by wooden structures, which of course have not survived. But in Charles II's reign an
improved type of decoy was introduced from Holland, and one made in
St James's Park, London. Decoys are recorded from the 13th century
which consisted essentially of V-shaped nets at one end of a pond, into
which the birds were driven, with the help of side nets leading to them.
The improvement was a scientific arrangement of nets and screens
along 'pipes' or channels leading off a pond (fig. 16, p. 218). Many
decoys were made in the fens of south Lincolnshire during the 18th
century, and 38 existed near Spalding, Boston, Wainfleet and Crowland.
They were also made on the Blackwater estuary in Essex, and then
spread to all parts. It was found that a straggling lake was not efficient;

the water area had not to be broad. Artificial decoys were evolved, and by the 19th century were made to a regular pattern.

The pond was 1 to 3 acres, dug out to 2 to 3 ft. deep, shelving at the sides and surrounded by trees and shrubs. From this pond ran 1 to

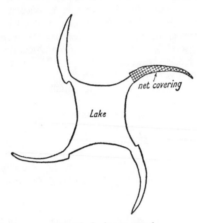

8 (usually 3 or 4) curving ditches called pipes, 60 to 70 yards long, tapering off at the far end; these were a foot to eighteen inches deep at the mouth, a few inches at the ends; they were screened in and covered with nets on iron hoops. The pipes had small channels or feeders to keep the water moving. The pond had steep banks rising sheer out of the water, 4 ft. 6 in. high, topped with shrubs and reeds; the pipes had banks on the inner side of the curve. A decoy therefore had the plan of a starfish with varying numbers of

FIG. 16. A decoy pond

arms. The authority on decoys, Sir R. Payne-Gallwey, writing in 1886, records 44 still in use in England, and 3 in Ireland; none are known in Scotland, except an unfinished one at the mouth of the Findhorn. But several times this number once existed. They are not all on the east coast, but occur also on parks in inland coonties, e.g. in Surrey at Virginia Water, Ottershaw and Pyrford (this one has four pipes, but is much overgrown and hard to make out—it was first mentioned by Aubrey in 1673). Most are in Lincolnshire, Essex, Norfolk and Suffolk; there are a few in Somerset (e.g. Sedgemoor), on the Severn (Berkeley), Yorkshire and elsewhere. One at Abbotsbury (Dorset) may possibly be monastic, although no doubt improved later; one at Hardwick Hall, Derbyshire, is of another type, consisting of an island cut through by a ditch, once netted. The most prolific of ducks was that at Ashby, Lincs. The ponds were of course used by the birds in the close season to breed and collect on.

Shooting-butts. On the mud-flats of Norfolk duck are shot from 'graves' dug in the mud, with ramparts thrown up on the side from which the birds are coming. On the Norfolk heaths the shooting-places were often screens of growing fir trees. On the moors of the Pennines and Scotland grouse are shot from batteries, lines of butts about 50 yards apart; these are circular, semicircular or horseshoe-shaped walls of peat or turf (or stone topped with turf); on a hillside they can be dug out and banked up (liggin-hoils). When decayed they can be hard to identify, except that they are usually in lines.

Mews, or houses for hunting-falcons, are represented at Farleigh Hungerford, Somerset.

Games. A stone at the head of the Afon Glan-Sais, Llanfairfechan (Caerns.), incised with three concentric squares, could be for a counter game of the Nine Men's Morris type. There is a wall for playing *fives* by the inn at Combwich, Somerset. A few early *tennis* courts survive, as at Falkland Palace, Fife.

Gibbet Stones. Stones projecting, often as much as 18 in., from the walls of a house, particularly in the North of England, are sometimes called gibbet stones. They have however nothing to do with gibbets, but are architectural, sometimes supporting tie-beams (if inside), sometimes purely ornamental (e.g. The Grange, Menston, Yorks. WR).

Golf Courses. If there are, or should be, deserted golf courses, their earthworks could be misleading in decay; greens, and the flat platforms of tees, are often artificially made or built up, and bunkers can be of several shapes and sizes.

Grooved Stones. Vertical grooving on a rock or prehistoric stone is almost certain to be due to natural weathering, the grooves being caused by water running down the rock and wearing away more along its softer planes than on its harder ones. It has however been suggested that some vertical grooving on certain Irish monuments could be artificial. There is a class of stone with artificial grooves; these are known as 'arrow-stones', but there is no means of knowing just what implements were sharpened on them to cause the grooves. The grooves are 3 to 10 in. long, on any face of the stone, in groups running in any direction, and sometimes meeting or crossing each other—quite unlike the more or less parallel striations right across the top face of a rock caused by glacial action. They are seen outside churches and mediaeval buildings, and some are prehistoric. Good examples are in Llanfairfechan parish, Caerns. One south-west of Camarnaint is a flat rock 8 ft. long and 3 ft. wide with over 100 grooves on its top. It may have some connection with the nearby stone axe factories of Graig Lwyd and its neighbours. Sharpening grooves may also be seen on church porches (e.g. Crail (Fife)).

Harbours. Prehistoric peoples landed at many points along the south and west coasts of Britain, but rarely made permanent harbours. In most cases it is not known precisely where they landed, although from the inland distribution of objects some of these places, such as South-ampton Water and the mouth of the Ribble, can be deduced. A known Iron Age port is at a little bay on the north shore of Hengistbury Head, Hants., in Christchurch Harbour; this is inside the protection of the Double Dykes. There is nothing to see here, by way of made landing-places, but the place has a powerful atmosphere. Actual harbours how-ever were associated with brochs and wheelhouses in Scotland, and with cliff-castles in Cornwall. At Midhowe (Orkney) rock-cut steps lead down from the broch to the narrow cleft which provided a haven. Roman jetties are found on the Fenland canals (depressions—barge docks; raised platforms—jetties (Stuntney; Somersham Dyke probably also). Queenhithe (London) represents the only survivor of a series of Saxon docks along the Thames. Mediaeval and later harbours can still be traced. A good example is Seaton Sluice, Northumberland, a disused coal and salt port, where there is a 17th century harbour, and a cut, 900 ft. long by 30 ft. wide, from the harbour to the sea (c. 1770).

Hill-figures and Crosses. A well-known type of monument in southern Britain is the figure cut in the chalk or limestone hills, and conspicuous for miles. This was a practice probably widespread in the Iron Age, although few such early examples remain. The early figures can all be shown to have a religious purpose, but later ones are either commemorative or merely ornamental.

The authentic early figures are: the White Horse at Uffington, on the Berkshire downs (pl. 10, p. 97). This is pre-Roman, say 1st or 2nd century BC. It is a stylised horse very like those on the Belgic coinage, that is, a deformation, through Celtic eyes, of a Greek model. It is generally regarded as a tribal emblem. Mr T. C. Lethbridge has recently claimed to have detected the former existence, on the Gogmagog Hills, near Cambridge, of a group of chalk-cut figures, also Celtic, represen-ting the sun's chariot and its horse, the moon goddess, and the evil god who periodically overcomes them and has to be overcome again by them (symbol of night and day, winter and summer). He considered that research would reveal other examples of such a group; records exist, for instance, of two 'giants' on Plymouth Hoe.

The Cerne Abbas Giant, Dorset, is an unmistakable fertility god, probably Celtic, but just possibly the Emperor Commodus (late 2nd century) as Hercules. He is a folklore character, centre of midsummer rites until quite recently. Above the Cerne Abbas Giant is the Trendle, a rectangular earthwork with two banks, and raised ground in the middle, which is said to have been used for maypole dancing. There are settlement sites near by. The Long Man of Wilmington (Sussex) is an enigmatic figure, for whom a large number of explanations, mostly fanciful, have been offered. The most recent is that he is a Swedish Odin (he resembles designs on the Sutton Hoo treasure), modified into a pilgrim figure by the mediaeval priory.

There must have been many more of these figures, lasting into the Middle Ages, but only a few records remain of some which were visible then; even then the date when they were first cut is in most cases quite unknown. In this category come the two successive Red Horses of Tysoe, a figure on Shotover Hill near Oxford (perhaps another 'giant'), and the two crosses near Princes Risborough, at Whiteleaf, and Bledlow on the Chiltern scarp. Both of these may be mediaeval, and that at Bledlow, an equal-armed cross, even Saxon; but again they may be 17th or 18th century follies. The cross at Ditchling (Sussex) commemorated the battle of Lewes in 1264, but was probably made later, by the monks of Shotover, as a point at which to pray for the fallen.

The 18th century saw a crop of horses, landscape 'improvements' or memorials to actual horses. Of these are the 1st and 2nd Westbury horses (although the first may be older; the 2nd dates from 1778). Then a long succession, all on the Marlborough downs—Cherhill, 1780; Pewsey I, 1785, Marlborough 1804, Alton Barnes 1812, Hackpen 1838, Devizes 1845 (no longer there), Broad Town 1863, Ham Hill 186? (gone); finally, Pewsey II, 1937. The Watlington 'mark' was a folly of 1764, not a sister of Whiteleaf and Bledlow, although it looks like that today. The Mormond stag (Aberdeenshire) was made about 1775.

In the 19th century more horses were cut—Osmington (Dorset) 1815; Litlington (Cambs.) 1838; Kilburn (Yorks.) 1857; Woolborough (Hants.) 1859; Litlington II, 1924; and possibly that on Rockley Down (Wilts.). Finally, in quite recent years there has been a crop, or rash, of various devices, war memorials, regimental badges and symbols (especially on Salisbury Plain), the Whipsnade lion, and the like, which may be regretted or enjoyed according to taste.

This is probably the place to mention the Glastonbury 'Temple of the Stars'. Mrs K. M. Maltwood, in 1935, proposed the ingenious theory of a series of great designs, mostly zodiacal, sprawling across the hills round Glastonbury, discernible as outlines made of natural features, filled in with woods and joined by old boundaries, roads and the like. The suggested date was Iron Age or Roman. This is attractive and original, and one or two of these figures look at first sight convincing; but the whole series places a very severe strain on credulity, and we must leave it in the air.

Horse-breaking Rings. A circular bank of earth, with no ditch, on Julliberrie Down, Chilham, Kent, was used for breaking-in horses.

Ice-houses. Before mechanical refrigeration was introduced in the mid-19th century, and in private houses later still, ice-houses were used in large houses for the storage of ice needed for keeping food fresh. A few may be late mediaeval, but they were not common until the late 17th century. They were in general use from the mid-18th century until the end of the 19th, and a few were in use in the 1920s; most date from before the railways. Natural ice was replaced in the 19th century by artificial. The ice was usually laid in layers of straw, and so stored it could be kept for a surprisingly long time, often all the year round. After railways came it could be brought to the house at any time,

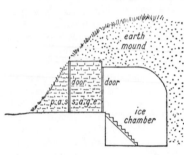

FIG. 17. An ice-house

for storage. Ice-houses were sometimes used for actual refrigeration of food, but usually only to store ice used in the house. They had to be dry as well as cool, and in this country were usually built underground. The chamber was often egg-shaped, either below ground surface, or covered with a dome of earth, with an entrance opening on to a passage to the chamber, or to steps down to it, as shown in Fig. 17.

Quite a large number survive, but few are recorded. A typical example is at Barrells Hall, Ullenhall (Warwickshire); its dome is about 10 ft. high, covering a brick structure with an egg-shaped chamber 17 ft. 6 in. high and 13 ft. 8 in. in diameter, entered by a short passage with an iron grille at the outer end and an oak door at the inner; the 'box' once had steps down to it, and a drain to carry away the melt-water. This one dates from between 1845 and 1850. I found one of this type recently at Shalford House, near Guildford, when looking for a dovecote. At Parden Hill Farm, Bishops Cleeve (Glos.), is a small stone ice-house on a bank, which may be monastic; at Blakeshall, Wolverley (Worcs.), is one cut out of a sandstone cliff; rectangular and beehive-shaped chambers are also found, and that at Croome Court (Worcs.) is not covered by a mound, but by a circular stone wall supporting a heavy polygonal timber and thatch roof. At Swakeleys, Ickenham (Middx.), an icehouse is built into the lower levels of a dovecote, which had a separate entrance reached by a ladder, on a platform round the top of the icehouse dome; nearly half of the 750 or so nesting boxes were below this level. A few free-standing icehouses exist, such as the round concrete one, covered with wattle inside and out, at Morden Hall, Surrey.

Inscribed Stones. The long palaeolithic period, so rich in art in France and Spain, produced nothing comparable in Britain; we have no cave paintings or engravings, and only a handful of pieces of bone inscribed with designs, e.g. a man's head in an animal mask, from Creswell. The Neolithic yields only the knobbed stone balls of the Rinyo-Clacton culture in Scotland (a good collection of these can be seen in the National Museum of Antiquities at Edinburgh, but their purpose is unknown).

Bronze Age. The earliest to concern the field-student are the designs carved, or rather pecked (i.e. a line is made up of a row of pits chipped from the rock-surface with a heavy stone tool, joining each other) on certain megalithic tombs of the Late Neolithic or Early Bronze Age. These are characteristic of the passage graves of the Boyne type, mostly in Ireland and Anglesey with extensive examples at New Grange (Co. Meath). and Barclodiad y Gawres (Anglesey). Patterns are carved on the stones of the passage and elsewhere, in a variety of forms, spirals, concentric ovals, branching designs, and others; they have affinities in Iberia, and have been shown to represent the eyes and breasts of the Mother Goddess, the human form, boats, trees, and other objects. This art, in several types and manners, had a long life in the highland zone, particularly in Ireland, Yorkshire, Northumberland, SW Scotland and Aberdeenshire. It appears on stones of the special type of circle enclosing a burial cairn known as Recumbent Stone circles in Aberdeenshire, in the form of 'cups', hollows pecked out in the stone, up to 3 in. across and to 1 in. or so deep. These circles derive, at some removes, from Boyne type tombs. An elaboration of this design, the 'cup and ring', where the hollow is surrounded by one or more concentric circles, often linked by or attached to wavy lines, is common in the succeeding Food Vessel period in the north of England; they can be seen on the hills along the Wharfe and Aire valleys in Yorkshire (e.g. at Ilkley), and in Northumberland (where the great carved slab at Routing Linn, near Doddington, gives a deep impression of Bronze Age religious experience) (pl. 9). They also exist in Argyll, Galloway, and in many barrows in Yorkshire, Dorset and elsewhere (e.g. on a chamber capstone at Clynnog Fawr, Caerns.); cups turn up from time to time on small rocks on the moors, and their full number is not yet recorded. They must be distinguished from hollows caused by water action, which usually have steeper sides and are deeper.

The famous 'drums' of chalk found in a Food Vessel child's grave at Folkton, Yorks., are carved with the face of the goddess (now in the British Museum). The discovery of carved representations of axes on some of the stones of Stonehenge has highlighted this practice, but it was known elsewhere before this; daggers and axes were pecked on a stone in a cairn at Badbury (Dorset), and axes are also known from cists in Crinan (Argyll), and elsewhere.

All this kind of material is peculiar to the Bronze Age, and the Iron Age has nothing to show like it, in spite of the flourishing Celtic art, which is essentially the province of the smiths and potters, and of the domestic crafts.[1]

Roman. The Roman period is flooded with inscriptions and carvings, some of them commercial, some native, and a few genuine works of art; the vast majority of these is now in museums, and there and in the standard books is the place to study them—they must be left in general outside the scope of this book. Hundreds of inscriptions are known, and they are of the greatest importance for the insight they give into the life of the province. Most of them are gravestones, altars, milestones and official inscriptions; dedications and military stones also. Some can still be seen in churches (e.g. at York; an altar to the spirit of the Wharfe at Ilkley), and in the military zone in the north and west. Some inscriptions have been found built into later walls, as in London. A few statues, mostly religious, can also be seen outside the museums; such are the statue of Mercury (or a Celtic god assimilated to him) in Aldborough church (Yorks. WR); and the very unusual carved slab set in the outside wall of the church at Copgrove, near Ripon, which represents either a priest with his sacrificial vessel and instrument, or a god with hammer and dish of abundance (pl. 9, p. 96). Both these examples may imply that the church stands on an earlier sacred site. Native works made in the Roman period include the famous Gorgon's head at Bath. (Native craftsmanship, often following Roman models, is to be seen on the mosaic floors found in the richer villas; most villas in fact have plain floors made of small brick cubes or tesserae.)

Celtic. A few, but important, inscribed stones date from the post-Roman period in the highland zone. These include the Castle Dor stone, near Fowey (Cornwall), which dates from the 6th century and commemorates Tristan, nephew of Cunomorus (Mark), a couple of heroes of legendary stature; also the Yarrow stone (near Yarrow village, Selkirkshire)—this is not easy to read, but is a memorial to two Celtic Christian princes, Nudus (Nudd) and Dumnogenus, sons of Liberalis, who died about AD 500. Cist and cairn burials once existed in the neighbourhood, and this tomb probably formed part of a burial ground of the late 5th and early 6th centuries. This period saw incursions of Irish into Cornwall, Wales and west Scotland, and these are broadly the areas of the **ogam** inscriptions. Ogam is a script consisting of lines, long and short, upright and diagonal, carved along the edge of a stone;

[1] but recently much Celtic sculpture and modelling is becoming known, including the remarkable carved heads from Yorkshire and elswhere.

this alphabet can be read, because many of the inscriptions are also repeated in Latin on the same stone (Fig. 18, below). Out of 54 known south of the Tweed, 30 are bilingual, and of these 27 or 28 date from AD 450 to 600; they go on into the 8th century. About 360 ogam stones exist, most of them in south-west Ireland (Cork, Kerry); there are 37 in south Wales, of which 16 are in Pembrokeshire (e.g. St. Dogmaels; Bridell); in Scotland they are widely distributed, including Shetland (Bressay), Aberdeenshire (Newton, a controversial e x a m p l e), Caithness (Latheron), and Perth (Abernethy) as well as Argyll (e.g. Poltalloch). About half the Scottish examples are late, from the 8th or 9th century. There are some important inscribed stones in Cornwall; Latin-ogam at Lewannick and St Clement—Latin only at St Columb Major, Lancarffe near Bodmin, St Hilary—the Christian chi-rho monogram at Lanteglos, South Hill, St Endelion; with ogam as well as St Kew and Minster, to name some of them.

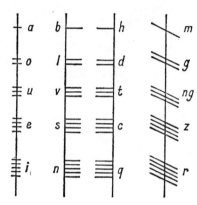

FIG. 18. The commoner letters of the ogam alphabet

Scotland has a unique set of stones in part of its Pictish area, north and east of the Forth. The southern Picts were converted to Christianity in the 5th century by St Ninian from Whithorn (Wigtownshire), where incidentally the 'Latinus stone' dates from about 450. By the 7th century the Picts were making very original 'symbol stones', carved with combinations of 14 symbols, crescent, V, Z, disc, serpent, fish, comb, mirror, and animals. These images are clearly not Christian, but there is doubt whether the stones, which must be memorials, were all pagan; certainly some of them have crosses, and some were reused for later crosses. There is a collection at Meigle, and one at Glamis. In the 8th century the Picts produced **cross-slabs**, with horsemen and apparently mythological scenes, but of broadly 'Celtic' type (Rossie: Meigle).

In the parts of northern England settled by Scandinavians in the 9th century there are memorial stones in the forms of '**hog-backs**'; (imitation 'houses of the dead'; example at Dewsbury—there are one or two in the South, e.g. at Bexhill); also 'bauta' stones which marked pagan graves. The ornate crosses of the Anglians and of the Celtic West are dealt with on p. 148.

Gravestones. Mediaeval and modern gravestones are a study in themselves, and need only be touched on here. Mediaeval cross-slabs, altar-tombs and monuments are essentially inside the church; but from the 17th century the churchyard comes to be what it is today. This was probably due to the expanding population and growing prosperity at that time, which meant that more and more people of the kind who would formerly have had monuments inside the churches had to be buried in the churchyard. The use of gravestones then spread to all who could afford it. The oldest are on the south side of the church, the north being unlucky and at first reserved for the unhallowed or the unbaptised, and only used later under pressure of space and lessening superstition. A survey of two or three old churchyards will provide examples of the various types of gravestone, and they need not be catalogued. There are the imposing altar and table tombs (e.g. that of the botanist Tradescant at Lambeth and the fine group at Thursley, Surrey), from the early 17th century; flat slabs ('ledger stones'); the long series of upright gravestones with inscriptions of great variety (epitaphs of the 17th and 18th century will repay collection); the 19th century figures of angels, crosses, etc., and the usual symbols of mortality and of immortality (17th and 18th centuries) such as skulls, cherubs, pyramids; and local or regional forms. Some of these represent the work of a particular mason, but many are traditional in a district; among these are the coloured 18th century gravestones of Monmouthshire (e.g. Llanvetherine), the slate gravestones of north Wales, with designs in an engaging folk-art; the wooden planks ('bed-boards') of the lowlands (e.g. Sussex); the iron of the Weald (e.g. Crowhurst); brick 'barrels' (e.g. W. Horsley, Surrey). Local stones are normally used, so that a graveyard in Cheshire, for instance, has a very different appearance from one in, say, Essex (where wooden 'headstones' are known). An interesting local variant is the use of rough chips of rock, uninscribed, except sometimes for a figure, perhaps a portrait, in relief, in the south-east of Scotland. Good examples can be seen at Ettrick and St Mary of the Lowes, both in Selkirkshire, and at Traquair (Peebles). Scottish cemeteries have run to enormous slabs of stone, and can give a very exotic effect; Dumfries is a good example, but the Necropolis in Glasgow is perhaps the most impressive. At the other end of the scale, but equally distinctive, are the small simple Quaker gravestones. Monuments inside churches (including incised slabs and brasses) are outside our scope, but there are wonderful collections, to begin a study, in York Minster and Westminster Abbey. (See pl. 31, p. 280).

Sundials. This section may finish with a brief look at incised symbols, etc., on the walls of churches. Sundials are the most conspicuous of these. A few mediaeval ones have survived; in the 14th century the day was divided into 24 equal hours (with the invention of mechanical clocks) and sundials on this basis begin to appear in the 15th century; elaborate ones of various kinds were made in the 16th, 17th and 18th centuries. A few portable dials were made, depending on the sun's height, but most of them are fixed, depending on the sun's position, and with style or gnomon parallel to the axis of the earth, whether horizontal or vertical. Mediaeval dials were not scientifically made like the later ones; they may be called **scratch-dials** or **mass-clocks** (after their usual function). They were once very plentiful; some 200 have been described in Somerset, and out of 50 churches examined in the Cotswolds 35 had dials, some having 2, one 6 and one 7. The Brading Roman villa (Isle of Wight) has a representation of a horizontal dial (on a pavement) with 12 parts or hours. Irish dials of the 7th or 8th centuries, on stone pillars, with four parts, are known. Saxon dials have four parts also (Escomb, Co. Durham); Bewcastle cross (Cumberland) has four parts each subdivided into three (late 7th century). Kirkdale church (near Kirkbymoorside, Yorks. NR), c. 1060, has four parts each divided into two, as have several others; some, like Warnford, Hants., have four parts in the lower half of a circle—this form should not be confused with Ordnance Survey bench marks, which themselves were first used in the 16th century. The dials need not actually be circular—only the lower half operates; and even quarter dials are seen, usually the west quadrant. Some have pieces of style projecting from the hole (e.g. Brockenhurst, Hants.). Mass-clocks usually have 24 thin incised lines, marking the beginning of the hours, whereas Saxon dials mark the middle. Some have holes, not lines (Binstead, Hants.). There are reversed dials in Hampshire, with the style bent upward.

Mass-clocks are usually on the south side of churches (West Clandon, Surrey), but sometimes on other walls and even inside (Shere, Surrey); near the south doorway is most usual (e.g. Shere, Surrey, has six here). The theory of sundials is complicated, and Green's book should be consulted. Sundials of the now familiar kind, with a dial affixed to a wall, are common on churches (e.g. Thursley, Surrey) and houses; they are also to be found on the tops of stone pillars, 3 to 6 ft. high, with dials either horizontal (e.g. in Garway churchyard, Herefordshire), or sloping (Dorstone village green—also Herefordshire); they are also met on spheres and other shaped figures, such as the elaborate one at Corpus Christi College, Oxford (1605).

Crosses, Masons' Marks, etc. Crosses can often be found incised on church walls (see p. 150). Graffiti of many kinds occurs on walls or pillars, signs, names, texts and the like. Finally, masons' marks, usually small geometric signs or letters, are common—great churches like Westminster Abbey and Ripon have large numbers.

Masons' marks can be used not only in the study of church architecture, but to trace the builders of domestic houses, bridges, etc. also —for instance, similar marks occur in two 16th century houses a few miles from each other, Tatefield Hall, Beckwithshaw, and Padside Hall, Darley (Yorks. WR), implying that the same architect had a hand in both. Note the masons' marks on old kerbstones.

Stones inscribed with matter of ephemeral importance are sometimes met with. At the entrance to Plumpton Rocks, near Harrogate, is a rock bearing the deeply-cut words 'Palliser the Hatter', and there is a similar one at Clint, a few miles to the north; Palliser was an enterprising Harrogate outfitter in the second quarter of the 19th century. In Derbyshire are several stones bearing references to biblical texts (e.g. Curber); these date from the late 19th century.

Figures can be seen carved on the walls of old houses (sometimes coming from still older buildings), e.g. a bird at Kettlewell, and a head at Ramsgill (Yorks. WR).

'*Meer-stones*', at boundaries of the runs of free lead-miners, with carved initials, can be seen, e.g. on Grassington Moor (Yorks. WR).

Laddered Posts. Wooden posts with stumpy triangular steps fixed up their sides (six each side) are to be found near coastguard stations, e.g. at Boscastle, Cornwall; Beer, Devon; Boulmer, Northumberland; Cippin (St Dogmaels, Pembs.). These are used by coastguards to practice the use of rocket life-saving apparatus—the post represents the mast of a ship, from the top of which a man hauls in the line of the rocket, fastened to a breeches buoy on which he can be 'saved'. They were introduced about 100 years ago, and, in spite of popular speculation, never had any other use.

Lighthouses and Beacons. The Romans introduced lighthouses into Britain, and built two high octagonal towers at Dover, made to take an open fire or beacon on their tops, to guide ships into the harbour. The next oldest is the early 14th century lighthouse on Chale Down, Isle of Wight (St Catherine's Oratory); some were maintained by monasteries, such as the Chapel of the Fire at Holy Island (Northumberland), a small building in which a fire was kept lit, to shine through the windows (pl. 22, p. 201). The 15th century east tower of Blakeney Church (Norfolk) seems to have been used as a beacon. Fire towers on the Roman model were common in the 17th century, and many survive, such as Tynemouth (c. 1608), Isle of May (1636), St Agnes (1680); there are two fine ones on the Farne Islands. The first waveswept tower, the Eddystone, was built in 1695-8, but the present lighthouse there is not the original. St Catherine's (IOW), was built in 1780, and

Bell Rock in 1807-10. Reflectors to increase the power of the light were first used in the Mersey about 1763, and from then on lighthouses develop into what we have today.

Land lighthouses or **beacons** were also used to guide travellers through forests or difficult country. These could be tops of church towers adapted, as at Monken Hadley (Herts.) or All Saints Pavement, York.; or they might be specially built towers, round or square with a lantern at the top. One built about 1770 survives on Lincoln Heath (Dunston Pillar, beside the Lincoln–Sleaford road); when no longer needed, the lantern was replaced by a statue of George III.

Look-out Posts, often on towers, are similar buildings. The Plummer Tower in Croft Street, Newcastle upon Tyne (13th century), is a restored survivor of 24 such towers in the district. A round stone tower on Caldy Island, Bristol Channel, with a deep embrasure, may have been a beacon or a look-out.

Lychgates occur in variety—some have slabs on which the coffin rested when it was received by the priest on reaching the churchyard (e.g. Chiddingfold, Surrey), and benches for the bearers.

Market Halls built on pillared arcades, such as Ross (Herefordshire) or Thaxted (Essex), derive from market crosses of the roofed type (e.g. Chichester), which later had rooms in the roof (Witney, Oxon).

Maypoles survive in a few villages, e.g. Aldborough and Nun Monkton (Yorks. WR); but these have of course in most cases been renewed, and the actual pole may not be old. Large stones with central hole or pit, lying on a village green, may be maypole bases. The festivities round maypoles have their origin in very ancient fertility rites.

Mazes are interesting and somewhat obscure survivals from the remote past; they probably represent prehistoric dancing-grounds on which were performed intricate dances representing the passage of the soul from life to death and back again, fertility, and other ideas. The Cretan and Egyptian labyrinths are well-known examples, and the name of Troy has also been associated with such rites. But there was a curious revival of mazes, after long disuse, in mediaeval times, sponsored by the Church; in several French and Italian cathedrals mazes were set into the floor, and the world-map in Hereford cathedral has a picture of one. Most British mazes were either made or restored in this period.

In Britain there were a large number, made of low turf walls (a few inches high), usually circular but in other shapes as well. The designs made by the low walls are in symmetrical curves or spirals. Some are near the sites of prehistoric villages or forts, not related to mediaeval or modern ones, which may reinforce the idea that these were restored and not newly-made. A fine example is at Camerton (Somerset); the Miz-maze on Breamore Down (Hants.) is in Celtic fields, and near a long barrow; among others are Troy Farm, Somerton (Oxon), Alkborough (Lincs.), Saffron Walden (Essex). Others may remain to be discovered in places with names like Mizmaze (e.g. near Old Sarum), or Troy Town. That at St Catherine's Hill, Winchester, inside the hill-fort, is square, and may be 17th century, not mediaeval. The terraces on Glastonbury Tor may be the remains of a three-dimensional maze.

The hedge-mazes found in gardens are only indirectly related to these—they derive immediately from the Italian geometrical style of gardening which spread in this country in the 16th century. There was one in Elizabeth I's reign at Theobalds Park, Cheshunt; the famous one at Hampton Court dates from William III.

Mills. Until the coming of steam-driven machinery and for some time afterwards, water and wind mills provided the main motive power for industry. Only a few are still working, but relics of many remain; 27,000 watermills once existed, and several thousand windmills, so the scope for finding traces or records of them is considerable.

Windmills are recorded in Britain from the late 12th century, and many still remain not unlike those common in the Middle Ages. More recently other shapes and structures were developed, but all are functional, and some very handsome. By the 17th century, when the oldest existing mills were built, the windmill was a common sight in both town and country. Not till the 19th century did their numbers diminish, when powered roller milling superseded the older types depending on natural forces. Rows of mills, used as landmarks also, stood along the coast, and their sites should be sought; from the mill owned by the Rank family in Hull in the mid-19th century, more than 20 others could be seen. Imports as well as new methods killed the old mills, and sub-mergence by the spreading towns; labour too left them as they declined. So there are now 2,000 derelict windmills, and less than 100 working, and these mainly on products other than flour.

Postmills. The earliest type of windmill was the postmill (fig. 19), where the whole structure revolves round a central post; this rises from a ground frame of two intersecting beams (cross-trees), usually resting on four piers of brick or stone, and is supported by sloping tie-beams. A fine example, showing this, is at Bourn (Cambs.). This lower section was later enclosed by a wall of brick or wood (the round-house), which provided storage space for the miller (e.g. Saxtead Green, Suffolk). Above this rises the superstructure, a framework of timbers, weather-boarded, depending from a 'crown-tree', a beam laid across the top of the post; the superstructure has three floors, the topmost for the grain-bins, the middle one for the mill-stones (the lower fixed, the upper

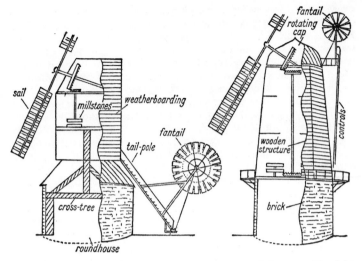

FIG. 19. Windmills. Sections of the two main types: *left*, post-mill; *right*, tower or smock-mill

rotating on it), the lowest for the reception of the flour into sacks. The stones are driven through geared shafting by the sails; these at first were canvas-covered, and had to be adjusted by hand to match varying wind-strengths; about 1770 the spring-sail was introduced, which had a series of shutters controlled by the action of the wind against springs. An almost fully automatic type was introduced in 1807, where the shutters were pre-set by means of a weighted rod, to a given limit of closing. The whole superstructure had to be turned, to bring the sails into the wind, and until the mid-18th century, this was done manually by a tail-pole projecting over the roundhouse. This needed constant attention to catch variations of wind, and in 1750 a 'fan-tail' was introduced which enabled the wind itself to move the tail-pole, by means of a small fan at the end of the pole at right angles to the sails, which, by gearing, moved a carriage rotating, often on a track, on the ground round the base of the mill.

Tower-mills and Smock-mills. In the late 14th century an improved type of mill was invented, the tower-mill (see fig. 19, p. 231 and pl. 32, p. 281). In this the greater part of the mill was stationary, with only a cap at the top, carrying the sails, and later a fantail as well, rotating. A tower-mill built of timber, usually octagonal, with cap sometimes overhanging, was called a smock-mill from its appearance; a fine example is the restored one at Cranbrook (Kent)—also Sutton Mill, Hickling (Norfolk). In these mills the tower could be more solidly built all the way up, and could be very large and high. Most windmills have four sails, but five, six and even eight were sometimes used. The speed of revolution varied, and that of the rotation of the millstones could of course be determined by gearing and governors. Both directions of rotation were used, and the length and area of the sails varied quite widely (up to 40 ft. long). Caps vary in shape regionally.

A few mills out of the hundreds which once existed are still to be seen, but most of these are either derelict or converted to dwellinghouses or other uses. At Clayton (Sussex) are two, 'Jack and Jill'; Jack is the remains of a tower-mill, used from 1866 to 1906, now a house—Jill a post-mill, out of use. At Outwood (Surrey) is a smock-mill, now ruinous, and a post-mill, built in 1665 and still working. Others are: Brill (Bucks.) 1668, idle; Chesterton (Warwickshire), Inigo Jones, 1632, built as an observatory and converted to a windmill later (a round stone building on six arches); Ashton (Som.), restored; High Ham (Som.), thatched cap; Terling (Essex), smock, in use. SE England, particularly Sussex and Kent, East Anglia and the Fylde are richest in windmills; most other counties have none at all (80 per cent of them are in Eastern England). But old pictures and prints show some that once existed, in many areas, even in towns, including London itself. On Wimbledon Common is a rare type, a hollow-post-mill, built in 1817. Essentially, mills were features of the grain-growing and low-rainfall areas of the country, and are rare in the west; in the Fens they were also used for drainage.

Sites of windmills, as well as actual remains of them, are still to be found. Mediaeval mills were usually built on a low flat round mound, to give maximum stability to the cross-trees and the base of the post. These mounds may be seen in conjunction with old field-systems, or near old manor houses or villages. They can be confused with barrows (as, for years, was one at Cattal, near York, until excavated); they sometimes had surrounding ditches, to get the earth to make them with, or quarry-pits near by. The cruciform channel which took the cross-trees can sometimes be made out. At Stanbridge (Beds., a county which once had 80 mills), is a mill-mound 63 ft. across, overlying earlier ridge and furrow. A few hundred yards west of this mound (which may go back to the 13th century), are the remains of a recent tower-mill, related to the modern village and road-system. Similar mounds are at Padbury, Nun Monkton (Yorks.), and elsewhere. They may not be linked to modern lanes, but to earlier field and lane-systems, now replaced. They are to be looked for on high ground, yet not far from the village, and near the grain-producing fields, which may themselves be overlaid and ignored by the existing villages and fields.

25. WALLING (B). *Above*, Iron Age type, made of irregular rough stones (Malham, Yorks.). *Below*, a typical 17th century enclosure wall (Gairloch, Ross & Cromarty)

26. WALLING (C). *Above*, a mediaeval cob wall, thatched to keep it dry (Ashwell, Herts.). *Below*, the pattern of 18th-19th century enclosure; stone walls and barns in valley pasture (Gunnerside, Swaledale, Yorks.)

Watermills were used in Roman Britain; by Domesday (1086) there were 7,500 (a 10th-century one was excavated in 1971 at Tamworth). They were manorial property, and tenants had to use the manor mill. In the later Middle Ages they were used not only for grain-grinding, but for fulling and other wool processes. The remains of the banks of the millrace and millpond can easily be recognised. In Sutton Park, Sutton Coldfield (Warwicks.) are 17th century millponds on the scale of hammer-ponds e.g. Bracebridge Pool. The water-power was used in three ways to drive the mill-wheel—overshot, breast, and undershot, according to whether the wheel is struck by the water above, slightly lower, or below; the wheel drives geared shafting not unlike that of a windmill. Watermills were later used for a wide variety of industries, such as paper, wool, collon; on the Wandle, calico-printing, snuff, oil, dyeing, brewing; in the Weald, iron; in Yorkshire, flint-grinding for china-making, cement. Wheels varied in size; Walton near Hull, is 36 ft. in diameter; Lothersdale (Yorks.) and Blisland (C'wall) are 50 ft. in diameter. The famous wheel at Laxey, Isle of Man (72 ft.) is exceptional; Mapledurham (Oxon) has a very wide wheel.

Watermills were supplanted by steam-power earlier than windmills, and in general only the remote corn-mills survived. Kent, Surrey and Norfolk once had a large number. Bexley is still in use; Farningham is a fine example, as is Houghton (Hunts.) and Castle Mill, Dorking. The Wandle, owing to its sharp fall in level, was intensely developed —in 1610 it had 24 mills and in 1805 it had 40. Hambleden, near Henley, is a fine mill; at nearly every lock on the Thames between Oxford and Marlow a mill once stood. Berkshire is rich in undershot wheels (Abingdon); Wales and the West have many overshot (Tewkesbury). Scotland has many mills, mainly for tweed-making, not only in the Border country, but in the west and the islands; the Water of Leith in and near Edinburgh, had several.

Click Mill, Orkney, although not itself very old, represents a very primitive type of watermill, with a horizontal wheel, which turns the upper millstone. This is in fact the earliest method of using power to turn a rotary quern. There are a few others in Scotland.

Tidal-mills are watermills using the rise and fall of the tides instead of a running stream. They were not only round the coast, but well up tidal rivers, such as two at Bromley-by-Bow, in East London. 23 were recorded in 1938, of which 10 were still using the tides. Notable examples are at Woodbridge (Suffolk), Thornington and Stambridge (Essex), Emsworth (Hants.), Beaulieu and Eling (Hants.), Pomphlett (Devon), and Carew and Pembroke in Wales.

Millstones are rounds of sandstone of varying diameters up to 3 or 4 ft. and 4 to 6 in. thick; the working surface is roughened by means of a pattern of lines cut about $\frac{3}{4}$ in. deep. Complete stones or fragments

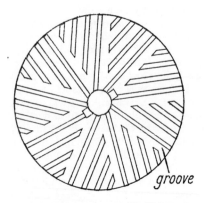

groove

FIG. 20. Millstone, showing the channels cut in the surface to spread the corn evenly. About 3 ft. across

turn up frequently, and are often seen as ornamental pieces in gardens. They should be sought in farm-yards as well as near mills, and fragments in stone walls (see p. 276). There is a large one embedded in the pavement in Mill Lane, Guildford. They mostly date from the 18th or 19th centuries. (See also querns, p. 276.) Millstones are used in some parts of the country as bases to put village names on (e.g. Dalby, Yorks.).

Stone blocks with holes cut in them, looking very like millstones, are sometimes seen on jetties for fixing bollards in (e.g. Brancaster Staithe, Norfolk).

Treadmills have been used for various industrial purposes since antiquity, and a few survive in this country, mostly dating from the 16th to 18th centuries. They have recently been studied by F. Atkinson, and classi-fied into vertical and horizontal wheels. Vertical wheels were worked either by men or animals; they include the well-known donkey-wheel at Carisbrooke Castle, IOW, for raising water from a well (others at Great Kewland, Kent, and Bovey Barton, Devon); man-power cranes at Guildford (see p. 196) and Harwich (the latter has two wheels, but is not in its original position); a hoist in Beverley Minster: and a dog-wheel at the George Inn, Lacock, Wilts., for turning a spit. Horizontal wheels, turned by horses or oxen, drove the machinery in three ways: *direct-drive* was used in mills for crushing various materials—bark, chalk, clay, ores, etc. (e.g. in cider-mills, and at a sandstone mill near Todmorden, Yorks.); axles were generally of a short type west of Severn and a long type east of Severn. *Rope-winding* was used for mine-shaft haulage or pile-driving, and *gear-turning* for threshing or working farm machinery ('gins'). Gins were often housed in special sheds, called ginhouses or wheelhouses, hexagonal or square projections from farm buildings, like the apse of a church, the roof supported by brick or stone pillars, and sometimes walled as well. Many of these survive, but no longer contain the wheel. They are found in many parts, e.g. the south-west of England and the Midlands, but are commonest in the north-east (North and East Riding and Co. Durham), e.g. Sawley

Hall, near Ripon, where there is a wheel for six horses. In Fife they are not apsidal, but semi-detached. The Scottish gin (whim) differs from the Tyneside (cog and rung) type.

Net-shops. The unique 18th century 'net-shops' at Hastings should be noted—tall wooden buildings for net-storage.

'Noosts' are open enclosures in Shetland to give shelter to boats in winter. In Shetland also can be seen the remains of fish-booths, stores and drying-beaches, dating from the Dutch and Hanseatic trade in the 16th and 17th centuries.

Oasthouses for roasting hops are a familiar sight in Kent and elsewhere, and many date from the 18th century. They are round in Kent, square in Surrey.

Park Walls are often worth a glance; some are fine pieces of 18th century stone-work or 19th century brick, and, enclosing park and often home farm as well, can stretch for miles (e.g. Petworth, Sussex; Hatfield, Herts.; and Holkham, Norfolk, which is nine miles long).

Peat Houses, for peat storage, are found in north Wales, but are rare; they are long narrow rectangular dry-stone buildings (e.g. Dwygyfylchi, Caerns.). The usual method of peat storage was a heap, often thatched, on a Peat Stool, or stone platform; these can be rectangular or round, and are very common, singly or in groups. They often retain the mound of peat, and can then look very like burial-mounds. **Peat tracks,** in mountain country (e.g. the Lake District), were laid for the passage of sledges hauling peat from the moors; they had a surface of turf laid on stone, and are about 7 ft. wide.

Pig-breeding. The sandy, wooded country of NW Surrey and NE Hampshire was a great pig-breeding area in the late Saxon and Norman periods (11th to 12th centuries). A few of the small rectangular earthworks in this area are probably the walls of **pig-styes** or **enclosures.** The uprooting power of pigs is such that strong fences, not only one but several, were needed to keep them in, and these enclosures have three or even four banks, on which fences were erected. Good examples are on Chobham Common (Surrey), three banks, about 100 by 80 ft.; another has the suggestive name of 'Bat's Hogstye', in Long Valley, Aldershot (Hants.).

Pillow-mounds. These are low, oblong mounds, usually from 50 to 90 ft. long by 20 to 40 across (but some are smaller), and 2 to 3 ft. high; most have a shallow ditch round them. The broad ones have flat tops; many also have grooves dug along or across them, or parallel ridges. They often occur in groups, and it has been noticed that many are not far from ancient forts, but this may be coincidence. They are widely distributed, and are found over most of southern England, with a few in the north and Wales.

Their purpose has been the subject of much speculation; indeed, if decayed they could be taken for long barrows. The late Mr Hazzledine Warren suggested, on the strength of baked sand in those at High Beech, Epping Forest (Essex), that they were the sites of Iron Age funeral pyres. But, in spite of difficulties, most of them are now generally regarded as being artificial rabbit warrens. The rabbit has been a source of food and fur since the late 12th century, and at times has been encouraged for these things. Warrens are frequently referred to in mediaeval documents, but their exact form does not seem to be known (some were fenced, to facilitate trapping). Some of these mounds, however, date from this period, although some are 18th or early 19th century. Some may have been used as warrens later, but some apparently were built as such. It is probably safe to take them all as warrens for practical purposes.

Good examples are those on Steeple Langford Cowdown, near Yarnbury (Wilts.) (other shapes also); Llanfihangel nant Melan (Radnor), over 30 on a slope, as many of them are; some in Glamorgan have been shown to be late mediaeval; those at Hutton-le-Hole (Yorks. NR) are said to be Napoleonic. Some long mounds at Llanelwedd (Radnor) have a rough stone trench running through the centre along the mound, and in Scotland rabbit-refuges were made in the form of long narrow mounds of turf with a tunnel inside. The grooves may have the same purpose. At Derry Ormond (Cards.) are circular mounds.

The enormous Thetford Warren had rabbit-enclosures surrounded by a bank of turf 4 ft. high, with reeds growing on it; rabbits were trapped in 'tipes'—pitfalls about 8 ft. deep, lined with flints, and closed by a trapdoor.

Plague Pits. The great plague epidemics of the past produced the problem of hastily burying large numbers of people. This was mostly done by way of plague-pits, which are usually pieces of flat ground which have never been built over, such as that now Charterhouse Square, London (Black Death), and the triangle of grass opposite the Victoria and Albert Museum (1665). Mounds covering plague-pits are at Twyford (Hants.), and see Riley's Grave, Eyam, Derbyshire.

The same problem resulted from a battle, and there are many traditions that barrows are where the dead of a local battle are laid. Local farmers turn up bones, arms, armour, cannon-balls, etc. on battlefields, and probably in most cases no mounds were raised. But there are references to barrows for battle-dead in saga literature, and battlefields might repay fieldwork. At Enborne, near Newbury, is a mound containing dead from the first battle of Newbury (1643), and others also exist.

Plantations. Not all patches of woodland represent the remains of primeval forest. In the Midlands, at the 18th and 19th century enclosures, *fox-coverts* (small woods and patches of gorse) were planted to provide hunting, the countryside having been too thoroughly cleared in earlier periods. The artificiality of ornamental clumps of trees in parks, and of forests of conifers, does not need stressing; sometimes they are planted in unnatural shapes, such as those in the form of a fleet of ships in the grounds of Douthwaite Hall, near Kirkbymoorside (Yorks. NR), and the attempt to trace out the name Victoria, in trees, on the Downs behind Brighton—a project which never got beyond the V. But conversely, evidence can often be seen of the spread of trees since early times; one of the Bronze Age circles on St Martha's Hill (Surrey) is in woodland probably planted at the end of the 18th century, and the hillforts of Loughton and Ambresbury are now deep inside Epping Forest (Essex).

Clumps of trees are often found planted on barrows or other sites in conspicuous positions (which does not help the excavator!). A well-known example is that on Chanctonbury Ring, Sussex. Clumps or rows of trees are often planted as windbreaks, or to screen an unwanted sight.

Platforms for Houses. A house situated at the lowest part of a slope may be built on a platform or terrace of earth projecting towards the river, to keep it out of reach of floods. This platform may then be ornamental—e.g. Eldinhope, Yarrow (Selkirkshire), where the platform has sides at a steep angle and sharp edges, and a perron in the middle of the long side. Conversely, a house may be built into a hillside or against a cliff, in which case a flat base may be cut back into the slope. Such terraces can be seen by themselves, when the former cottage has disappeared.

Pounds. Many villages possess pounds where stray animals could be kept till called for; these were just like those used locally for ordinary farming purposes, and their shape and material will vary accordingly, e.g. brick and square at Newnham on Severn (Glos.); stone and round at Hutton-le-Hole (Yorks. NR).

Pounder-stones were boulders used as anvils at smithies (e.g. Appletreewick, Yorks. WR).

Privies are known in prehistoric times, e.g. at Skara Brae, and from Roman Britain, as at Verulamium, but apart from those in abbeys and castles or a few towns, were rare in later periods until the 16th century. Those of the 18th century are worth a glance. They are usually small square brick or stone cabins with pointed, gabled or lean-to roofs. Many survive, but few no doubt are still used for their original purpose. They should be looked for behind old farmhouses or in villages. At a farm at Hutton-le-Hole (Yorks. NR) a fine example was in use till into the 1950s. It was a spacious room with a window, and had a wooden 'sociable' with two seats. It was approached from the house by a flagged path. At the back two access traps opened from the farmyard. A privy is combined with a dovecote at Abercamlais.

Railways and Tramroads. Working railways, and their equipment, are not in the scope of this book, but disused railways are, as their remains form features of the countryside.

The earliest tram-roads (railways have flanged wheels and flat rails, tramroads or wagonways flanged rails) were laid down in Notts., and soon after in Northumberland, by 1597 to carry coal from mines to staithes on the banks of rivers such as the Tyne, to be loaded into ships. Some of those in Co. Durham have been in continuous use for 300 years (the Causey Arch, a wagonway bridge at Tanfield, is probably the oldest railway bridge in the world (1727). The flanged wheel was used c. 1730 on the Prior Park wagonway at Bath; and flanged rails in 1776 at Sheffield. The early canal companies built tramroads as feeder lines, to save the expense of cutting branch canals. Traces of these can be found near old canals, such as the Somersetshire Coal Canal or the Ashby-de-la-Zouch Canal, or most of those in S Wales (Trevithick's locomotive was tried out on one of the latter). Longer railway lines were also built in some places to link two canals (e.g. the Cromford and High Peak, across Derbyshire, linking the Peak Forest and the Cromford Canals), or the Hay and Kington tramroads as a branch of the Brecon and Abergavenny Canal. The Stratford-on-Avon-Shipston-on-Stour horse-tramway can be traced near Ilmington (Warwicks.) as an overgrown green lane between hedges. Iron rails were used in 1767, but wooden and stone ones went on into the 19th century.

Mine and industrial railways can be found all over the country; there are several near Neath; and a long stretch of trackless but ballasted road runs across the moors from the derelict iron-mines in Rosedale (Yorks. NR). The line from Pateley Bridge (Yorks. WR.) to Scar (in Nidderdale) was laid, past Lofthouse, for the building of the reservoirs at the head of the dale, and taken up when these were finished. Its course, with tunnels, can still be followed. Indeed, unless these lines are deliberately removed their remains are permanent. The same can be said of the branch railways which have been going out of use for many years. Their green cuttings and embankments, punctuated by stations now used as houses, can be traced for miles. Good examples are the line from Galway to Clifden (Eire); the Bishops Castle line; the Lynton and Barnstaple.

Stephenson's railway from Whitby to Pickering (1835) at first followed the Eller Beck from Grosmont to just above Goathland; in 1865 this stretch was replaced by the present line, but the old line can still be seen, particularly at Beckhole. There is a tunnel with castellated entrances. The line was worked by horses until 1846.

The Surrey Iron Railways (the S.I.R., sometimes called collectively the Grand Surrey Iron Railways), being the first public lines in England, must be noticed in some detail. In order to obviate the shipping route through the Channel and round the Kent coast, dangerous during the Napoleonic war, a proposal was made for a canal from London to Portsmouth. This would have begun by following the Wandle valley, and would have reduced the water available to drive the 38 mills along this river (employing some 3000 people—the Wandle was the most industrialised river in England then). The opposition of the mills caused the plan to be changed to a railway, and an Act of 1801 authorised the Surrey Iron Railway, 9½ miles from the Wandle–Thames confluence at Wandsworth, along the Wandle to Mitcham, and on to Croydon, with spurs to factories, and a branch of 1¼ miles from Mitcham to Hackbridge and Carshalton. This was opened in 1803, and continued until 1846. No trace remains of this line, owing to later building, except for a few street alignments and possibly one or two bridges; from Mitcham to Croydon its course is used by the present railway. The S.I.R. was for freight, not passengers.

The next stage southwards was the Croydon, Merstham and Godstone Railway (Act of 1803, opened in 1805). This ran on from the S.I.R. at Croydon, and had a single track, with passing places, and a few stretches of double track. It, like the S.I.R., was strictly a plateway, that is, it used flat rails flanged on the inside, to keep the wagon, etc. wheels on; the rails were laid on stone sleepers about 16 in. square, leaving the centre of the track clear for the horses.

The C. M. & G. was projected to Reigate, with a branch to Godstone, but the investing public lost interest, and the line never got beyond Merstham. It ceased in 1838. From Pitlake, Croydon (whence the Croydon Canal Co. made a short railway to its basin in 1809), it ran along Church Road (then Tramway Road), and followed the western side of the main Brighton road to Coulsdon, then through Hooley to chalk and stone quarries at Merstham. An embankment and terracing can be seen at Coulsdon in the grounds of Cane Hill Hospital; at Dean Lane, Hooley, a cutting has been filled in, but three bridges remain along it, one buried up to its parapets; the cutting itself is to be seen in Dean Farm; Weighbridge Cottage is the old Toll and Weigh House; the course of the track is clear from the Jolliffe Arms Hotel to the quarries at Merstham, and a section of original retaining wall. A few other minor traces also survive along the route.

In certain cases earth removed from railway and canal cuttings was not used to make embankments elsewhere, but piled along the sides of the cuttings in ridges or mounds; such are the 'bumps' at Pinner (Middx.); there are a few oval mounds along the line just west of Beaulieu Road Station, Hants. It is interesting to recall that the railway embankments were made by the same methods as those used for making prehistoric banks, that is, by the emptying of basket-loads of earth from the top edge of the bank as it progressed. Some quarries for embankments may be filled by lakes (e.g. Weybridge, Surrey).

Railway tunnel mouths of the mid-19th century were often made ornamental, sometimes to tone in with a park landscape—a castellated pair is at Thrumpton, Notts.

Few early railway buildings are as impressive as stations like St Pancras, London, but early buildings, works and bridges can be seen in many places.

The quarry railway at Haytor (Devon), built in 1820, consists of a track of L-shaped granite setts; much of this can still be traced.

Ropeways. Where an incline is too steep to allow of a railway, a ropeway might be used, and a smooth plane running vertically up a hill to an old quarry may be the track of one. A good example is that to the old Scotgate Ash marble (delph) quarries above Pateley Bridge (Yorks. WR), which had a fall of nearly 600 ft.

Ribbon Walls ('crinkle-crankles'), are brick orchard walls, wavy in plan; the alcoves give shelter to fruit-trees. They are a feature of Suffolk, where there are nearly fifty, against about half that number in the rest of England. They date mostly from the early 19th century, but a few are late Victorian (e.g. Shackleford, Surrey).

Ridging on Roads. Ridging across an unmetalled lane can be caused by the repeated passage of cattle, which raises the surface soil in waves at right angles to the direction of movement. A cross-ridge on a hill-road can be for drainage (drainage-channels are sometimes cut across roads, not always covered over with stones).

River Crossing

Fords. Bridges were not built on minor roads or over minor rivers, and fords were therefore very common, as they still are. On large rivers they can still sometimes be seen close by the bridge that superseded them, as at Low Bridge, Knaresborough, where the lanes leading down to the ford are still there, although blind now. At Eynsford, Kent, the ford and narrow bridge, side by side, are both in use. Most fords are merely broad shallow places, but some are metalled like the road, and a few are paved. Recognisably Roman fords are still very rare; Iden Green, Kent —Kempston, Beds.; the latter was made of stone slabs, cemented, and partly held in place by rows of oak piles, 18 ft. apart, on the outside edges of the paved way; there were one or two posts in the centre also, presumably to separate the traffic lanes. Pre-Roman fords existed, and there were several on the Thames; Julius Caesar, in 55 BC, used one at Brentford, which was marked by lines of stakes (the Cowey Stakes).

Stepping Stones are an alternative to a primitive type of bridge in shallow water. Good examples at Bolton Abbey (Yorks.); Stanhope, Co. Durham; Ambleside, Westmorland; Studley Royal, near Ripon (18th century). A set over the Wylye in Wilton Park (Wilts.), raised on timber frames, is 19th century; those below Box Hill (Surrey) are modern.

Bridges. Primitive: early bridges of rope or wood have not survived, but a few stone slab ones still exist; single span (clam) or multiple span (clapper). Post Bridge, Dartmoor, is a clapper bridge of four large granite slabs resting on two piers and two abutments of rough rocks, unmortared. A clam spans the Wallabrook, a tributary of the Teign, and there is a clapper at Teignhead; a clapper at Linton in Wharfedale; both types at Wycoller (Lancs.); several in the Cotswolds; and the famous Tarr Steps over the Barle on Exmoor. Whether some of these were rebuilt, or even built, in say the 18th century, is not important; the type is prehistoric, and some of these survivors may have a very long history. (Pl. 29, p. 264.)

Roman: Most Roman bridges were wooden, but a few important ones had wooden roadways on stone piers; a model of that at Corbridge (Northumberland) is in the museum there, and remains of the abutments of such a bridge, where Hadrian's Wall crossed the N Tyne, can still be seen at Chollerford not far away. Similar bridges stood where the Wall crosses the Irthing, and at Newcastle, London, Rochester and elsewhere. A few small bridges are built of stone arches of Roman type; that at Castle Combe (Wilts.) may be genuinely Roman; Harold's Bridge at Waltham Abbey (Essex), and one at Preston, if later (and Harold's Bridge may be 14th century) are certainly of Romanesque inspiration.

Anglo-Saxon: Probably only repairs to existing Roman bridges were carried out in this period, and few if any new ones built.

Mediaeval: Fords were still the usual method of crossing rivers (many can still be seen close by an old bridge, and some of these were in use till quite recently; e.g. Knaresborough, Yorks.), as the many place-names ending in -ford show. The first mediaeval bridges tended to be built at two points on a river, the lowest where a bridge could succeed and an inland port established (London), another at the lowest point which could be forded in all weathers (Wallingford). London Bridge has a long and complex history rather outside our scope; Wallingford had a bridge in the 13th century, now much rebuilt. Many even important bridges were of timber, and began to be replaced by stone in the 13th century (e.g. Bristol, c. 1250; Chester, 1357; Stopham, Sussex, perhaps 1486; Congleton, Cheshire, not till 1784); even in the 15th century timber bridges were still being built.

Mediaeval innovations were the ribbed arch, which saved material, and the road recess continuing the cutwater upward; the mediaeval cutwater is pointed, but this is less efficient than the round form introduced in the 18th century. Twizel Bridge (Northumberland) is a fine ribbed bridge, and many ribbed arches exist, some incorporated into later work or widening; High Bridge, Knaresborough, for instance, shows three phases of building, which can be seen (from a boat) underneath its two arches. Good mediaeval bridges are too numerous to do more than mention a few: Eashing (Surrey), 13th century; Radcot and New Bridges, above Oxford; Elvet Bridge, Durham; Chapel Bridge, St Ives, Hunts.; Barnard Castle; Huntingdon; Dumfries; Ayr; Wadebridge, Bodmin, Bideford; Llangollen, are all variously characteristic (Pl. 29, p. 264.)

Every mediaeval bridge had its cross (mostly destroyed in the 16th and 17th centuries); many had chapels for the blessing of the traveller, collecting alms for maintaining the bridge, and even for regular services. The building and care of bridges was a strongly religious activity. Wakefield (c. 1358), Rotherham (1483), and St Ives (Hunts.) (1426), still have their chapels (although Wakefield is partly rebuilt); Bradford-on-Avon (Wilts.) has an oratory, used later as a lock-up and powder-magazine, and with its roof altered in the 17th century. A few bridges were fortified—Monnow Bridge, Monmouth, has a fine central tower gateway; Warkworth (Northumberland) has a tower at one end. An unusual bridge is the (disused) Trinity Bridge at Crowland (Lincs.), with three ways meeting in the middle (late 14th century). London Bridge had a chapel, houses, palace and water-wheels; the present bridge dates from 1831. High Bridge, Lincoln, has houses dating from c. 1540.

Renaissance to 18th century. Bridges continued to be built in the mediaeval manner as late as the 17th century (Wilton Bridge, Ross; St Neots; Berwick Old Bridge, 1611–24; Corbridge, 1674). The new styles of architecture began to be applied to bridges, however, before this; the Palladian ideas involved wide arches of Roman type, lighter piers, and less depth between arch and crown and parapet (Inigo Jones' bridge at Llanrwst; Lanercost, Cumberland; Barden Bridge, Yorks.;

Clare College, Cambridge (1640 or earlier)). From now on architects come by name into the story, such as William Edwards (Pontypridd bridge, 1750).

The landed proprietors built bridges widely on their estates, and many exquisite examples remain; Wilton Park, Wilts., 1737; Blenheim, 1711—only part of Vanburgh's very elaborate plan; Kedleston, Derbyshire, c. 1770 (Robert Adam); Chatsworth, 1762 (James Paine). Adam also built Aray Bridge, Inveraray, and Pulteney Bridge, Bath (1769). Gen. Wade's military bridges in Scotland should not be overlooked (Aberfeldy, 1733).

The Thames had a fine set of 18th century bridges, of which Chertsey (1785), and Henley (1786) may be mentioned. Smeaton and Mylne built many bridges at this time also, inaugurating the style of the later Industrial Revolution.

Industrial Revolution. A new epoch, led by engineers, was brought in by the Iron Bridge at Coalbrookdale in 1779, and lasted till the Forth Bridge in 1890. The later ones, and the modern concrete bridges, must be left out, but any study of bridges will inevitably lead on to them. The Iron Bridge, the first bridge in the world to be made almost wholly of iron, led to a revolution in civil engineering. Masonry of course continued in use, and bridges in the classical styles were made throughout the 19th century. Telford's canal bridges and aqueducts are dealt with in the canal section, but his Over Bridge, Gloucester, with its splayed arch, and his Dean Bridge, Edinburgh, may be referred to. He is perhaps best remembered for the Menai Bridge, an iron suspension bridge (1826, restored 1940). Brunel's Clifton suspension bridge just comes into this book, having been begun in 1836; we will not deal with the railway bridges. The wooden swing bridge at Selby (c. 1791) is an interesting survival. Notice bridges with built-in towpath.

Packhorse bridges well repay searching for. They date from the 14th to the 19th centuries, and are common in the North, where roads suitable for wheeled traffic were few, and where large quantities of goods were carried over not always easy country. The West Riding and Lancashire have most (e.g. New Bridge, Birstwith, Nidderdale, rebuilt 1822), but many counties have a few (Coombe Bissett, Wilts.; Eynsford, Kent, both mediaeval; Stow, Midlothian). Packhorse bridges are very distinctive; they usually have one high single arch, with a passage the width of a pavement, not a road, and often have parapets as well. At Ashford-in-the-Water (Derbyshire) there is one with three arches (The Sheepwash Bridge), which has a sheep enclosure joined to it to make the sheep ford the river. (Pl. 29, p. 264.)

Rock Basins ('bullauns' in Ireland) are oval or circular hollows in rock-surfaces, of an average size of 12 to 18 in. across by 6 ft. deep. Some of these may be natural, but many appear to have been made or used as mortars for the crushing of grain, herbs, nuts, etc., or stones; other uses have also been suggested. They seem to originate in at least the Roman period, and in the post-Roman in Ireland. They are common in Ireland (there are some 30 at Glendalough), and are found in Scotland (e.g. in Argyll) and Wales.

Cup-like cavities can be seen on rocks by the sea, formed by chopping up limpets for bait.

Ropewalks are the long low buildings used for making rope, which was twisted from several yarns by a man walking backwards manipulating a wheel and an apparatus of hooks. They were often 220 yards long but could be much longer (half a mile is recorded) or as little as 50 yards. Since the late 19th century rope-walks, although still used, house a mechanical process. Good examples at Bilston (Staffs.) and Cambridge, and an open-air walk at Dover. More could perhaps be traced by research at old centres of the industry such as Bristol and Newcastle.

Round Towers. The Round Towers of Ireland (and two in Scotland, Brechin and Abernethy) are bell-towers. They were however built in the 9th century, during the Viking raids, and combine this function with that of refuges. Several, when investigated in the 19th century, were found to contain human bones. Good examples are those at Glendalough, Kells, Kilkenny, Cashel, Cloyne and Roscrea in Eire, and Devenish, Co. Fermanagh in Ulster.

Rubbing-stones. Tall thin stones in fields, unlike the rough, irregular prehistoric monoliths, may be rubbing-stones for cattle. Both these and the monoliths may be associated with fertility customs. The wooden rubbing-posts set up by a Duke of Argyll on his Inveraray estates—which gave rise to the heartfelt slogan 'God bless the Duke of Argyll'—no longer exist. They were imitated elsewhere, e.g. by Sydney Smith at Netheravon.

Saw-pits. Heavy timber was sawn up, until the late 19th century, by means of saw-pits, in which a long saw was worked by a top-sawyer on a platform at the top, and a bottom-sawyer in the pit. These pits were not in the woods, but outside the local joiner's or wheelwright's, or in the yards of large houses or estates (example in the wheelwright's yard at Swallowfield, near Reading).

Sheep-enclosures are a familiar feature of the highland zone. They usually consist of unroofed circular or square 'rooms' of dry-stone walling. They are mostly of one 'room' only, but some consist of connected groups of compartments, or of an enclosure with a wall pro-

jecting from it, for shelter (short walls for shelter may stand by themselves). Some are backed against mountain walls, but most are free-
standing, and often in very isolated places. Some form pounds in
villages, others working-places on the farms where sheep can be dipped
and sheared. There are many varieties of local types. In south-east
Scotland the circle is the normal shape for 'beilds' or 'stells' ('fanks' in
W Scotland) with ovals also; there is a wide variety along the valley of
the Megget Water in Selkirkshire. Near the Devil's Beef-Tub above
Moffat (Dumfriesshire) is a ruined stell from which many of the stones
have been removed; this appears as an earth circle, and clearly confusion
could arise here. As the Border is crossed the shape changes, and in
Northumberland the enclosures are mostly square. But this is by way of
illustration only; the whole subject is a field for amateur observation, not
least from the point of view of the dry-stone walling. (See p. 210 for
creeps.)

Some Scottish 'fanks' may be protected plots (as in Shetland).

The Snowdon area has multicellular sheepfolds, with a large number
of conjoined 'rooms'; these are probably 18th century, and were built to
sort out mixed-up flocks belonging to several farms (e.g. Llanlechid).

The now deserted village on Hirta (St Kilda) is enclosed by a long
wall whose main purpose was to keep the sheep out.

Ruined houses on high ground in Wales are usually the remains of
hafods, sheep-farms on the high pastures used in the summer (18th
century). These are comparable to the shielings of Scotland.

Pools for washing sheep were sometimes made by damming a stream
with stones; these can be seen in hill-country, e.g. Hayshaw, near
Ramsgill, Nidderdale (Yorks. WR). A sophisticated one, with stone
channels, is at Thurlston (Notts.).

Shot Towers are tall square or round brick buildings, having a gallery
at the top, from which molten lead is poured through a grille into a
bath of water for cooling at the bottom. The shot tower at Chester
is still in use, but not that at Newcastle. Until its demolition in 1962,
a shot tower stood at the southern end of Waterloo Bridge, London.
Built in 1826, it was in use until 1949. The earliest is the square one at
Bristol (1782).

Staddle-stones are mushroom-shaped stone posts on which ricks, etc.,
are raised, to keep rats from them (Fig. 21), e.g. under barn, Pusey
(Oxon.), under dovecote, Milford (Surrey). They can be several
centuries old. They are often found used ornamentally.

Stocks are still common; Alfold (Surrey) and South Harting (Sussex)
have not only stocks, but a whipping-post as well. Waltham Abbey
(Essex) has a **pillory** in addition. A **cage** as a temporary lock-up is

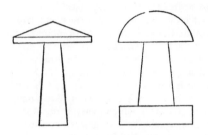

FIG. 21. Staddle stones

also to be found (Lingfield, Surrey; 1773).

Street Furniture. This is the convenient name given by architects to such things as signs, posts, railings and the like.

Bollards. A form of protection of buildings, of which railings are the extreme example, is the post or bollard, used to keep traffic off narrow pavements or out of pedestrian passages. A wide variety is met with, and London is very rich in them; some are of stone, some cast iron, some even wood. The Napoleonic war type of gun, or posts looking like these, were very popular, and are still to be seen; numbers are in the Tower of London district, and across the River in Southwark (Clink St., Bankside, etc.)[1]; there is a gay collection, painted black and white in Hanway Street, off Oxford Street, W1.

Bollaster. A special type of bollard is 'engaged' against a wall, and has been called a bollaster. These are from 1 to 3 ft. high, usually 1 or 2, and project about 6 in. from the wall. They are mostly of stone, but occasionally of wood. Their purpose is to keep vehicles off gateways, walls, etc. They can be seen, e.g. at the 17th century entrances of Gray's Inn, and of the Middle Temple (wood and stone); a number in Newman Passage, W1; on Holloway, Bath, against a raised pavement. In Queen Square, London, WC1, is an early 19th century pump protected by four bollards, three stone, one cast-iron, each having a low stone bollaster against it. Bollasters seem to start in the late 17th century, and were very common in the 18th, but there are many Victorian and modern ones also.

Railings. An intermediate stage between bollards and railings is the post and chain fence, or post and rail. Railings, being essentially parts of houses, or open spaces, are only doubtfully in the scope of this book, but come more into the history of the decorative arts of the 18th and 19th centuries. But being prominent features of the Georgian street scene (to protect people from falling into areas), they may be briefly noticed. The fancy heads of the uprights, with larger ones at intervals, are worth study. They are shaped in great variety: spears, flames, vegetable motifs (pine-cones, leaves, etc.), urns. Bedford Square and Great James St., London, WC1, have good examples, and the whole of

[1] real guns in the Borough, at the corner of Newcomen Street.

the Bloomsbury and Marylebone districts are full of them, as of course are Edinburgh and Bath, and other Georgian centres. By 1840 railings were getting heavier and less tasteful, like so much else.

With railings go torch extinguishers, foot-scrapers, bell-pulls, and the like. Note the iron clothes-posts of Edinburgh.

Pillar Boxes take their name from their original form of a Doric pillar. There is a good example at the foot of Jury Street, Warwick. They began in 1853, and were made in a variety of shapes (hexagonal, round, etc.) and apertures, many of which can still be found.

Ironwork on Public Buildings. A good deal of ornamental ironwork, some of it graceful and pretty, went into 19th century public buildings, such as market halls, railway stations and conveniences. Much of this still exists, particularly in country towns and unfashionable districts. There is for instance a circular urinal in the (old) Cattle Market by the Castle at Norwich; a urinal and staircase banisters at Severn Tunnel Junction (Mon.); and a seat at Eastleigh station (Hants.). In the same category, do not overlook *iron balconies*, which also show the sequence of decorative art (Chinese Chippendale, etc.).

Hitching-posts, Lamp-posts, Signposts, etc. Hitching-posts seem to be rare in this country, if they exist at all, but a plain wooden post with pointed top, to which a horse could be tethered, is at Tongham Vicarage, Surrey. Georgian and Early Victorian *lamp-posts*, some of great charm, are still to be found, some dating from the years round 1800. Such things as *drain-covers* and *coal-hole covers* show local variations. Ornamental wrought-iron gates must be omitted, except to say that gates and *gate-posts* can be very characteristic, and show regional styles; the round white posts of Ireland come to mind. Freakish gateposts are the jaw-bones of stranded whales in coastal districts.

Signposts, as opposed to milestones, originated in the Middle Ages and were erected somewhat at the whim of public bodies or private individuals. It was only in 1773 that they were made compulsory on highways. Examples from before this date are Broadway Hill, Worcs., 1669; Hopton, Derbyshire, 1705. A signpost in Devon, Otterton Cross at Bicton, is in the form of an ornamental square pillar, surmounted by a cross, which commemorates five martyrs burnt at the stake here; it has no arms, the directions being on tablets on the sides (1743). The latter feature occurs also at Cranleigh, Surrey. Local styles, in relatively modern signposts, can still be found in remote parts; in the Peak District they are raised on pedestals to keep the wording clear of the snow.

Notice-Boards, such as the interesting one at the entrance to Christ Church Meadow, Oxford, should be looked for.

Street-names can be of interest, and the Georgian kind with handsome deep-cut lettering on the wall at a corner are very satisfying. Bath is full of them, and I have seen them in small towns such as Barnard Castle (Co. Durham). Bath has name-tablets in great variety—with incised lettering; incised and painted in, with or without a painted border; painted on the wall; painted on wooden boards; metal plates, etc. In the large cities their survival is chancy, e.g. Church Street, Cardiff; Exton Street, London SE1 (tablets showing 'Church Street' and 'Alfred Place'). Names with letters in relief are well represented at, say, Adelaide Street, London WC2. London has some dated tablets: such as Marsham Street, SW1 (1688); Great James Street, WC1 (1721); May's Building, St Martin's Lane, WC1 (1739); Rathbone Place, W1 (1778).

Coade Stone, a kind of terracotta largely based on kaolin, was a very popular material for statuary, house ornament, etc., from the 1770s to the Regency (the makers, Coade and Selly, were in business from 1769 to c. 1840). It was made in moulds, and hence was much cheaper than carved stone, yet very durable; it could be painted. Bedford Square, London WC1, is ornamented with plaques and reliefs in this material.

Memorial Stones are sometimes met with, not only in town streets, but on country roads, commemorating people or events. Such are a stone in a wall at Wrotham (Kent) on the spot where an officer was shot dead by a deserter in 1799; that near the source of the Tweed, in memory of the guard and driver of the Moffat mail-coach, lost in a blizzard in 1831; near by, at the Devil's Beef Tub, is a modern stone to a Covenanting Martyr of the 17th century. The Smithfield martyrs, and William Wallace, are remembered at Smithfield, London, by modern stones; the Rufus Stone, in the New Forest, where William II died, is well known. Dedicatory inscriptions on wayside fountains and the like are often worth attention. A monolith at Harrogate commemorates the completion of the Leeds turnpike road. Memorials to events sometimes take the form of *monuments*, often large and imposing; one of the best-known is the Monument in London, set up by Wren at the place where the Great Fire of London started in 1666. Such monuments are to be seen also on hilltops or battlefields. The Lansdowne monument is inside the hillfort of Oldbury Castle, Cherhill (Wilts.).

Statues to distinguished men, in streets or squares, must be omitted, although some of these are placed in remote countrysides also, such as that to James Hogg at St Mary's Loch, Selkirkshire.

Some Inn-signs are old, and can be very handsome (e.g. The Castle, High Street, Battersea). Old *traders' signs*, such as *barbers' poles*, still occur; one painted red and white (some have blue as well) survives in Bishopthorpe Road, York. There are two at Clare (Suffolk). Most types of sign were abolished in 1762, because they were dangerous; other countries, and even Scotland, have more variety than England.

27. WALL FEATURES. *Above*, a cow-creep in a stone wall, with a sheep-creep at ground level. The upper stones can be removed (Grassington, Yorks.). *Below*, a bee-bole in a 17th century wall, for keeping beehives sheltered and off the ground. The bricks measure $9'' \times 2''$, a size no longer used (Guildford, Surrey)

28. QUARRYING. *Above*, the "hills and holes" left by mediaeval stone-working (Barnack, Northants.). *Below*, the remains of an 18th-19th century lime-kiln, with the quarry spoil-heaps (Gwbert, Cardiganshire)

Milestones make a rich study, and there are still a large number to be seen, with a very wide measure of local variety. They were used by the Romans; most of the survivors of these are of course in museums, but a few are still in situ, such as the possible example one mile from Dorchester (Dorset) at Stinsford. Four in Cornwall are very near their original positions (e.g. Trethevey). The London Stone (Cannon Street), once thought to be the point from which the Romans took the mileage of their roads, is now held to be of unknown origin and purpose. They were not again used in Britain until the turnpike roads were built; a few roads had marks or stones from 1663 (Dover road); 1708 (Great North Road), but genuine milestones were erected in the 1720s (Trumpington, Cambs., 1727); an Act of 1744 made them compulsory on most roads, and another in 1766 extended their use to all. Many stones of this period survive, and some have very pleasing layouts and lettering. (White Stone (Herefordshire) 1700; Henley in Arden (Warwicks.) 1748, on a tablet in a wall.) They range from the low painted stone ones of SE Scotland, and slate in N Wales, to monumental white specimens, as one near Ascot (Berks.), and the 'White Lady' stone at Thames Ditton (Surrey), by the Orleans Inn near Esher (1767). Most are about two feet high. Some are of cast-iron, or plaques affixed to posts (New Forest area). Milestones continued to be erected throughout the 19th century, and their date can usually be deduced from the style and lettering. Spellings, in the earlier ones, can be wild; many were made by local craftsmen; abbreviations are still common—Cor for Corbridge, or even just C; B for Bodmin; (at Tickhill) Wor 10 Lon 157, for Worksop and London.

Sometimes a lot of knowledge was presumed; Sarum for Salisbury may be familiar, but Barum for Barnstaple is not; nor is Shaston for Shaftesbury! There is a series in Yorkshire where the mileage shown is the 'customary' mile, which itself varies, but which is usually between $1\frac{1}{3}$ and 2 statute miles, no doubt to comfort the traveller; for example, a stone in Rudding Lane, near Harrogate, still in its original position, reads: Knaresborough 2 miles, Spofforth 2 miles, Harrogate 1 mile, Leeds 9 miles; the actual mileages are 3, 3, 2, and 14. There were still recently over 50 such stones in the West Riding alone.

Lime-trees were planted about 1700 as mileposts from Salisbury to Shaftesbury, and some still remain.

Property Marks are symbols, arms, crests, letters or inscriptions, either at the boundaries or estates or on the walls of individual properties. They may be on posts or stones, like the City of London marks on iron posts or pyramids in Epping Forest, Hadley Woods, etc.; initials set up at the edge of newly enclosed land, e.g. on Rigton High Moor (Yorks. WR), in the 1770s. Mediaeval monasteries often incised a cross on a stone, as on Fountains Earth Moor. Property marks may also be on

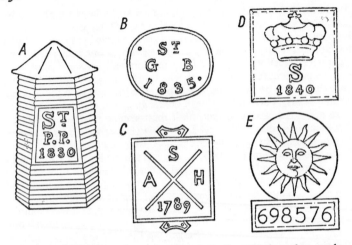

FIG. 22. Boundary and property marks. *A*, *B*, *C*, parish boundary marks—
A is a short iron post, *B* and *C* wall-plaques; *B* has the initials of the parish,
C its badge (the St Andrew's Cross) as well. *D*, an estate boundary mark—
here the crown and letter stand for the Lord Southampton. *E*, an insurance
mark (the Sun)

plaques of metal, more or less decorative, affixed to a wall. When I was a
boy the words 'French Hospital' on such a plaque in a suburban road
puzzled me until I discovered that they denoted the owner of the
property, which in this case belonged to the French Hospital in London.
Schools and other bodies often have elaborate armorial or pictorial
plaques, some of them 18th century. Houses built on estates are often
marked with monograms, initials, arms, etc. plaques, or on stones like
milestones. One of the latter type is on the London road at Guildford,
near Abbotswood, on the former boundary of Stoke and Worplesdon
parishes. The London parishes usually have wall-plaques with initials
and date (St G. 1787), and little groups of these of different dates can be
found; stumpy posts also occur, as in Woburn Square, WC1. The
ancient cities, such as Norwich, with its 47 parishes, have many of these
plaques; Norwich has over 100 still in situ, mostly of lead, but a few of
iron (Fig. 22, above). Some street bollards are also parish boundary
posts, like that at the Holborn end of Chancery Lane, London WC2.
The western boundary of the city is marked by Holborn Bars, two
stone monoliths carved with the city shield.

A special kind of post is that known as a 'wine and coal post', or a
City Post. These were set up as a result of an Act of 1861, which continued earlier Acts and levied a duty on coal and wine brought into

London; the money was used for the improvement of the metropolis. The boundary of the Metropolitan Police District was taken as defining the area covered by the Act, and posts were set up accordingly along this line, on roads, railways and canals where they crossed it (and, although not compulsorily under the Act, at other points too). The posts bear the arms of the City of London (the cross and dagger), and the inscription ACT 24 AND 25 VICT. CAP 42. An example can be seen on Epsom Common.

Between 2 and 3 Taviton Street, London WC1, are two plaques of coarse stone, one with a ducal coronet over a letter B, the other with a baron's coronet over an S. These were placed there in 1840–41, when the boundary of the Duke of Bedford's and Lord Southampton's estates was adjusted.

A prominent tree is sometimes used as a boundary mark—as the Shire Oak, Headingley, Leeds (the old tree survived until 1941, and has been replaced).

A special type of mark is that of a mediaeval trade guild, such as that of the wool industry at Lavenham, Suffolk, a mitre over a fleur de lys in plaster on the house walls—this is the sign of St Blaise, patron of wool-combers.

Insurance marks should be noted, small plaques usually high on a house, in the form of the badge of the company, e.g. the Sun.

Mounting Stones, squared blocks of stone, usually stepped, sometimes on both sides, are to be seen not only at the gates or doors of country houses and churches, but also in urban settings, such as in Hyde Park, London, Royal Crescent, Bath, and Burford (Oxon.). There is a three-step stone, built of dry-stone walling, outside Yarrow Church (Selkirkshire) (a 'loupin'-on stane'). The Duke of Wellington had one set up for him outside the Athenaeum in Waterloo Place, London, in 1830; it is long and low, with steps at each end.

Tethering-rings, set in stones, are found also at church and house gates (e.g. Peterchurch, Herefords.).

Packing-stones are like rough mounting blocks, in two steps. They are found by the sides of roads rising out of valleys, in Yorkshire, Monmouth and elsewhere. They are on the left-hand side going up the hill; the man carrying the pack sat to rest on the lower ledge and rested his pack on the upper.

Raised pavements can still be seen in some old towns, e.g. Dorking, Surrey (pl. 30, p. 265).

Unmodernised Road Surfaces are of course becoming increasingly scarce. Stone setts are still common in the Midlands and North, and there are quite a number of streets so paved in London. They have been retained in the High Street of Guildford (Surrey). Elm Hill, Norwich, has a cobbled surface. Cobbled pavements can be seen at Little Walsingham (Norfolk), and kerbsides in Broad Street, Ludlow (Salop). Some brick pavements survive, as at Tunbridge Wells (Kent). Original pavements of flat rectangular stones of irregular size (and very pleasing effect) still exist, as in Bloomsbury, London WC1, e.g. the south side of Russell Square; and in Bath (e.g. North and South Parades). Very large flag-stones can be seen under the Arches, London WC2. Wood block road-ways have not yet all disappeared, as in Upper Thames Street, London EC4 (July 1960). Biddenden (Kent) has pavements of 'Bethersden marble'. Paving of sheep or deer bones, now rare, still exist in a few places (e.g. at almshouses at Wantage, Berks.). See pl. 30, p. 265.

Tilting-posts or quintains, were posts with a movable horizontal arm from which hung a sack of straw, or some such target, for tilting at with a long pole. One survives at Offham, Kent (late mediaeval).

Toll Houses can still be seen on 18th century turnpike roads and at the end of bridges. They are cottages, with a door on to the road, and often ornamental in architecture and octagonal, etc., in shape. (By the bridge, Dorchester, Oxon; on the turnpike, east of Marlborough.) The first tollgates were at Wadesmill, Herts, in 1663.

Watchmen's Huts. The body-snatching trade of the 18th and early 19th centuries, for the supply of material to the anatomy schools, for which recently-used graves were reopened, led to the erection of watchmen's huts (or 'boxes') in churchyards. There is a fine stone example at Wanstead (Essex). Crail (Fife) has a mortuary for protecting the dead before burial. Hudds are clergymen's portable graveside shelters (Friskney, Lincs.).

Weathervanes have been in continuous use since the Middle Ages, and perhaps earlier; they were known to the Romans. They occur in a wide variety of forms, from the familiar cock on a church spire, to the heraldic device on the outbuildings of a great house, or a fanciful shape on some farm. Many survive from the 16th century or before.

This list of odds and ends cannot be exhaustive: there are for example many small buildings which could be so described, such as lock-ups, fire-engine houses, bakehouses, brewhouses, pest houses, teazle towers, tortoise houses, root-houses, eel-houses, deer-larders; also dole stones in the churchyards on which benefactions were placed; plague stones on the edge of villages, where food for the stricken villagers was left; church marks, names of the farmers, etc., who were responsible for the upkeep of the stretch of fence round churchyard or glebe where their name appeared; chains to keep cattle out of churches, etc. The reader can make his own collection.

DECEPTIVE NATURAL FEATURES[1]

Erosion-gullies are a feature of steep slopes in certain conditions. They descend the hillside vertically, and are V-sectioned. They should not be mistaken for hollow ways, which have flat bottoms. Gullies can be deceptive where the hillside is now wooded, and erosion slowed up, thus filling the gully-bottom with earth. Gullies in open country can be seen in Wessex (e.g. Uffington, Berks.), and in the Black Mountains, (Breck.); and on wooded slopes in the Chilterns, e.g. at Chinnor, but these may be tracks of the old London-Oxford road.

It is possible for natural causes to produce features imitating the ramparts of a hillfort on a steep slope; on Pitch Hill, Ewhurst (Surrey), successive **landslips** have formed horizontal banks across the hillside, with the appearance of fort banks. Outcrops can also look like terraces.
 In mountain country a gully down a slope, edged by low banks, may look like a way of human origin, but is really the track of a **rock-slide**.

Sink-holes and swallow-holes, in limestone country, sometimes look like mineral workings, but have no lips or spoil-heaps.

Stabilised Dunes. Vegetation growing on a damp patch on sandy soil may become covered by drifting or wind-borne sand, which in turn is keyed by more vegetation, and so on; this process can form ridges or mounds, which can look very like barrows. Some mounds at Thursley, Surrey, long thought to be barrows, were only recently shown to be dunes. The successive layers of vegetation show as black streaks in the sandy soil.

Terracettes. It has recently been pointed out by Dr G. H. Dury that the narrow horizontal steps across a steep hillside, usually known as 'sheep-paths' or sheep-tracks, are formed not by sheep, but by soil-creep. They should be called terracettes. Sheep and cattle use them of course, but sheep-paths which run obliquely do not form steps. The banks at Avebury and Maiden Castle have prominent examples, and they can be found everywhere. Sometimes a stepped scar in a steep valley-side, as at Hutton-le-Hole (Yorks. NR), can look like an amphi-theatre.
 Several natural objects can look like barrows, such as moraines and outcrops (as can the remains of crop, peat, etc., stacks or even ruined buildings).

[1] see also the effects of glaciers, pp. 35-39.

CHAPTER 3

Types of Field Antiquities: Surface Finds

A walk in the country, or even digging in the garden, is not infrequently enlivened by the finding of small objects on the ground, some of which may well be the remains of the activity of earlier generations of men. Not all people are first interested in archaeology by some conspicuous earthwork, and this may be their introduction. The names of cultures, etc., are more fully defined in the Background sections.

FLINT

Flint implements are perhaps the best-known of surface finds, and can indeed be picked up over a great deal of Britain, especially in the lowland zone. Flint is a very hard rock, but has special properties which made it convenient for the making of prehistoric implements. It is a concretion of almost pure silica (silicon dioxide), accumulated in cavities in chalk left by the decay of various marine animals such as sponges and sea-urchins, or collected round hard objects. Traces of these animals can sometimes be seen inside a lump of flint. Flint is usually translucent; it has a very close texture, and often looks like solid glass; it can be of various colours, black from the boulder-clay of the Yorkshire coast, honey-coloured from the Wolds, blue-black, grey, brown or banded with white from further south; reds and yellows are also found. Some of these colours are very local in origin, and tools made in them can be traced across country, giving evidence of trade or migration.

Flint is found in layers in the Upper Chalk, either in slabs (tabular) or in nodules; these nodules have a thin rough whitish crust called *cortex*. Under the prolonged action of chemicals in the soil (technically, the leaching of silica from between quartz crystals by alkaline solutions), flint gradually changes colour, starting with the surface and working inward, until in thinnish places the new colour goes right through the piece; the effect, called *patination*, is at first milky mottling (pale blue-grey and white), thickening to dead white. Patination varies in colour with the composition of the soil (e.g. on greensand it is pale brown, and in gravel 'ochreous', red and yellow), and in rate of growth, even in two spots close together, so that it is not always a good guide to age, even relative age. But as a rough rule a mesolithic piece (say 5000 BC) will be whiter than a neolithic flint (say 2000 BC) from the same field. Flint is not only fairly easy to work, once the skill has been acquired, but is a pleasure to handle—the texture of a flake surface is extremely smooth to the touch, more like glass or porcelain than stone.

The working of flint depends on its peculiar properties of flaking, which it shares in various degrees with glass, obsidian and chert, all forms of silica. If a slab of flint is struck sharply at right angles to the surface it does not crack or split, but a cone drops out from the point of impact. If the piece is a nodule, it tends to behave in the same way, but the strength of the cortex prevents the formation of a cone, and produces a fracture which bends in and then out again, giving a shell-like appearance to the flake surface. In more detail, a struck flake has definite and regular characteristics (fig. 23; p. 256)—a *striking platform*, where the blow was struck; a *bulb of percussion* just below it, with a *flake scar* where the flake is detached from the core; little cracks radiating from the point of percussion; transverse *ripples* where the forces within the flint conflict, accompanied by tiny vertical fissures reflecting the strains; sometimes the edge of the flake opposite to where the blow was struck is curved over and inward in a *hinge-fracture* (when the force of the blow is not strong enough to go straight through the piece). Not all of these signs are always present completely, but usually several of them are, and often all. The implement will then be finished to the particular shape aimed at by the maker, which may involve further trimming of the piece by detaching other flakes, and the making of a cutting edge by means of small flaking vertically from the edge. In general, no flake should be accepted as genuine unless these three features are present, regular flaking characteristics, defined and intentional shape, and secondary working.

The prominence of the bulb and other signs of flaking depends on the angle at which the blow was struck, which in turn depends on the technique of striking used, and the sort of flake, core or blade which was aimed at. These factors vary with the culture. For an account of the cultures mentioned here see pp. 41–82.

The earliest cultures (Abbevillian) used stone hammers held in the other hand, which produced a wide flaking-angle (i.e. the angle between the striking platform and the flake surface) and a strong bulb; later (Acheulian) wooden bars were used, producing shallower flaking; Clactonian implements were made by indirect force, that is, by placing the nodule on an anvil-stone and striking it above with another stone, the flake being struck off the core by the rebound from the anvil— this produced flakes of classical characteristics. Levalloisian technique was by way of preparing a core by flaking it all round, before detaching a large complete tool with one blow. The Upper Palaeolithic cultures used thin narrow blades, made by pressure, that is, by forcing small flakes off (with very shallow bulbs) with bone spatulas; this continued throughout the Mesolithic. Neolithic and Bronze Age flintwork is on larger flakes, but has much secondary flaking, often very fine and close, and, later, stepped or scaled along the edges and over the upper surface. The bulb side is usually left untouched.

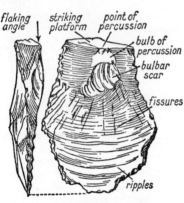

FIG. 23. The flaking of flint

Natural forces can also fracture a nodule of flint; the crushing of stones against each other in a glacial moraine, or the smashing of stones against each other on a beach or in a river bed, or by rocks falling on them from a height, are obvious ways; ploughs, and animals or wheeled traffic, can crush flints in a field or on a road. Frost can penetrate cracks in the cortex, and prise off a flake or a 'pot-lid' (a round piece); heath fires can shatter a nodule into a cluster of fragments. These causes, however, do not always produce all the characteristics, and the flake surface is not usually so smooth to the touch; the flake-angle with crushed flints tends also to be more obtuse than with human flints. Frost fractures are flattish, with minute cracks; their surface may be pitted. But caution should be observed; one always picks up dozens of flints hopefully, but retains few, if any. (See pl. 16, *b, d.*)

The famous *eoliths*, once thought to be very early man-made flints, have now been shown to be due to natural causes. Even genuine flints can be very crude; prehistoric man often picked up a piece, shaped it to do a particular job, and threw it away. These ill-formed pieces can be recognised by the marks of wear along their edge, minute nibbles which give a series of tiny but regular bumps to the thumb-nail if rubbed along the edge of the flint. This wear is normally on one side of the edge of flint only; natural wear is irregular, and overlaps on to both sides indiscriminately.

Flint implements can be found on the surface in fields, heaths, etc., particularly in chalk, sand or gravel country, and in most parts of the country; also in gravel pits, and even in heaps of gravel brought for road-metalling. Ditching, etc., operations, and building work, should always be examined. Rabbit-scrapes frequently throw up flints and other small objects from barrows and Roman sites. Look on gentle hilltops and south-facing slopes, but not on heavy, damp lower ground;

29. BRIDGES. *Above*, the oldest form, a clapper bridge; *centre*, mediaeval — with characteristic pointed cutwaters and road recesses; *below*, a simple packhorse bridge without parapets (14th century onwards)

30. PAVEMENTS. *Above, left,* a mediaeval paved path ; *right,* "a raised pavement" following the road's original contours. *Below,* 18th century cobbles with later flagstones

absence of implements on likely sites may be due to thick tree-cover in early times. Flint occurring in non-flint country should always be examined—it may have been brought by man. The best areas, which of course correspond to the areas of easy settlement for early man, are the chalk, gravel and limestones of the south-east half of England, the moors of Devon, Cornwall, and Yorkshire, both the Pennines and the North York Moors. Fields should be quartered slowly and carefully, and every flint which appears to show the characteristics mentioned above picked up. The best conditions are after rain, or in frosty weather, when the soil is broken down and stones exposed. Helping a farmer to hoe a field is a good method! A high proportion of waste flakes and chips will always be found. Burnt flints (grey to black, and crazed with a fine network of black lines; see pl. 16, c) if evenly distributed over a field, probably came either with lime spread in the 18th or 19th century, or from a fire; but if concentrated in a small area may represent the site of a human settlement. Implements may accompany such a concentration. Implements are often found in one part only of a field, also representing an area of settlement. The great quantity of implements found, say handaxes, compared with the very small population, is of course due to the enormous length of time involved.

It should be remembered that not only the fields but the stones on them belong to the farmer or landowner, and in strict law permission is necessary to take them away. But few farmers will object to one's walking across a field and picking up flints. Gates should of course be shut, and no damage done to growing crops. In practice searching should be done after ploughing and in winter and spring, in any case not after crops have started to show. Permission should be sought for a prolonged search—this may also have the advantage that the farmer may be interested himself, and may know a great deal about the surface finds on his land, and where they can be found.

Flint and stone axes, and arrowheads, are sometimes found in farm buildings, as charms (like horseshoes by the door) to keep misfortune away from the cattle. The way of life in some periods suggests other places to look besides fields: such as, for the Palaeolithic, gravels, beach exposures of boulder clay, etc., moraines (exposed by lakes and reservoirs), and river beds (where the implements are rolled, that is, worn smooth by water and striking against other stones); for the Mesolithic, rock shelters, also on heaths and moors—here patches of broken ground should be examined, including paths and tank-tracks.

The main types of implements (fig. 25, p. 260) which may be expected are:

Abbevillian, rough handaxes on cores, often with patches of cortex showing, with zigzag edges due to alternate deep flaking.

Acheulian, handaxes with shallow flaking and fairly straight edges; these can be quite large—they are ovate (oval) to begin with, with a 'twisted' or double-curved edge like an S in reverse. Later they are pear-shaped, and finished with a narrow or pointed end; some of these are made on thick flakes. In this stage also scrapers on flakes and thick blades can be found. On gravel soils they are patinated yellow and brown (ochreous).

Clactonian, a variety of tools on rough, heavy flakes, with prominent flaking at a wide angle. These are mostly scrapers with the straight or curved edges worked and worn; the upper surface may have cortex, the lower is usually the untouched flake-surface. Rough points and end-scrapers also; an interesting tool is the chopper, made from a crude pebble, chipped off from both sides to make an edge, a tool of very primitive ancestry.

Levalloisian tools are similar, but often have a prepared platform, flaked before the tool is detached from the core. Flakes made from these tortoise cores are worked all over their upper surfaces. Points are common.

Mousterian combines handaxes with pointed or rounded ends with large flakes with finely-worked edges. Small discoidal core-scrapers; triangular points, the edges worked for use as knives; side-scrapers with curved edges, sometimes D-shaped.

Upper Palaeolithic (mostly Creswellian in Britain) tools are quite different, being made on thin and small blades and cores. The blades, whose upper side is made by means of long parallel flaking, are finished to a variety of forms; points, awls, borers (where the wear will be on alternate edges at the tip); knives, side-scrapers, saws, where the long edges are worked; end-scrapers; blades with bites out of the sides, for spoke-shaves; a variety of burins, that is, blades with thin chips removed from one end, to form a tiny transverse edge; core-scrapers or 'push-planes' made of stumpy or long cores, with one side prepared by long parallel flaking to make a cutting edge at the round flat bottom of the core—this type, and some of the others, lasts into the Mesolithic.

Mesolithic tools are in two traditions, Sauveterrian on the moors, Maglemosian in the forests. The Sauveterrian are mostly microliths, very small blades made for mounting in wooden handles, sometimes several to one tool. These are in many forms, often geometric—triangles, crescents, trapezes, etc.; they were made from the shaped end of a blade whose remainder was snapped off, making the 'microburins' which are thus not implements at all. Tiny thin slivers of flint may have battered backs, one edge finely chipped along, to prevent its wooden haft splitting. Saws and awls are common, and non-geometric blades. Core-scrapers and small tanged arrowheads. The Maglemosian and Horsham cultures share many of these forms, but add the heavy tools needed for tree-clearing and digging; these are picks and adzes, 'maceheads',

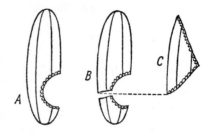

FIG. 24. Stages in the making of a mesolithic tool. A blade of flint is notched on one side (*A*); it is then snapped off at the narrow part (*B*), leaving, below, a reject piece, or 'micro-burin'; the upper part is then worked into a geometric shape (*C*)

probably digging-stick weights, and axes and arrowheads with their edge transverse to the body of the flint, made by detaching a flake (tranchet); these can be resharpened simply by detaching another transverse flake. The 'Horsham point' is worked along one edge and has a hollow (incurved) base. Small round (thumb-nail) scrapers are very common on mesolithic sites.

Neolithic and Bronze Age flintwork is different again, being on heavier blades and rough flakes. Much of it is just flakes picked up, roughly worked to give a cutting edge, used, and discarded. The forms are therefore not very uniform in execution, but fall into scrapers, both side and end, knives, borers, points, saws; many scrapers are round or oval, larger than the mesolithic ones. Arrowheads go from the primary neolithic leaf forms (long, stumpy, pear-shaped), to the small tranchet forms of the secondary Neolithic (with variants such as lopsided types), to the tanged and barbed types of the Bronze Age, including the large, finely flaked, triangular Wessex type. Flint axes appear, long parallel-sided types like the stone ones, and sharpening flakes from these can be found. Hollow scrapers and sickle-blades (with the characteristic gloss caused by cutting corn-stalks). Discoidal knives, partly polished, are Food Vessel types, as are slug knives; flint daggers, imitating metal forms, are Beaker forms. The secondary Neolithic has a variety of special forms—picks and axes, tranchet derivative arrows, fabricators (long bars of flint with rounded end, of doubtful purpose), core-scrapers, square-ended, discoidal and waisted scrapers (the latter perhaps hoes).

Flint continued to be used for implements right into the Middle Ages, e.g. for marking and cutting glass, but cannot be distinguished from the rough neolithic flakes. **Gunflints** however are distinctive—they are square or oblong, unpatinated, used in flintlock guns in the 17th, 18th and 19th centuries; they are still made for the foreign market at Brandon, Suffolk, three miles from the ancient flint mines of Grimes Graves (fig. 26, p. 262).

Flint implements can sometimes be bought in antique shops, and

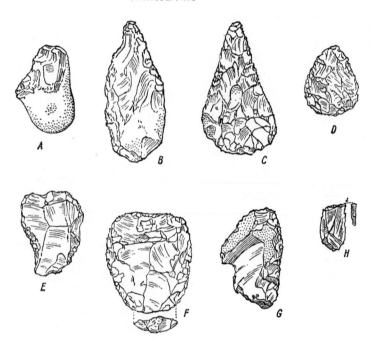

FIG. 25. Types of flint implement

A early palaeolithic pebble tool
B Abbevillian axe
C middle Acheulian axe
D twisted ovate (with s-shaped edge)
E Clactonian flake-tool
F Levalloisian flake-tool (with end-view of prepared striking platform.
G palaeolithic side-scraper
H upper palaeolithic burin
I palaeolithic/mesolithic core-tool ('push-plane')
J microlith (Forest culture)
K geometric microliths
L mesolithic end-scraper
M neolithic scraper (with end view)
N Bronze Age round scraper (disc)
O discoidal knife (Beaker), with polished edge
P slug knife (Food Vessel), and section
Q flint dagger (A Beaker)
Arrowheads: R, transverse; S, lopsided; T, leaf; U, tanged-and-barbed; V, Wessex type

MESOLITHIC

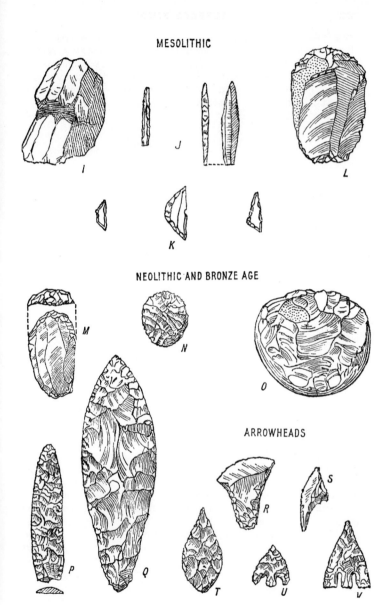

I   J   K   L

NEOLITHIC AND BRONZE AGE

M   N   O

ARROWHEADS

P   Q   R   S   T   U   V

gaps in collections can be filled in this way, but only with full usefulness if the exact provenance is known. Here though one must beware of fakes; the 19th century collectors' market gave rise to several people, such as Flint Jack at Whitby or George Glover in the London area, whose work is often highly skilled, and sometimes hard to tell from the real thing. The form can give them away, but an expert should be consulted if there is any doubt.

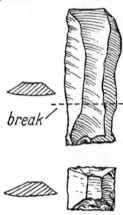

FIG. 26. A gunflint, made from part of a straight blade. *Above,* upper surface and section of the blade; *below,* the finished gunflint, snapped off and reshaped

STONE

Apart from flint, implements were also made of stone, the best-known of which are the polished stone axes of neolithic times (fig. 27). These are made in a variety of rocks, including greenstones and volcanic ash, the grey stone of Graig Lwyd, diorite and other hard rocks. In the highland zone, where flint was scarce or had to be imported, many hard rocks were used for ordinary tools, quartzite, hard limestones or even sandstones, and occasionally slate and ironstone. The commonest substitute for flint is the opaque, grey or brown siliceous rock **chert**, found in the Pennines and further north. Chert has flaking properties very similar to those of flint, but not quite so controllable; it produces tools of the recognisable forms, but rather rougher in shape and finish. There are distinctive local types of stone axe, such as in Shetland and Cumberland.

Round or oval pebbles were used as slingstones and potboilers.

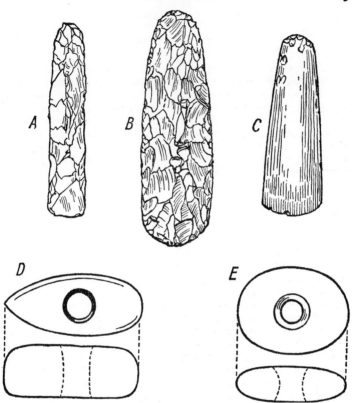

FIG. 27. Stone axes. *A*, 'Thames pick', late mesolithic; *B*, neolithic flint axe; *C*, neolithic polished axe; *D*, Early Bronze-Age axe-hammer; *E*, mesolithic 'mace-head'. (*D* and *E*, top-view and side section)

Unflaked nodules of flint served as hammerstones—these acquired an easily recognisable surface, battered and contused (pl. 16, *c*). Perforated stones could be net-sinkers or weights. Stone discs may be hunting equipment, or could be road-bowls (see p. 207). Quartzite pebbles, polished on one side, can come from the mould-boards of ancient ploughs. Sharpening and grinding stones are often found.

BONE AND WOOD

Bone was used for implements, but will not often be found on the surface; the main types are shoulder-blades as shovels, antler levers in flint-mines, harpoons, thin slivers as awls and needles, and heavy pieces sliced off to form wedges. Many things, such as needles and combs, were made of bone in the Middle Ages. Humanly worked bones can be found among the profusion of bones and flints which strew the foreshores at Clactonian sites like that at Jaywick, Essex. Here the late Hazzledine Warren also found a pointed and fire-hardened stick, but wooden tools and utensils have of course mostly perished, except on wet sites like foreshores and bogs, or in wells.

BRONZE

Bronze tools and weapons are often found in digging operations all over the country. Perhaps the commonest are **axes**, which follow a dating sequence (fig. 28) starting with a simple flat type in the Early Bronze Age, hafted on to a right-angled stick split to embrace the axe, and bound with string. This developed flanges along the sides, to grip the haft more firmly. Then, in the Middle Bronze Age, the 'palstave' appeared by the addition of a stop-ridge between the flanges to prevent the haft driving down too far and splitting. By the Late Bronze Age this had become a sturdy tool with a loop on one side of the stop-ridge to attach a cord to for even greater firmness. In the Late Bronze Age also there were introduced new types, the winged axe, in which the flanges were folded over as wings to grasp the haft; and the socketed axe, where the whole axe was now a hollow container for a solid haft, tied to the head by means of cord through the loop. This type, which is very commonly found, has a thickened neck for greater strength, and ornaments on the faces consisting of raised lines and dots (the Yorkshire type has three of these), or curving lines to imitate the wings of the winged axe. The Breton type is plain with square section. Socketed axes are sometimes known to country people as candlesticks or cream-jugs. Other bronze implements are **daggers**, the early ones with either tangs or rivets to attach them to the pommel; **swords**, which are rapiers in the Middle Bronze Age, some with long chapes of metal to protect the ends of the scabbards, and leaf-shaped types in the Late Bronze Age, that is, widening out towards the end of the blade—these have tongues in one piece with the blade, on which plates of wood, bone, etc., were fastened as a grip, and short winged chapes. **Spearheads** also evolve from tanged to socketed types, some having loops

at the base of the blade, or openings in it. There is also a variety of
tools, chisels, gouges, hammers, knives, sickles, razors, tongs, hooks,
etc.; harness pieces; pins with various types of head, rings, armlets, etc.
In the Late Bronze Age there were travelling smiths, who collected
broken or worn-out tools on their travels and remade them into new

EARLY BRONZE AGE

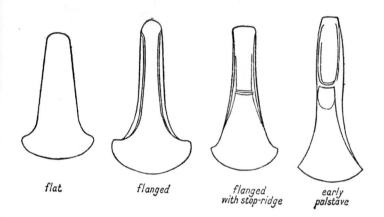

flat   *flanged*   *flanged*   *early*
                                   with stop-ridge   *palstave*

MIDDLE AND LATE BRONZE AGE

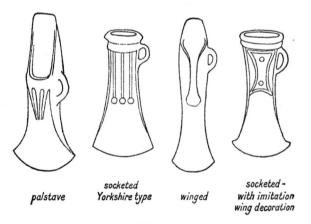

                socketed   *socketed -*
palstave   *Yorkshire type*   *winged*   *with imitation*
                                              wing decoration

FIG. 28. Bronze axes

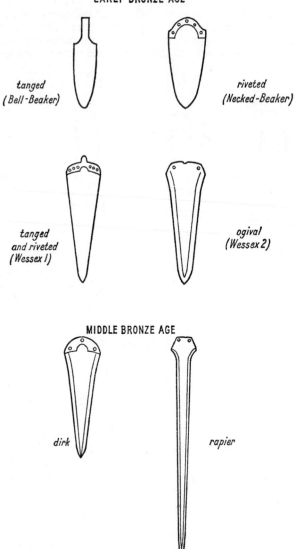

FIG 29. Daggers and swords

LATE BRONZE AGE

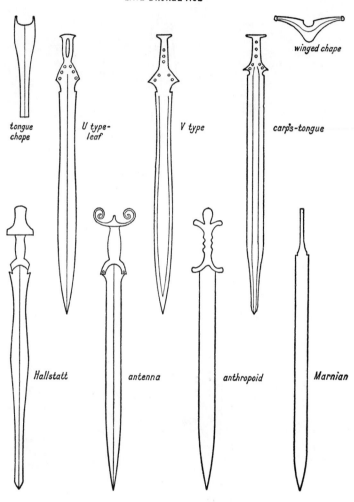

winged chape

tongue chape

U type-leaf

V type

carp's-tongue

Hallstatt

antenna

anthropoid

Marnian

IRON AGE

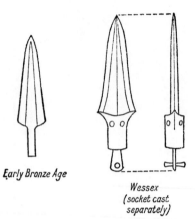

TANGED

Early Bronze Age

*Wessex
(socket cast
separately)*

SOCKETED

loop
←for
thong

*Middle
Bronze Age 1*

basal
loops

*Middle
Bronze Age 2*

ornamental
"lunate"
holes in
blade

*Late
Bronze
Age*

*Roman
and
later*

FIG. 30. Spears

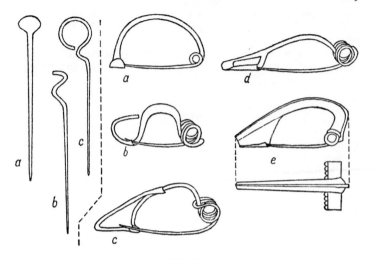

FIG. 31

Pins. *a*, Wessex bulb-headed, Early Bronze Age; *b*, Swan's-neck, Iron Age A;
c, ring-headed, Iron Age B
Fibulae (brooches or safety-pins). *a*, Hallstatt, Iron Age A; *b*, *c*, *d*, La Tène,
Iron Age B–C, showing development of catch-plate; *e*, Roman, seen from
the side and above, showing covered springs

ones. If their stock-in-trade was lost it forms a hoard, which can contain
a wide variety of things. Hoards still turn up, and if a broken tool is
found, it may mean that a hoard is lying not far off. An interesting
point is that the bronze used for tools in the Late Bronze Age has a lead
content absent from those of the Middle Bronze Age.

IRON

Iron tools, etc., are in a great profusion of forms, and the tools of the
Belgae, and even more, the Romans, are very similar to a carpenter's
or blacksmith's set today. Special Iron Age types are currency bars,
long strips of metal with pinched-in ends, cauldrons, buckets, mirrors,
some elaborately decorated in the flowing Celtic styles; daggers and
swords with elaborate pommels and scabbards; pins, both of the 'safety'
type, in a dated sequence, and straight types with bent or ring heads;
torques and personal ornaments; harness and chariot-fittings; helmets,
shields; small objects like statuettes and human and animal features

for the tops of staffs, temple buckets, braziers, etc., or ceremonial cauldrons. This list could be extended, and the range of objects should be seen in museums.

Corrosion is of course likely to have affected most finds of metal objects, and expert help should be sought in cleaning and restoring them.

POTTERY

Many other things can be found on the surface, of which pottery is perhaps the most important. Most pottery is only revealed by excavation, but sherds occasionally turn up in fields, and, more richly, on the sites of Roman towns, etc. Many come from farm middens spread as manure on the fields. It is not practicable here to list all the hundreds of pot-forms created from the Neolithic onwards, and only brief notes of the main characteristics can be given. Domestic pottery up to the Middle Ages was usually very coarse, but in most periods there have been better wares; the variety of forms increases with each period to the present, but already in Roman times there was a considerable number. Early pottery was stiffened by the addition to the clay of little pieces of stone, chalk or shell, called grit or backing; sometimes this was such as to disintegrate in the firing, leaving tiny holes in the fabric. Most early pottery was black or buff; red patches, extending sometimes to a side or even a whole pot, were caused by uneven firing, oxidation due to air getting into the kiln. Certain pottery is coated with a thin layer of clay called slip, for greater impermeability or for ornament; from Roman times onwards glazes are also used. The main features are:

Neolithic. Smooth, well-fired, round-bottomed, often grit-holes; buff or grey. (Pl. 17*a*, p. 160.)

Secondary Neolithic. Coarse, thick, black ware with white grit or spongy; heavily ornamented with 'maggots' of cord, bird-bones, stick-ends, finger-nail; round or round-pointed bottoms; built up in rings (but ring-building occurs as late as the Iron Age). Also grooved and rusticated ware. (Pl. 17, *b*, *c*.)

Beaker. Fine buff; B types thinner than A and C; rouletted or incised designs, and horizontal cord lines in B2; flat bottoms. (Pl. 17, *d*. *e*.)

Food Vessel. Thick, coarse, buff, corky, often blackish, gritted; incised or cord ornament.

Urns. Like Food Vessels, sometimes very coarse indeed. Pygmy vessels may be hard and smooth. (Pl. 17, *f*.)

Late Bronze Age. Thick buff, globular, barrel or bucket urns, raised ridges. (Pl. 17, *g*.)

Early Iron Age, A and B. Both rough and smooth types, buff or

NEOLITHIC

Windmill Hill

SECONDARY NEOLITHIC

Mortlake

Rinyo-Clacton (grooved ware)

EARLY BRONZE AGE I

Beakers

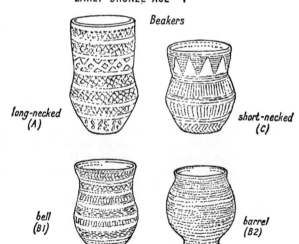

long-necked (A)

short-necked (C)

bell (B1)

barrel (B2)

FIG. 32. Types of pottery I

blackish, some burnished, some haematite-coated; south-western
B, black smooth, with curvilinear incised ornament. Flat-based,
except for omphalos (hollow) bases in south-east. (Pl. 18, *a*, *b*.)

Belgic. Wheel-made, black and red, some buff, smooth and hard;
foot-rings, bead-rims. (Pl. 18, *c*, p. 161.)

Roman. A wide variety of bowls, dishes, jugs, jars, etc. of all shapes
and sizes: 'Samian' or *terra sigillata*, fine hard red, burnished, with moulded designs; special types, such as Castor, black or dark grey with barbotine decoration (raised designs stuck on); wavy or folded ware. New Forest ware is sometimes hard grey with a purple glaze, or soft and buff, with circles and wavy stripes in reddish paint or stamped rosettes; Crambeck ware, from Yorkshire, is buff or blackish with white grits with red-brown paint. Some pottery from Colchester (1st century) is lead-glazed. Most Roman pottery, however, is 'coarse' ware, native-made, and often reflecting older traditions: much of it is grey or brown, buff or nearly white; incised decoration is common, often in criss-cross lines; there are also stamps and raised blobs. Some pieces are quite thin and well-made; at the other

EARLY BRONZE AGE 2

Food vessels

Yorkshire type   Southern type

Pygmy Types

Aldbourne cup   "grape cup"

"incense cup"

FIG 33. Types of pottery II

extreme are the *amphorae* and *mortaria*, for wine-storage and
pounding of food respectively, which are very thick buff. Dales
ware is hard and smooth, black or brown; Derbyshire ware gritty,
grey, red inside, with 'goose-flesh' texture. Samian was imitated
in the 4th century, with Red ware. There is a type with metallic
silver-grey finish. The variety is bewildering until one is familiar
with it. (Pl. 18, *d* to *g*.)

Anglo-Saxon, pagan (AD 450–650), again has a number of domestic
types, with a few more formal. Domestic wares are black, grooved
and burnished, thick black or grey rusticated, thick black plain;
grey with roulette ornament, rough grey-buff, buff-black plain;

cinerary urns are continental in appearance, black, with raised bands and stamped decoration.

Middle Saxon. 650–850. 7th century pottery imported into Cornwall is red, either soft with stamps or hard, plain or finger-nailed; also combed amphorae. Jutish pottery in Kent is often white or pink. East Anglia imported wheel-made pottery from the Rhineland, *Later*, 850–c. 1100, thick plain black types were common, some with white grits. Pingsdorf ware from the Rhineland, grey, painted, was imported in the 11th century, and also imitated; the earliest wheel-made glazed ware in Western Europe was found at Thetford; it is yellow, pale green or orange, some with red on orange (10th–11th century); another late Saxon type has straw backing, and St Neots ware is shelly. Stamford ware (lead-glazed) lasted from the 11th century to the 13th.

Mediaeval and later. Plain wares continue, but lead-glazing is more common, and can frequently be picked up. The colours are yellow, green (often apple-green), brown; designs are stamped, incised or painted. Coarse ware is buff, black, grey or brown. Painted ware was imported from France, lustre from Spain. Tall flagons are common. These types continue into the early 17th century. Distinctive pottery was made by the Cistercians. (Pl. 19, *a* to *d*, p. 192.)

Stoneware was imported and then imitated in the late 16th century; the Rhenish flagons with a human mask on the neck, called Bellarmines, are common. This sort of pottery led to the English salt-glazed stonewares of the 17th and 18th centuries, grey or brown mottled or speckled. (Pl. 19, *e, f*, p. 192.)

Tin-glazed earthenware or Delft, with bold underglaze patterns, mostly in blue, came in also at this time, and from about 1630 was widely made in England, where its popularity is still high. In the 17th century also we meet slip-ware, usually dark brown with patterns of yellow slip; marbled ware, in which the slip has been joggled when soft to make an effect like that of certain papers; horizontal blue and white lines; dark blue with pale blue irregular blotches; heavy dark brown glazes are common, and purple is met with. The popular art of Staffordshire begins in the 17th century, and holds its own till the late 19th; we are scarcely concerned with the finer pottery and porcelain of this period, but sherds will sometimes turn up. Bone china and ironstone ware appear in the early 19th century, as does transfer-printed pottery. The mass of Victorian domestic wares need no description; the fields are liberally strewn with them, and with fragments of bottle, flower-pot, etc.,

In general, rims, bases and decoration give most information about old pottery, and should be concentrated on.

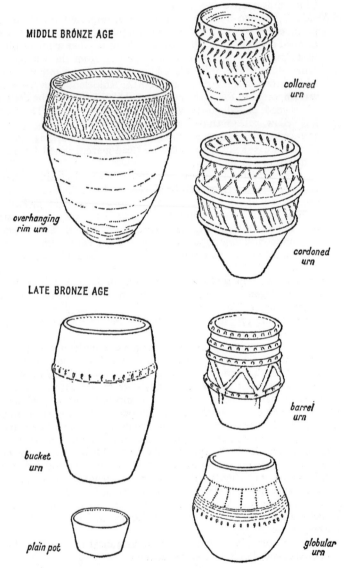

MIDDLE BRONZE AGE

collared
urn

overhanging
rim urn

cordoned
urn

LATE BRONZE AGE

bucket
urn

barrel
urn

plain pot

globular
urn

FIG. 34. Types of pottery III

IRON AGE A

*high-shouldered
situla*

*deep-shouldered
bowl*

IRON AGE B

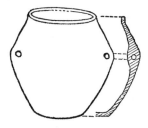

bead-rim jar

*jar with
countersunk handles*

*bowl with
curvilinear
decoration*

IRON AGE C

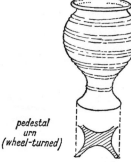

*pedestal
urn
(wheel-turned)*

butt-beaker

FIG. 35. Types of pottery IV

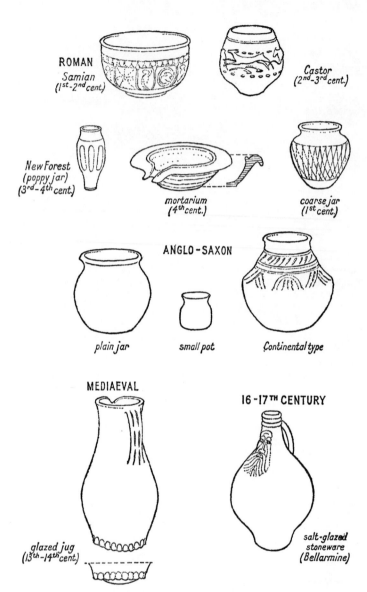

ROMAN

Samian
(1st-2nd cent.)

Castor
(2nd-3rd cent.)

New Forest
(poppy jar)
(3rd-4th cent.)

mortarium
(4th cent.)

coarse jar
(1st cent.)

ANGLO-SAXON

plain jar

small pot

Continental type

MEDIAEVAL

16-17TH CENTURY

glazed jug
(13th-14th cent.)

salt-glazed
stoneware
(Bellarmine)

FIG. 36. Types of pottery V

BUILDING MATERIALS

Building materials, such as bricks, tiles and plaster, found in quantity in a small space, point to the likelihood of a former building, and this should be followed up. Pre-Roman houses will not leave a mark on the surface, but Roman ones will; they were usually built of half-timbering filled with lath and plaster or wattle and daub, on stone footings or in stone packings, and this kind of building continued virtually until the 17th century. In some areas 'cob' is found, sticky mud mixed with moss and hair. In Brightwell churchyard, Berks., is a stretch of cob wall (mixed with straw), thatched, which may be 12th century or even earlier (pl. 26, p. 225). Clay-lump pisé is used in Norfolk.

Bricks. Roman bricks are made in many sizes; variation is to be expected, as bricks shrink up to 10 per cent of their dimensions, apart from the effect of hand-making. Ordinary small bricks are $5 \times 2\frac{1}{2} \times 1$–$1\frac{1}{2}$ in.; for hypocaust pillars square bricks of $8\frac{1}{2}$ in. sides were used, with larger sizes for the tops and bottoms of 11 in., 17 in. and 23 in. square, the latter 3 in. thick. For wall courses a size of 17 in. $\times$ 11 in. was used, and there are other shapes, such as quadrants and hexagons. Roman bricks have a smooth, rather soapy feel, being, like their tiles, fired less hard than modern ones. Brickmaking died out with the Romans, and was reintroduced from Flanders about 1220. These were large bricks, $10\frac{1}{2}$–$12\frac{1}{2} \times 5$–$6 \times 1\frac{3}{4}$–$2\frac{1}{4}$ in.; later a size 8–$9\frac{3}{4} \times 3\frac{3}{4}$–$4\frac{1}{4} \times 1\frac{3}{4}$–$2\frac{1}{2}$ in. was used. Dutch bricks, from about 1400, are smaller still, 6–8×3–$3\frac{3}{4} \times 1\frac{3}{8}$–$1\frac{3}{4}$ in. Until the 16th century there was no recognised standard, and the so-called Tudor brick was in use until the 18th century. Several attempts were made to regulate brick sizes, and to increase them: 1571—$9 \times 4\frac{1}{4} \times 2\frac{1}{4}$ in.; 1625—$9 \times 4\frac{3}{8} \times 2\frac{1}{4}$ in.; 1725—$9 \times 4\frac{1}{4} \times 2\frac{5}{8}$ in. But there were overlaps and variations, and size cannot be used as reliable evidence of date. The present size is usually known as $9 \times 4\frac{1}{2} \times 3$ in., but there are still variations—the length is strictly $8\frac{3}{4}$ in., the width $4\frac{9}{16}$; the thickness is $2\frac{5}{8}$ in. in the south of England, $2\frac{7}{8}$ in the north, from $1\frac{3}{4}$ to $3\frac{1}{8}$ in Birmingham, and up to $3\frac{1}{2}$ in Scotland. Brickwork becomes very common after the late 17th century. Special bricks were sometimes used for paving yards, etc., such as the small yellow ones $6 \times 3 \times 1$ in., of the late 17th century. (See plates 24, p. 217, and 27, p. 256.) Bricks can have makers' marks and dates. 'Frogs' were used from the 1830s.

Tiles were used extensively by the Romans. Roofs had two kinds, rectangular flat (*tegulae*) with two opposite edges turned up $12 \times 18 \times 1$ in.; these were linked by curved cover tiles (*imbrices*). Hot-air piping in walls and under floors was made of box-tiles which often had regular patterns of incised lines to serve as keying for the plaster. Small cubes

277

of brick or tile, *tesserae*, with side about ¾ in., were used for flooring, and turn up in large numbers on any Roman site. More elaborate floors, with mosaic patterns, used pieces of coloured stone as well. Before bricks were reintroduced, Roman tiles were often used in churches and houses of the 11th and 12th centuries (e.g. Bradwell, Essex, Compton, Surrey, and St Albans Cathedral). Tiles were used for roofing extensively from the 16th century, and evolved into the present forms, flat 10½ × 6½ × ½ in. (with many derivative shapes), curved, one fitting over the next (pantiles), and Spanish (semi-circular, laid alternately to fit into each other), with curved ridge-tiles as well. Drain-tiles, met frequently in fields, can be pipes or semi-circular. Tiles for roofing are unglazed, but glazed and encaustic tiles were used from the Middle Ages for decoration, both on walls and floors—these hardly concern us here. 'Mathematical bricks' are tiles of various shapes to cover walls (e.g. Guildford House, Guildford).

Stone. Roofing can also be by wooden 'tiles', called shingles; or by stone slabs—these were used by the Romans, and very commonly in the Middle Ages and later (e.g. the stone of Collyweston and Horsham). Stone and flint (cut or cobbles), according to the local supply, was also used for the walls. Cut flint can be arranged in patterns with stone, in alternate squares (chequer), or in complicated designs (flush-work, as at Long Melford church, Suffolk). Slate is an essentially 19th century roofing material. Roman walls and ceilings were often rendered with plaster, sometimes covered with painted designs; floors could be made with a material of crushed brick and plaster mixed called *opus signinum*.

GLASS

Glass varies in colour with its age and composition. Roman glass is greenish, brownish or yellowish with vivid iridescence. Saxon, found in Kent (imported partly from France) and elsewhere, is clearer and whiter. From 1226 onwards it followed the techniques of Normandy, using potash, and is mostly greenish. English glassmaking was enriched from Lorraine in the 16th century and later from Venice (clear soda glass); these two traditions merged in the 17th century, when lead was used as an additive. All these kinds can be picked up; among the many bottles of the last two centuries some interesting early 19th century examples can be found. (See also p. 126.)

QUERNS AND VARIOUS SMALL OBJECTS

Querns and millstones (fig. 37) or part of them, can be found not only in farmyards, but in hedgerows and, in the north, built into stone walls. Sandstone rubbers and sharpening stones, often cigar-shaped, can be picked up in fields; most date from the 18th and 19th centuries. Clay loom-weights and spindle-whorls may be neolithic or later. Fragments of tools or farm implements, horse-shoes of different types and sizes; knives and forks (two-pronged forks came into common use about 1730); nails, staples and a variety of bits of iron, will always turn up. Hand-made forged nails only ceased to be made in the early 19th century. Fragments of arms and armour (e.g. of the Wars of the Roses and the Civil War) turn up on battlefields. Cannon-balls are found on the site of battles, and can be picked up on near-by farms. They were made in twelve sizes (i.e. weights); iron or bronze was used from about 1350 until the mid-19th century, but stone balls, usually granite, were also used from *c.* 1350 to the 17th century. Small objects like buttons (metal buttons, often with decorated head, were used in quantities in 18th and early 19th century dress); buckles; pins and brooches (the safety-pin type was used in the Iron Age); traders' tokens and commemorative medals; coins (used from Belgic times—cannot be described in detail here). Oyster shells are very common indeed on Roman sites; the Romans ate large quantities of shellfish; but some oyster-shells were spread on the fields for liming in the 18th century. Small clay objects like bobbins, wig-curlers, and clay pipes, turn up in old gardens; pipes also in the fields.

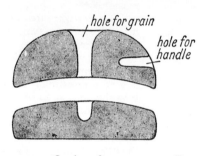

FIG. 37. Section of a rotary quern (Iron Age or Roman)

labels in figure: hole for grain; hole for handle

CLAY TOBACCO-PIPES

Clay tobacco-pipes are important archaeologically, as they can be dated to within 20 or 30 years by their shape (Fig. 38), and in many cases by their maker's mark. In certain cases, such as rubbish pits, they can be used for dating in the absence of coins; being fragile they have only a short life, and were usually thrown away soon after they were made. The trade was well established by the end of the 16th century; pipes of this date were only about 3 in. long, and had very small bowls. By 1650 bowls were larger, and pipes about 8–11 in. long; decoration was common, and makers' initials were placed on the bowl. By 1700 they were larger still, and were sometimes fully signed and dated, with often elaborate decoration. In the 18th century the flat foot was replaced by a spur, on which the maker often put his initials, or some symbol; lengths reached 15 or 18 in. Bowl-shape varied also, getting longer and larger; 17th century pipes have the bowl at an obtuse angle to the stem, pointing away; this angle reduces until in the 18th century the bowl is nearly upright. After 1800 pipes grew smaller again. The manufacture of clay pipes died

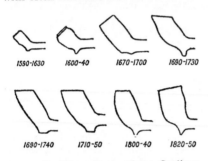

FIG. 38. Clay tobacco pipes. Outlines showing the development of bowl forms

out in the mid-19th century, except for a few small centres. The main centres were London and Bristol, but by 1650 Chester, Hull, Broseley and other towns joined in the trade. Full lists of makers, and dates, are still being built up by local museums and collectors.

Farm rubbish-heaps should not be overlooked; many interesting objects of all periods have been found in them.

CLEANING AND MARKING

All surface finds should be cleaned gently and carefully, and should be marked in Indian ink with the find-spot (map-reference) date and initials. White ink if the object is dark. A dab of varnish will protect the marking. Gummed labels should not be used—they eventually come off. Coins and other unmarkable objects should be kept in little envelopes, which can be marked, or in specially designed cases. Local museums, archaeological societies or public libraries are always glad to hear about surface finds.

Part III: The Technical and Legal Aspects of Archaeology

CHAPTER I

The Techniques of Archaeology

The purpose of archaeology, despite the questions that excavators are asked as they dig, is not primarily to find things, but to reconstruct and understand the life of past ages and peoples. Its main tool is excavation, the methodical uncovering, layer by layer, of the remains of a living-place, tomb or other evidence of past life, and the interpretation of the results. The methods it uses to interpret what it finds are partly those which have been evolved especially by and for archaeologists, partly the techniques of other sciences which are related to the study of the past or its conditions, or which can be used for this purpose. Thus for the Stone Ages, geology and its relatives have to be called in; for more recent periods, methods which are almost those of history, linked with the laboratory techniques of pure science, might have to be used. In this section the most important of these techniques will be very briefly described, as a background to the study of field monuments. It is not the purpose of this book to be a detailed guide to techniques, and the reader is referred to the many works which give such information (see p. 341).

EXCAVATION

Excavation is the basic means of getting at the broad facts of a site. It depends on the principle of *stratigraphy*, which is that an object left on or in the soil at any given time will be found at a lower level than one deposited later (so a ditch or pit is dated by its *lowest* content, a mound or hoard by its *latest*). Of course many things can happen to upset this ideal order, but the excavator must begin with this assumption. He works by uncovering the layers from the top, that is, in the reverse order from which they were laid down. From the successive layers he can construct a sequence of events on the site—buildings succeeding each other, with perhaps intervals of destruction or desertion, development of tools, weapons, ornaments and the like, even changes of custom or social habit. For his object all the time is not to find things unrelated to their background, but to get inside the life and thought of the people who made the things he is digging up. Of course, what he finds will never be the complete picture—perishable things will rarely have survived, and what he sees will be only a small part of what was actually used. But from these things none the less he has to build up the best story he can. Each layer may contain a group of objects; these, when supplemented by objects found on other sites which can be dated to the same period or people, form a *culture*, that is, the assemblage of the utensils of a given people, time and place. By arranging the cultures of the successive layers in order, a relative chronology can be drawn up; this merely says that culture A was earlier than culture B. This can be supported by the succession of developmental stages of objects themselves (e.g. the axe). To arrive at an absolute dating other methods have to be used, either comparison with culture of similar type elsewhere, which have already been dated by reference to a third known fact (e.g. a tool in Britain imported from say Bohemia, where tools of this type can be shown to be derived from tools in say Anatolia, which can be dated by a picture on a Hittite seal found with a pot made in Egypt in the reign of a particular pharaoh whose place in actual history is certain). This sounds complicated, but is not so far-fetched as might appear. Or scientific techniques may have to be used. The excavator needs therefore not only knowledge of the results of archaeological research, but may have to call in a variety of experts to provide facts which excavation by itself could not give. Part of the art is to know when this is necessary, if the full value of the site is to be got; part is skill in excavating and interpreting, which are to some extent flairs. In any case the best excavators are those who have asked the right questions of the site, and have therefore got helpful answers; knowing not only how to dig, but where—a point well illustrated by, say, Sir Mortimer Wheeler's investigation of Roman stations in India. Actual digging is preceded by a survey of the site, and accompanied by full notes, records, plans and sections, photographs and drawings, soil samples, etc. The act of removing the layers of the site automatically destroys evidence, which can never be found again; so the excavator is responsible to posterity and to his calling for extracting the utmost from the site in the course of destroying its original structure. It is therefore the practice to leave, where possible, part of the site unexcavated, so that later workers, with improved techniques, can reinterpret it in years to come.

AIR PHOTOGRAPHY

One of the most important aids to field archaeology is air photography. This has been developed markedly since the First World War; its lines were laid by two pioneers, O. G. S. Crawford and Major Allen, both now deceased, and have been built on by Dr St Joseph, Mr Bradford, Mr Rhodes, Mr A. Baker and others in Britain, M. Poidebard and others in France. The air photograph is now an indispensable adjunct, not only to large-scale exploration, e.g. the discovery of say Roman forts in Scotland, but to the excavation of a site, the surroundings of which it can illuminate and help to explain.

The Air Ministry have prepared a National Survey on a scale of 1 : 10,000 (about 6 in. to a mile), based on vertical photographs, and this can be seen at certain libraries or on request under safeguards; sheets can be bought quite reasonably. A few firms produce photographs of certain areas also. Vertical photographs are used for maps; the sheets overlap, and by the use of a stereoscope a clear round image can be got. Indeed, a stereoscope is essential to get the best out of the photographs. An oblique view has its value for general appreciation of a site in its setting, or a landscape. Air photography is used for the demonstration of known sites in their contexts; the study of whole areas; discovery of unrecorded sites, both above ground and buried; preservation of records of sites about to be destroyed by building works, etc. It can give a complete picture of a culture, e.g. patterns of related farms; Celtic fields in relation to Roman villas; a deserted village with its fields, trackways, common-lands: it can therefore help in assessing ancient populations, settlement and ecology. It can discover fresh sites, e.g. ring-ditches or levelled barrows, forts, farms, deserted villages; it can help in appreciating terrain, and in reconstructing the replacement of an earlier landscape by a later; and in the understanding of submerged lands. Valuable as all this is, it must be followed up by work on the ground, and the indications checked and investigated; the interpretation of air photographs is by no means easy, and unless it is checked on the ground they can be quite misleading.

The archaeological information on an air photograph is given by marks representing differences in vegetation or soil. *Vegetation-marks* (often called crop-marks): earth, once dug, never resumes exactly its old denseness, and is for ever looser, more porous and more permeable than the surrounding land. It therefore forms a deeper soil, which holds moisture in its lower levels when the rest of the soil is parched. This enables vegetation of all kinds to grow richer, higher and greener than the rest, especially in times of drought. Rooting-depth is what matters to a plant, and some roots, even those of weeds, can penetrate

283

to a surprising depth. So ditches, post-holes and the like can be seen by darker, greener growth. Cereal crops may grow as much as twice as large over an old ditch as on undisturbed ground. The cycle of cereal growth is important; some times of year give better results than others. Barley is the best for this purpose, wheat and oats next, rye not so good. Of the non-cereals, lucerne and clover are good, as are horse-beans; beet, turnips and potatoes give variable results. The best appearances are in drought, or at least after three or four weeks of dry weather; in wet weather colour differences tend to be reduced; in wind the colour of plants is altered and distorted. Apart from colour, higher crops produce shadow-effects in slanting light; even the stubble from these crops shows up differently. Grass-marks are rarer, but possible in certain conditions—the henge at Arminghall, Norfolk, was discovered by grass variations. Weeds, too, often give good results. The soil of ancient settlements contains considerable quantities of phosphates, which can stimulate rich and dark plant growth.

The opposite effect is produced by buried roads, walls, etc., which reduce the depth of soil available to plants growing over them; in dry weather these plants suffer, grow poorer and lighter, and *parch-marks* result. Buried Roman roads produce lines of both types, dark over the side ditches, light along the road itself. A rare effect is caused when building rubble, containing lime from its mortar, corrects the acidity of certain soils, and thus stimulates plant growth—this occurred at a Roman house at Cavenham, Suffolk.

Another type of mark is the *soil-mark*. When earthworks or barrows are levelled, or when grass is stripped, or on bare (ploughed) land, differences in soil-colour become apparent. Mounds or banks give light marks on darker ground—i.e. the subsoil, containing less humus, is uncovered; ditches, with their humic filling, show up dark (humus is darkest when wet) (pl. 15, p. 152). *Damp-marks* are produced by buried ditches retaining moisture—this contrast only occurs in dry weather.

Shadows are often thrown by high crops, banks, etc.; they can often reveal field-boundaries, lynchets, etc., when the sun is very low. *Highlights* on grass, etc., are the reverse of shadows, and often just as revealing. Grass or bare earth are best for this effect; heather blurs it, and so does bracken—the Bronze Age earth-circles on St Martha's Hill, Surrey, well-defined on the ground, are quite invisible in the Air Survey photograph, because of the bracken cover. White frost or light snow will often lodge in otherwise indiscernible hollows, and reveal low banks, as will low slanting sunlight. Shallow flooding too can sometimes bring out differences of relief, when banks protrude above the water.

The vast majority of markings and features in most landscapes, however, are non-archaeological, and great skill is needed to interpret all the complex details of an air photograph. Such features are modern plough-lines across a field, often in regular rows, or radiating from a point at a turning-place or headland; cultivation across superimposed geological strata gives curved lines along the contours; modern ditches levelled off may be deceptive; subsoil brought to the surface by plough-ing (e.g. a knoll levelled off) makes light marks which could resemble levelled tumuli (the tops of old sand-dunes look like these too); white dots may be sheep on bare patches of ground, black dots cattle or bushes: ploughing on the edge of a slope can make a soil-mark along a contour, which can look like an enclosure or levelled hillfort; fissures in gravel subsoil can look like field boundary ditches; old watercourses, natural creeks, ditches, even springlines, etc., can be deceptive; fungus or vegetation rings ('fairy rings') must be identified as such; old ponds, hut-sites, etc., often show up; finally, one can be deceived by places where trees have been removed, or where haystacks, heaps of manure, fertiliser, etc., have stood.

No one air photograph is likely to show all there is to see; indeed, most show nothing at all, except where differences of level (e.g. banks) exist. Conditions vary so much that the ideal, rarely achieved, is to have photographs taken from different heights, at different times of day, and seasons of the year, over several years. At last, and just once, something new may show up. Most of the effects described above can be seen, but not so well, from a hill or other high place (the steeper and higher the better). Conditions must be waited for and taken advantage of also. A good example of this was during Mr Hope-Taylor's excava-tions of Anglian buildings at Yeavering, Northumberland. A likely area was cleared of turf, and was almost quite featureless; but after rain, and from a tower erected specially for observation and photography, a soil-pattern emerged which revealed a complicated network of foundation-trenches for wooden buildings of different periods, and post holes, all quite invisible otherwise. This not only shows the need to get the right conditions, but also, incidentally, the possible fruitlessness of trial trenches unless the pattern is already known. The exceptionally dry summer of 1959 enabled Dr St Joseph's systematic air surveys to detect hundreds of new sites of all kinds. This also greatly altered the then known distribution patterns, e.g. on the Suffolk–Essex borders some 40 barrows had been recorded, in a few small areas only, and not in the valleys; the air survey found some 200 more, spread more widely, and along the gravels of the Stour and other rivers also. Unexpected numbers of sites, including farm enclosures and pit alignments, have also been located on the gravels of the Midland rivers, Trent, Welland, etc., with a concentration round Maxey, Northants. Results like this show how prehistory is dependent on the evidence available to it; up to 1959 conclusions had to be based on only a fraction of the now known facts, and are bound to be revised.

A new application of photography is *photogrammetry*—recording from vertical photographs instead of laborious drawing.

Another special application of photography to archaeology may be mentioned in passing, although its main use so far has been in Italy. The Italians, faced with the mass excavation of extensive Etruscan cemeteries, often containing hundreds of solidly built stone tombs, have shortened their work by inspecting the inside of the burial chambers, and so seeing whether the tomb is worth the labour of excavation. They use a device consisting of a pole which can be inserted through the tomb walls into the burial chamber; the pole carries on its end a tiny camera and flash apparatus, which can be operated from the other end. A photograph of the burial chamber can be taken, and examined at leisure.

DISCOVERY

There are many techniques of discovery. The simplest is that of *bosing*, which is merely striking the soil with a heavy stick, beam or beetle, vertically and at frequent intervals. Undisturbed ground gives out a dead sound on striking; but ground once disturbed never recovers its original consistency, and returns a dull thump to the blow. Mr Curwen used this method in Sussex to locate barrow–ditches, flint–mines, etc.; and Mr Lethbridge reconstructed with it a complicated group of figures cut on the slopes of the Gogmagog Hills. A similar method is *probing* with an iron rod. Here disturbed soil is easier to penetrate than undisturbed; and soil over a buried obstacle, say a wall-footing, is harder to penetrate than that away from the obstacle. A less primitive way of doing this is by the *electrical resistivity* method. Electrodes are inserted in the ground at regular say (4 ft.) intervals, and a current passed between them. The amount of voltage, i.e. electrical pressure, at the end of the circuit depends on the resistance of the ground, or, put another way, on the amount of moisture in the soil. If the soil is permeable a smaller drop in voltage is recorded, and vice versa. The electrodes are progressively moved along the line under survey, and the readings of the instrument set down in the form of a graph, whose fluctuations indicate the buried features. So a high reading (a peak in the graph) means a high resistance, say a buried wall, and a low one a ditch or pit. Natural features are of course included as well, so excavation is necessary to check the indications. But much time can be saved with this instrument. The original form, the megger, has now been developed by Mr A. J. Clark into a compact and very sensitive transistorised instrument, and a machine in one piece is now in use.

It should be said that *dowsers* claim to be able to find many kinds of objects, as well as water.

Recent research into the *magnetic* properties of soils have suggested a new method which is now being developed by Dr M. J. Aitken. There are two different effects; one, that clay contains iron oxides, which are themselves faintly magnetic—when these are baked to make pottery, or the walls of a kiln, this magnetism is fixed, and differs from that of the surrounding soil (see below). Pieces of iron slag in an old rubbish-pit will also be appreciably magnetic. The other fact, still not fully understood, is that disturbed soil, as in a ditch or pit, containing humus (the acids of which may convert the traces of iron oxide in the soil to a more highly magnetic form), is more magnetic than subsoil—gravel is hardly magnetic at all. A device called a proton magnetometer, in which hydrogen protons (in water) are gyrated faster by the magnetic forces mentioned above than by less magnetic soil, has been constructed, and with its aid Dr Aitken has located ditches and pits as well as kilns and remains of burnt houses. This is of great importance, for without it, it would be impracticable to investigate, say, the rubbish-pits which are dotted about inside the walls of a hillfort, short of an effort of digging normally quite out of the question. This method was successfully used in 1959 by Dr Aitken to trace a ditch at Verulamium.

A successful alternative was tried out in 1966; this uses a new type of metal detector which responds to the magnetic viscosity in humus in pits, etc.

Several types of mine-detector, and machines working on the asdic principle (where an impulse is reflected back from an object or hard layer) have been tried with varying success.

Soil-analysis, developed by Dr I. W. Cornwall, is another valuable aid to archaeology. Soil can be studied both physically and chemically, and the climate and other conditions under which it was formed can be determined. The size and nature of the grains can show whether it is a wind-borne loess, or a mud, clay or sand of marine or fresh-water origin, or is a glacial deposit derived from the rocks of a given area. Chemically, soils are classified by their humus and other content (brown-earths, podsols, etc.) which indicate climatic and cultivation conditions. Some of the features of the structure of barrows, formerly puzzling, are now seen to be due to podsolization, that is, the leaching down, in sandy soils, of the iron salts in the top layer, which produces a typical pattern of humic, leached, and iron layers. Soil-analysis can also determine buried soils, by their traces of humus, and can say whether the soil under a barrow has once been ploughed. The excavator now takes samples of soil from any part of the site where analysis will tell him some fact not otherwise obtainable. Related tests are those for the *phosphate* contents of soils; an ancient settlement site has a high proportion of phosphates in its soil, which can be a useful cross-check on indications shown in air photographs. Tests for phosphates and fats can also detect the former presence of a body, where an acid soil has removed visible traces. Bone silhouettes in soil can be detected by photography in ultra-violet light.

Petrology is called in to identify the rocks used in stone axes, or the clays used in pottery, and their provenance. Much work has been done, particularly by the South-Western Group of Museums, in taking thin slices from stone axes, and by macroscopic, microscopic and spectroscopic study, to find the outcrops from which they were quarried. In this way a large number of groups has been drawn up (e.g. the Cumberland lavas, Cornish greenstones, etc.) and the prehistoric trade in axes illuminated. Similarly, the source of the bluestones of Stonehenge was shown to be the Presely Mountains of Pembrokeshire. *Spectrography* is used to examine pottery, glazes etc. *X-rays* were used at Stonehenge in 1958 to make sure that there were no internal cracks in a stone 5 ft. thick before it was re-erected; the agent used was a radio-active isotope of sodium. Other uses of X-rays include radiography (e.g. of bones), diffraction analysis, and projection microscopy. The determination of food refuse, including animal and fish bones (and the age at which animals were killed), nuts, grain, etc., essential for understanding the economy of ancient peoples, needs specialist skills; as does the metallographic analysis of the metals from which tools were made and their origins (copper, bronze, iron).

Statistical methods are being applied to problems such as the incidence of types of implement, variations of form and technique, etc., within a culture; e.g. the flaking angle of naturally fractured flints compared with that of humanly made tools.

Experiments have been made at Cambridge in the use of *computers* to solve problems of distribution in time and place of, say, pottery types in the various phases of the Bronze Age. (see page 60.)

The Dutch have developed a method, of particular usefulness on sandy soils, whereby a *plastic* is sprayed over features in the soil (e.g. furrows, post-holes): when this has hardened it is removed as a sheet containing a very thin layer of soil; the result is a full-scale image of the features, which can then be conveniently in this form studied or preserved elsewhere.

Underwater exploration techniques, so successful with sunken Greek ships and Mediterranean harbours, are being extended to Britain, although our colder and less transluscent waters are an obstacle. More besides the Roman ship sunk in the Thames estuary, the Spanish galleon at Tobermory, and King John's jewels in the Wash, might be explored in this way; sunken lands, such as those off Scilly, are apt candidates. *Caving* also has its own methods, some of which have been used to investigate ancient remains in caves.

The original firing temperature of pottery can be found by studies of the expansion and shrinkage of clays. The origin of flint can be determined by its trace elements (e.g. flint from Spiennes has high levels of phosphorus, Grand Pressingny of iron, Grimes Graves of potassium), so the movements of flint implements can be followed.

31. GRAVESTONES outside churches begin in the 17th century. *Top*, stone, with the popular symbolic carving of the time. *Centre*, Wealden cast-iron, from local workings now extinct. *Below*, painted wooden 'bedboard' (cheaper than stone) of the 19th century

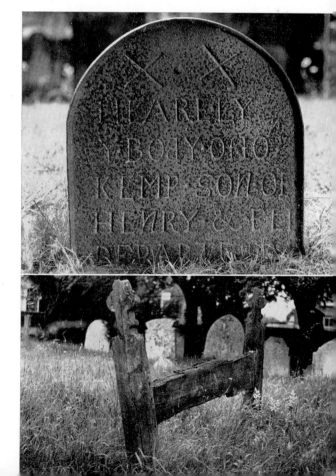

32. *Above*, a disused tower-mill (19th century) behind the stump of a mediaeval village cross. *Below*, survival of a primitive device in the mid-20th century: turf enclosure wall and windbreak protecting a dwelling (New Forest borders, Hants.)

DATING

Turning to methods of dating, again many laboratory techniques are being developed or applied to archaeology, and supplement field methods. *Tree-rings*, the rings of annual growth, which vary in thickness according to the weather of each year (the wetter the thicker), can be arranged, for a given region, in a pattern of thickness. A scale of dates can then be built up, backwards from the present, by taking trees of overlapping age; against this scale a series of rings from a beam in an old house, etc., can be set, and its date read off. A. W. G. Lowther has been very successful in dating mediaeval houses, wharves, etc. in this way; the method is much used in America to date huts of Indian and pre-Columbian cultures, but it has limitations. Recent work on tree-rings shows that they may not always be reliable for absolute dating; there are too many possibilities for extra rings to form, for indistinct divisions between rings, etc.

Varves are the layers of silt deposited in a glacial lake at the foot of a glacier; the amount of material deposited will vary from year to year, and each year's layer will contain coarser grains at the bottom and finer at the top (taking longer to settle). Each varve extends further than the one before as the ice-front recedes. Here again a pattern can be built up and dates assigned. In this way the Swedes and others, starting in 1878 with the pioneer, Baron de Geer, have been able to date the final recession of the last glaciation and subsequent periods.

Post-glacial climatic history, however, on which much archaeological dating depends, has been most firmly established by *pollen-analysis*. The outer skin of pollen-grains is very resistant to decay; moreover, the pollen of each plant differs markedly in shape and size from others. So pollen found in old soils or in bogs can be collected and counted by species of plant. The result can be plotted, and for each climate-period since the last glaciation a pattern of vegetation can be built up. This will show the proportion of various trees, say pine, birch and hazel, at a given time; this will be succeeded by other combinations, and so on. The pattern so obtained shows the setting in which man's cultures were set. A new method of dating, still in development, is by the rate of growth of certain species of lichen on stones.

A method which has attracted great attention recently is the use of *radio-active carbon* ($C14$). This depends on the fact that the earth is continually being bombarded by neutrons carried in the cosmic radiation. Some of these meet nitrogen atoms ($N14$) floating in the upper atmosphere, and convert them to radioactive carbon ($C14$). The heavy $C14$ atoms become oxidised to CO_2, and are absorbed by plants, animals and men. The $C14$ bears a fixed ratio to the ordinary $C12$, so the amount of C14 in a living body is known (proportionately). Radio-active substances have the characteristic of gradually losing their additional electrons and reverting to their original atomic weight, a process which takes place at a regular rate for each element. So after a living organism dies, it ceases to absorb carbon, and the amount of C14 in it will gradually decrease at a steady rate, and from this the date of death can be calculated. In 5568 years ± 30 (the estimate has been progressively refined), only half the original amount of C14 (the half-life) will be left, in 11,140 a quarter, and so on. The specimen to be dated has to be burnt to convert it into sooty carbon (after various processes), which is spread on a Geiger counter, and its radio-activity emissions counted; from the result the age of the specimen can be calculated. The method involves a margin of error due to many causes, but a fair accuracy is now obtained for dates within about 70,000 years ago. This margin is always expressed as part of the date obtained—e.g. a piece of palm wood from Qumran (the Dead Sea Scrolls), expected on other grounds to date from just before AD 68, was given a C14 age of $1,940 \pm 80$, a very close result (these figures represent years ago).

It has been clear for some years that the build-up of radiocarbon in living things is not constant over the millenia (the causes of these variations are still obscure), and that consequently dates based on C14 do not always agree with those derived from other sources. A method of calibrating C14 dates was found by checking them against the age of the rings of the very long-lived Californian tree, the bristlecone pine, which could be fitted to cover the last 7000 years. Samples of dated tree-rings were cross-dated by C14, and a comparative graph constructed (by Suess in 1967) back to 5100 BC. (Using the 5568 half-life, which is in general use, although a half-life of 5730 ± 40 is even more accurate). This shows that, from about 1300 BC backwards, the C14 dates diverge from the true dates, until by 4000 BC they are some 5-600 years too young (by 6000 BC the gap narrows again). Oddly enough, dates for the Aegean, Egypt and places east are not far out; the discrepancy gets bigger as one goes north-west to Britain.

The implications of this for British prehistory are catastrophic, as Dr Colin Renfrew (1970) has pointed out. The first farmers now arrived before 4000 BC, and copper was in use about 2500. The old theory that all civilisation was diffused from the Near East (as Childe has been loosely interpreted), no longer holds in literal form. Metallurgy arose earlier in the Balkans than in the Aegean, and there are three foci for it. The megalithic tombs of NW Europe are an independent invention (in France), and precede the Pyramids by a millenium (some British henges, and Silbury, are contemporary with the Pyramids, about 2500 BC. The Wessex culture (*c.* 2000 BC) precedes that of Mycenae (*c.* 1500), so the links hitherto assumed between them must be reconsidered. And so on. A new framework will need to be worked out in the next few years, and British prehistory will enter a new phase.

Other elements have radio-active isotopes which can be used in the same way, but these are mostly used for dating rocks, and the age of the earth itself, and have no practical archaeological value (the main elements so used are radium, helium, thorium, uranium, and their lead-ratios, rubidium and strontium). But a rock-dating method which has its use in archaeology is that based on *potassium-argon*. Radio-active potassium (K40) occurs with potassium in rocks. It has a half-life of 1.3×10^9 years, and decays into calcium-40 and argon-40, which can be measured by means of a mass-spectrometer. Using this method, the age of the hominid *Zinjanthropus*, found in Bed I at Olduvai in Africa, a bed of early Pleistocene age, has been determined as about $1\frac{3}{4}$ million years.

Geological dates are also obtained by calculations from solar radiation (see p. 34), and from the rate of sedimentation, weathering, soil-formation, erosion, denudation—these methods are subject however to a considerable margin of error.

Some of these long-distance methods have an application to the Pleistocene period, and so to archaeology.

A method of dating documents by radioisotopes to reveal the water-marks has been applied to the Vinland map.

There are various methods of great importance involving trace-elements. *Fluorine* is found free in the form of ions which wander along in the ground-water and penetrate bones they may happen to meet. This happens at a known and constant rate, so that the longer a bone has lain in the soil the more fluorine it contains. This method was used by Dr Oakley to check the age of Piltdown skull and jawbone, and the associated fauna (it has now been counter-checked by C14). It proved that the skull was that of a fairly ancient man (although he had been doctored to match the gravel in which he was found), while the jaw was that of a modern ape; this celebrated forgery was exposed by a combination of scientific techniques. The fluorine method is most useful for comparing the ages of two bones from near each other in the same patch of soil: different soils produce different rates of fluorine penetration, so cannot easily be compared. It is of no use in limestone soils, because calcite prevents the spread of fluorine in the bone tissues. A somewhat similar principle, in reverse, is used in dating by the organic *nitrogen*, or carbon, content of bone, which decreases after death. This was also used in the Piltdown case; an old bone should have more fluorine and less nitrogen, a recent one the reverse. *X-ray crystallography* can distinguish new bone or tooth tissue from fossilized tissue. *Radiometric assay* depends on the fact that, in Oakley's words, 'uranium circulating in the blood-stream is fixed in the phosphatic mineral matter of bones by replacement apparently of the calcium atoms in the hydroxyapatite'. The same process goes on when a bone is buried in the ground, and uranium reaches it in the percolating ground-water. So the longer a bone has been buried the more uranium it can have. For instance, a modern bone has less than 1 part per million of uranium (U_3O_8), whereas the Piltdown skull had 3 parts (showing it to be not much older—the Swanscombe skull had 27 parts, and early Pleistocene elephants have had as many as 600). A rough time-scale can be constructed from all these methods, and they can be used to check each other and refine on the date given by any one of them.

A technique is being developed at Leeds University for the dating of *parchments*, that is, untanned skins, based on the shrinkage temperature of the collagen fibres in the skin. These fibres degenerate with age, and the older the parchment the lower the temperature at which they will begin to shrink. So materials of different ages, say, Bronze Age rawhide axe-hafting, 5th century BC letters, the Dead Sea Scrolls, and mediaeval documents can be arranged in chronological sequence; the data so obtained, as in most of these techniques, can be used to check dates arrived at by other methods. This method of course gives only the date when the parchment was made, not of the writing on it.

Archaeomagnetism is a new dating technique evolved in England and France, and still being developed, notably by Dr Aitken at Oxford. Many rocks, including clays, contain oxides of iron and are feebly but appreciably magnetic. When heated the magnetism decreases, and vanishes at the Curie-point (500–600°C.). If it is then cooled below this point it becomes remagnetised, at the *present* intensity and direction. Clay objects such as walls and bottoms of pottery kilns, whose original positions can be determined, can (subject to certain technical complications which are being gradually overcome) be so heated and cooled, and the difference between the two readings, of the magnetic fields before and after treatment, measured. From the results of several such processes a scale can be constructed of readings representing specimens of known date, say kilns of Roman, mediaeval and 18th century dates, this can then be used to ascertain the date of other, undetermined, objects. Pots are not so good for this method of dating as pieces of kiln, because of the varied and usually indeterminable position in which they were fired, or, in some cases, to which they slipped inside the kiln. But, as with all these methods, greater precision is to be expected as work proceeds.

Thermoluminescence can also be used for dating. If a material contains some radio-active impurity, the emitted particles ionise a large number of electrons, some of which are trapped at lattice imperfections. There is an accumulation of energy, which can be released by thermal agitation, and whose magnitude is proportional to the time since the last heating. The method can be applied to pottery, which need not be in situ, and can be quite small. The precision is not better than $\pm 10\%$, but is good enough, e.g. to distinguish Iron Age from Saxon pottery.

Thermoluminescence is now being applied to the dating of bones and the detection of fakes.

It has recently been discovered that *glass weathers* by way of very thin periodic layers, rather like those of trees. Dr R. G. Newton (Sheffield) is developing a method of dating old glass by this means. The rate of growth of patina can be used to date a flint (*hydration rind dating*).

CLEANING AND PRESERVATION

The cleaning and preservation of finds is also getting more and more into the laboratory, and little need be said about it. The amateur should not attempt to clean his own finds with stiff brushes, etc.; the most that should be done is to wash them gently and carefully. If, as with metal, they are corroded or fragile, the local museum will treat them. Mention may be made here of the now standard use of polyvinyl acetate and substances with similar properties; objects, after special cleaning, are steeped in this, and a surface layer is formed which keeps out air, and hence decay and rust, without affecting the appearance of the object. This can be applied to metal, bone, wood and pottery, and is an important advance in technique. A matter from time to time in the public eye is the removal to museums, for treatment and re-erection, of mosaic pavements from Roman sites. Several methods have been tried for this; they depend in principle on canvas or some such material being stuck to the upper side of pavement while it is still on the ground; the pavement is then detached from its base of mortar and rolled up on the cloth like a carpet. It can then be moved and detached at leisure. Special techniques have had to be developed to deal with Roman wall plaster, which is usually in a fragmentary condition, to reconstitute the painted design, to fix the colours, and to rebuild the plaster.

PUBLICATION

Finally, it may be mentioned that a very important technique of archaeology is the prompt and efficient publication of the results of excavation or study; without this no comparative survey or basic research, leading to the periodical rewriting of prehistory which is one of the functions of the subject, would be possible. The framing of a useful and objective report is not easy, but its value far outweighs the effort.

CHAPTER 2

How Sites get Buried

It is often asked why ancient sites are so commonly buried under several feet of soil. (From the archaeologist's point of view a protective covering of earth has advantages, except in very destructive soils.)

In the country there are three main agencies, (*a*) the deposition of minute particles of sand, rock-dust, etc., by rain and wind; (*b*) the action of earthworms, which burrow down, loosen and aerate the soil, drag surface objects like leaves underground, and, most important, throw up casts of earth on to the surface. They also undermine heavy objects like stones, walls, etc., so that they sink. Individually their effect would be negligible, but there are so many thousands to the acre that their combined effect is very considerable. Darwin, in a famous piece of research, *The Formation of Vegetable Mould through the Action of Worms* (1881) showed that they caused the soil level to rise at the rate of ·2 in. a year (although this is partly weathered off again); (*c*) the growth of plants on the surface. These die and decay, and increase the humus content of the topsoil, in which the successive generations of plants grow and repeat the process.

The rate of all this varies with the soil conditions and the climate, but the average Roman villa (1700 years old) is between 3 and 4 ft. down. (A subsidiary, but archaeologically important, effect of earthworms is to displace small objects, such as fragments of pottery, and draw them down to a lower, and perhaps differently dated, level—this calls for caution on the excavator's part.)

In order to learn more of the processes involved in the life of earthworks (silting, soil-creep, consolidation, weathering, action of vegetation and earthworms, etc.), the British Association, supported by other bodies, has begun a long-term experiment in which banks and ditches of controlled dimensions will be built by hand methods, and examined at intervals over the next 128 years. The first of these was made on chalk-down soil near Marlborough (Wilts.) in 1960.

An exception to the sinking of an ancient soil-surface is when it is protected by, say, a barrow from weathering, ploughing, etc., and hence can be higher than the surrounding soil. Weathering of soil has removed most traces of neolithic and Bronze Age houses.

On town sites the processes are different, although earthworms are a factor here too. But the reason why Roman London is 25 ft. below the present street level, and tells (artificial mounds, remains of towns) in the Near East can be over 100 ft. high, is that floors were usually of earth, covered with mats or rushes. Rubbish was trodden in, and every so often a new layer of soil, and more mats and rushes, were laid down. Houses were mostly built of timber with fillings of plaster, wattle and daub, or even compressed mud, or rubble. When a house was replaced, or if it was burnt (as happened not infrequently), its materials, instead of being carted away, would be spread over the site, and the next house built upon them. So the levels would gradually rise over the centuries. The street levels rose also, and many town churches are now entered down steps. The successive levels can be distinguished in section— they show up as different layers in the soil—and can be dated by the small objects, pottery, coins, etc., which had fallen into and been incorporated into the compressed remains of each house or occupation layer. Thus the history of a town, often very complex, can be unravelled by excavation. [1]

Again, the rate of growth varies locally, but the average English town has risen some 10 ft. since Roman times (e.g. the Roman road surface of Stonegate, York., is about 10 ft. below the present road; a mosaic floor at Winchester was 8 ft. below); London, with closer building than most Roman towns, more intensive occupation, frequent fires, and rapid rebuilding, over twice as much. But the low Roman levels in London are partly due to the sinking of the land since Roman times.

[1] Buried features which have subsided may cause cracking in modern houses, and may be traced by this.

CHAPTER 3

The Law

Field antiquities are affected by two main branches of the law, and it is as well to know what these are, and to be familiar with their broad principles.

ANCIENT MONUMENTS ACTS

The Ancient Monuments Act of 1913 and 1931, which apply to Scotland as well as England and Wales, lay on the Ministry of Works (who may be advised by certain learned societies and other bodies), the duty of making and publishing a list of monuments the preservation of which is of national importance; these include a wide variety of structures and sites, such as barrows, forts, earthworks, Roman remains, castles, churches, abbeys, crosses, bridges and many other objects. A monument on the list may not be demolished, altered or added to by its owner without the Ministry's consent, and a preservation order may be made if it is in danger of damage or destruction. The Ministry or a local authority may acquire or become guardians of a monument if that is the best way to preserve it, or may help the owner to do so. Access by the public to a monument is usually easy, but if it is in private hands permission may have to be asked; if in public ownership a small fee is sometimes charged, and there may be stated hours when it can be visited. Any person who injures or defaces a monument is liable to a fine of five pounds or a month's imprisonment, plus payment for the damage done. This provision may cover unauthorised excavation also. The implementation of these Acts is in the hands of the Chief Inspector of Ancient Monuments and his staff at the Ministry of Works, who will always give advice and help in connection with the listing and preservation of a monument.

TOWN AND COUNTRY PLANNING ACTS

Under Section 29 of the 1947 Act, which continues Section 11 of the 1932 Act, a local planning authority (e.g. a county council) is empowered to make orders for the preservation of buildings of 'special architectural or historic interest' in its area, excluding churches or buildings already included in the Schedules drawn up by the Ministry of Works under the Ancient Monuments Act. Lists of buildings worthy of such preservation are prepared under Section 30 by the Ministry of Housing and Local Government, for the guidance of local planning authorities. Crown lands are not covered by these lists. Some planning authorities (e.g. Surrey County Council) have published lists of sites, monuments and buildings in their area, of historic or architectural interest, which may cover items listed by the Ministry of Works and the Ministry of Housing and Local Government, as well as others considered to be of importance.

TREASURE TROVE

The other relevant law is that of *Treasure Trove*. Under this the Crown becomes the owner of gold or silver (in coin, plate or bullion) that has been *hidden* in the soil or a building and of which the owner cannot be traced. But the legal position is not as simple as this might imply, and still forms the subject of lawyers' debates. It may be helpful to outline the problems. There are several ways of parting with one's goods or chattels. They can be *abandoned* as being no longer wanted, for instance; in this case they become *res nullius*, belonging to no-one, and anyone who wishes to claim them may do so. They can be *lost*, like an odd coin; here the title in them remains with their owner, and if you find them and keep them without making an effort to find the owner and restore them to him you may be committing larceny. They can also be *hidden*, like a hoard or treasure buried in times of trouble and meant to be recovered; here also the title remains with the owner. It all depends on the facts; if these events take place today there is usually little difficulty in deciding the right legal position and course of action, but if the events took place two thousand years ago, it is often far from easy, and sometimes quite impossible, to find out what the true facts are. The important point is that the Crown's title to gold and silver as treasure trove arises only in cases of 'hiding', e.g. where prima facie it appears that the hoard was hidden *animus revocandi*—with an intention to return and recover it, and where the true owner cannot now be traced. If there is apparently no element of hiding, e.g. odd coins found on the surface of the soil, the items will probably not be treasure trove belonging to the Crown, but may belong to the owner of the land.

But there is another class—objects deposited in a grave or given to the gods; for instance, the treasure in the Saxon royal tomb at Sutton Hoo, or objects thrown into a sacred lake or holy well. These are not hidden, but openly laid in the grave, etc., with the knowledge and consent of all; and there is no intention of recovering them. So they do not appear to

belong to the Crown as treasure trove, and the decision in the Sutton
Hoo case reflects this—here the treasure was judged to be the property
of the ground landlord. She subsequently gave the treasure to the
Nation, but 'this does not of course affect the decision.

Under an Act of 1887 (repeating very old practice), the coroner of the
district where the find is made has the duty of holding a public enquiry
into the ownership of the object and the bona fides of the finder. If the
finder of gold or silver reports it immediately to the local coroner
(which can be done through the Police or the Director of the British
Museum), he is allowed its full market value if it is retained by the Crown
or a museum, or alternatively the articles are returned to the finder; if
some only are retained, the value of these is paid. The coroner often
calls in experts to help him reach his decision, such as officials of the
British Museum. A finder can be sure of fair treatment and a good price;
all finds, not only those of gold or silver, are sent by the coroner to the
British Museum for valuation. Full declaration of finds also adds to
knowledge; the object may be of great scientific as well as intrinsic
importance; other associated objects, not gold or silver, may be even
more important. Concealment is an offence. Finds made in the City of
London, such as the Roman silver from the Mithraeum, may be claimed
back from the Crown by the City Corporation, and are placed in the
Guildhall Museum. Finds elsewhere go either to the British Museum,
if of national importance, or to a local museum, or may be shared;
copies of objects, particularly coins, are sometimes given to the finder.

The above applies to England; in Wales the rules are the same,
except that the National Museum takes the place of the British Museum.
In Northern Ireland the Ministry of Finance takes possession on behalf
of the Crown, and deposits the treasure trove in a N. Ireland museum.

In Scotland the position is quite different. Here objects do not have to
have been hidden, and the *animus revertendi*, the intention to return
(and recover), is not the essence of the matter, as it is in England. *All*
finds are treasure trove, and all treasure trove, whether gold or silver
or not, belongs to the Crown, which does not have to establish its title
in the courts. There is therefore no coroner or jury. The Procurator-
Fiscal takes possession. The National Museum of Antiquities values the
finds, of which those not of gold or silver are often given back to the
finder. There is no special procedure for reporting, but of course all
finds should be declared immediately.

Moves are on foot (still continuing in 1971) to improve the legislation
for the control of the disposal of portable antiquities, and for treasure
trove. And since January 1970 licences have been required for the
export of any antique (except coins) recovered at any time from the
soil of the UK.

CHAPTER 4

Scheduled and other Monuments

The Ministry of Works publish a list of the monuments scheduled under the Ancient Monuments Acts (see p. 296), with occasional additional lists (there is a separate one for Scotland). These lists, although containing only those monuments which are scheduled, are a quite invaluable source of knowledge for the amateur on the best sites in his county, and cover a wide variety, from earthworks and barrows to crosses, wells, castles and abbeys. They are recommended possessions. Many counties also issue lists of ancient sites, buildings etc., whether scheduled or not.

The lists reveal an astonishing profusion of monuments in certain counties, such as Argyll, Caithness, Kirkcudbright, Orkney, Perthshire, Sutherland, and Wigtownshire in Scotland; Cornwall, Devon, Dorset, Gloucestershire, Hampshire, Norfolk, Northumberland, Shropshire, Somerset, Sussex, Wiltshire and Yorkshire in England, and Carmarthen, Denbighshire and Pembrokeshire in Wales. But this does not mean that counties with only a few entries in the list, such as Peebles or Holland, have little to show. The lists contain over 11,000 items, but there are a very large number of antiquities not scheduled, not only prehistoric or Roman, but mediaeval and later also. Some counties indeed are very rich in types of monuments not frequently listed, such as churches and houses; Essex, for instance, with not very many ancient sites, has some 750 noteworthy mediaeval or Tudor houses. And many of the objects mentioned in this book are for various reasons unlikely to be listed anyway. Even so, the lists provide an admirable introduction to field archaeology, by giving good and representative examples of many important types of monument; as many as possible should be visited.

Not all listed monuments are so labelled, particularly those in private ownership, and the ordinary passer-by, and sometimes the farmer himself, may be unaware that a particular site is of national importance; although the Ministry are of course well aware of this problem, and are doing their best to solve it. One inference from this state of affairs is to treat *all* ancient sites with great care, and not to damage them or scratch about in them just to see what can be picked up. Conversely, if you see, or hear of, monuments being damaged, either accidentally or wantonly, do not hesitate to report the matter to the local library, archaeological society, or the police, whether the site is scheduled or not. In remote parts a barrow could be ploughed out, or a stone circle destroyed, before those concerned are aware or steps can be taken to protect it, and the vigilance of all is necessary if the remaining monuments are to be properly looked after and handed on to our successors.

Building and road works, and the like, should also always be watched to see if any antiquity lies in the path of the bulldozers. Sites and finds are constantly coming to light all over the country, sometimes in the most unexpected places. The exposure of Roman sites by the bombing and rebuilding of towns such as London, Canterbury, Exeter and Winchester is well known, and their investigation has enabled a great deal of knowledge to be recovered. But excavations of a purely commercial kind are going on all the time, on building sites (such as that at Walbrook, London, on which the Mithraeum was found), gravel pits, housing estates, road works, etc., and these frequently reveal ancient sites (Iron Age pits, huts, a temple such as at Heath Row aerodrome (London airport), Roman burials), and finds (flints, coins, pottery). Similarly, farming operations such as ditching and field draining can also cut through ancient remains. It is therefore a good plan to watch any such works in your neighbourhood; make yourself known to the foreman and his men, ask to see any find they have made, and try to assess its importance. Anything of real interest should be at once reported to the local museum, library or archaeological society, who may be able to arrange for an experienced archaeologist to keep the site under review as well; he will probably be glad to have your help. Reporting is better than trying to cope with the situation yourself; it may prove very large, or the finds may need expert treatment to get them out or preserve them, or the firm doing the work may have to be approached to allow emergency excavation to be undertaken. Contractors are usually very sympathetic and helpful in cases of this kind, in spite of the inconvenience to their work which may be involved, but approach from some official quarter is usually necessary before the desirable arrangements can be made. The great value of amateur observation of likely sites can be illustrated by that of the French 19th century pioneer of the Palaeolithic, Boucher de Perthes (a customs official), who by watching for years the gravel quarries near Abbeville was able to establish the great age of human artifacts; also by the dentist Mr A. T. Marston, who by similar observation of the gravel pits in the Thames terraces at Swanscombe, Kent, had the supreme good fortune, not only of recovering a sequence of Acheulian and Clactonian material, but also the fragments of the human skull which is the earliest known remains of a man of *Homo sapiens* type.

In general, a visit should be paid to any monument or site, of whatever type or importance, which you happen to be within reach of; only so can a wide knowledge be built up. It should however not be forgotten that most sites are on private land, much of it farmed. Strictly, then, the owner's or farmer's permission should be asked to visit such a site, but this is not always possible; if asked it is rarely refused; most owners are very pleased that people should take the interest to see the site. Care should of course be taken to avoid doing any damage to gates (which should always be shut after you), hedges, crops, etc. Standing grass (for hay) or crops over an inch or two high should not be walked on. If you have not got permission to cross private land, and damage is done, or birds disturbed, you are risking legal action against you as a trespasser or under the game laws. Flints etc. picked up on a field belong to the owner of the land, but normally he will not object to your keeping them if asked; he probably has enough stones on his land already! Of course, a few owners are interested in antiquities themselves, but that is a risk one has to take!

Part IV: Aids and Suggestions

CHAPTER I

Following Up

The amateur will do well to confine himself, at least at first, to acquiring a detailed knowledge of the antiquities of his own district, or of a fairly small area, which he can visit frequently and get to know thoroughly. He should familiarise himself with its history and prehistory, and with its monuments and finds; to understand these a broad background will be found necessary, but naturally this will grow slowly and perhaps piecemeal as his interests develop or change. For all this full use must be made of local libraries, museums and societies. Private notes should be kept, and built up. On such a basis most amateurs have been trained, and it is surprising what they have been able to accomplish. The main sources of information are outlined below.

PUBLIC LIBRARIES

These can be used in two ways, either to borrow general works from or for special collections. If the local library or branch does not stock a particular work, it can be ordered, for fourpence or so, through the National Central Library service, whereby any library can draw on the combined resources of most of the libraries in the country. It is therefore very rarely that a book cannot be obtained. The library in most towns of any size also usually has collections of books on local history; these may be kept in a special place, but can always be consulted. A vast amount of information can be got from these collections, which, besides books, usually have newspaper cuttings, old prints, manuscript notes, pamphlets, etc. They often contain works not in the libraries of the local archaeological society (see below), and should be used in conjunction with these. The larger towns also have county or local *archives* or record deposits, which contain old registers, estate records and maps, wills, and a variety of documents which may bear on the former state of the district, from the Middle Ages onwards.

MUSEUMS

Museums should be freely consulted. The staff welcome enquiries, and are very glad to see, advise on, and note finds. The collections, even in the smaller museums, will usually be general as well as local, including reserve stocks of flints, pottery, etc., which one can ask to see. If one is allowed to handle these reserve sherds, flints and small objects, so much the better; it is important to get the feel of things as well as to know what they look like.

Museums of course vary greatly in size and scope. They may be classified into:

   local, usually small, but often including rare and interesting things (e.g. Harrogate);

   county, collections of medium size, drawing on finds and excavations of which some may be important, and often having good reserves (e.g. Salisbury);

   regional, which have fuller type-series and more comparative material (e.g. Bristol);

   national, as in London, Edinburgh, Cardiff and Dublin, and to some extent also Oxford and Cambridge, whose wealth of material is very great;

   there are also *site museums*, as at Avebury or Verulamium (St Albans), containing only material derived from that site, but often giving a comprehensive, stimulating picture of a whole period; and

   specialised museums, dealing with a limited range of subjects, such as the Museum of English Rural Life at Reading, the folk-museum at St Fagan's, Cardiff, or the Wellcome Historical Medical Museum, London, which has a palaeolithic collection.

In all there are some 900 museums in England, Wales and Scotland; a useful list is published annually, *Museums and Galleries in Great Britain and Northern Ireland* (Index Publications). Many of the more relevant museums are mentioned in their place in the Sites to Visit section (pp. 308-347).

SOCIETIES

The organisation of British archaeology is based on the archaeological societies, which provide the impetus and facilities for much of the research carried on outside the Universities. There are several advantages in belonging to one of them: they usually have a library, containing other societies' journals, works on local antiquities, some often of a kind rarely found elsewhere, general reference works and maps; some of them have a museum, or run one jointly with the local authority; they hold meetings, often addressed by highly competent archaeologists, or at which local matters are discussed; they run excursions to sites, etc.; they excavate and watch local sites; they publish notes and reports; and they provide a forum in which a member can get help with his problems. For all this the annual subscription is only a guinea or two, often less for members under 21.

Again, there are several types of society:

the *county* society, usually in the county town, is the normal unit, and the smallest capable of having all the facilities described. Some of these, particularly in large counties or areas, have subsidiary sections for localities or subjects, which can often be joined separately from the parent society;

local, covering only a town and its immediate neighbourhood (e.g. Leatherhead);

groups organised by certain museums (e.g. Bradford); *sections* of non-archaeological societies, e.g. a natural history society, as at Croydon; *school* societies;

the *national* societies are either general like the British Archaeological Association, the Royal Archaeological Institute, The Society of Antiquaries of Scotland, the Cambrian Archaeological Association; or cover a restricted field, such as the Prehistoric Society, the Society for the Promotion of Roman Studies, the Society for Mediaeval Archaeology; the Newcomen Society, for the history of technology; the Railway and Canal Historical Society. These hold meetings of very high value, and have library facilities or access to them; their journals and publications are of the highest standard. The annual subscription to these is two guineas or so. The senior society, the Society of Antiquaries of London, has a magnificent research library, and sponsors much excavation and research; its fellowship is by election in recognition of work in or for archaeology.

All these county and national societies, and many of the local ones, are co-ordinated, for purposes of concerted action when required, and to encourage a rationalised programme of research, by a body called the Council for British Archaeology, composed of representatives of the societies. Regional groupings, for more limited purposes, also exist, such as that which includes the various societies in Yorkshire.

The majority of current work—excavation reports, notes, reviews, comparative studies—appears in the periodical literature issued by societies. All the societies, except the smallest, and even some of these issue typewritten sheets, publish a journal, usually annually, but sometimes more often. A list of the national journals, and other periodicals, is on p. 342.

The amateur should not be put off by the mass of literature. One must be selective at first, but in time it will fall into perspective and be seen for what it is, a source in which one can look for the facts one wants.

TRAINING

Systematic training is to be had at the classes run by the Workers' Educational Association, the Extra-Mural Departments of Universities, and some local authorities. Some of these classes lead to certificates or diplomas, and some courses spread over four years. University diplomas and degrees proper are not in our scope, and details will be found in Dr Kathleen Kenyon's *Beginning in Archaeology* (1961 edition). Summer schools, residential courses and training digs are run by Universities, Field Centres and other bodies. Less formal touch can be kept with current thinking and developments by listening to the monthly programmes on the wireless, 'The Archaeologist'. Series are also run covering a particular period in more detail; television also caters for the subject, not only in popular programmes, but by occasional feature programmes dealing with a particular excavation or technique.

MAPS AND RECORDS

Maps are an essential tool, and should be freely used. The largest scale in ordinary use is the Ordnance Survey 6 in. to a mile, which shows a surprising amount of detail, including field boundaries. The 2½ in., which is based on a photographic reduction from the 6 in., with the National Grid superimposed, is quite suitable for normal purposes, and has advantages. The 1 in. is good for surveys of fairly large areas, but too small to mark every minor find without overcrowding and illegibility. It is a good thing to have two maps of the same area; one should be taken on walks, and notes made on it, of all archaeological features seen, and all small finds; also all sites which cannot be easily seen, such as those revealed by air photographs. These notes can later be transferred to the other map, using Indian ink in small print, with a thin nib or mapping-pen. Symbols should be used for the different kinds of site or find, to avoid overloading the map with descriptive entries. There is no universal code of symbols, which indeed would not be practicable for all the purposes and periods involved, so one's personal set must be evolved. This can be built up from the standard works, and the distribution maps therein. At the same time a card index should be kept; one card for each find or site, showing details, measurements if possible, location, with grid reference, date, present where-abouts, if a small find, and any published reference, if something known already. A photograph should also be taken if possible, and kept with the card index.

For industrial sites the record should contain a note of the sources, e.g. a firm's accounts, plans, sections and maps, illustrations and photo-graphs, bibliography, if any, and other evidence, such as local hearsay. The Council for British Archaeology has initiated a general guide to these monuments, which will cover the types, distribution, significance, and methods of recording them.

From time to time, and at once if a new find or discovery has been made, you should let your local society, museum or public library know what you have found. They may advise reporting some of the entries to the Archaeology Officer of the Ordnance Survey, who is re-sponsible for putting authenticated material on the maps, thus making it available to all, and building up a corpus of knowledge (future editions will show more and more antiquities of all kinds). Incidentally, the Ordnance Survey publish a series of specialised maps for archae-ologists, which, with their introductions, are of the greatest value. These cover Ancient Britain, Roman Britain, The Dark Ages, Monastic Houses, and a few special areas; the Iron Age is in preparation, and the Southern section has already appeared. A guide to these is *The Historian's Guide to Ordnance Survey Maps* (National Council of Social Service, 1964). Recent special maps are those of Hadrian's Wall (1964) and the Antonine Wall (1970).

EXCAVATION

When a new site is found, it should only be excavated under the super-vision of a recognised expert. The local society will advise on this, and will put through all the often delicate negotiations which are required, permissions from the interested parties and authorities, and arrange-ments for the dig itself, including the proper equipment. The amateur will be welcomed at the dig. Excavation needs training and a certain skill, and automatically destroys the evidence as it goes along; the temptation to indulge in it without proper organisation should therefore be resisted. Casual poking on a site with a stick or trowel should also be avoided; this may damage or destroy evidence in the shape of pottery or structures which may happen to lie just below the surface. Similarly, the use of metal detectors for 'treasure-hunting' is inimical to archae-ology and should be avoided.

FOLKLORE

Finally, no opportunity should be lost of talking to those who know the countryside and its antiquities, including country people who may not have any formal training. Some know a great deal; practically all are willing to hold forth. Of course, gossip is not all of equal value and may lead to nothing; but some may be very rewarding. Gossip also may touch on folklore, which should not be overlooked as a source of one kind of information on ancient monuments, that is, how they have struck later peoples. Some of it enshrines memories of the remote past, some is pure fiction. Stories of fairies and the like may refer to gods or former peoples, and old customs such as games, dances, and rites on ancient sites may be echoes of old religions. Customs such as the seasonal dances at Helston (Cornwall) or Abbots Bromley (Staffs.), or the well-dressing at Wirkworth (Derbyshire) have a long history. Details cannot be given here, but careful note should be taken of all such stories or customs, and expert advice sought as to their value. There is a periodical on this subject, *Folklore*. Similarly, *place-names* can be illuminating as to the whereabouts and nature of ancient sites, but this again is a tricky subject and needs expert knowledge for correct interpretation. A special branch of this are the popular names given to barrows, hillforts, etc. (see p. 164). Indeed, *all* information, however unlikely, about an old site, should be noted, and sifted with expert help; it may add a new fact to knowledge. Much remains to be done, and much can be done by the amateur.

CHAPTER 2

Sites to Visit

It is of course not possible here to indicate more than the most important visible monuments, those forming the basic and essential examples of the main types dealt with in this book. The areas most thickly settled by early man have been mentioned on pages 32–33; the broad geological features of the country, as outlined on pages 29–32, should be borne in mind. Certain areas are relatively devoid of ancient monuments, others very rich—the richness due not only to the nature of the soil, but to other factors such as trade or industry, and in some cases to the accident of survival. Whole counties, on this strictly selective basis, will not have many major sites, but in many of them are smaller or less important sites, and the hints given in this book should enable the reader to find and enjoy them for himself. Few parishes actually have nothing at all. A complete list is, in any case, impossible; the number of monuments represented by the examples given in this book must be of the order of 50,000. The best beginning is the lists issued by the Ministry of Works (*List of Ancient Monuments*—England and Wales and Scotland separately), which gives over 11,000 items, and the Ordnance Survey map of Ancient Britain, with its index.

The reader should visit as many as he can of the sites listed below, and use them as mental yardsticks for appreciating the others which he will find at every turn. The *best centres or districts* for seeing early monuments (which are to an encouraging extent in areas favoured for holidays) are appended to the list.

Many of these sites are in private hands, and permission to visit them should always be sought if possible.

ABBREVIATIONS

P	Palaeolithic	S	Anglo-Saxon or Scandinavian
M	Mesolithic		
N	Neolithic	*Med*	Mediaeval (11th to 15th centuries)
B	Bronze Age		
I	Iron Age	*Mod*	Modern (16th century onwards)
R	Roman		
D	'Dark Ages' (Celtic, Sub-Roman, post-Roman or Pagan Saxon)	*Mus*	Museum containing important archaeological collection

SOUTH-WEST ENGLAND (map 1, p. 350)

Devon, Cornwall, Scilly

Devon. A few sites in the *eastern* part—Broom quarries with palaeoliths, Farway round barrow group, Hembury and Blackbury hillforts,—but most concentrated on *Dartmoor*. Settlement sites at Grimspound and Foales Arrishes (B, 1); groups of huts, enclosures, circles, standing stones, stone rows, etc., at Shovel Down, Merrivale, Ditsworthy Warren Trowlesworthy Warren, Erme Valley (B); N hut group, Legis Tor; hillforts, Milber Down, Cranbrook, Prestonbury Castle (1); promontory fort, Bolt Tail, 1; Lydford, earthwork (D); Copplestone Cross, near Crediton (D). Bridges, Postbridge, Barnstaple, Bideford; crosses, North Bovey; open fields, Braunton. Haytor tramway. Centres: Honiton area, Chagford, Tavistock and south, Bideford area, Exeter (*mus*), Plymouth (*mus*). Other *mus*, Torquay, Morwellham, Sticklepath.

Cornwall. Two regions, eastern and Penwith—has a large number of settlement sites and small forts, and a vast profusion of crosses and inscribed stones (D and *med*). The *Bodmin Moors* have several stone monuments of the Bronze Age: circle, Stripple Stones; The Hurlers; group of stones, huts, circles, etc., Rough Tor; burial chamber, Trethevy; round barrows, Braddock Down; circle, Duloe. Ogam stones, Lewannick, D. *Central area:* cliff castle, Trevelgue; hillfort, Castle an Dinas; fort, Castle Dore; stone avenue, Nine Maidens (St Columb Major). *West:* hillfort, Carn Brea; fogou (subterranean refuge, 1), Halligye. A great concentration in *Penwith*: villages and huts, Madron (Chysauster; also fort, Chun Castle); St Cleer; Sancreed (Carn Euny, with souterrain); Zennor. Stone circles, Madron (Nine Maidens); St Buryan (Merry Maidens); Wendron; Zennor. Standing stones, Burras; Trenuggo; Boleigh. Courtyard house (1), Porthmeor; cliff castle, Gurnard's Head. Iron Age rounds, Gwennap; St Just. R milestones, Gwennap; Trethevy near Tintagel. Well, Madron; St Cleer; crosses and inscribed stones (D). Lanivet; Madron; St Buryan; St Cleer; St Ives; Wendron. Well-house, Luxulyan. Falmouth, the King's Pipe (17th century tobacco burner). Centres: Bodmin Moors area; St Columb Major; Penzance. *Mus*: Penzance, Zennor.

Scilly (St Mary's), has a few burial chambers (Bants Carn), and a village (Bants Carn).

WESSEX (map 2, p. 351)

Hampshire, Isle of Wight, Berkshire, Wiltshire, Dorset, Somerset

Hampshire. Silchester, site of R town (walls and amphitheatre); Litchfield, barrows, Ladle Hill camp (N, B); Quarley Hill fort (I); Danebury, hillfort (I) and long barrows (N); Winchester, hillfort on St Catherine's Hill (I) and maze (*med*); Flower Hill, disc barrow. Portchester castle (R and *med*); Bournemouth, double dykes on Hengistbury head (I); Breamore, long barrow (N) and Mizmaze (*med*). Southampton, *med* walls, etc., and wine cellars; earthwork Barley Copse, Crondall; barrel tombs, Froyle; multiple bedboard, Yateley; charcoal sites, New Forrest (e.g. Monk Ash, Wood and Church Moor); Farley Mount, folly. Centres: Kingsclere area, Stockbridge area, Winchester (*mus*). Other *mus*: Christchurch, Alton.

Isle of Wight, Brading R villa. St. Catherine's Oratory (*med* lighthouse), Chale; Calbourne (water) mill; Yarmouth Castle (Henry VIII fort). *Mus:* Carisbrooke Castle.

Berkshire. Lambourn, Seven Barrows (B) and cross, (*med*); Ashbury, Wayland's Smithy, chambered tomb (N); Uffington, White Horse (I) and fort; Blewbury, barrows (B) and fort (I); Inkpen, barrows (I), fort, section of Wansdyke (D); Grim's Bank; *med* cob walls, Blewbury and Brightwell; barn, Great Coxwell; dovecote, Bisham; Thames bridges at Abingdon, etc. Centres; Ashbury, Lambourn, Wallingford. *Mus:* Reading (Silchester material—R) and *mus* of English Rural Life.

Wiltshire. In some respects the richest county in England, falls archaeologically into two main areas, centred on Avebury (*mus*) and Stonehenge: In the former (*northern*) are Avebury henge itself, with the West Kennet Avenue (B); the Sanctuary on Overton Hill, and barrows (B); Silbury Hill (B); Windmill Hill camp, N; the East Kennet and West Kennet chambered tombs, N; and innumerable round and long barrows; Wansdyke (D) runs from Savernake Forest to near Bath, south of the Avebury district, and passing Knap Hill camp (N). In NW Wilts. also are Castle Combe, cross (*med*); Bradford on Avon, Saxon church, tithebarn and bridge; Lacock, dovecote and conduit house (*mod*); *med* causeway, Kellaways; Ashton Keynes, four crosses (*med*); Bishopstone N., lynchets (S); Devizes, flight of locks on canal west of town: *mus*. B, I; Savernake canal tunnel; pumphouse, Crofton; Cricklade, town walls (D) and churchyard cross. The *southern* area culminates in Stonehenge (B), with cursus (N); Durrington, N camp and Woodhenge (B); there is a vast profusion of barrows of all kinds on Salisbury Plain, good groups at Winterbourne Stoke, Wilsford; hillforts at Old Sarum (with Norman castle and cathedral), Figsbury Ring, Yarnbury, Scratchbury and Battlebury near Warminster, Whitesheet Castle near Mere, Chiselbury, Winklebury (all I); near Mere are Pen Pits (I quarries) and round barrows; double dyke on Win Hill (I). Centres; Marlborough, Chippenham or Devizes, Salisbury (*mus*).

Dorset. Another crowded county, and again in two parts, north-east and south-west. The *north-east* is really part of the Wiltshire chalk block; this Cranborne Chase area is very rich in barrows, field-systems, enclosures, e.g. the Tarrants, Pimperne (long barrow) and Pentridge (Oakley Down); here is the Dorset cursus, N (Wyke Down), and Bokerley Dyke (I), and just south is Knowlton with enclosures, one of which contains a church; hillforts at Hod Hill, Hambledon Hill, Spettisbury, Badbury, hill-slope fort at Buzbury; Wareham has Saxon fortifications. In the *south-west* is Dorchester (*mus*, N, B, I, R), with R villa and Maumbury henge/amphitheatre (B, R): Maiden Castle, the greatest British hillfort, with N camp, very long barrow and R temple inside; and fine barrows nearby; Chalbury and Eggardon hillforts; The Grey Mare and her Colts chambered tomb (N) near Abbotsbury, which also has a duck decoy (*mod*); Nine Stones (B circle), Winterbourne Abbas; the area west of Dorchester is very rich in barrows; open fields, Portland (*med*); bowling green and dovecote, Melcombe Bingham; Cerne Abbas, hill-figure, I; old quarries, Kimmeridge (R). *Med* bridge, Wool, with 19th century inscription. Centres: Blandford, Dorchester. Other *mus*: Farnham (Pitt-Rivers, Cranborne Chase material, N, B, I, R).

Somerset. Mostly concentrated in the Mendips, but a western group in the Quantocks and on Exmoor. Bath, besides the R bath (*mus*), is a rich centre of Georgian detail. In the hills just south, are Stanton Drew, stone circles, avenue and cove (B); Stony Littleton, chambered tomb (N); Cadbury hillfort (I); Wraxall R villa. *The Mendips:* Gough's Cave, Aveline's Hole, and Wookey Hole, all inhabited caves (P, I, R); *mus*, Gough's Cave; Gorsey Bigbury, henge, (B); Priddy circles (B); hillforts at Maesbury, Dolebury and Worlebury, I; R amphitheatre and forts, Charterhouse; round barrows at Blagdon, Cheddar, Chewton Mendip and Priddy. *South of Mendip:* Brent Knoll hillfort (I); marsh villages, Meare and Glastonbury (*mus*); barrows near Wells (B). *S. Somerset:* hillforts, Cadbury (? Camelot) and Hamdon Hill (I). *Quantocks:* hillforts, Ruborough, Castle Ditch, Trendle Ring. *Exmoor:* Bat's castle; Withypool Hill, stone circle (B); pack bridges, Winsford, Withypool (Tarr Steps), N on; also Horner and Allerford. Crosses at Dunster, Crowcombe, etc.; Bruton, dovecote, bridges. Norton St Philip, dovecote. Centres: Bath, Cheddar area, Glastonbury area, Exmoor area. Other *mus*: Taunton Castle, Wells (caves).

SOUTH-EAST ENGLAND (map 3, p. 352)

London, Middlesex, Kent, Surrey, Sussex

London. The most important museums for our purpose are: British, all
periods to s, and *med* and *mod* pottery and glass; Natural History,
evolution of man and P, M; Geological; Guildhall, R and *med*; London,
R, S, *med*, *mod*; Horniman, ethnology and P, Wellcome, P. Street furniture, etc., can best be seen in the Bloomsbury and Marylebone districts.
Canal scenery, Regent's Park to Little Venice; railway scenery, Euston
to Camden Town; docks and wharves, St Katherine's, Southwark and
Bermondsey. A few items of interest: tower mill, Brixton; horse ramp,
Brewer St; paving-stones Charing Cross arches; gas-lamps, West-
minster (and sewer-gaslamp, Carting Lane); gun bollards, Borough;
pavement crane, Greek St; B barrow, Hampstead Heath; the 'Roman
Bath'; Highgate Cemetery; the Mithraeum, Queen Victoria St.
Transport *mus*, Clapham.

Middlesex. Grim's ditch, Harrow Weald (I). *mus:* Brentford, Gunners-
bury, Tottenham.

Kent. P rock-shelter, Oldbury, Ightham; Kentish group of megalithic
tombs (N), especially Coldrum and Kit's Coty House near Aylesford;
hillforts, I, Oldbury, Bigbury; R remains, Richborough; R lighthouse,
Dover; R fort, Reculver; R walls. etc., Rochester; R villa, Lullingstone;
R remains, Canterbury; Jutish barrows (D), Barham and Derringstone
Downs; *med* bridges, Yalding, Aylesford; *med* cross, Ebbsfleet; wind-
mill, Cranbrook; Martello towers, Folkestone; boat-shed, Sheerness;
Northfleet, cement kiln; Faversham, Chart Mills (gunpowder).
Centres, Canterbury (*mus*, pre-R, R, S, *med*), Aylesford, Dover. Other
mus: Maidstone, Deal Castle (for Henry VIII coastal defences).

Surrey. M hut, Abinger (also *med* motte); bell barrow, Wotton (B);
triple barrow, Elstead (B); earth circles, St Martha's Hill (B); I enclosure,
Chobham (Bee Garden); I–R fields, D barrows, Farthing Down, Couls-
don; hillforts of the greensand, especially Anstiebury, Holmbury and
Hascombe (I); the greensand has a large number of hollow ways, some
ancient—note the very deep gully on Winterfold Heath; R villa,
Farnham; *med* moated site, Boughton Hall, Send; *med* bridges on
Wey, e.g. Eashing; *med* cross, Lingfield; cultivation terraces, Hut Hill,
Wisley; furnace pond, Imbhams, Haslemere; paved paths to churches,
Okewood, Charlwood; *mod*, Dorking Mill; garden terraces and grotto,
Albury Park; post-mill, Outwood; treadmill crane, *med* clunch mine,
Guildford; turf lock, Sutton Green; course of Surrey Iron Railway,

Merstham; course of Wey and Arun Canal, south of Bramley. Centres:
Guildford (*mus*), Reigate. Other *mus*: Haslemere, Charterhouse School,
Farnham, Weybridge.

Sussex. The ancient sites are mostly concentrated along the South
Downs. *Eastern:* N camp, Coombe Hill; N long barrow, Hunters
Burgh; B long barrow and *med* cross, Alfriston; hillfort and fields, I,
Caburn, R terrace-way, Firle; hill-figure, ?I or S, Long Man of Wilming-
ton; R fort, Pevensey; folly, Dallington. Towermill, Polegate; postmill,
Cross in Hand; iron graveslabs, Wadhurst; donkey wheel, Sedles-
combe; R road, Holtye. *Central:* Black Rock, raised beach, etc.; N
flint mines, Harrow Hill; N flint mines and I hillfort, Cissbury; I hillfort,
Chanctonbury; Devil's Dyke, I; S fort, Burpham; *med* hammer ponds,
St Leonard's Forest; windmill, Shipley. *Western:* N camp in I hillfort,
The Trundle; Bow Hill, a large group, including round barrows, double
bell-barrow, hill-slope fort, spur-ditches, covered ways, hut-sites,
etc. (N, B, I, R); N long barrow, Up Marden; Iping, group of round
barrows or ? stabilised dunes, R road, *med* bridge; B barrows, Devil's
Jumps, Treyford; terrace-ways, Harting-Treyford area; I dykes,
Boxgrove and Lavant; R villa and section of Stane Street, Bignor (*mus*);
R palace, Fishbourne; *med* cross, Chichester; *med* bridge, Stopham;
church on mound, Chithurst; canal tunnel, Hardham. Centres: Lewes
(*mus*), Worthing (*mus*, S, N), Chichester (*mus*). Other *mus*: Brighton,
Weald and Downland, West Dean.

EAST ANGLIA (map 4, p. 353)

Norfolk, Suffolk, Essex

Norfolk. Not many monuments, except round barrows on the heath
country (e.g. Weasenham and Weeting), but a few of great importance:
N flint mines, Grimes Graves, Weeting; long barrow, West Rudham;
ironworks, Holkham and Warham (this? re-used by Danes); R town
(walls and earthworks), Caister St Edmunds; Foss Ditch, near Weeting
(D); S cathedral and earthworks, North Elmham; *med* motte, Thetford;
pumphouse, Little Walsingham; church on mound, Holkham; windmills, Huntset, Reedham, Cley, Burnham Overy; urban details, Norwich; the Broads (*med* turbaries) Centres: Norwich (*mus*), Thetford
(*mus*), Wells.

Suffolk. R barrow, Eastlow Hill; R fort, Burgh Castle; D barrows, Sutton
Hoo; many *med* moated sites; *med* crosses, Bungay, Lavenham,
Mildenhall; tide-mill and steelyard, Woodbridge; windmills, Paken-
ham, Saxtead Green; packhorse bridge, Moulton; disused railway and
quays, Blythburgh. Centres: Bury St Edmunds (*mus*), Southwold.
Mus, Ipswich.

Essex. The richest county for *med* moated sites—nearly every parish has at least one. The classic Clactonian type-site is not visible, but at Lion Point, Jaywick, is a Clactonian exposure on the foreshore. The important Belgic capital of Camulodunum is represented by earthworks and barrow at Lexden; the R town by walls, gates, and temple remains at the Castle (Colchester, *mus*); R barrow, Mersea Island; Saxon Shore fort, Bradwell (R); hillforts, Wallbury, near Bishops Stortford; Ambresbury Banks and Loughton Camp, Epping Forest (I); R barrows, Bartlow Hills, Ashdon; I and R and *med* saltings, on Blackwater near Maldon; S earthworks, Maldon; maze, Saffron Walden (*med*); moated site, Writtle (King John's Palace); Pleshey, motte and bailey, and protective earthworks round village (*med*); Waltham Abbey, Stoney Bridge (*med*); windmill, Bocking; pillow mounds, High Beech; Greensted church has a unique example of Saxon timber building; Tilbury Fort (16th century). Centres: Colchester, Chelmsford (*mus*, R). Other *mus*: Southend, Walthamstow, Chingford.

SOUTH-EAST MIDLANDS (map 6, p. 355)

Northamptonshire and Soke of Peterborough, Cambridgeshire, Isle of Ely, Huntingdonshire, Hertfordshire, Bedfordshire, Buckinghamshire

Northamptonshire and Soke of Peterborough. Standing stones (B), Castor (Robin Hood and Little John); long barrow, Woodford; hillfort, Hunsbury, Hardingstone (I); R town, Castor and Water Newton (Hunts.); R and *med* quarries, Barnack; important S. churches, Earl's Barton, Brixworth, Barnack; Farthingstone, motte and bailey, and earthwork (*med*); Geddington, Eleanor Cross (also Hardingstone) and Bridge. Centres: Peterborough (*mus*), Kettering. *Mus:* Northampton, Stoke Bruerne (canal *mus.*).

Cambridgeshire and Isle of Ely. Round barrows, Bourn (also post-mill) Chatteris (B); Wandlebury hillfort; ringditch, Chatteris (I); Waterbeach, Car Dyke (R canal); Devil's and Fleam Dykes (D, across Icknield Way); Fen waterways, e.g. Bedford Rivers; Soham, steelyard; Stretham, pumphouse. Centres: Cambridge (University Museum of Archaeology and Ethnology); Chatteris-Ely area.

Huntingdonshire. Round barrows, Chesterton, Great Stukeley; R town, Water Newton; bridges on Ouse (e.g. St Ives); Hilton, maze and monument. Centre: Huntingdon. *Mus:* St Ives.

Hertfordshire. Long and round barrows, Therfield Heath; R barrows, Six Hills, Stevenage; Belgic town site, Prae Wood, St Albans (I); I earthworks, Wheathampstead (Devils' Dyke) and St Albans, Beech

Bottom; R city, St Albans, with walls, theatre, houses, etc., and *mus*; Royston, The Cave (? denehole, adapted for hermitage, *med*), Waltham Cross (Eleanor cross). Centres: St Albans, Royston.

Bedfordshire. Round barrows, Dunstable Downs, Totternhoe; Caddington, hut circles, Blow's Downs (1); Willington, dovecote and moated site (*med*); packhorse bridge, Sutton (*mod*); Maiden Bower, Houghton Regis (1 fort). Centre: Dunstable area. *Mus*: Luton, Bedford Modern School.

Buckinghamshire. Bledlow, S barrows and hillside cross (*med*); Princes Risborough, Whiteleaf Cross; Cholesbury hillfort (1); Grim's Ditch, Great Hampden and Lacey Green; Tattenhoe, deserted village (*med*)— also Quainton and Quarrendon. Centres: Chilterns area, Aylesbury.

SOUTH-WEST MIDLANDS (map 6, p. 355)

Oxfordshire, Warwickshire, Gloucestershire, Worcestershire

Oxon. Barrow and Hoar Stone, Enstone (B); long barrow and standing stone, Lyneham; the Rollright Stones, circle with associated stones (B); S barrow, Asthall; R town site, Alchester; R villa, North Leigh; Grim's Ditch, Enstone and Kiddington; village site, *med*, Kiddington; dovecote, Minster Lovell; bridges, Culham, New and Radcot; stone fences, e.g. Kelmscot. Centres: Oxford (Ashmolean and Pitt-Rivers museums), Chipping Norton.

Warwickshire. Hillforts, Beausale, Oakley Wood (Bishops Tachbrook), Corley (Burrow Hill), Oldbury, Solihull (Berry Ring); Chesterton, R station, deserted village, tower mill (Inigo Jones); cross, Knightlow Hill; Wappenbury, fort of uncertain date; Solihull, motte and moat; motte, Brinklow; Rugby, mill mound; Guy's Cliffe, rock-cut chambers; many bridges, e.g. Clopton, Hampton in Arden (packhorse). R fort reconstructed at Baginton. Centres: Birmingham, Warwick, Nuneaton; *mus*, Birmingham City and Science.

Gloucestershire. Very rich in barrows, including some of the best of the Severn-Cotswold family—fine examples at Uley (Hetty Pegler's Tump, which can be entered), Sudeley (Belas Knap, with forecourt), Notgrove, Rodmarton, Brimpsfield (West Tump), Gatcombe; round barrows numerous, e.g. Swell; hillforts along the Cotswold edge, Leckhampton, Haresfield, Uley, Old Sodbury; R villas, Chedworth, King's Weston; bridges, Bourton on the Water; mills, Tewkesbury; Upper Swell. Industrial remains, Stroud area; tramroad track, Keynsham; tombs, Painswick; weathercock, Winchcomb; market hall, Tetbury; gable crosses, Down Ampney. s church, Deerhurst. The part of the county *west of Severn*, largely the Forest of Dean, is a separate district, with a very different character; small fort, Little Dean, (12th century); late 4th century temple and buildings, Lydney; Offa's Dyke along the east bank of the Wye, from Tidenham to beyond Staunton; R iron workings, Scowles, near Lydney; early 19th century dock, Bullo Pill; D chapel, Blackley; crosses, Lydney, Clearwell; holy well, near Flaxley; R road, Blackpool Bridge; 17th century water garden, Westbury. Centres: Northleach, Stroud, Bristol, Lydney. *Mus*: Bristol, Chedworth, Gloucester, Cirencester, Lydney (private).

Worcestershire. Hillforts, Bredon, Woodbury; linear earthwork, Shire Ditch, Malvern (I); several crosses, e.g. Ripple; dovecote, Kyre; 18th century canal port, Stourport; Forge Mill (needles), Redditch. Centres: Malvern, Evesham. *Mus*: Worcester, Stourbridge (glass), Avoncroft (buildings, Stoke Prior).

NORTH MIDLANDS (map 5, p. 354)

Rutland, Lincolnshire, Leicestershire, Nottinghamshire, Derbyshire, Staffordshire

Rutland. Moated sites, Empingham, Whissendine; dovecote and bridge, Empingham; maze, Wing; stocks and cross, Oakham.

Lincolnshire. Holland: Trinity bridge and crosses, Crowland; s sea wall, 'Roman Bank'; Boston, warehouses. Centre: Spalding (*mus*). *Kesteven:* hillfort, Honington; s crosses, Digby and Stoke Rochford; packhorse bridge, Scredington. Centre: Grantham, Stamford (townscape). *Lindsey and Lincoln City:* important groups of long barrows, including Claxby (Deadman's Graves), Langton (Spellow Hills), Swinhope (Hoe Hill), Walmsgate (Beacon Plantation); settlement site, M, N, B, Hall Hill, West Keal; Risby Warren (M, N, B); R fort, Horn castle; s barrow, Burgh le Marsh; *med* town site, Torksey; R remains, Lincoln; R canals, Car Dyke, from Peterborough to Lincoln, Foss Dyke, Lincoln to the Trent; s sea-walls and *med* saltings, Marsh Chapel and Saltfleet area (Sea Dyke); High Bridge, Lincoln; Maze, Alkborough. Centres: Lincoln, Scunthorpe (*mus* at both), Skegness, Grimsby.

Leicestershire. R remains, Leicester; s stones, Breedon; several crosses, e.g. Mountsorrel, Sproxton; motte and bailey and moated site, Gilmorton (also deserted village, Cote de Val); a large number of moated sites; fishpond, Kirby Hall site, Frisby-on-the-Wreak; Breedon-on-the-Hill, hillfort enclosing s church. Centre: Leicester (*mus*).

Nottinghamshire. Cresswell Crags, P rock shelters and caves; crosses, Linby (*med* and 17th century); moats and fishponds, Rolleston; Sibthorpe, *med* sites and dovecote; Civil War earthworks, Wiverton Hall; open fields, Laxton. Centres: Nottingham (Castle, *mus*, caves and cellars), Worksop. Other *mus*: Newark.

Derbyshire. Most of Creswell Crags are in Derbys., including Pin Hole Cave and Mother Grundy's Parlour; the *Peak District* between Matlock and Buxton is rich in barrows, both round and chambered, and stone monuments—barrows, Minning Low, Ballidon; Hob Hurst's House, Beeley; Five Wells, Taddington; henges, Arbor Low, ?unfinished; Bull Ring, Dove Holes; stone circles, Harthill Stones; Nine Ladies, Stanton; a few hillforts, e.g. Mam Tor, Castleton (?LBA); hermitage, Harthill; several crosses, e.g. Bakewell; many bridges, e.g. Ashford, Derby (with chapel); Cromford, mills and village; Bonsall, cross; Haddon Hall, packhorse bridge and terraced gardens; Hartington, dewponds; Tissington, well; Melbourne, the Iron Arbour; lock-up, Smisby. Centres: Buston, Matlock.

Staffordshire. Thor's Cave (I and R), near Hulme End; hillforts, Berry Ring, Bradley; Castle Ring, Cannock; R site, Wall (*mus*); Ilam, crosses and bridge; watermills, N of Stone; Abbots Bromley, market cross, iron and wood gravestones, the Horns; gardens, Shugborough. Centres: Stafford, Lichfield, Ashbourne (just in Derbyshire). *Mus*: Stoke on Trent (ceramics), Shugborough.

SOUTH WALES, with Monmouthshire and Herefordshire
(map 8, p. 357)

Monmouthshire, Herefordshire, Brecknockshire, Glamorgan, Carmarthenshire, Pembrokeshire, Cardiganshire, Radnorshire

Monmouthshire. A few barrows and circles, of which Portskewett long barrow and Harold's Stones, Trelleck (group of standing stones) may be cited; hillforts, such as Llanmelin and Sudbrook; R towns, Caerwent; R legionary fort, with amphitheatre and civil village, Caerleon (*mus*); several churchyard crosses, e.g. Grosmont, Raglan, Trelleck (also wayside cross); motte, Trelleck; *med* village site, Mathern; bridge, Monmouth (with gate tower); holy well, Trelleck, and pool, Mathern; Civil War earthwork, Penrhos, Caerleon. Moat, Hen Gwrt (Llantilio Crossenny); Raglan castle, paved court and bowling green; Skenfrith, dovecote in church tower, and stone tower on motte; cast iron bridge, Chepstow. Centres: Chepstow, Trelleck, Monmouth. *Mus*: Newport.

Herefordshire. A county with much fine detail: Arthur's Cave (Whitchurch), P and M; megalithic tomb, Arthur's Stone, Dorstone; several fine hillforts. Herefordshire Beacon and Midsummer Hill on the Malverns, Coxall Knoll, Croft Ambrey and Pyon Wood (Aymestrey), Bach Camp (Kimbolton), Wall Hills (Thornbury), Credenhill, Sutton Walls (inside ruined), Aconbury, Capler, Ethelbert's Camp (Dormington); R town site, Weston under Penyard; Offa's Dyke, Lyonshall and other places; a large number of mottes, e.g. Kilpeck, Huntington; crosses, Hereford, and several churchyard crosses (e.g. Tyberton); mound, dancing floor or moot, King's Caple; church, Kilpeck; dovecote, Garway; sundials, Garway, Dorstone; Pembridge, market hall with ancient stone (see also bell-tower); battle burial mound, Mortimer's Cross (1461); market hall, Ross; Goodrich, rock-cut moat, military lockup (?), Y Crwys; dovecote, Eardisland; inn on old Tramroad, Tram Inn; ironwork, Great Malvern Station. Centres: Hereford (*mus*), Leominster.

Brecknock. Group of megalithic tombs—Gwernvale, Ty Isaf, Ty Illtyd; stone circle, Cerrig Duon; hillforts, Crug Hywell, Castell Dinas (Talgarth), an I fort with *med* castle in it; many mottes—Talgarth (three). Bronllys; R forts, Brecon Gaer and Y Pigwn; D inscribed stones, Trallong, Llanddetty, Llandefaelog fach. Centres: Brecon (*mus*), Crickhowell, Talgarth.

Glamorgan. Rich in barrows, round and Severn–Cotswold type, and in forts and settlements, mostly near the coast between Cardiff and Port Talbot, and in Gower. *Eastern area:* long barrows, Tinkinswood, St. Lythans; round barrows and standing stones, Llanrhidian; promontory fort, Castle Ditches, Llantwit Major; hillforts, Port Talbot (six), Y Bwlwarcau (Llangynwyd); Caerau; R fort, Cardiff; D crosses, etc., Llandough, Llantwit Major, Llangan, Merthyr Mawr (and dipping bridge); D monastic site, Llantwit Major. *Western area:* B cave, Goat's Hole, Paviland; meg. tombs, Arthur's Stone, Parc Cwm (Parc le Breos); standing stone, Samson's Jack; hillforts, The Bulwark, Cil Ifor; D sculptured stone, Llanrhidian. Centres; Cardiff, Llantwit Major, Port Talbot, Gower. *Mus*: Cardiff (National Mus.), Margam Abbey (D).

Carmarthenshire. A large number of round barrows, and some of the simple west Welsh type stone burial chambers. P cave, Coygan; barrows, Conwil-Elvet, Llangeler; burial chamber, Gwal y Filiast (Llangynog, also Meini Gwyr stone circle); standing stone, Hirfaen Gwyddog (Llanycrwys); hillfort, Carn Goch (Llangadock); R gold workings, Dolaucothi; D inscribed stones, Laugharne, Eglwys Gymmyn; dovecote, Kidwelly (Coleman); Civil War earthworks, The Bulwarks, Carmarthen. Centres: Llandovery, St Clears.

Pembrokeshire. **One** of the richest counties in Britain, particularly for megalithic tombs, post-Roman inscribed stones, holy wells, settlement sites, and castles in the south. *South*: standing stone, Harold's Stone. Bosherston; I promontory fort, Nab Head; fort, Roman Castle; rath, Marloes; R cave, Longbury Bank; D crosses, Carew, Penally; D inscribed stone, Caldy Island; D settlement site, Gateholm Island; settlement (?), Skomer Island. *North*: megalithic tomb, Pentre Ifan, near Nevern; burial chambers, Llech y Tribedd, near Nevern, Carreg Coitan Arthur and Cerrig y Gof (five chambers round a circular mound), near Newport; Carn Llidi, near St David's Head; standing stones, Bedd Morus, Lady Stone; stone row, Parc y Meirw; stone circle, Gors Fawr; forts, St David's (Clegyr Boia; Castell Heinif, promontory fort, also Penpleidian); Carn Ingli; many raths and small forts. Settlements, St David's Head; source of Stonhenge bluestones, Carn Meini, Presely Mountains. D inscribed stones and crosses, Nevern, St Dogmaels, St David's; D chapel, well (restored) and stones, St Non's; *med* cross on rock, Nevern. Limekilns (18th century), e.g. Parrog; square farm ponds, e.g. Treriffith near Nevern; holy well, Llanllawer; corbelled hut, Llanwnda. Centes; Tenby, Dale area; St David's, Newport-Nevern area.

Cardiganshire. The west of the county has sites etc. not unlike those of Pembrokeshire, the north like central Wales. Barrows and stones, Melindwr; Yspytty Cynfyn; hillfort, Pen Dinas, near Aberystwyth; D inscribed stones, Penbryn, Llandewi Brefi, Llanwnnws; cairns on Plynlimon; coracles on Teifi. Centres: Cardigan, Aberystwyth.

Radnor. Some barrows; stone circle, the Fedw, Glascwm; standing stones, Four Stones, near New Radnor; R practice camps, Llandrindod Common; Offa's Dyke, south of Knighton; D cross-slab, Llowes; mottes, e.g. Knighton, Painscastle. Centre: Presteigne.

NORTH WALES, with Shropshire and Cheshire (map 7, p. 356)

Shropshire, Cheshire, Montgomeryshire, Flintshire, Denbighshire, Merioneth, Caernarvonshire, Anglesey

Shropshire. Like Herefordshire, a county of hillforts and border castles, but also rich in round barrows. Barrows at Myndtown and Ratlinghope (one a disc); stone circles, Clun (also standing stone), Chirbury (Mitchell's Fold and Hoar); forts, Caer Caradoc (Church Stretton), Bury Ditches (Lydbury N), Norton Camp (Culmington), Caynham, The Wrekin, Old Oswestry; caves, Church Stretton. Great Ness; R town, Wroxeter; R fort, Walltown, Neen Savage; Offa's Dyke passes through the county in the Clun Forest area, and west of Oswestry; Wat's Dyke is parallel to it from Oswestry to the Dee; mottes, e.g. Stanton Lacy, Betws-y-Crwyn; sundial and gates, Madeley Court; pyramidal dovecote, Tong; Madeley, the Ironbridge (1779); Coalbrookdale, early ironworks (scene of Darby's use of coke for smelting, 1709); cockpit, Lydbury North; first iron-framed mill, Shrewsbury (1796). Centres: Oswestry, Shrewsbury, Ludlow (*mus*).

Cheshire. Megalithic tomb, Bridestones, Congleton; hillforts, Helsby Hill, Maiden Castle (Bickerton); defensive work, Oak Mere (?); R shrine, Chester; crosses, Sandbach, Macclesfield; bridge, Chester; earthworks (s), Toot Hill, near Macclesfield; Styal (industrial village). Centres: Chester, Macclesfield. *Mus*: Chester.

Montgomery. Stone circles, Llanbrynmair; hill forts, Ffridd Faldwyn (Montgomery), Beacon Ring (Trelystan); Breiddin and Bausley (three); I settlement, Craig Rhiweirth, Llangynog; D slab, Meifod; Offa's Dyke, Churchstoke to Llandysilio. Centre: Montgomery-Welshpool area.

Flintshire. Caves, Tremeirchion; circle and barrows, with Offa's Dyke, Holywell racecourse; stone circle and stone, Penbedw Park, Cilcain; round barrows, Ysceifiog; hillforts, Moel Hiraddug (Cwm), Moel y Gaer (Bodfari and Northop), Pen y Cloddiau (Nannerch); Wat's Dyke, Holywell to Hope; D slab cross, Maen Achwyfan, Whitford; well, Holywell; castle mounds, Flint. Centres: Holywell, Mold.

Denbighshire. A large number of round barrows, e.g. Llangollen (also stone circle and earth circle), long barrow, Capel Garmon; earth circles, Capel Hiraethog (Gyffylliog); circular platform, Rhyd Sion Wynn (Llanrhaiadr yn Cinmerch); stone rows, Pentre Foelas; ancient village, Cefn Banog (Clocaenog); Offa's Dyke, Brymbo to Glyntraian; Wat's Dyke, Gwersyllt to Ruabon; hillforts, Pen y Corddyn (Abergele), Parc y Meirch (Dinorben), Foel Fenlli (Llanbedr), Castell Dinas Bran; D cross-stones and inscribed stones, Gwytherin, Llangerniew, Llantysilio (Eliseg's Pillar), Pentre Foelas; churchyard cross, Derwen; well (Ffynnon Fair) Cefn, and caves; cockpit, Denbigh (Hawk and Buckle Inn); dovecote, Denbigh; Civil War earthwork, Denbigh; bridges, Pentre Foelas; canal aqueduct, Pont y Cysylltau (Chirk); R practice camps, Castell Collen. Centres: Abergele, Denbigh, Llangollen.

Merioneth. Megalithic tombs, Carneddau Hengwm, Llanaber; circles, Caer Euni (Llanderfel), Llandrillo; hillforts, Caer Drewyn (Corwen), Dinas Melin y Wig (Gwyddelwern); ancient village, Muriau y Gwyddelod (Llandanwg); R fort, Tomen y Mur (Maentwrog); D inscribed stones, Towyn, Dolmelinllyn, Talsarnau; ring motte, Llanfor; bridges Dolgellau, Llanbedr; *med* house site, Llys Bradwen, Llangelynen; *med* paved track, Roman Steps, Bwlch Tyddiad. Centres: Harlech, Dolgellau.

Caernarvonshire. Falls into two very different halves, Snowdonia, and the Lleyn peninsula. *Snowdonia*, including the coast from Conway to Bangor, has Graig Lwyd, site of stone axe factory (N); stone circles, standing stones, arrow stones, etc. Llanfairfechan; hillforts, Conway (Caer Lleion), Beddgelert (Pen y Gaer); R marching camp, Pen y Gwryd; D inscribed stones, Penmachno. *Lelyn*: cairn, Yr Eifl; a series of forts from Dinorwic to Carn Fadron, by Dinas Dinlle and Garn Bodfean; R fort, Caernarvon; several village sites (I, R date, to post-R), especially round Llanaelhaiarn, and dominated by the hilltop site of Tre'r Ceiri; holy well and D stone, Llangybi. Group of antiquities at Clynnog Fawr, including megalithic tomb with cup-marks, Bachwen, one with traces of mound, Penarth; standing stone and round cairns; fort; St Beuno's well; D cross-stone, sundial; bridge. Centres: Conway, Bettws y Coed, Caernarvon, Clynnog, Criccieth-Portmadoc area. *Mus*: Caernarvon; Bangor (Penrhyn Castle, slate industry and loco-motives).

Anglesey. Important megalithic tombs, Bryn Celli Ddu (and standing stone), Brynyr Hen Bobl (both Llandaniel Fab), Barclodiad y Gawres (Aberffraw, with mural art); Penrhos Lligwy (also Bodafon hut groups, and Din Lligwy fortified village); forts and hut circles, Holyhead; R fort, Holyhead; R defended settlement, Caer Leb; D inscribed stones, Llangadwaladr, Llansadwrn, Penmon; well and dovecote, Penmon; cashel, Priestholme; Parys mine buildings and port, Amlwch. Centres: Menai Bridge, Amlwch, Holyhead.

YORKSHIRE AND LANCASHIRE, (map 10, p. 359)

City of York. City wall, partly on line of wall of R fortress; R tower (Multangular Tower); S barrow, Lamel Hill; castle mound, Clifford's Tower; *med* river wall. *Mus*.

East Riding. M settlement site, Star Carr, Seamer; many round barrows, e.g. Duggleby Howe, Kirby Grindalythe; Willy Howe, Thwing; Huggate Wold; Thixendale; Danes' Graves (I), near Driffield: mono-lith in churchyard, Rudston; linear earthworks, Aldro, Huggate; Danes Dykes, Flamborough; sanctuary limit stones, Bishop Burton, Bentley and Walkington; S cross, Nunburnholme; many deserted villages, e.g. Burton Constable, Cowlam, Kilham; Flamborough, old lighthouse. Centre: Great Driffield. *Mus*: Hull (Mortimer).

West Riding. The *southern Pennines* have the important hillforts of Carl Wark and Wincobank, near Sheffield, and Almondbury near Huddersfield; near the latter also much M material has been found (e.g. Marsden); quern workings, Wharncliffe; stretch of R road, Blackstone Edge; S earthwork, Roman Ridge, Rotherham—Wath-on-

Dearne area; Catcliffe, glass cone (1740); Abbeydale Forge, Sheffield. A *northern* group of sites is in Upper Wharfedale and Craven; B inscribed stones, Ilkley, Addingham, Baildon; stone circles, Baildon, Bradfield, Ilkley (Twelve Apostles, Burley Moor), Yockenthwaite; I settlement sites, Grassington, Arncliffe, Craven; hillfort, Ingleborough; P cave, Victoria Cave, near Settle. The Devil's Arrows, B monoliths, Boroughbridge, are part of the complex sites on the NR side of the Ure. R remains, Aldborough. Crosses, S. Ilkley; *med*, Ripley; Aldborough (battle memorial); Boroughbridge. *Med* caves, Knaresborough. *Med* house site, North Rigton. Studley Royal, 18th century gardens and pavilions. Monk Wall, Fountains Abbey. *Mod* lead mines, Greenhow and Grassington; monastic iron workings, Ramsgill; line of disused railway, Pateley Bridge to Scar. 19th century well-house, Harrogate. Dyke, Aberford. Bolton Abbey, table tombs and fishpond; Pateley Bridge, very large mill-wheel, Corn Close; line of ropeway, Scotgate; Park Rash (Kettlewell), Brigantian rock-cut defences; Ribblehead, drumlin field; Dent, Grassington, Middlesmoor, Haworth, cobbled streets; Linton, packhorse and clapper bridge, and sheep-stile at churchyard; witches' seat on chimney, Feizor. North Deighton has a barrow (Green Howe), a motte (Howe Hill), lynchets, and a dovecote. The riches of the West Riding defy listing—few parts of England have more variety of monuments. Centres: Sheffield (*mus*), Huddersfield (Tolson *mus*), Ilkley, Grassington, Settle, Ripon, Knaresborough or Harrogate. Other *mus*: Leeds (Kirkstall), Bradford, Rotherham, Ripon (Thorpe Prebend House), Skipton, Harrogate, Wetherby, Halifax, Doncaster.

North Riding. A very large number of barrows on the *North York Moors* —Eskdaleside (also stone row, High Bride Stones), Fylingdales, Hutton Buscel area (with circles), Farndale-Rosedale area, Castleton area (cairn group, Danby Rigg), Moorland crosses, e.g. White Cross (Fat Betty), Danby; Ralph Crosses, Westerdale. R road, Wheeldale Moor; R practice camps, Cawthorn; R signal stations, Scarborough, Goldsborough. Linear earthworks, Scambridge Dykes (Ebberston, ?s), Hutton Buscel, Farndale and Boltby Scar (promontory forts); hillfort, Eston Nab. I settlement, Scarborough; D sundial, Kirkdale; jet workings, Scugdale (along outcrop); drove road, Hambleton Hills; bridges, Danby, Glaisdale. Pillow mounds, Hutton-le-Hole. Chimney and course of old railway, Rosedale. Sneaton beacon.

In the *Pennine* part of the county are the groups of henges at Thornborough and Hutton Moor; I fortifications, Stanwick; R forts, Bainbridge; Rey Cross (marching camp). Bridges: West Tanfield, Greta Bridge. *Med* house site, Topcliffe on Swale. Centres: Pickering, Eskdale (Ripon), Richmond (Barnard Castle). *Mus*: Malton, Middlesborough, Scarborough, Whitby, Ryedale Folk *mus*, Hutton-le-Hole (see glass furnace and cruck cottage).

Lancashire. B burial circle, Bleasdale Circle; stone circles, Briercliffe, Lowick, Turton, Worsthorne; settlement site, Kirby Ireleth; crosses, Whaley, also group in Line Valley: bridges, Wycoller, Newby; hogback stone, Heysham; Dog Holes Cave, Warton; duck decoy pond, Hale. Centres: Lancaster (*mus*). Other *mus*: Manchester, Liverpool, Ribchester (R site), St Helens (Pilkingtons, glass).

NORTH OF ENGLAND (map 9, p. 358)

Westmorland, Cumberland, Durham, Northumberland

Westmorland. Henges, Mayburgh, Yanwath (King Arthur's Round Table); stone circles, Barton, Casterton, Crosby Ravensworth, Shap; hillfort, Castle Crag, Bampton; settlement sites, Crosby Ravensworth (Ewe Close, Burwens, and others), Hugill, Kentmere, Waitby, Crosby Garrett. R fort, Low Borrowbridge. D cross, Casterton; R road, High Street. Bridge, Kirkby Lonsdale; plague-stone, Penrith. Centres: Kirkby Stephen, Windermere, Penrith.

Cumberland. Stone circles, Long Meg and her Daughters (Hunsonby), Eskdale, Millcm, Castlerigg (Keswick), and others; settlement, Lazonby; Burnscar, Eskdale; hillfort, Carrock Fell; R forts, Bewcastle, Hardknott Castle (Eskdale) Walls Castle (Ravenglass); Ambleside; the Roman Wall crosses the county from the Solway north of Carlisle to Willowford, and sites are visible at Banks Burn (section of wall), Birdoswald (fort), Poltross Burn (milecastle), Willowford (bridge abutment); caves and inscribed rocks, Wetheral, inscriptions, Rock of Gelt (Brampton). D crosses, Bewcastle, Gosforth, Penrith (with hogbacks). Scots Dyke, Kirkandrews (16th century); cobbled pavements, Kirkgate, Cockermouth; spinning galleries, Coniston, etc. Centres: Carlisle (*mus*), Penrith, Ravenglass.

Co. Durham. Hillfort, The Castles, S. Bedburn; R forts, Piercebridge, South Shields; R aqueduct, Lanchester; S inscription, Jarrow; Nevill's Cross, Durham; bridges, Durham, Barnard Castle. Centre: Durham. *Mus*, Beamish Hall.

Northumberland. A very rich county, particularly in Bronze Age inscribed stones, hillforts and border castles, not to mention the Roman Wall. Barrows, Debdon, Doddington, Bewick Moor, Windy Gyle; stone circles, Cartington, Duddo, Garleigh Hill (Hesleyhurst, with stone rows and round barrows), Simonburn; Ilderton; standing stones, Ford, Haltwhistle, Harnham, Holystone, Yeavering; incised rocks (B), Chatton and Doddington, particularly Roughting Linn and Dod Law, and other places; cairns (N, B), Kielder; hillforts, at least 90—fine examples at Yeavering Bell (with hut-circles), **Lordenshaws** and Garleigh Moor (with cup-and-ring stones), Dod Law, Old Bewick; settlement sites, plentiful in the Cheviot area, also, e.g. **Gunnar Peak**, near Chollerton; R sites, forts, Risingham (with rock-cut relief), High Rochester, Dere Street, camps at Chew Green; Hadrian's Wall—runs from Willowford to Wallsend, and the full system is visible in many places, some spectacular, e.g. Walltown Crags (with turret), Henshaw (with milecastle), Housesteads (fort), Carrawburgh (Mithraeum and well), Chesters (fort and bridge abutments), Corbridge (base storehouses); S monastic site, Farne Islands (also two 17th century lighthouses); lighthouse, Holy Island; Percy's Cross, Norham cross; bridges, Corbridge, Twizel, Warkworth (with gatehouse); dovecotes, Bamburgh and several places between Embleton and Berwick; 16th century fortifications, Berwick; shot tower and 13th century lookout, Newcastle. Model village on plan of abbey, Blanchland (1750); hirings hall, Stamfordham; lead mines, Allenheads. Centres: Hexham, Wooler, Belford area. *Mus*: Newcastle (University), Corbridge, Chesters, Housesteads, Berwick, Chesterholm (R *vicus*).

SOUTH-EAST SCOTLAND (map 11, p. 360)

Roxburghshire, Berwickshire, Selkirkshire, Peeblesshire

Roxburghshire. A concentration of settlements and forts of I and R date along the Cheviot foothills, e.g. the great multiple fort of Woden Law, and lesser ones at Bonchester Hill (multiple), Park Law, Swindon Castles, Hownam Law, Blackburgh Hill, Shaw Craig; and very impressive is the fort on Eildon Hill North; settlement sites at Buchtrig Mote and Hayhope Knowe; R practice camps and siegeworks, Pennymuir (Woden Law); R inscriptions and D cross, Jedburgh Abbey; D hillfort, Ruberslaw; site of old Roxburgh, near Kelso; 17th century cross, Melrose. Centres: Cheviot area, Jedburgh–Hawick area (Galashiels).

Berwickshire. Long cairn, The Mutiny Stones, near Longformacus; several hillforts, Earn's Heugh (Coldingham); Edin's Hall (and broch), Cockburn Law and Preston Cleugh, near Duns; Longcroft and Addinston, Lauder; Black Hill, Earlston; D hogbacks, St Helen's Kirk, Cockburnspath (also market cross); D homestead site with hut remains, The Haerfaulds, near Lauder; dovecote, Mertoun House, St Boswells. Centres: St Abbs, Duns, Lauder.

Selkirkshire. Hillfort and broch, Torwoodlee, near Galashiels; fort, The Rink, R fort and camp, Oakwood; D inscribed stone, Yarrow; many old roads, e.g. Dryhope–Tushielaw–Buccleuch drove-road; *med* house site, Dryhope; rock-splinter gravestones, St Mary's of the Lowes (Yarrow) and Ettrick; site of gold washings (? *mod*), Glengaber; variety of sheep-beilds, along Megget Water. Centres: Galashiels, Yarrow.

Peeblesshire. B cairn, Corse Law; I hillforts, Cademuir Hill, Dreva, Milkeston Rings; R forts, Lyne; R roads, Edston; Carlops to Lyne Water; drove-road south of Peebles. Centre: Peebles.

THE LOTHIANS (map 12, p. 361)

East Lothian. Several hillforts, Traprain Law (Prestonkirk), with standing stone; The Chesters (Drem) (multiple defences and hut circles); The Hopes (Gifford) (multiple); Hare Law (Yester), vitrified; Black and White Castles (Garvald); dovecotes, Dunbar and Preston-pans; cross, Prestonpans; Gifford cross and pump. Centres: Lammer-muir area, Haddington.

Midlothian. B cup and ring marked rocks, Tormain Hill, near Ratho; several hillforts, e.g. Corsehope Rings, Castle Law (Abernethy) with earthhouse; Kaimes Hill (multiple defences), Castle Greg, with en-closure; earthhouse, Crichton Mains; R bathhouse, Inveresk, Mussel-burgh; D inscribed stone, Cat Stane, near Kirkliston; Dalmahoy; St. Triduana's wellhouse, Restalrig, Edinburgh; D fort, artillery mounds, Leith Links; dovecotes, Corstorphine and Inveresk; bridge and market cross, Musselburgh. Centre: Edinburgh (National Museum of Antiquities).

West Lothian. Henge and cairn (B), Cairnpapple Hill; forts, Bowden Hill and Cockleroy; Craigie Hill; R carvings, Eagle Rock, Cramond; D stones, cross-shafts and hogbacks, Abercorn Church; Torphichen Preceptory refuge stone; sundial, Old Dundas Castle; dovecote, New-liston. Centres: Queensferry, Linlithgow.

SOUTH-WEST SCOTLAND (map 11, p. 360)

Dumfriesshire, Kirkcudbrightshire, Wigtownshire, Ayrshire, Lanarkshire, Renfrewshire

Dumfriesshire. In the *east* side of the county several stone circles, e.g. Loupin Stanes, Eskdalemuir; Clochmabenstane, Gretna; hillforts along the White Esk, Bessies Hill, Castle O'er, Bailie Hill; hillfort and R siegeworks, Burnswark; R fort, Birrens; R fort, Raeburnfoot, and road, Rae Burn to Borthwick Water; R road, N. of Moffat; Ruthwell Cross (D). In the *Nithsdale* area: stone circle, Holywood; hillforts, Barr's Hill, Tynron Doon; R fortlet, Durisdeer; many castle mounds and mottes, e.g. Annan; *med* bridge, Dumfries, and fish-weir; also churchyard with very massive tombstones—a good example; ford cross, Thornhill; embankment of Solway viaduct (1869-1934), Annan. Centres: Moffat, Eskdale area, Annan area, Dumfries, Nithsdale area. *Mus*: Dumfries, Thornhill (Grierson).

Kirkcudbrightshire. A very rich county for megalithic tombs, stone circles, etc., cup and ring marked rocks, and for forts of many kinds, both Iron Age and post-Roman. Long chambered cairns, Cairn Avel, Carsphairn; Boreland; horned cairns, Cairnholy, Kirkdale; round chambered cairn, White Cairn, Bargrennan; large round cairn, White Cairn, Corriedow; cairns and circles, Caulside, Anwoth; stone circles, Claughreid, Kilmabreck, and Glenquicken, Creetown; B sculptured rocks, Brockcleugh, Tongland, and High Banks, Kirkcudbright; vitrified fort and symbol stone, Trusty's Hill, Gatehouse; forts, Dungarry and Suie Hill, Auchencairn; fortified enclosure, The Moyle, Barnbarroch; market cross, Kirkcudbright; Mote of Urr, near Castle Douglas (*med*); horse ramp, Cardoness Castle. Centres: Kirkcudbright (*mus*), Gatehouse.

Wigtownshire. Like Kirkcudbright, very rich in stone monuments and forts. Long chambered cairns, Mid Gleniron (New Luce); cairns, Lingdowie and Cairnerzean Fell; stone circle, Torhouskie; cup and ring marked rocks, Broughton Mains (Sorbie); standing stones with incised crosses, Laggangarn; forts include hillforts at Barsalloch Point, Cruise Bank Fell, Bennan of Garvilland, Doon of May (vitrified); promontory forts, Dinnans, Burrow Head, Crummag Head, Larbrax; St Ninian's Cave, near Whithorn (D). Centres: Whithorn (*mus*, D), Stranraer–Glenluce area.

Ayrshire. Chambered cairns, Balmalloch; Cuff Hill; burial chamber Hailie; cairns, Blackside; vitrified forts, Kemplaw; Kildoon Hill; Portencross; market crosses, Prestwick, Cumnock, Kilwinning; bridges, Alloway (Auld Brig o' Doon), Ayr (Auld Brig o' Ayr). Centres: Largs, Ayr.

Lanarkshire. B cairns, Corse Law; Dungavel Hill; hillforts, Camps Water; Cow Castle; D inscribed stones, Govan Church; bridges, Bothwell Bridge, Lanark Old Bridge; Glasgow Necropolis, massive tombstones; Leadhills, mining village and curfew bell; New Lanark (complete mill town, 1784). Centres: Glasgow, Lanark. *Mus*: Glasgow (Art Gallery, Hunterian and Transport).

Renfrewshire. D crosses, Inchinnan; Barochan (Houston). Centre: Paisley (*mus*).

WEST HIGHLANDS (map 13, p. 362)

Bute, Argyll

Bute. *North Bute*: stone circle and standing stone, Kingarth, where is also St Blane's Church (D), a beehive cell; vitrified fort, Dunagoil; hillfort, Barone Hill. *Arran*: several stone circles, etc., and neolithic tombs: circles, Machrie Moor; burial chamber, Tormore; long chambered cairn, Carn Ban; long horned cairn, Giant's Grave (Whiting Bay). *Cumbrae*: Lighthouse. Centres: Rothesay, Brodick.

Argyll. One of the main areas for B cup and ring marked rocks, and also rich in Celtic crosses. There is a great concentration in the *Crinan* district, with a three-mile long cairn cemetery from Kilmartin south; carved stones, Achnabreck, Cairnbaan, Kilmichael Glassary; avenue and henge, Ballymeanoch; cairn with cists and axe carvings, Ri Cruin; embanked circle, Temple Wood; gallery grave, Nether Largie south. Numerous standing stones some with cup-marks (Kintraw, and near Dunadd). Forts Luing, Duntroon (vitrified), Dunadd (D), Dun Garraron (? *med*). D carvings, Kilmartin; monastery, Eileach an Naoimh. Canal and harbour, Crinan. *Knapdale* has a Celtic cross at Keills and several forts; *Kintyre* has a cairn at Corriechrevie; chambered cairn (N), Kilkeddan; horned cairn, Blasthill; promontory fort, Balemacruma; vitrified forts, Dun Skeig and Carradale. *Islay*, gallery grave, Port Charlotte; Celtic cross, Kildalton; horizontal water mill, Balmavicar. *Cowal* area: chambered long cairn, Ardmarnock; vitrified fort on small island, Caisteal Aoidhe. *Lorne*: cairn, Achananearn; vitrified fort, Dun mac Uisneachan. *Appin*: broch, Lismore (Tirefour). *Mull*: rich in duns, galleried duns, brochs, promontory forts, cliff castles, (duns, Dun Aisgain (Bhurig), Dun Ara, Dun Nan Ceard, Aros; broch, Torloisk). Stone setting and barrow, Ardnacross; stone circle, Loch Buie. Wishing well, Ardura. Drove road and cattle ports, Croag and Grass Point. Deserted village and market, near Stronbuy. *Iona*: D monastic site, cells, corpse-road, crosses (St Martin's). Centres: Crinan area (Lochgilphead), Tarbert, Loch Etive area, (Oban), Mull.

SOUTH AND EAST HIGHLANDS (map 14, p 363)

Fife, Kinross-shire, Perthshire, Angus, Clackmannanshire, Stirlingshire, Dunbartonshire

Fife. Several B monuments and I forts. Cairn, West Lomond; cup and ring marked stone, St Margaret's Stone, Rosyth; remains of stone circle, Lundin Links; hillforts with multiple defences, East Lomond, Dunshelt, Clatchard Craig, Norman's Law; D sculptures, Wemyss Caves; hogback, near Inchcolm Abbey; symbol stone, Lindores (Newburgh); dovecotes, Creich, Rosyth; market cross, Kincardine (and folly, Dunmore Park (The Pineapple)); Falkland Palace, tennis court, doocot. *East Neuk*: Crail, harbour, arrow stone, mortuary, two caves with pilgrims' crosses. Mile and direction posts; ginhouses. St Andrews (castle), underground passage (mine and countermine). Centres: Tayside area, Kirkcaldy, Dunfermline, St Andrews or Crail.

Kinross-shire. Cairn and hillfort, Dumglow. Centre: Kinross.

Perthshire. A large county, but most of its visible monuments are in three areas, Strathmore, Strathearn and the Tummel–Garry district. *Strathmore*: B cup-marked stone, Macbeth Stone, Belmont; vitrified fort, Barry Hill; fort and earthhouse, Dunsinane; earthhouse, Pitcur; R frontier work, Cleaven Dyke; D symbol stones, Meigle *mus*. *Strathearn*: N long cairn with cist, Rottenreoch; hillforts, Castle Law, Abernethy; Castle Law, Forgandenny; R road, Culdees; large R fort, with multiple ditches, Ardoch—also R camps; D cross-slab, Fowlis Wester church; D fort, St Fillans Hill; round tower and symbol stone, Abernethy. *Tummel-Garry*: B cairns, Monzie Farm; Strathgroy (Sithean); Dunfallandy (also D cross-slab); B stone setting, Clachan an Dirich; I forts, Aldclune. There is also a broch outside these areas at Coldoch, Doune. In addition to these major sites, Perthshire is very rich in standing stones and stone circles (e.g. Scone, Monzie). There is a concentration of N and B sites in the Tay valley (Loch Tay to Dunkeld —triple stone circle, Kenmore; N barrow, Pitnachree). Dunkeld, bridge. Centres: Coupar Angus, Crieff, Pitlochry, Doune.

Angus. Has a variety of monuments, mostly in and round Strathmore. Several circles and standing stones, e.g. Corogle Burn, near Cortachy; earthhouses, Barns of Airlie; Tealing; hillforts, White and Brown Caterthun (Menmuir); vitrified forts, Finavon, Laws of Monifieth; R camp, Kirkbuddo; several symbol stones, e.g. Aberlemno, and D cross-slabs, e.g. Kirriemuir, Glamis; round tower, Brechin. Centres: Brechin, Forfar.

Clackmannanshire. Clackmannan market cross and 'Clackmannan' Stone (Stone of Manau, ? date), bridge, Tullibody. Centre: Alloa.

Stirlingshire. Broch, Torwood; sections of the Antonine Wall, Polmont and Falkirk, with R fort, Rough Castle, near Falkirk; Stirling Old Bridge; Airth market cross; Westquarter dovecote; remains of king's garden, Stirling. Centre: Falkirk or Stirling.

Dunbartonshire. Cup and ring marked rock, Auchnacraig (Duntocher); most of the Antonine Wall is in this county—visible sections at Bar Hill (with fort), Bearsden, Duntocher (Golden Hill fort), New Kilpatrick and Cumbernauld (with Croy Hill fort). Centre: Bearsden–Kirkintilloch, Kilsyth area.

WESTERN ISLES (map 15, p. 364)

Eigg, I fort on very impressive site, An Sgurr. *Skye*: chambered cairn (N) and fort (I), Rudh an Dunain; cairn (B), Kensaleyre; brochs, Dun Beag, Dun Hallin and several others; I fort with outer boulder defences, Dun Gerashader and many others; early *med* ecclesiastical remains, Annait, near Dunvegan. *North Uist*: N chambered cairns, Barpa Langass and Barpa nam Feannag; wheelhouses, Vallay Strand. *South Uist*: N chambered cairns with rings of pillar stones, Reineval and Loch a' Bharp (also Dun Bharpa on Barra). Barra Head, Sron an Duin, promontory fort in very wild position. Teampull Mor (Howmore), *med*, ecclesiastical remains. *Lewis*: the major monument of Callanish (stone circle, cairns and megalithic avenue); stone circle, Garynahine; brochs, Dun Carloway (well preserved), Dun Cromore.

MORAY FIRTH AND EAST (map 16, p. 365)

Nairnshire, Morayshire, Banffshire, Aberdeenshire, Kincardineshire, Inverness-shire

Nairnshire. Vitrified fort, Dun Evan; Boath doocot, Auldearn. Centre: Nairn.

Morayshire. D water tank, Burghead (The 'Roman Well', King Street); D cross-shaft, Sueno's Stone, near Forres. Elgin, arcaded houses (17th century); planned town, Fochabers (1798). Centres: Burghead, Forres, Elgin (*mus*).

Banffshire. N long cairn, Longman Cairn, Gamrie; stone circles, e.g. Rothiemay; symbol stones, St. Peter's church, Inveravon. Centres: Banff, Strath Avon.

Aberdeenshire. Very rich in stone circles, with a few henges, and the 'recumbent stone' type. Stone circles, Loanhead of Daviot; Old Keig; Midmar Church; Cullerlie; Sunhoney; henge and standing stones, Broomend of Crichie; round cairn, Memsie, near Fraserburgh; hillforts, Barmekin of Echt; Mither Tap of Bennachie; vitrified forts, Dunnideer, Tap o' Noth; earthhouses, Muirs of Kildrummy, Glenkindie; D cross-slab, Maiden Stone, near Inverurie; symbol stone, Inverurie churchyard—there are many of these in the county; Aberdeen, Bridge of Dee and Brig o' Balgownie; 'Consumption Dykes' (stone walls), Kingswells. Centres: Aberdeen (*mus*), Inverurie, Kildrummy area.

Kincardineshire. Several stone circles, e.g. Eslie; ogam stone, Nether Auquhollie (Rickarton); R camp, Raedykes. Centre: Stonehaven.

Inverness-shire. The main concentrations are round Inverness itself, part of the Moray Firth series of neolithic tombs, etc., and on the islands, including many brochs. *Inverness* district: N chambered cairns, Clava, Druidtemple, Torbreck, Essich Moor, Belladrum, Culburnie; vitrified forts, Dun Mor, Craig Phadrig. Later sites include Knocknagael Boar stone, Inverness (D); Culloden Battlefield, near Inverness. Centre: Inverness. In the *west* of the county, Dun Telve and Dun Troddan, Glenelg, well-preserved brochs.

NORTH SCOTLAND (map 17, p. 366)

Ross and Cromarty, Sutherland, Caithness

Ross and Cromarty. Most of the monuments form part of the important Moray Firth group. *Moray Firth/Cromarty*: N chambered cairns, Carnurnan, Balnaguie, Woodhead, Midbrae, Heights of Brae, Mill-craig, Kinrive; N burial chambers, Mains of Contin, Ballachnecore, Strath Skiath; vitrified fort, Knockfarill (Strathpeffer); D cross-slab, Nigg. *Dornoch Firth*: N chambered cairns, Ardvanie, Lechanich; B cairn, Red Burn; stone circles (B) and symbol stones (D), Edderton, *Loch Broom area*: broch and vitrified fort, Dun Lagaidh; broch, Dun an Ruigh Ruadh. Centres: Dingwall–Cromarty–Invergordon area, Tain, Ullapool.

Sutherland. Very rich in stone monuments, forts, brochs and settlements. *South*: round horned cairn, (N) Spinningdale. *East*: round and long cairns, Kinbrace; B cairn, Carn Liath; B cairns and stone settings, Learable Hill (one stone has an inscribed cross); brochs, Kintradwell, Castle Cole; earthhouse, Salscraggie Lodge. *West*: broch, Clachtoll. *North*: Strathnaver is very rich in horned and round cairns (Skail, Skelpick, Borgie, and above Syre); brochs (Dun Viden); settlements; stones (Clach an Righ); clearance village, Rossal. Near Tongue is a good broch (Dun an Maigh); B carved rock and *med* island fort, Loch Haken. Further west, earthhouse, Laid; Dun Dornagil (broch). Centres: Helmsdale, Bettyhill (Strathnaver).

Caithness. Extremely rich in cairns and stone monuments, and brochs. Some major examples are: long horned cairns and stone rows, Camster; round horned cairn, Ormiegill; stone setting, Achkinloch; stone rows, Mid Clyth, Lybster; wags or galleried dwellings (I), Yarrows (also broch), Forse, Langwell; brochs, Skirsa Head, Ness, Nybster. Centres: Wick-Latheron area, Duncansby Head area. *Mus*: Thurso.

NORTHERN ISLES (Map 18, p. 367)

Orkney. These islands have a very large number of stone tombs and other monuments, some of very great importance. Among the finest are: *Mainland*: chambered cairn, Wideford Hill; group of stone circles with henge affinities) and cairns, including Unstan, Stenness; chambered tomb in round cairn, Maes Howe (with runic inscription; N stone village, Skara Brae; horned cairn, Head of Work; broch, Gurness; earthhouse, Rennibister; D monastery, Deerness; Click Mill, Dounby; Viking house sites, Brough of Birsay. *Hoy*: rock-cut tomb (N), Dwarfie Stane. *Rousay*: N long stalled cairn, Blackhammer; double chambered cairn (one above the other), Taversoe Tuick; broch and cairn, Mid Howe. *Eday*: long stalled cairn, Calf of Eday. *Westray*: chambered cairns, Holm of Papa. Centres: Kirkwall (*mus*), Stromness (*mus*), Rousay. *Mus*: Skara Brae, Gurness.

Zetland (*map* 18, p. 367). *Mainland*: N ? temple, Stanydale; heel-shaped chambered cairn, Vementry; chambered cairn, Ronas Hill; brochs, Mousa, Clickhimin, Dalsetter, Burland (on defended promontory); I village and Viking houses, Jarlshof (Sumburgh); mounds of burnt stones, ? cooking places, Skelberry; steatite workings, Burn of Catpund. *Whalsay*: defensive work with causeway on small island, Loch of Huxter. *Yell*: broch, Hoga Ness. Centres: Lerwick, Sumburgh. *Mus*: Lerwick, Jarlshof.

NOT SHOWN ON MAPS

Isle of Man. Manx antiquities fall largely within Irish traditions. N burial monuments, Cashtal yn Ard; Meayll; King Orry's Grave; hillforts, South Barrule (?LBA); Cronk Sumark; coastal forts, Cronk ny Merriu; Close ny Chollagh; Balladoole (with Viking ship burial and chapel; Celtic and Norse houses, Braaid; keills, Maughold (with Celtic and Norse crosses); crosses, Kirk Michael; Tynwald Hill (moot); round tower, Peel; Civil War fort, Ballachurry; waterwheel, Laxey; execution mound, Castletown.

Channel Islands. The archaeology of the islands is part of that of France rather than of Britain. Ancient Guernsey has strong links with Brittany, Jersey with Normandy.

PARTICULAR AREAS FOR SPECIAL SUBJECTS

Flint Mines: Sussex, Norfolk.

Causewayed camps: Wessex, Sussex.

Henges and cursuses: Wessex, Derbyshire, Ripon area, Aberdeenshire.

Stone circles: N. and E. Scotland, Devon and Cornwall, Pennines, Lakes.

Megalithic tombs: Cotswold, SE. Wales, N. Scotland and Orkney; simple chamber tombs, Pembrokeshire.

Long and round barrows: Wessex (Berks., Wilts., Dorset), Yorkshire (N. York Moors, Wolds).

Bronze Age inscribed stones: Yorkshire (Wharfedale), NE. Northumberland, Argyll.

Iron Age settlements: Wessex, Sussex, Pennines (Craven and Wharfedale).

Bronze and Iron Age settlements and various stone monuments: Dartmoor, Cornwall.

Linear earthworks: Wessex, Chilterns, E. Yorkshire.

Hillforts: Wessex, Surrey, Sussex, Chilterns, W. Midlands, Welsh Borders, S. Pennines.

Round forts: Cornwall, Galloway; brochs, etc., N. Scotland, Hebrides, Orkney and Shetland.

Dark Age inscribed stones and crosses: Pembrokeshire, Cornwall, SW. Scotland, E. Scotland, Argyll.

Holy Wells: Caernarvonshire, Pembrokeshire.

Mottes: Welsh borders (particularly Herefordshire, Shropshire).

Moated sites: Essex, Suffolk.

Deserted villages, ridge and furrow, (mediaeval): Northants, Bedfordshire, N. Bucks, N. Oxon, S. Warwicks.

Stone walls: Pennines, N. Wales, Galloway, Cotswolds.

Georgian and Regency urban detail: Bath, London (Marylebone and Bloomsbury), Edinburgh, Brighton.

Early Industrial sites: Staffordshire, Shropshire.

OUTSTANDING SITES

Flint mines; Grimes Graves (Norfolk).

Causewayed camp: Knap Hill (Wilts.).

Henges: Stonehenge and Avebury (Wilts.), Thornborough (Yorks. NR).

Megalithic tombs: West Kennet (Wilts.), Belas Knap and Hetty Pegler's Tump (Glos.), Barclodiad y Gawres and Bryn Celli Ddu (Anglesey), Maes Howe (Orkney). Rock-cut tomb, Dwarfie Stane (Orkney).

Long Barrow: Pimperne (Dorset).

Round Barrows: Duggleby Howe (Yorks. ER).

Mixed Barrow group: Winterbourne Crossroads (Wilts.).

Roman barrows: Bartlow (Cambs.)

Saxon barrows: Sutton Hoo (Suffolk).

Artificial mound: Silbury Hill (Wilts.).

Stone circles: Rollright Stones (Oxon), Brodgar (Orkney), Torhousekie (Wigtowns.), circles, avenue, cairns, Callanish (Lewis).

Stone avenue: Avebury; *standing stones,* Devil's Arrows (Yorks. WR).

Cairn Cemetery; Danby Rigg (Yorks. NR).

Bronze Age sculptured rocks: High Banks (Kirkcudbright), Roughting Linn (Northumberland), Crinan.

Temples: neolithic, Stanydale (Shetland); classical type, Lydney (Glos.); Celtic type,

Maiden Castle (Dorset); Mithraeum, Carrawburgh (Northumberland).

Hillforts: Maiden Castle (Dorset), Woden Law (Rox.), Ingleborough (Yorks. WR, for site), An Sgurr (Eigg), for site; vitrified forts, Finavon (Angus), Dunagoil (Bute).

Promontory forts: Danby Rigg (Yorks. NR), Barra Head (for site).

Belgic type defences: Stanwick (Yorks. NR).

Fortified towns: Tre'r Ceiri (Caernarvons.), Din Lligwy (Anglesey).

Roman forts: Housesteads (Northumberland), Ardoch (Perthshire); Saxon Shore forts, Portchester (Hants.), Richborough (Kent); supply base, Corbridge (Northumberland).

Roman camps; Hod hill (Dorset); practice, Cawthorn (Yorks. NR).

Brochs, Mousa, Clickhimin (Shetland), Mid Howe (Orkney), Dun Carloway (Lewis). *Wheelhouse,* Vallay Strand (N. Uist); *wag,* Forse (Caithness); *earthhouses,* Rennibister (Orkney), Crichton (Midlothian); *courtyard house,* Pothmeor (Cornwall); *fogou,* Halligye (Cornwall).

Stone villages: Chysauster (Cornwall), Skara Brae (Orkney), Jarlshof (Shetland), Tre'r Ceiri (Caerns.).

Linear earthworks: Devil's Dyke

(Cambs.), Scamridge Dykes (Yorks. NR), Wansdyke.

Hill-figure: White Horse, Uffington (Berks.); Cerne Abbas Giant (Dorset); Long Man, Wilmington, (Sussex).

Roman roads: Ackling Dyke (Dorset), Blackstone Edge (Yorks. WR), Wade's Causeway (Yorks. NR).

Roman fortified frontier: Hadrian's Wall.

Roman villa: Chedworth (Glos.)., Fishbourne (Sussex), Lullingstone (Kent).

Roman baths: Bath.

Roman theatre: St Albans, Caerleon.

Celtic fields: Fyfield Down (Wilts.).

Lynchets (cultivation terraces): Bishopstone North (Wilts); upper Wharfedale (Yorks. WR).

Crosses: Celtic, Iona (Mull); Anglian, Bewcastle (Cumbs.), Ruthwell (Dumfries.); covered, Castle Combe (Wilts.); churchyard, Iron Acton (Glos.).

Re-used site: Old Sarum (Wilts.)— I, R, S, *Med.*

Saxon town defences: Wallingford (Berks.), Wareham (Dorset).

Mottes: York, Thetford (Norf.).

Bridges: Clapper, Postbridge (Devon); *Med.*, Eashing (Surrey), Dumfries, Twizel Bridge (Northumberland), Wakefield (with chapel), Monmouth (with gate-tower); 18th century, Henley (Oxon); Ironbridge (Salop), first iron bridge; Selby (Yorks.), wooden, swing; packhorse, Birstwith (Yorks. WR).

Georgian urban detail: Bath, Edinburgh, London.

Georgian landscaped gardens: Studley Royal (Yorks. WR), Wilton (Wilts.), Stourhead (Wilts.).

Victorian urban detail: Glasgow.

CHAPTER 3

Books to Read

The order of subjects in this list of books is that adopted in the text itself. Thus further reading on the historical and cultural background is followed by books on specific topics and concludes with those on the archaeology of the different regions and localities.

In making this selection I have listed only those books which seem to me the most worth-while: many have been omitted, either because they cover much the same ground as works already mentioned or because they are not strictly relevant here.

The list is confined as far as possible to fairly recent books, and mentions few articles in learned journals, although the latter are often the only place where a particular subject is dealt with. In any case the books, whether written for those with no previous knowledge or for the expert, usually give references to other books and to articles, so that they provide a starting point which can be left as far behind as one wants. Latest editions should be read where possible; archaeology has developed so rapidly since the 1920s, and is still developing. A very useful general book list is issued by the Council for British Archaeology (1960). The general subject of this book is well covered in *Field Archaeology, Some Notes for Beginners*, issued by the Ordnance Survey (1963).

THE TWO ZONES

Sir C. Fox: *The Personality of Britain* (1959 edition) is the pioneer work; for the structure of Britain in relation to settled land, Dudley Stamp: *Britain's Structure and Scenery* (1949), or A. E. Trueman: *Geology and Scenery in England and Wales* (Penguin, 1949). The current problems in this field are well set out in G. H. Dury: *The Face of the Earth* (Penguin, 1959). J. Hawkes: *A Land* (Penguin, 1959) is an introduction from a very personal angle.

CLIMATE

C. E. P. Brooks: *Climate Through the Ages* (1949); H. H. Lamb: *The Changing Climate* (1966); for the physical aspects of the ice ages, see the relevant chapters in a book on geology, such as A. Holmes: *The Principles of Physical Geology* (1945); for the effects of climate on early man, F. E. Zeuner: *Dating the Past* (1958), although a somewhat difficult book, is by far the most complete: Ian Cornwall: *Ice Ages—Their Nature and Effects* (1970) is a useful introduction.

MAN'S INFLUENCE ON THE LANDSCAPE

This is best covered by W. G. Hoskins: *The Making of the English Landscape* (1957); also Dudley Stamp: *Man and the Land* (1955). H. J. Fleure & M. Davies: *A Natural History of Man in Britain* (1970 ed.) with good bibliography, is a classic revised.

THE CULTURES OF BRITAIN

There are a great many books, not all of equal authority, giving introductions to archaeology, both general and British in particular. A brief general work, which outlines the broad principles, should be read first, followed by detailed accounts of British matters and of special fields. Some of the outlines are: K. P. Oakley: *Man the Toolmaker* (1961); Grahame Clarke: *Archaeology and Society* (1957) and *From Savagery to Civilisation* (1946). These should be followed by J. and C. Hawkes: *Prehistoric Britain* (Penguin 1958); in more detail, V. G. Childe; *Prehistoric Communities of the British Isles* (1947). The late Professor Childe wrote many books of great importance, any of which can be read with profit; his last works, and in many ways the most important, were the 6th edition of *The Dawn of European Civilisation* (1957), which sets Britain in its wider context, and the easier companion to that not very easy book, *The Prehistory of European Society* (Penguin, 1958). There is now Stuart Piggott's *Ancient Europe* (1965), and Clark and Piggott: *Prehistoric Societies* (1970), Robin Place: *Introduction to Archaeology* (1968), and Derek Roe: *Prehistory* (1970). An excellent picture-book is S. Thomas: *Pre-Roman Britain* (1965).

See also V. G. Childe: *Scotland before the Scots* (1946); S Piggott: *Scotland before History* (1958); S. Piggott ed: *The Prehistoric Peoples of Scotland* (1962); A. J. Raftery: *Prehistoric Ireland* (1952); I. Ll. Foster and Glyn Daniel ed; *Prehistoric and Early Wales* (1965).

For the techniques of **hunting, farming** etc., see J. G. D. Clark: *Prehistoric Europe: The Economic Basis* (1952). A useful reconstruction of life in the Palaeolithic is in Chapter 9 of J. D. Clark's *The Prehistory of Southern Africa* (Penguin 1959). Grahame Clark: *The Stone Age Hunters* (1967), is an excellent introduction. For the evolution of man, although outside the scope of this book, see chapters 3 and 4 of J. D. Clark's book, and W. E. Le Gros Clark: *History of Primates* (British Museum—Natural History 1958), or in more detail, W. Howells: *Mankind in the Making* (1960), and C. S. Coon: *The Origin of Races* (1963). The latest factual surveys are K. Oakley: *Frameworks for Dating Fossil Man* (1969), and M. H. Day: *Guide to Fossil Man* (1965).

For the **Palaeolithic**, M. C. Burkitt: *The Old Stone Age* (1955) and John Wymer: *Lower Palaeolithic Archaeology in Britain* (1967); for art and religion, A. Laming: *Lascaux* (Penguin 1959). For the **Mesolithic**, the standard works are still J. G. D. Clark's *The Mesolithic Age in Britain* (1932) and *The Mesolithic Settlement of Northern Europe* (1936); also A. D. Lacaille: *The Stone Age in Scotland* (1954); H. L. Movius: *The Irish Stone Age* (1942). The position in the south of England is summarised in W. J. Rankine: *A Mesolithic Survey of Southern England* (Surrey Arch. Soc. Research Paper No. 4, 1956); new light is thrown by J. G. D. Clark: *Star Carr* (1964).

For the **Neolithic,** general background in V. G. Childe: *What Happened in History* (1943); the standard, but somewhat technical book, is S. Piggott: *The Neolithic Cultures of Britain* (1954); a short introduction is Sonia Cole: *The Neolithic Revolution* (British Museum—Natural History, 1959).

There is no work dealing exclusively with the **Bronze** and **Iron Ages;** Childe's *Prehistoric Communities* (see above) is still basic, up to 1400 BC. D. L. Clarke: *Beaker Pottery of Great Britain & Ireland* (2 vols, 1970), though technical, will be standard for years to come. For the Iron Age see S. S. Frere, ed: *Problems of the Iron Age in Southern Britain* (Univ. London Institute of Archaeology, 1961), and A. L. F. Rivet, ed; *The Iron Age in Northern Britain* (CBA, 1967). Much is available on the Iron Age Celts, such as T. G. E. Powell: *The Celts* (1958). For Celtic Art, S. Piggott and G. E. Daniel: *A Picture Book of Ancient British Art* (1951); in more detail, Sir C. Fox: *Pattern and Purpose* (1958). A useful gallery of tool etc. types is the British Museum handbook *Later Prehistoric Antiquities of the British Isles* (1953).

Roman Britain is best introduced by I. A. Richmond: *Roman Britain* (Penguin, 1963), which has an extensive bibliography from which most aspects of the life of Roman Britain can be followed up. For the objects, see the B. M. handbook *The Antiquities of Roman Britain* (1958) and R. G. Collingwood & Ian Richmond: *The Archaeology of Roman Britain* (1969). More recent general books are: A. Birley: *Life in Roman Britain* (1964); Grace Simpson: *Britons and the Roman Army* (1965); J. S. Wacher, ed.: *The Civitas Capitals of Roman Britain* (1966); and C. Thomas, ed.: *Rural Settlement in Roman Britain* (CBA, 1966). Also I. A. Richmond, ed.: *Roman and Native in North Britain* (1958).

The **Sub-Roman** period has no comprehensive study yet, but an introduction is Geoffrey Ashe, ed.: *The Quest of Arthur's England* (1968), with more detail in D. B. Harden, ed: *Dark Age Britain* (1956), and Nora K. Chadwick: *Celtic Britain* (1963); Isabel Henderson: *The Picts* (1967). The history of R.B. is now newly covered in S. S. Frere: *Britannia* (1967).

For the **Saxon** period, P. Hunter Blair: *An Introduction to Anglo-Saxon England* (1956), to whose bibliography may be added E. A. Fisher: *Introduction to Anglo-Saxon Architecture and Sculpture* (1959), D. Wilson *The Anglo-Saxons* (1960), and J. N. L. Myers: *Anglo-Saxon Pottery and the Settlement of England* (1969). See also A. Shetelig: *Viking Antiquities in Great Britain and Northern Ireland* (1950–4); J. Brøndsted: *The Vikings* (Penguin, 1960); also H. Arbman: *The Vikings* (1961). Major sites, including Star Carr, Lullingstone and Sutton Hoo, are described in R. L. S. Bruce-Mitford editor: *Recent Archaeological Excavations in Britain* (1956). A more 'popular' general work is Geoffrey Bibby: *The Testimony of the Spade* (1956). There is no comprehensive study of the **Mediaeval and later** antiquities covered by this book. For general interest G. E. Daniel's *A Hundred Years of Archaeology* (1950) and now his *The Origins and Growth of Archaeology* (1967), should not be missed. Some of the original documentary sources will be found in C. W. Ceram: *The World of Archaeology* (1966).

CAVES

J. W. Jackson in *British Caving* (editor C. H. D. Cullingford, 1962 ed.).

SETTLEMENTS, FARMS AND VILLAGES

This subject is rather scattered, but see particularly Hoskins' *Making of the English Landscape*, Clark's *Prehistoric Europe*, Rivet's *Town and Country in Roman Britain*, and the references in Childe's *Dawn*. The classic report on **Iron Age farms** (Little Woodbury) is G. Bersu in *PPS* for 1938. M. E. Seebohm: *The Evolution of the English Farm* (1952); also R. Whitlock: *A Short History of Farming in Britain* (1964). For **deserted villages,** M. W. Beresford: *The Lost Villages of England* (1954), brought up to date as M. Beresford & J. G. Hurst, eds.: *Deserted Medieval Villages* (1971); for **agriculture,** E. C. Curwen: *Plough and Pasture* (1946); H. C. Bowen: *Ancient Fields* (1961). Sites on gravel are dealt with in *A Matter of Time* (Royal Commission on Historical Monuments, 1960). For **fogous,** see Evelyn Clark: *Cornish Fogous* (1961), and F. T. Wainwright: *The Souterrains of Southern Pictland* (1963). For **Brochs,** E. W. MacKie in *Proceedings of the Prehistoric Society*, XXXI, 1965, 93. **Villas,** A. L. F. Rivet: *The Roman Villa in Britain* (1969)—H. C. Bowen's Chapter in this gives new views on Iron Age farms and farming.

QUARRIES, MINES AND INDUSTRIES

The histories of technology should be consulted, such as *A History of Technology*, edited by Singer and others (Oxford for ICI, 1954 to 1958); also T. K. Derry and T. I. Williams: *A Short History of Technology* (1960). Clark, in *Prehistoric Europe*, deals with flint, stone, bronze and iron. **Iron** is well dealt with also in H. R. Schubert: *A History of the British Iron and Steel Industry* (1957); valuable chapters on 17th and 18th century ironworking are in A. Raistrick: *Quakers in Science and Industry* (1950); and a special study is H. Straker: *Wealden Iron* (1924). For **other metals,** L. Aitchison: *A History of Metals* (1960). For **glass** see G. H. Kenyon: *The Glass Industry of the Weald* (1967), and generally, E. Barrington Haynes: *Glass Through the Ages* (Penguin 1959). **Industrial archaeology** is now receiving systematic study. General books are K. Hudson: *Industrial Archaeology* (1966); J. P. M. Pannell: *Techniques of Industrial Archaeology* (1966); and for background, W. H. Calloner and A. E. Musson: *Industry and technology* (1963). Regional studies like K. Hudson: *Industrial Archaeology of Southern England* (1965); and D. Smith: *Industrial Archaeology of the East Midlands* (1965). Several counties are publishing lists, e.g. Herts, Beds, Staffs, the NE, Devon. Aubrey Wilson: *London's Industrial Heritage* (1967). *The Industrial Archaeologist's Guide*, 1969-70 and every two years, has useful lists of relevant museums, literature and sites.

ROADS

Little has been done on prehistoric roads, and two well-known books, R. Hippisley Cox: *The Green Roads of England* (1944), and A. Watkins: *The Old Straight Track* (1945), should be treated with caution. A new study is H. W.

Timperley and Edith Brill: *Ancient Trackways of Wessex* (1965). For **Roman roads** see I. D. Margary: *Roman Roads in Britain* (1967 ed.), also, for the detail of an area, his *Roman Ways in the Weald* (1965); the Viatores: *Roman Roads in the South-East Midlands* (1964); B. Berry: *A Lost Roman Road—Bath to Poole* (1963). For **mediaeval and enclosure roads** see Hoskins' *Making of the English Landscape*. See also A. R. B. Haldane: *The Drove Roads of Scotland* (1952), K. J. Bonser: *The Drovers* (1970), and generally, A. E. Boumphrey: *British Roads* (1939).

CIRCLES, CROSSES, HOLY PLACES

For **cursus**, R. J. C. Atkinson in *Antiquity* (1954). **Henges** are introduced in a technical report, by R. J. C. Atkinson, C. M. Piggott and N. K. Sandars: *Excavations at Dorchester, Oxon*, 1st Report (1951); for **Stonehenge,** see R. J. C. Atkinson: *Stonehenge* (Penguin 1960). Brief accounts of Stonehenge, Woodhenge, Avebury and other important sites are given in R. J. C. Atkinson: *Stonehenge and Avebury and Neighbouring Monuments*, an illustrated Guide (HMSO, 1959). Avebury is fully treated in Isobel Smith: *Windmill Hill and Avebury* (1965). The other side of Stonehenge study is in G. S. Hawkins: *Stonehenge Decoded* (1965); this has led to a lively controversy in *Nature*—see articles by F. Hoyle and C. A. Newham on 30 July, 1966; and by D. H. Sadler on 10 September, 1966; and, on the other side, *Antiquity*, September and December, 1966. The mathematics of stone circles, and their use as observatories, is dealt with in Alexander Thom: *Megalithic Sites in Britain* (1967). For **temples** see the chapter on religion in Richmond's *Roman Britain*, and M. J. T. Lewis: *Temples in Roman Britain* (1966). **Holy wells** are dealt with patchily, but a good introduction is Francis Jones: *The Holy Wells of Wales* (1954). For **crosses**, well-illustrated introduction, Aylmer Vallance: *Old Crosses and Lychgates* (1920); L. Stone: *Sculpture in Britain; The Middle Ages* (Pelican History of Art, 1955).

BURIAL

For **barrows** generally, L. V. Grinsell: *The Ancient Burial Mounds of England* (1953); more detail on all aspects of round barrows is given in Paul Ashbee's *The Bronze Age Round Barrow in Britain* (1960). An excellent recent study of a **long barrow** is Stuart Piggott: *The West Kennet Long Barrow* (1962). See now P. Ashbee: *The Earthen Long Barrow in England* (1970). Although prescientific, W. Greenwell's *British Barrows* (1877) can still be very profitable. For **Megalithic tombs,** Glyn Daniel: *The Prehistoric Chamber Tombs of England and Wales* (1950), and, in wider setting, *The Megalithic Builders of Western Europe* (1958); Audrey Shore Henshall: *The Chambered Tombs of Scotland* (vol. 1, north and east, 1963); T. G. E. Powell et al: *Megalithic Enquiries in the West of Britain* (1969). **Ritual** in pre-historic and Roman Britain is dealt with in a series of articles by Dr J. X. W. P. Corcoran in *ANL* in 1958 and 1959. Iron Age **religion** is dealt with in Anne Ross: *Pagan Celtic Britain* (1967), and Saxon in Brian Branston: *The Lost Gods of England* (1957).

MILITARY WORKS

Hillforts are dealt with mostly in scattered articles, of which the first of importance is that by C. F. C. Hawkes in *Antiquity*, 1931. See now *The Iron Age and its Hillforts* (Southampton Univ. 1971). Books dealing with the Iron Age should be consulted; see also chapters in S. S. Frere editor: *Problems of the Iron Age in Southern Britain* 1961. Similarly with **Roman forts.** For **Hadrian's wall** see J. Collingwood Bruce's *Handbook to the Roman Wall* (XII edition, 1966). For **mottes**, see B. Hope Taylor's report on Abinger in *Arch. J.*, 1950 and D. F. Renn's article in *Antiquity*, 1959. H. G. Ramm, R. W. McDowall & Eric Mercer: *Sheilings and Bastles* (1971).

LINEAR EARTHWORKS

Sir C. Fox in *Antiquity* III (1929), pp. 134–54: also O. G. S. Crawford: *Archaeology in the Field* (1953); and L. V. Grinsell: *The Archaeology of Wessex* (1958). A. H. Allcroft: *Earthwork of England* (1908) is still of value. See also Sir C. Fox: *Offa's Dyke* (1955). P. A. Jewell ed.: *The Experimental Earthwork on Overton Down, 1960* (B.A. 1963).

CANALS AND MARSHES

For **canals**, E. C. R. Hadfield: *British Canals* (1966) and regional studies; also L. C. T. Rolt: *The Inland Waterways of England* (1964); P. A. L. Vine: *London's Lost Route to the Sea* (1965). For **sites submerged**, O. G. S. Crawford in *Antiquity* (1927); and F. J. North: *Sunken Cities* (1957); also J. M. Lambert and others: *The Making of the Broads* (Royal Geog. Society Research Series No. 3, 1960). For **the fens**, A. K. Astbury: *The Black Fens* (1958).

ODDS AND ENDS

These are often helpfully dealt with in the columns of *Country Life* and *The Field*; see also the Notes in the county journals. Courtney Dainton: *Clock Jacks and Bee Boles* (1957) mentions many odds and ends. **Bee-keeping.** The Bee Research Association has issued a pamphlet on *Bee-Boles*. **Boats** have been studied by T. C. Lethbridge and J. Hornell. **Carts and farm equipment.** J. Geraint Jenkins: *The English Farm Wagon* (1961). Philip Wright: *Old Farm Implements* (1961). **Dovecotes.** A. O. Cooke: *A Book of Dovecotes* (1920), while incomplete, is a useful introduction. **Dry-stone walls.** F. Rainsford-Hannay: *Dry Stone Walling* (1957), and A. Raistrick: *The Story of the Pennine Walls* (1946). **Follies**, etc. Barbara Jones: *Follies and Grottoes* (1953). For garden features see books on country houses. **Fowling.** The operation of decoy-ponds is set out in Sir R. Payne-Gallwey's *The Book of Duck Decoys* (1886); old encyclopedias of field sports should be referred to on fowling generally. **Hill figures.** M. Marples: *White Horses and other Hill Figures* (1949), and T. C. Lethbridge: *Gog Magog* (1957). **Ice-houses.** The only study I know, except a few articles, is a rather inaccessible monograph by F. W. B. Yorke: *Ice-houses* (1955). **Inscribed stones.** Bronze Age, H. Breuil in *Proceedings of the Prehistoric Society of East Anglia* for 1934. Pictish, S. Cruden: *The Early Christian Pictish Monuments of Scotland* (1957); **Sundails,** A. R. Green: *Sundials* (1926) and two recent books, Frank W. Cousins: *Sundials* (1970), and Rene R. J. Rohr: *Sundials* (1970). **Graves.** Frederick Burgess: *English Churchyard Memorials* (1963). **Mazes.** W. H. Matthews: *Mazes and Labyrinths* (1922); articles in *Antiquity*, 1932. **Mills.** A brief survey is C. P. Skilton: *British Windmills and Watermills* (1947); more detail in Rex Wailes: *The English Windmill* (1954). The Wind and Watermill section of the Society for the Protection of Ancient Buildings is now publishing a series on this subject. See also Stanley Freese: *Windmills and Millwrighting* (1957); Leslie Syson: *British Watermills* (1965). **Pillow-mounds.** See O. G. S. Crawford: *Wessex from the Air*, p. 18. **Railways.** H. G. Lewin: *Early British Railways* (1925) goes up to 1844; general introductions are W. H. Boulton: *The Railways of Britain* (1950), and Jack Simmons: *The Railways of Britain* (1961). See also F. G. Bing: *The Grand Surrey Iron Railway* (1931). For tramroads, B. Baxter: *Stone Blocks and Iron Rails* (1966). **River crossing.** Eric de Maré: *The Bridges of Britain* (1956) or G. Bernard Wood: *Bridges in Britain* (1970), and, for more detail, the regional studies of H. Jervoise, *The Ancient Bridges of the North, etc. of England.* **Street furniture.** This is scattered widely in articles, etc.; I do not know of a book covering the whole subject. Some of the ground is covered in R. Lister: *Decorative Cast Ironwork in Great Britain* (1960). For **Inn signs,** J. Larwood and J. C. Hotten: *English Inn Signs* (1951). **Weather-vanes.** A Needham: *English Weathervanes* (1953). The National Benzole Books: *Bridges; Monuments; Follies* (1963) will be found useful, also the Discovering series. Wine and Coal Posts *London Archaeologist,* (Spring 1969).

SURFACE FINDS

For **flint**-working and types, K. P. Oakley, *Man the Toolmaker*, or the British Museum handbook, *Flint Implements* (1956). For **building materials,** see Norman Davey: *A History of Building Materials* (1961); A. Clifton-Taylor: *The Pattern of English Building* (1965); J. T. Smith: *Timber-framed Building in England* (Arch. J., CXXII, 1966); N. Lloyd: *A History of English Brickwork* (1925). **Pottery** is covered only in a disjointed way. For prehistoric, see the various books on archaeology listed above; for later periods, R. J. Charleston: *Roman Pottery* (1950); *Romano-British Coarse Pottery* (CBA, 1964); *Anglo-Saxon Pottery: A Symposium* (CBA, 1961, reprinted from *Med. Arch.,* 111, 1959); B. Rackham: *English Mediaeval Pottery* (1947); *Guide to English Pottery and Porcelain* (British Museum, 1923), or W. B. Honey: *English Pottery and Porcelain* (1945). **Small finds** are well illustrated in the catalogue of the London Museum, e.g. *Mediaeval* (1968). **Coins.** J. G. Milne, C. H. V. Sutherland and J. D. A. Thompson: *Coin Collecting* (1951); a general survey is R. A. G. Carson: *Coins* (1962). For pre-Roman coins, article by D. F. Allen in *Problems of the Iron Age in Southern Britain* (1961). **Clay pipes,** Adrian

Oswald in *ANL* Sept. 1961, the *Connoisseur Concise Encyclopaedia of Antiques* vol. IV (1959), *J.B.A.A.* (vol. 33, for 1960), *ANL* 1964-5 (7, 10 and 11), Lawrence Harley: *The Clay Tobacco Pipe in Britain* (Essex Field Club, 1963).

TECHNIQUES

Excavation is covered by K. Kenyon: *Beginning in Archaeology* (1964); R. J. C. Atkinson: *Field Archaeology* (1953); Sir Mortimer Wheeler: *Archaeology from the Earth* (Penguin, 1956); R. J. C. Atkinson: *Archaeology: Methods and Principles* (1965); G. A. Webster: *Practical Archaeology* (1963). Useful and practical information, particularly for rescue work on lowland sites, in *Notes on Archaeological Technique* (Ashmolean Museum, 1957). Leslie Grinsell, Philip Rahtz and Alan Warhurst: *The Preparation of Archaeological Reports* (1966).

Stratigraphy: see Mortimer Wheeler: *Archaeology from the Earth* (1961), and E. Pyddoke: *Stratification for Archaeologists* (1961).

Air photography: see J. S. P. Bradford: *Ancient Landscapes* (1957); the pioneer application to archaeology is O. G. S. Crawford: *Wessex from the Air* (1928), and its full development, M. W. Beresford and J. K. S. St Joseph: *Mediaeval England: An Aerial Survey* (1958). J. K. S. St Joseph, ed.: *The Uses of Air Photography* (1966); Leo Deuel: *Flights into Yesterday* (1971). For the ordinary kind of photography, M. B. Cookson: *Photography for Archaeologists* (1954).

For **dating methods,** F. E. Zeuner: *Dating the Past* (1958); the advanced scientific methods which are rapidly developing are dealt with in M. A. Aitken: *Physics and Archaeology* (1961)—reports on current work in this field should be read in periodicals such as *Nature* and *Antiquity*. See also W. F. Libby: *Radio-carbon Dating* (1955). A new general introduction to principles is S. Piggott: *Approach to Archaeology* (1959). The account of the uncovering of the Piltdown forgery, J. S. Weiner: *The Piltdown Forgery* (1955) is of great interest. I. W. Cornwall's two books on special aspects are important: *Bones for the Archaeologist* (1956), and *Soils for the Archaeologist* (1958). The current synopsis is D. R. Brothwell and E. Higgs: *Science in Archaeology* (1969); other important surveys are R. F. Tylecote: *Metallurgy in Archaeology* (1962); L. Biek: *Archaeology and the Microscope* (1963); H. Hodges: *Artifacts* (1964); D. R. Brothwell: *Digging up Bones* (1963); G. W. Dimbleby: *Plants and Archaeology* (1967). Articles on the new C14 dating have appeared in *Antiquity*, March 1970, *Current Archaeology*, Jan. 1970, and *World Archaeology*, Oct. 1970.

Preservation is rather outside our scope, but the standard work is H. J. Plenderleith: *The Conservation of Antiquities and Works of Art* (1956).

The CBA have brought out two handbooks, Handbook of Scientific Aids and Evidence for Archaeologists (1970), and Archaeological Site-index to Radiocarbon Dates (1971).

FOLLOWING UP

The national archaeological journals are:

Antiquaries' Journal; referred to as Ant. J.—published by the Society of Antiquaries of London. This carries synopses of all current journals, British and foreign. The Society also produces *Archaeologia* (Arch.) irregularly (this has long articles), and a series of Research volumes, each dealing with one site or subject.

Archaeological Journal (Arch. J.)—Royal Archaeological Institute.

Journal of the British Archaeological Association (J.B.A.A.)—mostly post-Roman.

Proceedings of the Prehistoric Society (P.P.S.)—has occasional summaries of recent work.

Journal of Roman Studies (J.R.S.)—Society for the Promotion of Roman Studies, with a valuable annual summary of the year's work on Roman Britain. Replaced by *Britannia* from 1970.

Mediaeval Archaeology (Med. Arch.)—Society for Mediaeval Archarology.

Post-Mediaeval Archaeology (Post-Med. Arch.)—Society for Post-Medieval Archaeology.

Transactions of the Newcomen Society—history of technology.

Industrial Archaeology

The University of London Institute of Archaeology issues an *Annual Report*, now *Bulletin*.

The well-known quarterly *Antiquity* is of great value in airing current matters of concern; it gives full weight to field antiquities, through the interests of its founder, the late O. G. S. Crawford.

Published irregularly for many years, the *Archaeological News Letter* (A.N.L.) carried news of excavations and local matters besides general articles. There is now *Current Archaeology*, every two months from March 1967.

Then there are the county and local journals, too numerous to list, which normally publish matter relating to the county, etc., but sometimes general papers as well. County magazines, such as the *Dalesman* and the *Essex Countryside*, often carry relevant features. Some of the county societies issue research papers separately.

Occasional articles on archaeological subjects appear in the *Bulletin of Celtic Studies* (which also has summaries of work in Wales), *Nature, Caving,* the *Museums Journal*, and the journals of related subjects, such as anthropology and geology; also in the *New Scientist*.

The Council for British Archaeology (C.B.A.) issues annual bibliographies of articles in all these journals, lists of offprints which can be bought, and monthly lists of excavations, summer schools, etc.—also an annual list of Discovery and Excavation in Scotland (1958 onwards), and a similar one for East Anglia and the East Midlands and now *British Archaeological Abstracts* (twice a year, from 1968).

Outside England, there are:

Proceedings of the Society of Antiquaries of Scotland (P.S.A.S.).

Archaeologia Cambrensis (Arch. Camb.)—Cambrian Archaeological Association.

Ulster Journal of Archaeology (U.J.A.)—Ulster Archaelogical Society.

Proceedings of the Royal Irish Academy (P.R.I.A.).

Journal of the Royal Society of Antiquaries of Ireland (J.R.S.A.I.).

For **maps** see page 306. See also the useful *National Trust Atlas of England and Wales* (1964).

A useful list of **museums** is *Museums and Galleries of Great Britain and Northern Ireland* (Index Publications, annual); also Jack Simmons, *Transport Museums* (1970).

For **folklore,** L. V. Grinsell's *Ancient Burial Mounds of England*; a good general introduction is Eleanor Hull: *Folklore of the British Isles* (1928). For **place-names** see the county volumes of the English Place-Name Society, and A. H. Smith: *English Place-Name Elements* (1956); the *Concise Oxford Dictionary of English Place-Names*; articles in *Antiquity*, 1927 and 1943; and two recent general introductions, K. Cameron: *English Place-Names* (1960), and P. H. Reaney: *The Origin of English Place-Names* (1960).

SITES TO VISIT

Generally speaking, and with exceptions, the usual kind of guide or county book does not deal fully, if it deals at all, with the sort of monuments covered in this book, although it is often very good indeed on history and architecture. A public library will be able to advise on books not listed here, and will have the county and local journals.

A good beginning are the Lists of Ancient Monuments in England and Wales published by H. M. Stationery Office for the Ministry of Works, which lists some 9000 scheduled monuments; there are similar lists for Scotland. These may be followed by the growing and remarkable series of short guides to those monuments, sites and buildings in the charge of the Ministry of Works, which can be visited. The Royal Commission on Historical Monuments (England), and its counterparts in Wales and Monmouthshire and Scotland (RCHM and RCAHM), have resumed issue in the last few years of their county surveys, which set a very high standard and are of the greatest value to field archaeologists, not only for their descriptions of sites, but for the introductory matter. The Victoria County Histories are also being completed or reissued, on modern lines. The National Parks Commission Guides cover field sites.

Apart from these official publications, some series of county books are relevant; among these may be mentioned the County Archaeology Series, published by Methuens in the 1930s; although in some respects out of date, they give a lot of facts, and some counties are covered in no other way. N. Pevsner's *The Buildings of England* (Penguin) are useful, particularly for some counties. There is now a series of Regional Archaeologies (S.W. Scotland, Severn Basin, Yorkshire, South Wales, etc.).

Relevant books are listed below.

ENGLAND

J. Hawkes: *Guide to Prehistoric and Roman Monuments in England and Wales* (1951); Nicholas Thomas: *A Guide to Prehistoric England* (1960)—a companion guide to Roman sites is in preparation; L. Cottrell: *Seeing Roman Britain* (1956); for later periods, Arnold Fellows: *England and*

Wales—A Traveller's Companion (1964) (replaces *The Wayfarer's Companion*). The Regional Archaeology series is a useful one.

London and Middlesex. C. E. Vulliamy: *The Archaeology of Middlesex and London* (1930); John Summerson: *Georgian London* (Penguin, 1962); Ralph Merrifield: *Roman London* (1969). *Londinium*—A Practical Guide to the Visible Remains of Roman London (Classical Assoc. 1970).

South-east. G. J. Copley: *An Archaeology of South-East England* (1958)—covers north of the Thames as well, roughly as far as the Chilterns; I. D. Margary: *Roman Ways in the Weald* (1948); Ronald Jessup: *South-East England* (1970).

Kent. R. F. Jessup: *The Archaeology of Kent* (1930); *Pre-Roman, Roman and Mediaeval Canterbury* (Canterbury Excavation Committee, 1954); G. W. Meates: *Lullingstone Roman Villa* (1955).

Surrey. D. Whimster: *The Archaeology of Surrey* (1931); K. Oakley, A. Rankine and A. W. G. Lowther: *A Survey of the Prehistory of the Farnham District* (Surrey Arch. Soc., 1939); J. Hillier: *Old Surrey Watermills* (1957).

Sussex. E. C. Curwen: *The Archaeology of Sussex* (Methuen, 1954); Peter Hemming: *Windmills in Sussex* (1936). Barry Cunliffe: *Fishbourne* (1971).

Wessex. L. V. Grinsell: *The Archaeology of Wessex* (1958); C. Cochrane: *The Lost Roads of Wessex* (1969).

Hampshire. J. Heywood Sumner: *The Ancient Earthworks of the New Forest* (1917); J. B. Calkin: *Discovering Prehistoric Bournemouth and Christchurch* (1966); *A Survey of Southampton and its Region* (B.A. 1964).

Berkshire. H. J. Peake: *The Archaeology of Berkshire* (1931); G. C. Boon: *Roman Silchester* (1957).

Wiltshire. *Victoria County History*, vol. 1 (1957); H. de S. Shortt, editor: *City of Salisbury* (1957); J. Heywood Sumner: *The Ancient Earthworks of Cranbourne Chase* (1913); for Stonehenge, Avebury, Silbury, West Kennet, etc., see p. 339.

Dorset. *Dorset* (RCHM, 3 vols.). C. Taylor: *Dorset* (1970).

South-West. *Air-photographic Archaeology in the South-West* (CBA, 1965). Aileen Fox: *South-West England* (1964).

Somerset. D. P. Dobson: *The Archaeology of Somerset* (1931); N. Pevsner: *N. Somerset and Bristol*, and *South and West Somerset* (Penguin). Barry Cunliffe: *Roman Bath* (1969). Robin Athill: *Old Mendie* (1971).

Devon. N. Pevsner: *South Devon* (Penguin); R. Hansford Worth: *Dartmoor* (1967); Dartmoor National Park Guide (HMSO, 1957): W. G. Hoskins: *Devon* (1954); and *Two Thousand Years in Exeter* (1960). L. V. Grinsell: *The Archaeology of Exmoor* (1970); Crispin Gill, ed.: *Dartmoor, a New Study* (1970). H. Harris: *The Industrial Archaeology of Dartmoor* (1968).

Cornwall. H. O'N. Hencken: *The Archaeology of Cornwall and Scilly* (1932); W. G. V. Balchin: *Cornwall* (1954); F. E. Halliday: *A History of Cornwall* (1959); N. Pevsner: *Cornwall* (Penguin); C. Thomas and Peter Pool: *The Principal Antiquities of the Lands End District* (West Cornwall Field Club Guide, 1959); A. J. Langdon: *Old Cornish Crosses* (1896); *Shell Guide to Cornwall* (J. Betjeman) (1964). Frank Booker: *Industrial Archaeology of the Tamar Valley* (1967). Vivien Russell: *West Penwith Survey* (1971).

Scilly. B. A. St J. O'Neil: *Ancient Monuments of the Isles of Scilly* (HMSO, 1961).

East Anglia. R. Rainbird Clarke: *East Anglia* (1960).

Suffolk. A. Suckling: *An Index to the History and Antiquities of the County of Suffolk* (1953); Charles Green: *Sutton Hoo* (1963). R. L. S. Bruce-Mitford: *The Sutton Hoo Ship Burial* (BM Handbook, 1968).

Essex. M. R. Hull: *Roman Colchester* (Colchester and Essex Museum, 1947).

Cambridgeshire. Sir C. Fox: *The Archaeology of the Cambridge Region* (1948). RCHM, vol. 1 (1967).

Buckinghamshire. J. F. Head: *Early Man in South Buckinghamshire* (1955).

Bedfordshire. J. Dyer, etc.: *The Story of Luton* (1964); C. L. Matthews: *Ancient Dunstable* (1963).

Oxfordshire. *The Oxford Region* (1954); K. Allison, M. W. Beresford, J. G. Hurst et al.: *The Deserted Villages of Oxfordshire* (Leicester Univ., 1965).

Warwickshire. *Birmingham and its Regional Setting* (1950).

Gloucestershire. O. G. S. Crawford: *Long Barrows of the Cotswolds* (Bellows, 1925); *Bristol and its Adjoining Counties* (British Association, 1955); Forest of Dean National Forest Park Guide; Cyril Hart: *Archaeology in Dean* (1967). See also Somerset. L. Grinsell: *Prehistoric Sites in the Mendip, South Cotswold and Bristol Region* (1966). R. A. Buchanan & Neil Cossons: *The Industrial Archaeology of the Bristol Region* (1969).

Lincolnshire. C. W. Phillips; in *Arch. J.*, xc and xci (1933–4); H. Dudley: *Early Days in North-West Lincolnshire* (1949); M. W. Barley: *Lincolnshire and the Fens* (1952). B. Whitwell: *Roman Lincolnshire* (1970).

Leicestershire. W. G. Hoskins: *The Heritage of Leicestershire* (1949); C. D. B. Ellis: *History of Leicester* (1948). Elizabeth Black: *A Guide to Leicestershire Archaeology* (Leic. Mus. 1970).

Nottinghamshire. RCHM, *Newark on Trent—The Civil War Siegeworks* (1964).

Derbyshire. N. Pevsner: *Derbyshire* (Penguin); Peak National Park Guide; Nellie Kirkham: *Derbyshire Lead Mining* (1968).

Cheshire. E. J. Varley and F. W. Jackson: *Prehistoric Cheshire* (1940); *Historical Atlas of Cheshire* (1958); F. H. Thompson: *Deva, Roman Chester* (Grosvenor Museum, Chester, 1950), and *Roman Cheshire* (1965).

Shropshire. N. Pevsner: *Shropshire* (Penguin).

Yorkshire. F. and H. W. Elgee: *The Archaeology of Yorkshire* (1933). A. Raistrick and B. Jennings: *A History of Lead Mining in the Pennines* (1965); A. Raistrick: *Prehistoric Yorkshire*; *The Romans in Yorkshire*; *The Anglo-Saxons and Danes in Yorkshire* (Dalesman, 1964).

York. *Eburacum* (RCHM, 1962). *Roman York from AD 71* (1971).

East Riding. M. Kitson Clark: *A Gazetteer of Roman Remains in East Yorkshire* (Yorks. Arch. Soc., 1935).

West Riding. N. Pevsner: *Yorkshire: The West Riding* (Penguin); E. T. Cowling: *Rombald's Way* (1946—mid-Wharfedale); *Sheffield and its Region* (British Association, 1956); G. G. Watson: *Early Man in the Halifax District* (Halifax Scientific Soc., 1952); J. A. Petch: *Early Man in the District round Huddersfield* (Tolson Mus., 1924); the bulletin issued by the archaeology group of the Bradford City Museum is very useful; Cuchlaine A. M. King: *The Yorkshire Dales* (Geographical Assoc., 1960). *Yorkshire Dales National Park Guide* (1971).

North Riding. F. Elgee: *Early Man in NE Yorkshire* (1930); H. Rowantree:

A History of Scarborough (1930); J. G. Rutter: *The Archaeology of Scarborough and District* (Scarborough Mus., 1956); T. H. Woodwark: *The Crosses on the North York Moors* (Whitby Lit., and Phil. Soc., 1962); R. H. Hayes and J. G. Rutter: *Wades Causeway* (Scar. & Dist. Arch. Soc. Res. Rpt. No. 4, 1964); J. McDonnell, ed.: *A History of Helmsley, Rievaulx and District* (1963); *North York Moors* (National Park Guide, 1966).

North-West. A. E. Smailes: *North England* (1960); J. C. Bruce: *Handbook to the Roman Wall* (12th edn., 1966). W. Robinson: *A History of Man in the Lake District* (1967).

Lancashire. W. G. Hoskins, ed.: *Lancashire* (English Landscapes).

North-East. W. G. Collingwood: *Northumbrian Crosses of the pre-Norman Age* (1927), and see North-west.

Northumberland. N. Pevsner: *Northumberland* (Penguin).

WALES

W. J. Lewis: *Lead Mining in Wales* (1967).

Brecon. Brecon Beacons National Park Guide (1967).

Monmouthshire. V. E. Nash-Williams: *The Roman Legionary Fortress at Caerleon* (Nat. Mus. of Wales, 1952).

Glamorgan. J. G. Rutter: *Prehistoric Gower* (Welsh Guides, Swansea, 1948).

Flintshire. Ellis Davies: *Prehistoric and Roman Remains in Flintshire* (1949).

Denbighshire. Ellis Davies: *Prehistoric and Roman Remains in Denbighshire* (1929).

Caernarvonshire. *Caernarvonshire* (RCAM, vol. I, East; vol. II, Central); Snowdonia National Park Guide (HMSO, 1958). Frances Lynch: *Prehistoric Anglesey* (1970).

South-west. Donald Moore, ed.: *The Land of Dyfed in Early Times* (1964).

SCOTLAND

O. G. S. Crawford: *The Topography of Roman Scotland North of the Antonine Wall* (1949); J. W. Small: *Scottish Market Crosses* (1900). R. Feachem: *Guide to Prehistoric Scotland* (1963); John Butt: *The Industrial Archaeology of Scotland* (1967). W. Douglas Simpson: *The Ancient Stones of Scotland* (1965).

Roxburghshire. *Roxburghshire* (RCAHM).

Peeblesshire. *Peeblesshire* (RCAHM).

Selkirkshire. *Selkirkshire* (RCAHM).

Central. Handbook to the Antonine Wall (Glasgow Arch. Soc., 1970).

Clackmannan. A. I. R. Drummond: *Old Clackmannanshire* (1953).

Fife. Ivor Dowse: *Pittenweem* (1964).

Stirlingshire. Inventory of Stirlingshire (RCAHM, 1965).

Argyll. *A Preliminary Handbook to the Archaeology of Islay* (Islay Archaeological Survey Group, 1960); Ivor R. Dowse: *Iona* (1964). Marion Campbell: *Mid-Argyll* (1970).

Perthshire. *Ancient Monuments on Tayside* (Dundee Mus. 1970).

North. Orkney and Shetland (RCAHM); *The Northern Isles* (ed. F. T. Wainwright, 1962); *The North-East of Scotland* (British Association Survey, (1963).

Orkney. V. G. Childe: *Skara Brae* (Kegan Paul, 1931); Hugh Marwick: *Ancient Monuments in Orkney* (HMSO, 1952).

Zetland. J. R. C. Hamilton: *Excavations at Jarlshof, Shetland* (HMSO, 1956), and *Excavations at Clickhimin* (1968).

OTHER PLACES

Isle of Man. A. M. Cubbon: *The Ancient and Historic Monuments of the Isle of Man* (1967).

Channel Islands *The Archaeology of the Channel Islands*, two volumes, by T. D. Kendrick on Guernsey (1928) and J. Hawkes on Jersey (1939).

Northern Ireland. *Ancient Monuments in Northern Ireland in State Charge* (1928); *Ancient Monuments in Northern Ireland not in State Charge* (1956); *Archaeological Survey of County Down* (1964) and E. R. Green: *The Industrial Archaeology of Co. Down* (HMSO, 1963).

Irish Republic. S. P. O'Roirdain and G. E. Daniel: *New Grange* (1964); Peter Harbison: *Guide to the National Monuments of Ireland* (1970); Estyn Evans: *Prehistoric and Early Christian Ireland—a guide* (1966).

I have omitted from this list the very numerous books, articles and reports on single sites, but references to these will be found in the general works.

Glossaries. C. Trent: *Terms used in Archaeology* (1959); J. Stewart: *Archaeological Guide and Glossary* (1960).

REGIONAL MAPS

The maps which follow illustrate the *Sites to Visit* section (see page 308)

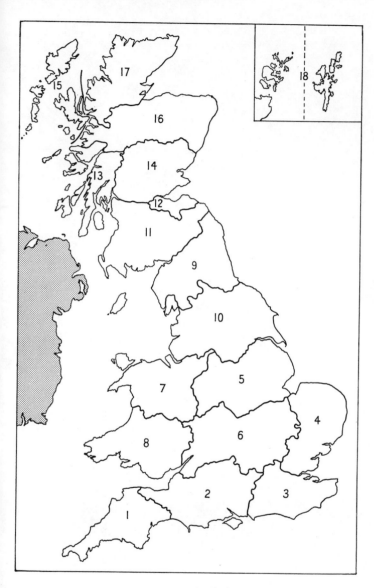

Key map of Britain

349

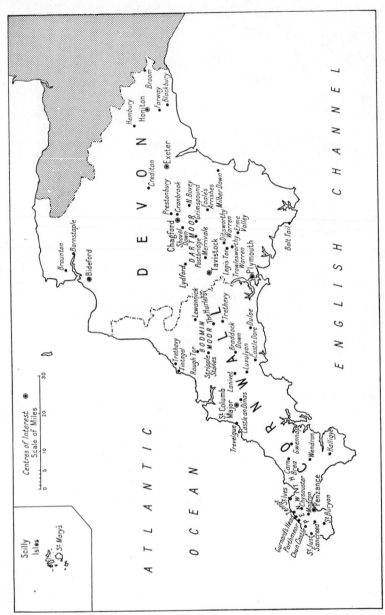

1. South-West England

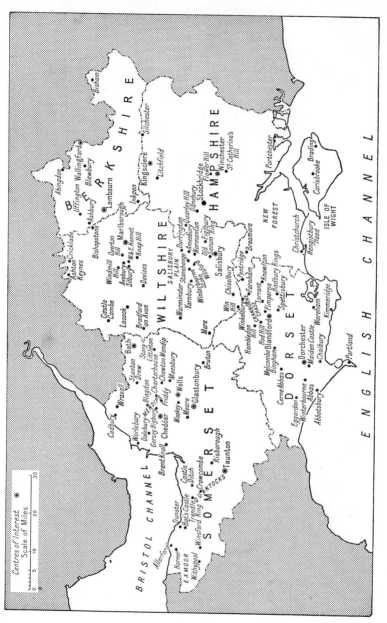

2. Wessex

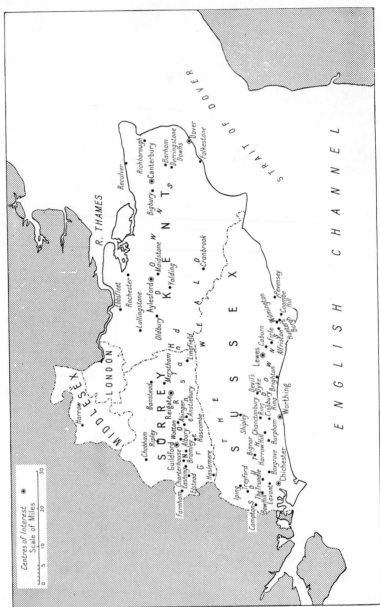

3   South-East England

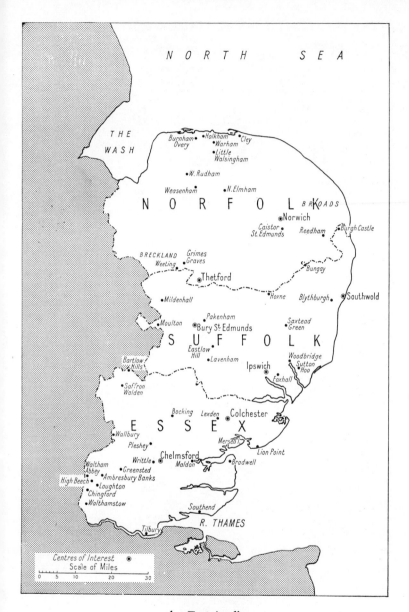

NORTH SEA

THE WASH

Burnham Overy • *Holkham* • *Cley*
Warham
Little Walsingham

W. Rudham •

Weasenham • *N. Elmham* •

N O R F O L *BROADS*

⊚ *Norwich*

Caistor St. Edmunds • *Reedham* • *Burgh Castle*

BRECKLAND *Grimes Graves*
Weeting •

⊚ *Thetford* *Bungay*

Mildenhall • *Horne* *Blythburgh* • ⊚ *Southwold*

Pakenham *Saxtead Green*
Moulton • ⊚ *Bury St Edmunds*

S U F F O L K

Eastlow Hill
Bartlow Hills *Lavenham* *Woodbridge*
⊚ *Ipswich* *Sutton Hoo*
Foxhall
Saffron Walden

Bocking • *Lexden* ⊚ *Colchester*

E S S E X

Wallbury •
Pleshey • *Mersea I.*
Lion Point
Writtle • ⊚ *Chelmsford*
Waltham Abbey *Maldon* • *Bradwell*
High Beech *Greensted*
• *Ambresbury Banks*
Loughton
Chingford
• *Walthamstow* *Southend*

Tilbury *R. THAMES*

Centres of Interest ⊚
Scale of Miles
0 5 10 20 30

4. East Anglia

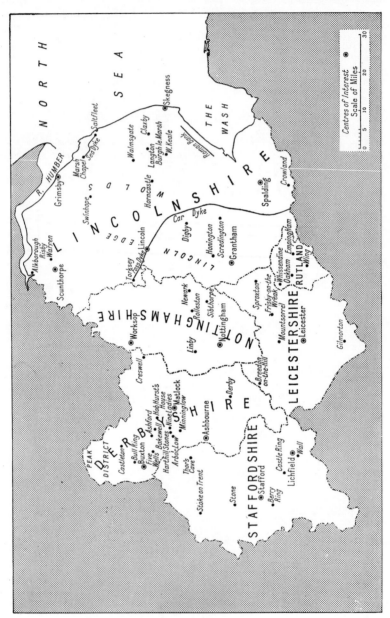

5. North Midlands

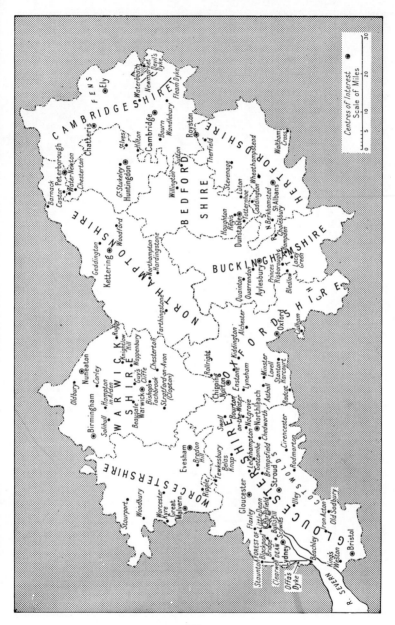

6. South Midlands

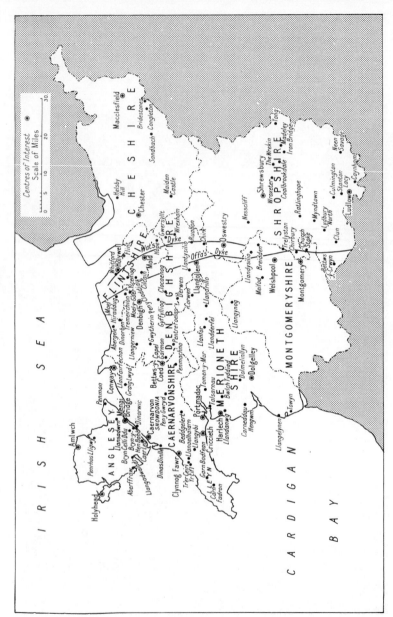

7. North Wales and borders

8. South Wales, and borders

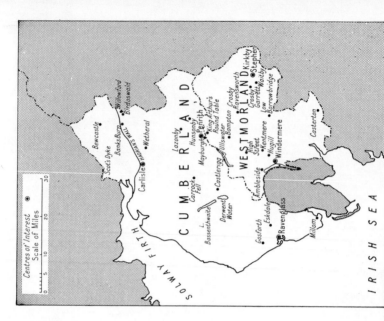

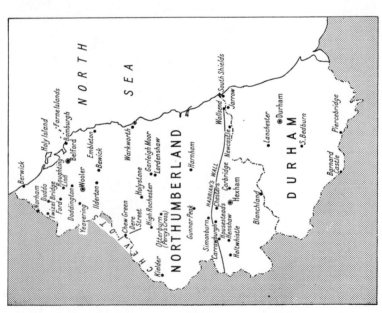

9. The North of England

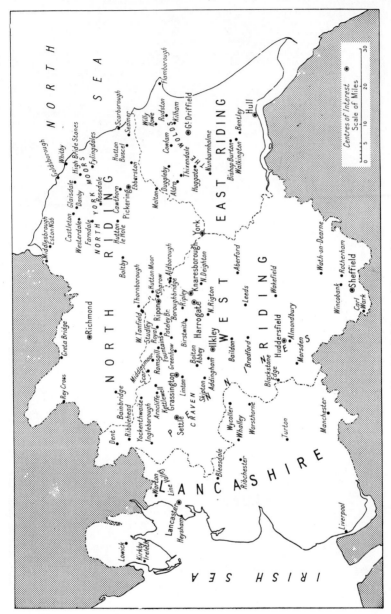

10. Yorkshire and Lancashire

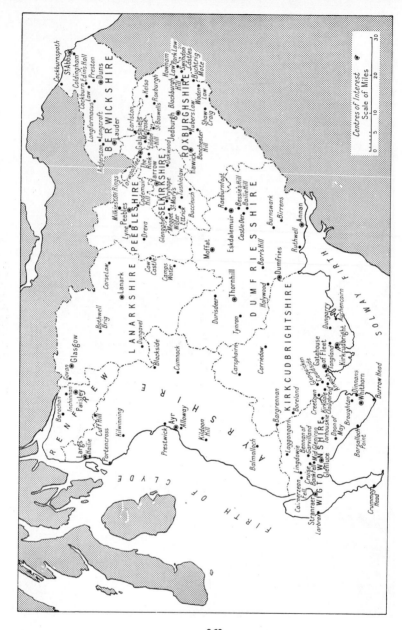

11. South Scotland

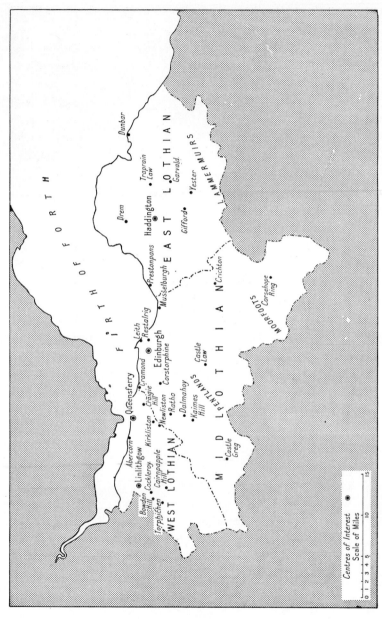

12. The Lothians

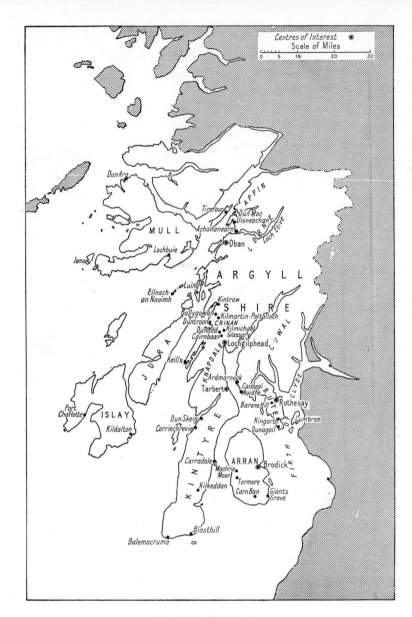

13. West Highlands

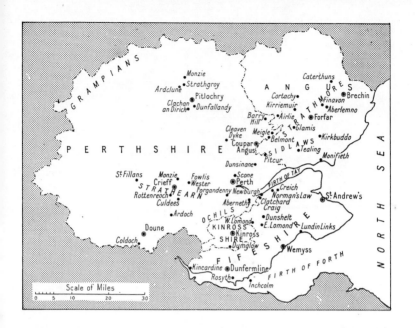

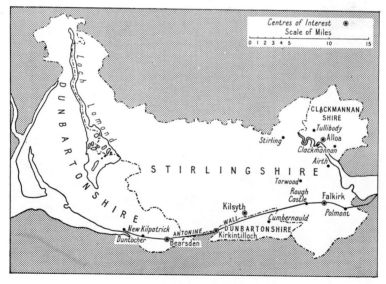

14. South and East Highlands

363

ATLANTIC

OCEAN

E. Loch Roag

Carloway

Callanish

Garynahine

Cromore

L E W I S

H A R R I S

THE MINCH

N.UIST

Barpa nam
Feannag

Barpa Langass

Dun Hallin

Kensaleyre

Dunvegan

Dun Gerashader

Dun Beag

Howmore

S.UIST

Reineval

Loch a'Bharp

S K Y E

Rudh an Dunain

Dun
Bharpa

BARRA

(Sron an Duin)
Barra Head

EIGG   An Sgurr

Centres of Interest   ◉
Scale of Miles
0 5 10 20 30

15. Western Isles

364

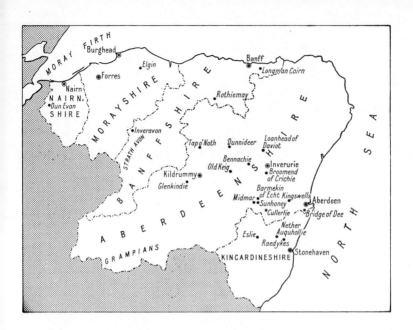

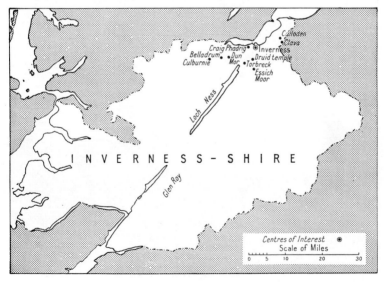

16. Moray Firth and East

365

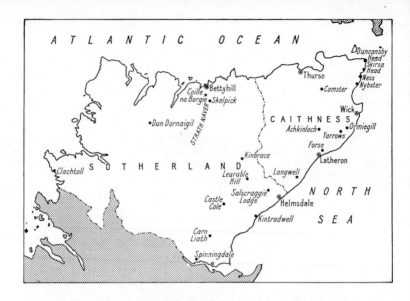

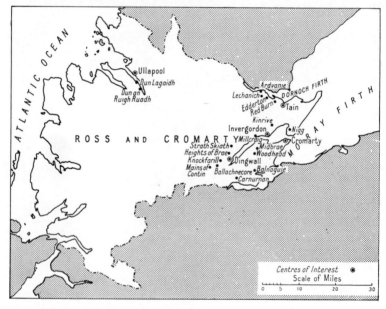

17. North Scotland

366

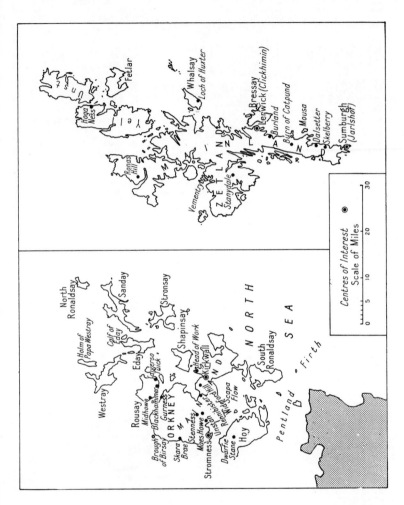

18. Northern Isles

INDEX OF PLACES

This is an index to British places mentioned in the body of this book: further places of importauke may be found in the 'Sites to Visit' section, pages 308-34.

Counties are indicated only: (1) for place names which occur in more than one county; (2) for sites which are not named after their own town or parish.

INDEX OF SUBJECTS